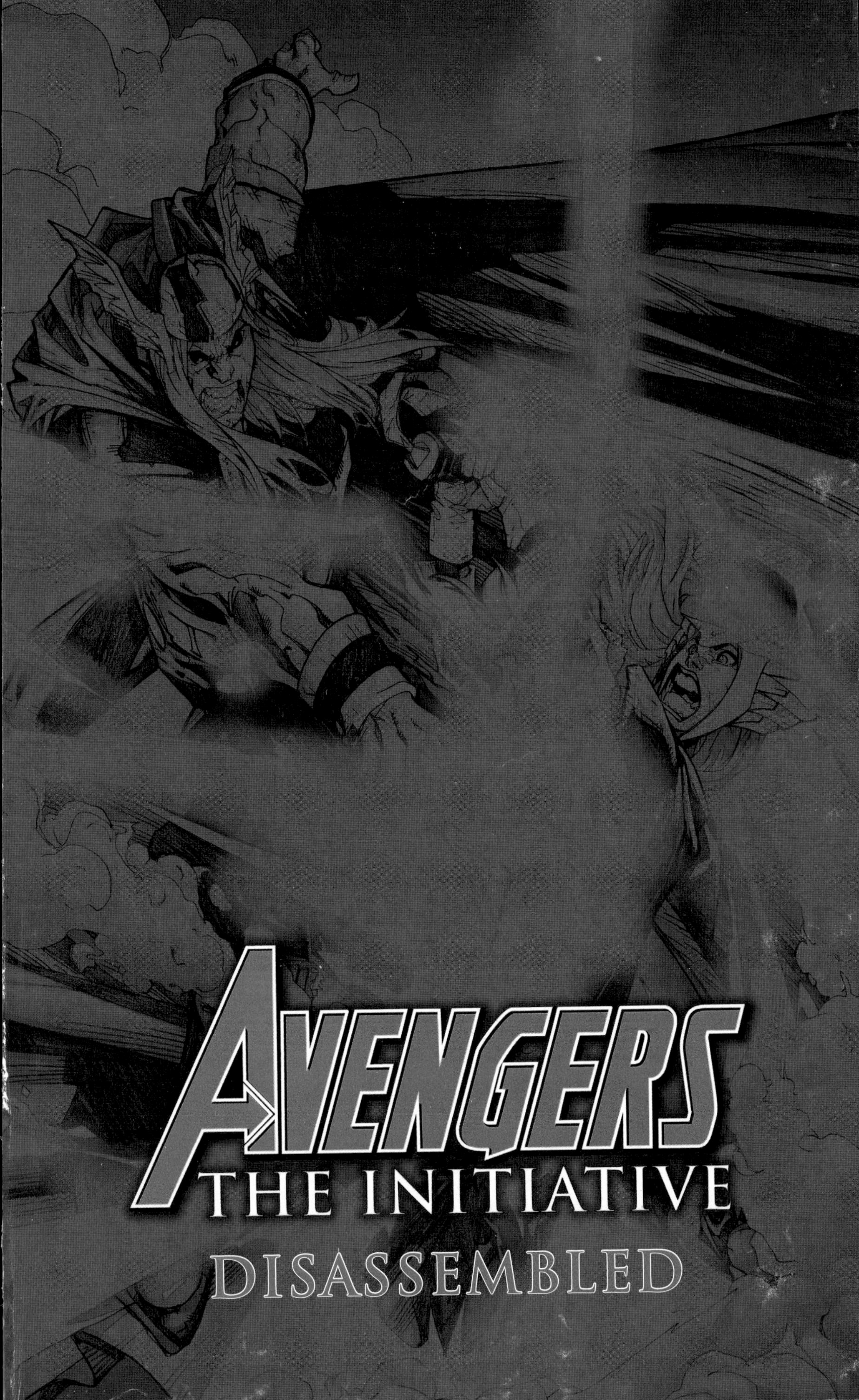

AVENGERS
THE INITIATIVE
DISASSEMBLED

AVENGERS
THE INITIATIVE
DISASSEMBLED

ISSUE #20
WRITERS: DAN SLOTT & CHRISTOS N. GAGE
PENCILER: STEVE KURTH
INKER: DREW HENNESSY
COLORIST: MATT MILLA
COVER ART: MARK BROOKS

ISSUES #21-25
WRITER: CHRISTOS N. GAGE
ARTIST: HUMBERTO RAMOS
COLOR ARTIST: EDGAR DELGADO
COVER ART: HUMBERTO RAMOS & EDGAR DELGADO

AVENGERS: THE INITIATIVE FEATURING REPTIL
WRITER: CHRISTOS N. GAGE
ARTIST: STEVE UY
SPECIAL THANKS TO CORT LANE & HUMBERTO RAMOS
COVER ART: HUMBERTO RAMOS & EDGAR DELGADO

LETTERERS: VIRTUAL CALLIGRAPHY'S JOE CARAMAGNA
WITH CHRIS ELIOPOULOS (ISSUE #25)
EDITOR: JEANINE SCHAEFER
EXECUTIVE EDITOR: TOM BREVOORT

AVENGERS: THE INITIATIVE — DISASSEMBLED. Contains material originally published in magazine form as AVENGERS: THE INITIATIVE #20-25 and AVENGERS: THE INITIATIVE FEATURING REPTIL. First printing 2009. Hardcover ISBN# 978-0-7851-3151-9. Softcover ISBN# 978-0-7851-3168-7. Published by MARVEL PUBLISHING, INC., a subsidiary of MARVEL ENTERTAINMENT, INC. OFFICE OF PUBLICATION: 417 5th Avenue, New York, NY 10016. Copyright © 2008 and 2009 Marvel Characters, Inc. All rights reserved. Hardcover: $24.99 per copy in the U.S. (GST #R127032852). Softcover: $19.99 per copy in the U.S. (GST #R127032852). Canadian Agreement #40668537. All characters featured in this issue and the distinctive names and likenesses thereof, and all related indicia are trademarks of Marvel Characters, Inc. No similarity between any of the names, characters, persons, and/or institutions in this magazine with those of any living or dead person or institution is intended, and any such similarity which may exist is purely coincidental. Printed in the U.S.A. ALAN FINE, EVP - Office Of The Chief Executive Marvel Entertainment, Inc. & CMO Marvel Characters B.V.; DAN BUCKLEY, Chief Executive Officer and Publisher - Print, Animation & Digital Media; JIM SOKOLOWSKI, Chief Operating Officer; DAVID GABRIEL, SVP of Publishing Sales & Circulation; DAVID BOGART, SVP of Business Affairs & Talent Management; MICHAEL PASCIULLO, VP Merchandising & Communications; JIM O'KEEFE, VP of Operations & Logistics; DAN CARR, Executive Director of Publishing Technology; JUSTIN F. GABRIE, Director of Publishing & Editorial Operations; SUSAN CRESPI, Editorial Operations Manager; ALEX MORALES, Publishing Operations Manager; STAN LEE, Chairman Emeritus. For information regarding advertising in Marvel Comics or on Marvel.com, please contact Mitch Dane, Advertising Director, at mdane@marvel.com. For Marvel subscription

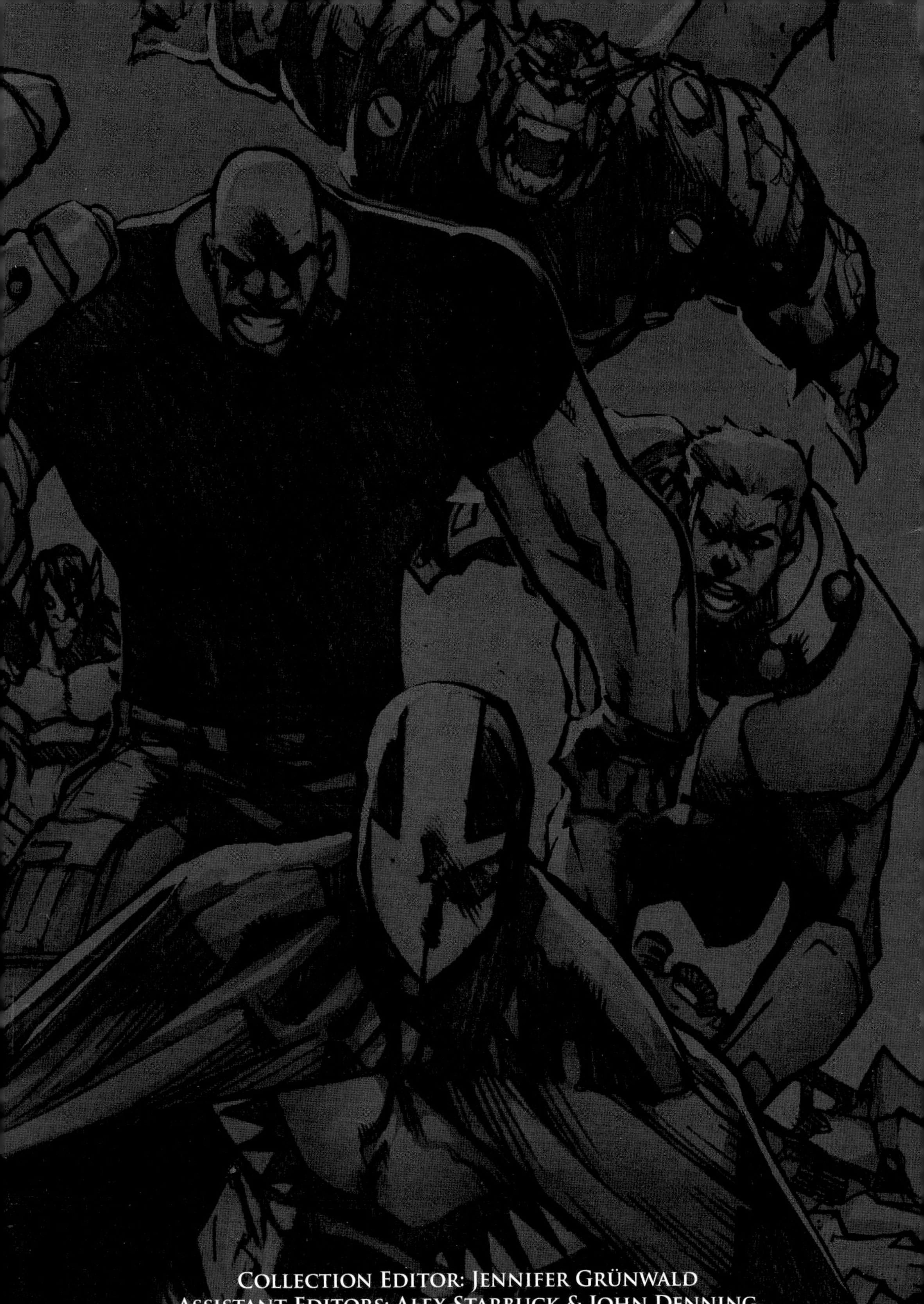

Collection Editor: Jennifer Grünwald
Assistant Editors: Alex Starbuck & John Denning
Editor, Special Projects: Mark D. Beazley
Senior Editor, Special Projects: Jeff Youngquist
Senior Vice President of Sales: David Gabriel

Editor in Chief: Joe Quesada
Publisher: Dan Buckley
Executive Producer: Alan Fine

AVENGERS THE INITIATIVE

AFTER STAMFORD, CONNECTICUT WAS DESTROYED DURING A TELEVISED FIGHT BETWEEN THE NEW WARRIORS AND A GROUP OF DANGEROUS VILLAINS, A FEDERAL SUPERHUMAN REGISTRATION ACT WAS PASSED. ALL INDIVIDUALS POSSESSING PARANORMAL ABILITIES MUST NOW REGISTER WITH THE GOVERNMENT. TONY STARK, A.K.A. IRON MAN, HAS BEEN APPOINTED DIRECTOR OF S.H.I.E.L.D., THE INTERNATIONAL PEACEKEEPING FORCE. HE HAS SET IN MOTION THE INITIATIVE, A PLAN FOR TRAINING AND POLICING SUPER HEROES IN THIS BRAVE NEW WORLD, INTENDED TO POSITION A LOCAL SUPER HERO TEAM IN EACH OF AMERICA'S FIFTY STATES.

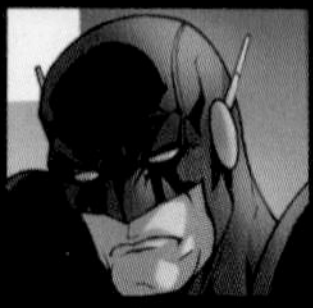
YELLOWJACKET

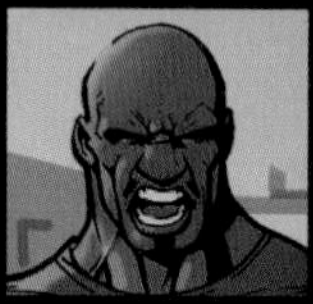
GAUNTLET

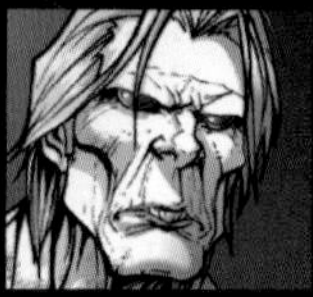
BARON VON BLITZSCHLAG

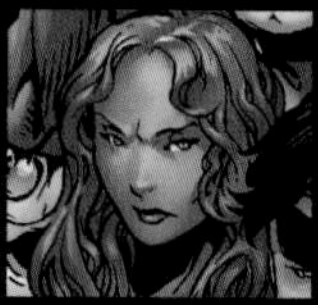
TIGRA

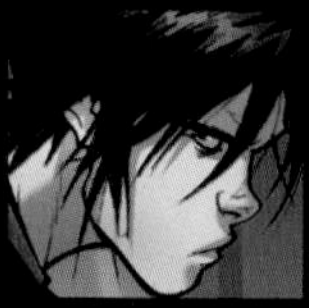
TRAUMA

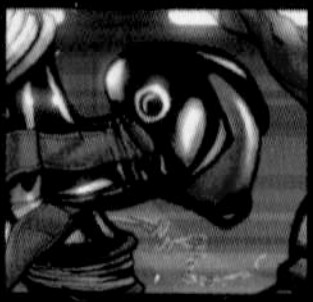
MUTANT ZERO

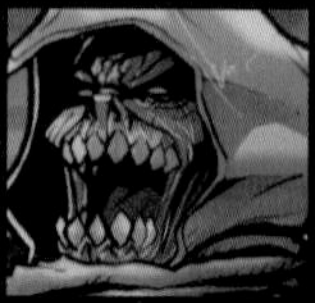
TASKMASTER

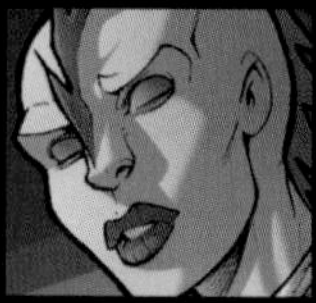
KOMODO

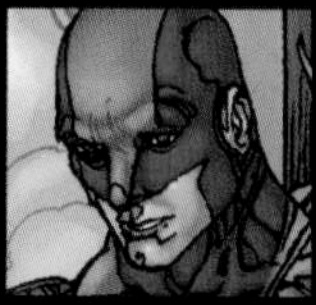
HARDBALL

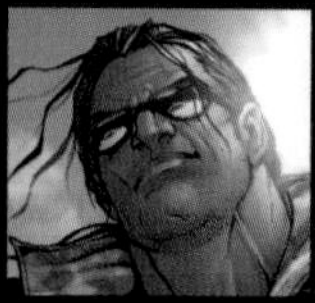
RYDER

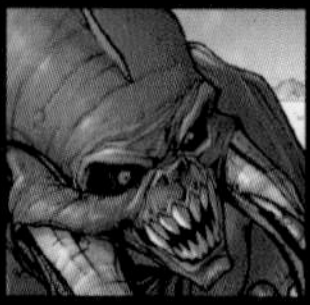
RIOT

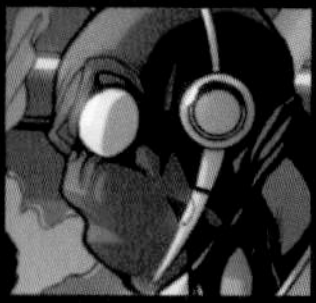
ANT-MAN

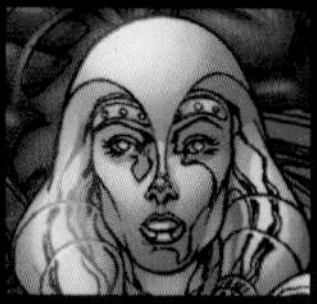
JOCASTA

In the aftermath of the Skrull invasion, Camp Hammond has been hit the hardest. Some of its staff and dozens of members of the Fifty State Initiative had been replaced by Skrull impersonators, the full extent of which has finally been revealed as the real heroes have been returned to Earth.

And no one has been hit harder than Director Hank Pym, a.k.a. Yellowjacket, who has returned to Earth to find his entire life turned upside down by the Skrull imposter...and the love of his life, Janet Van Dyne, dead by the Skrull-Hank's hand.

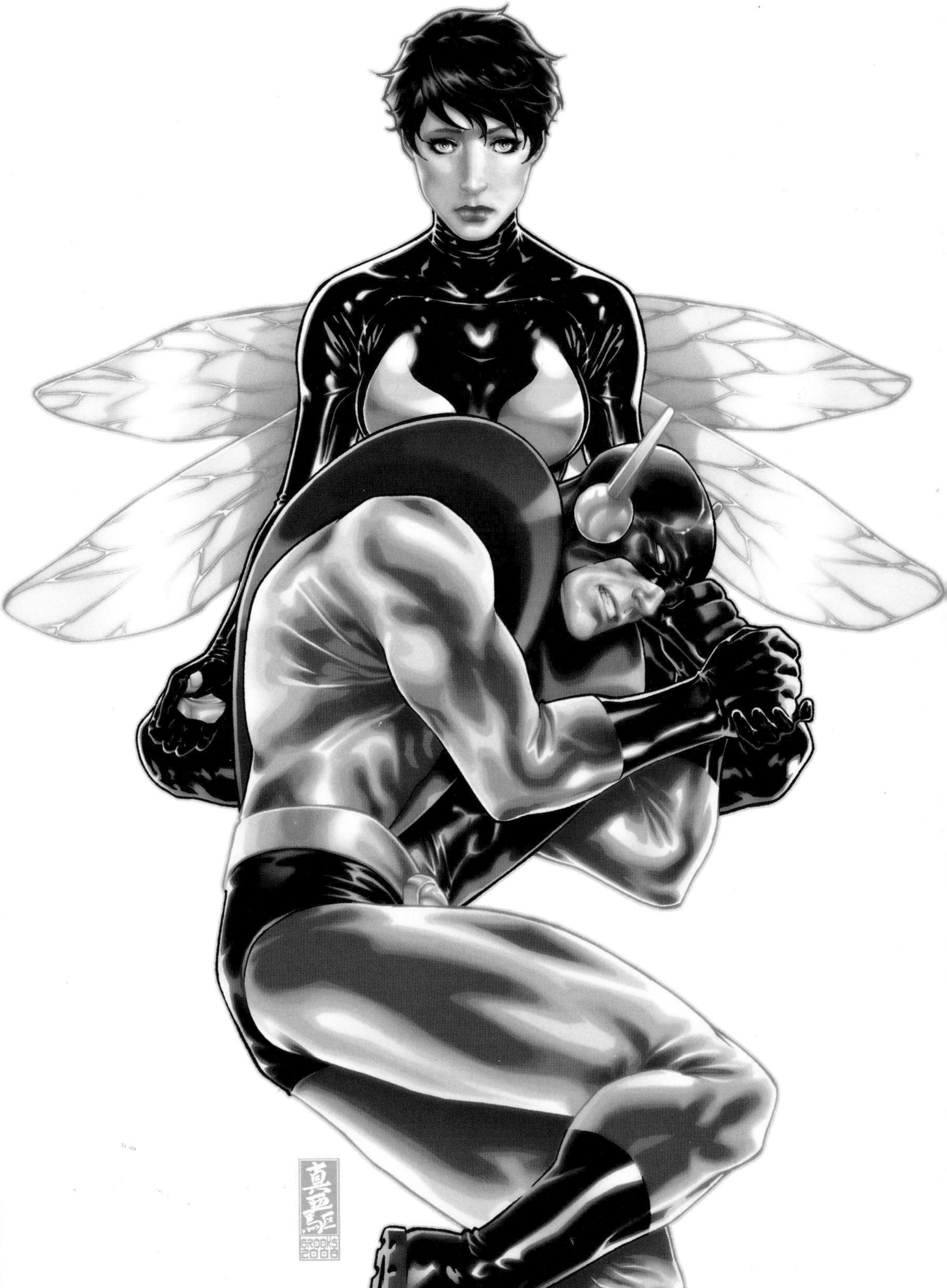
BROOKS
2006

#20

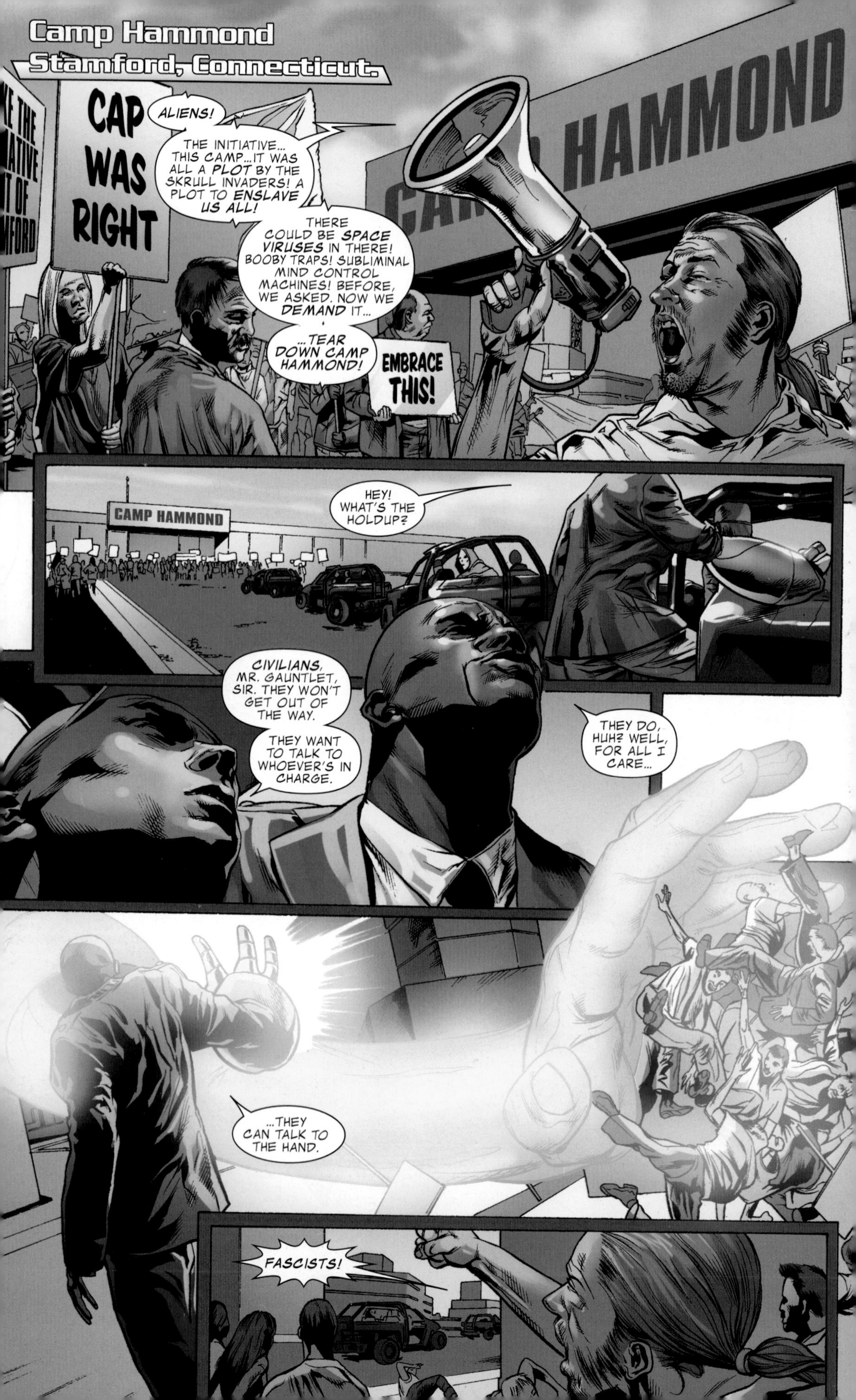
Camp Hammond
Stamford, Connecticut.
CAP WAS RIGHT
CAMP HAMMOND
ALIENS!
THE INITIATIVE... THIS CAMP...IT WAS ALL A PLOT BY THE SKRULL INVADERS! A PLOT TO ENSLAVE US ALL!
THERE COULD BE SPACE VIRUSES IN THERE! BOOBY TRAPS! SUBLIMINAL MIND CONTROL MACHINES! BEFORE, WE ASKED. NOW WE DEMAND IT...
...TEAR DOWN CAMP HAMMOND!
EMBRACE THIS!
CAMP HAMMOND
HEY! WHAT'S THE HOLDUP?
CIVILIANS, MR. GAUNTLET, SIR. THEY WON'T GET OUT OF THE WAY.
THEY WANT TO TALK TO WHOEVER'S IN CHARGE.
THEY DO, HUH? WELL, FOR ALL I CARE...
...THEY CAN TALK TO THE HAND.
FASCISTS!

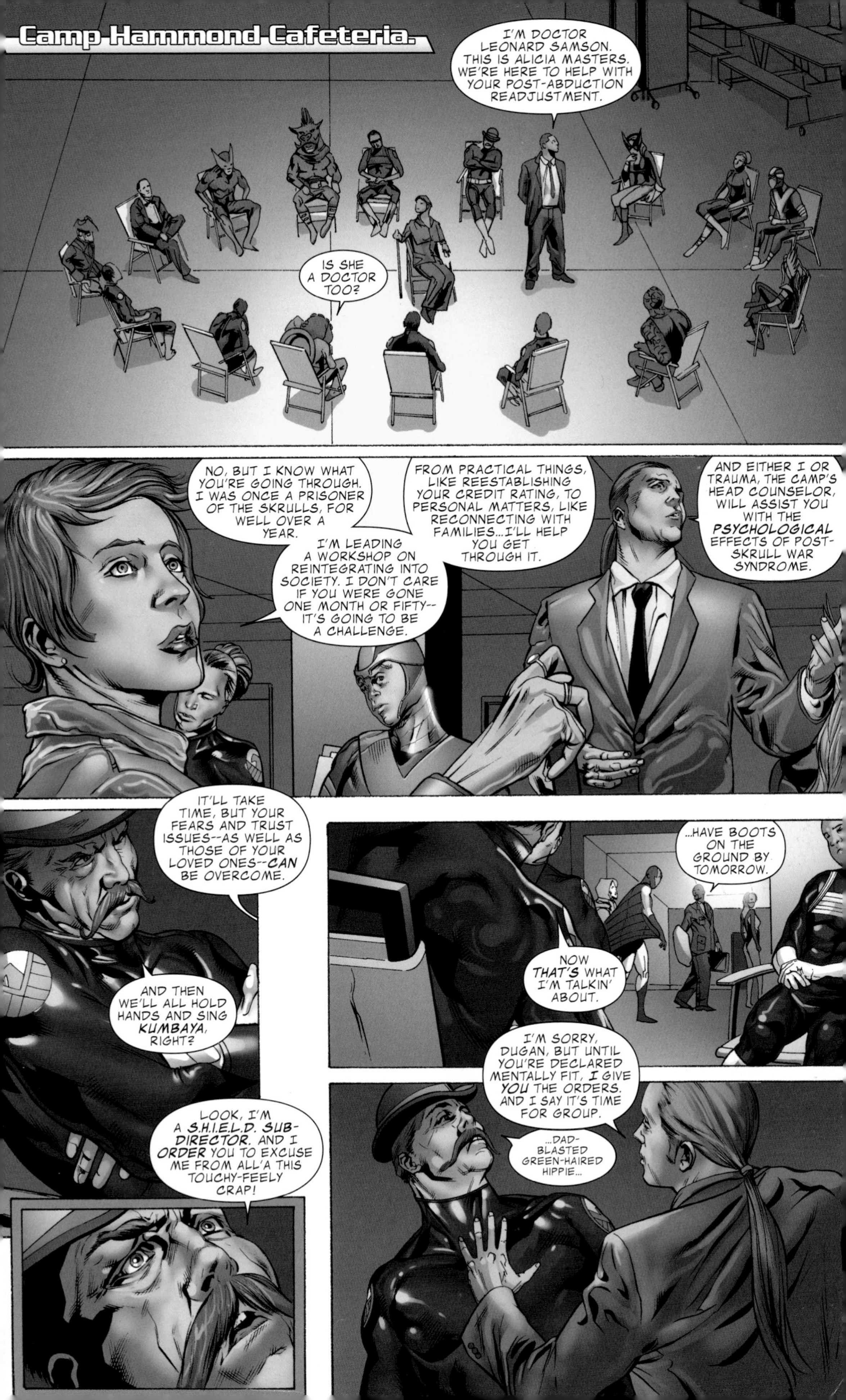
Camp Hammond Cafeteria.
I'M DOCTOR LEONARD SAMSON. THIS IS ALICIA MASTERS. WE'RE HERE TO HELP WITH YOUR POST-ABDUCTION READJUSTMENT.
IS SHE A DOCTOR TOO?
NO, BUT I KNOW WHAT YOU'RE GOING THROUGH. I WAS ONCE A PRISONER OF THE SKRULLS, FOR WELL OVER A YEAR.
I'M LEADING A WORKSHOP ON REINTEGRATING INTO SOCIETY. I DON'T CARE IF YOU WERE GONE ONE MONTH OR FIFTY--IT'S GOING TO BE A CHALLENGE.
FROM PRACTICAL THINGS, LIKE REESTABLISHING YOUR CREDIT RATING, TO PERSONAL MATTERS, LIKE RECONNECTING WITH FAMILIES...I'LL HELP YOU GET THROUGH IT.
AND EITHER I OR TRAUMA, THE CAMP'S HEAD COUNSELOR, WILL ASSIST YOU WITH THE PSYCHOLOGICAL EFFECTS OF POST-SKRULL WAR SYNDROME.
IT'LL TAKE TIME, BUT YOUR FEARS AND TRUST ISSUES--AS WELL AS THOSE OF YOUR LOVED ONES--CAN BE OVERCOME.
AND THEN WE'LL ALL HOLD HANDS AND SING KUMBAYA, RIGHT?
...HAVE BOOTS ON THE GROUND BY TOMORROW.
NOW THAT'S WHAT I'M TALKIN' ABOUT.
LOOK, I'M A S.H.I.E.L.D. SUB-DIRECTOR. AND I ORDER YOU TO EXCUSE ME FROM ALL'A THIS TOUCHY-FEELY CRAP!
I'M SORRY, DUGAN, BUT UNTIL YOU'RE DECLARED MENTALLY FIT, I GIVE YOU THE ORDERS. AND I SAY IT'S TIME FOR GROUP.
...DAD-BLASTED GREEN-HAIRED HIPPIE...

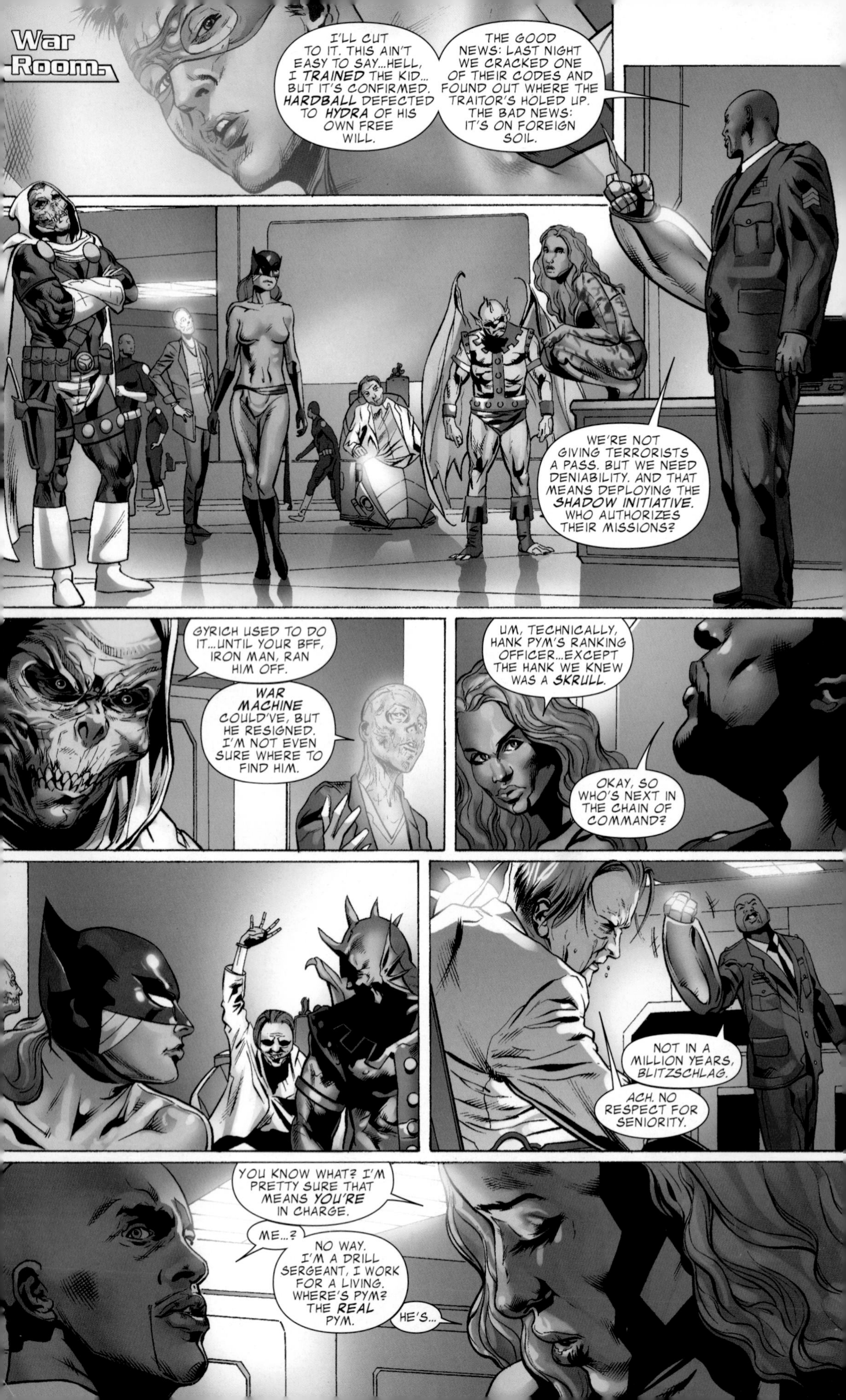
War Room.
I'LL CUT TO IT. THIS AIN'T EASY TO SAY...HELL, I TRAINED THE KID... BUT IT'S CONFIRMED. HARDBALL DEFECTED TO HYDRA OF HIS OWN FREE WILL.
THE GOOD NEWS: LAST NIGHT WE CRACKED ONE OF THEIR CODES AND FOUND OUT WHERE THE TRAITOR'S HOLED UP. THE BAD NEWS: IT'S ON FOREIGN SOIL.
WE'RE NOT GIVING TERRORISTS A PASS. BUT WE NEED DENIABILITY. AND THAT MEANS DEPLOYING THE SHADOW INITIATIVE. WHO AUTHORIZES THEIR MISSIONS?
GYRICH USED TO DO IT...UNTIL YOUR BFF, IRON MAN, RAN HIM OFF.
WAR MACHINE COULD'VE, BUT HE RESIGNED. I'M NOT EVEN SURE WHERE TO FIND HIM.
UM, TECHNICALLY, HANK PYM'S RANKING OFFICER...EXCEPT THE HANK WE KNEW WAS A SKRULL.
OKAY, SO WHO'S NEXT IN THE CHAIN OF COMMAND?
NOT IN A MILLION YEARS, BLITZSCHLAG.
ACH. NO RESPECT FOR SENIORITY.
YOU KNOW WHAT? I'M PRETTY SURE THAT MEANS YOU'RE IN CHARGE.
ME...?
NO WAY. I'M A DRILL SERGEANT, I WORK FOR A LIVING. WHERE'S PYM? THE REAL PYM.
HE'S...

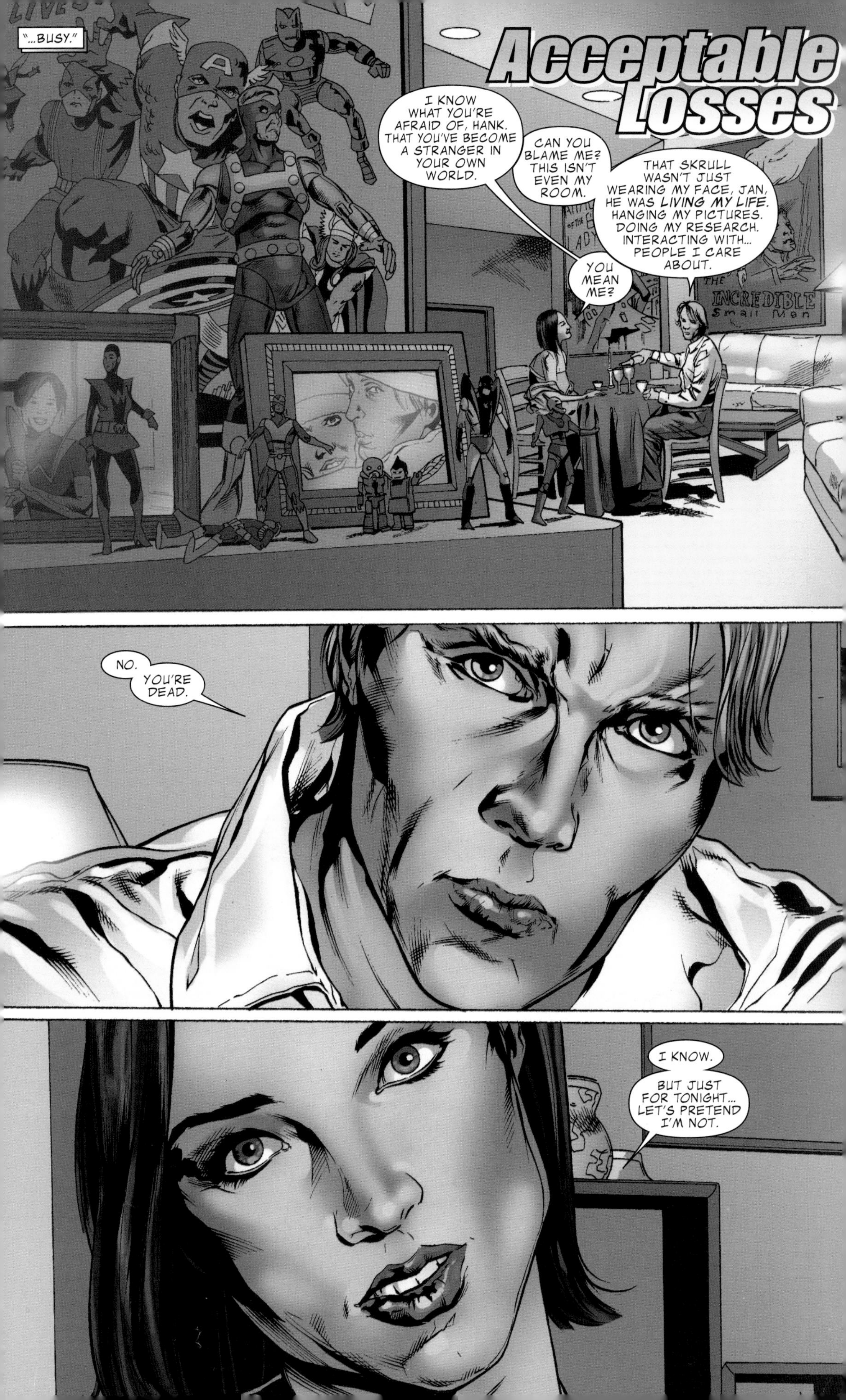
"...BUSY."
Acceptable Losses
I KNOW WHAT YOU'RE AFRAID OF, HANK. THAT YOU'VE BECOME A STRANGER IN YOUR OWN WORLD.
CAN YOU BLAME ME? THIS ISN'T EVEN MY ROOM.
THAT SKRULL WASN'T JUST WEARING MY FACE, JAN, HE WAS LIVING MY LIFE. HANGING MY PICTURES. DOING MY RESEARCH. INTERACTING WITH... PEOPLE I CARE ABOUT.
YOU MEAN ME?
THE INCREDIBLE Small Men
NO.
YOU'RE DEAD.
I KNOW.
BUT JUST FOR TONIGHT... LET'S PRETEND I'M NOT.

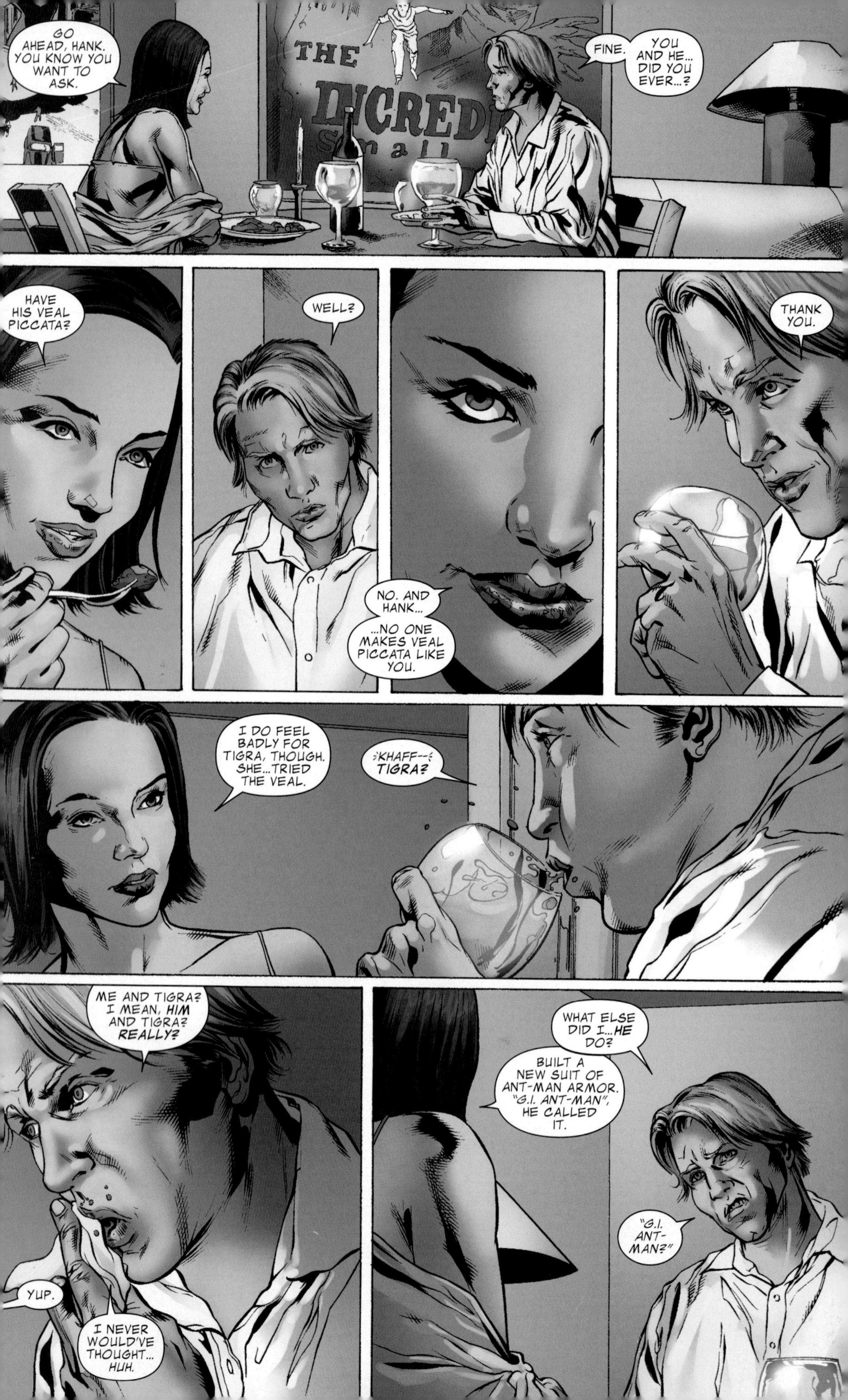
GO AHEAD, HANK. YOU KNOW YOU WANT TO ASK.
THE INCREDI Small
FINE.
YOU AND HE... DID YOU EVER...?
HAVE HIS VEAL PICCATA?
WELL?
NO. AND HANK...
...NO ONE MAKES VEAL PICCATA LIKE YOU.
THANK YOU.
I DO FEEL BADLY FOR TIGRA, THOUGH. SHE...TRIED THE VEAL.
KHAFF-- TIGRA?
ME AND TIGRA? I MEAN, HIM AND TIGRA? REALLY?
YUP.
I NEVER WOULD'VE THOUGHT... HUH.
WHAT ELSE DID I...HE DO?
BUILT A NEW SUIT OF ANT-MAN ARMOR. "G.I. ANT-MAN", HE CALLED IT.
"G.I. ANT-MAN?"

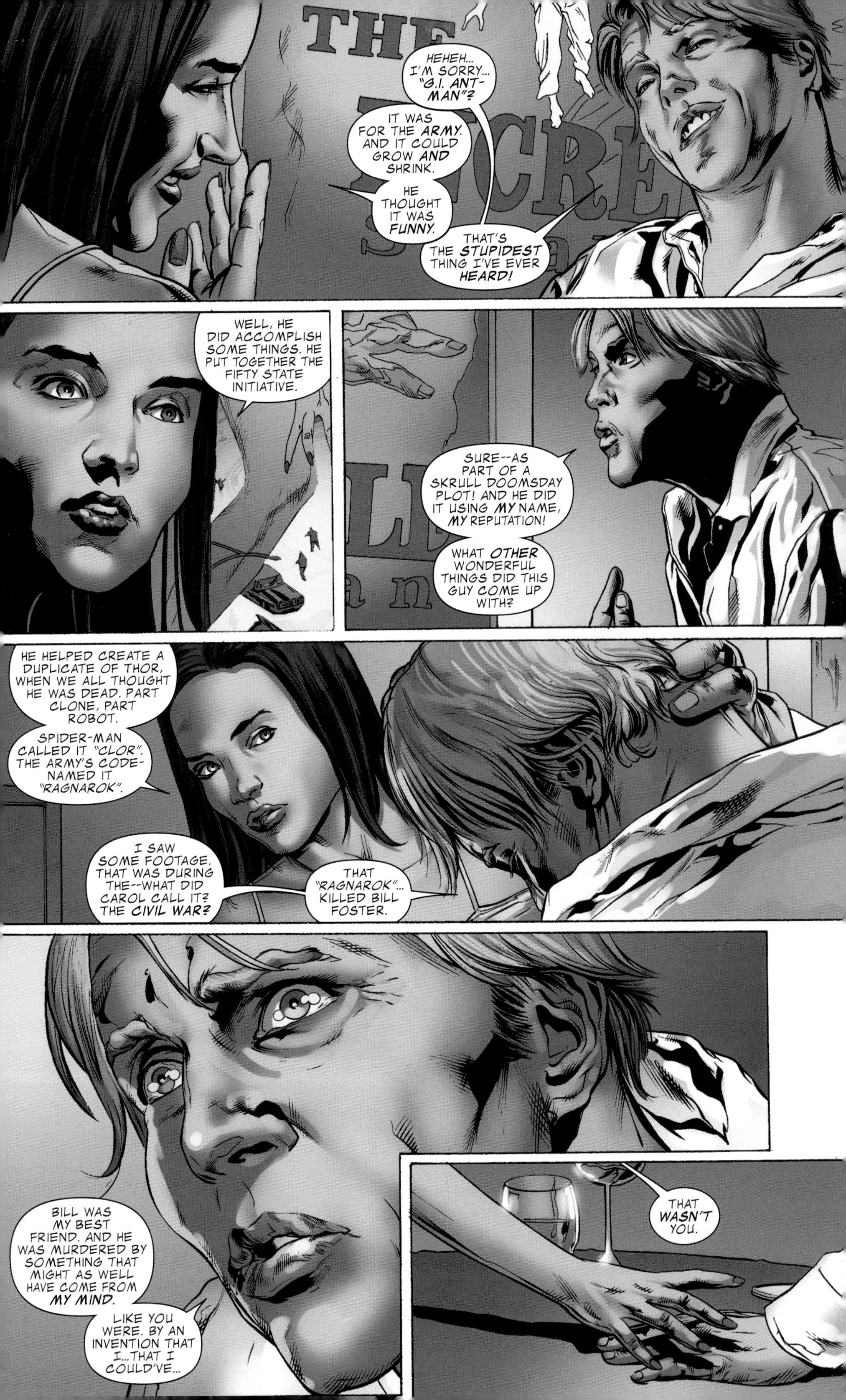
HEHEH... I'M SORRY... "G.I. ANT-MAN"?
IT WAS FOR THE ARMY. AND IT COULD GROW AND SHRINK.
HE THOUGHT IT WAS FUNNY.
THAT'S THE STUPIDEST THING I'VE EVER HEARD!
WELL, HE DID ACCOMPLISH SOME THINGS. HE PUT TOGETHER THE FIFTY STATE INITIATIVE.
SURE--AS PART OF A SKRULL DOOMSDAY PLOT! AND HE DID IT USING MY NAME, MY REPUTATION!
WHAT OTHER WONDERFUL THINGS DID THIS GUY COME UP WITH?
HE HELPED CREATE A DUPLICATE OF THOR, WHEN WE ALL THOUGHT HE WAS DEAD. PART CLONE, PART ROBOT.
SPIDER-MAN CALLED IT "CLOR". THE ARMY'S CODE-NAMED IT "RAGNAROK".
I SAW SOME FOOTAGE. THAT WAS DURING THE--WHAT DID CAROL CALL IT? THE CIVIL WAR?
THAT "RAGNAROK"... KILLED BILL FOSTER.
BILL WAS MY BEST FRIEND. AND HE WAS MURDERED BY SOMETHING THAT MIGHT AS WELL HAVE COME FROM MY MIND.
LIKE YOU WERE. BY AN INVENTION THAT I...THAT I COULD'VE...
THAT WASN'T YOU.

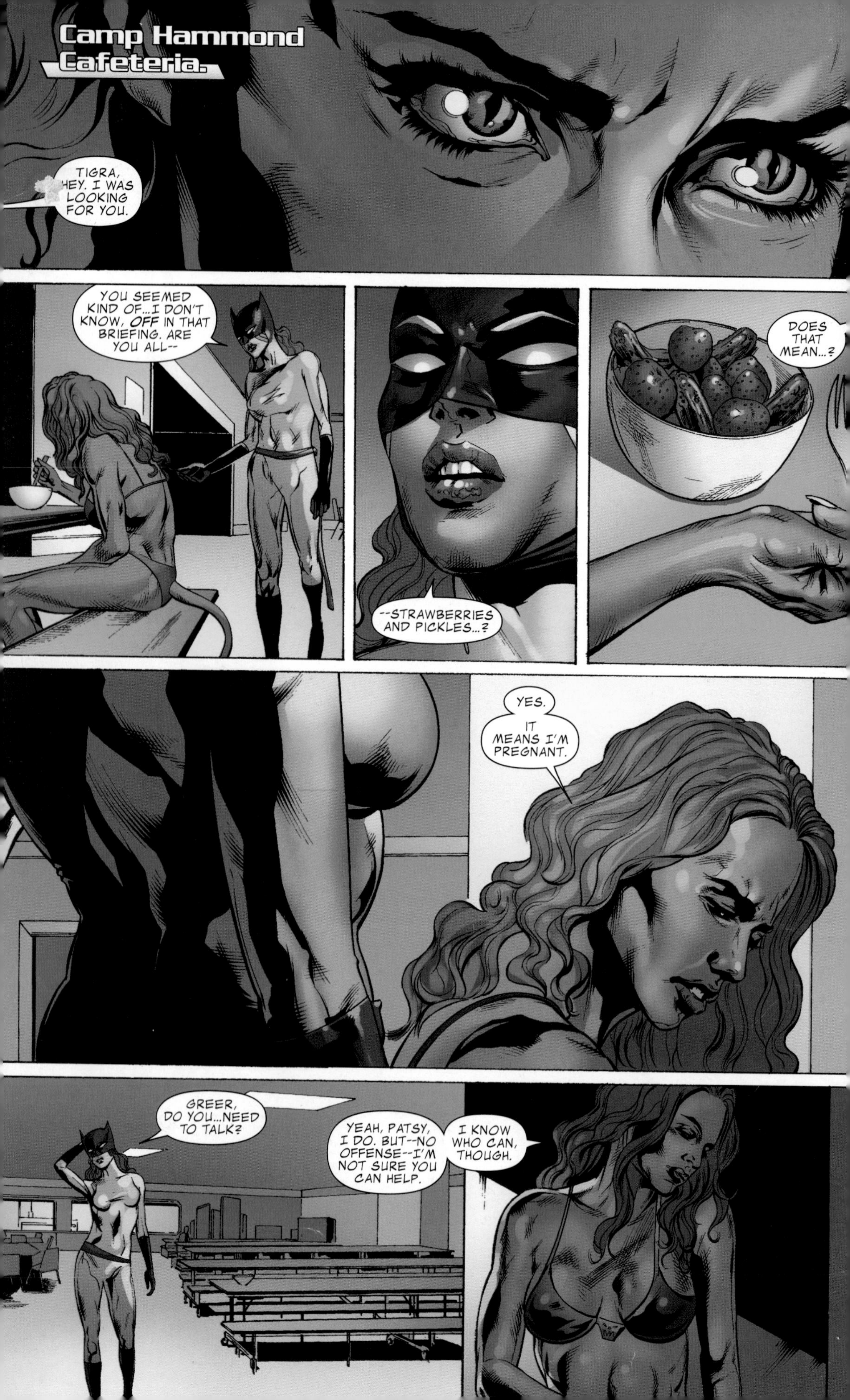
Camp Hammond Cafeteria.
TIGRA, HEY. I WAS LOOKING FOR YOU.
YOU SEEMED KIND OF...I DON'T KNOW, OFF IN THAT BRIEFING. ARE YOU ALL--
--STRAWBERRIES AND PICKLES...?
DOES THAT MEAN...?
YES.
IT MEANS I'M PREGNANT.
GREER, DO YOU...NEED TO TALK?
YEAH, PATSY, I DO. BUT--NO OFFENSE--I'M NOT SURE YOU CAN HELP.
I KNOW WHO CAN, THOUGH.

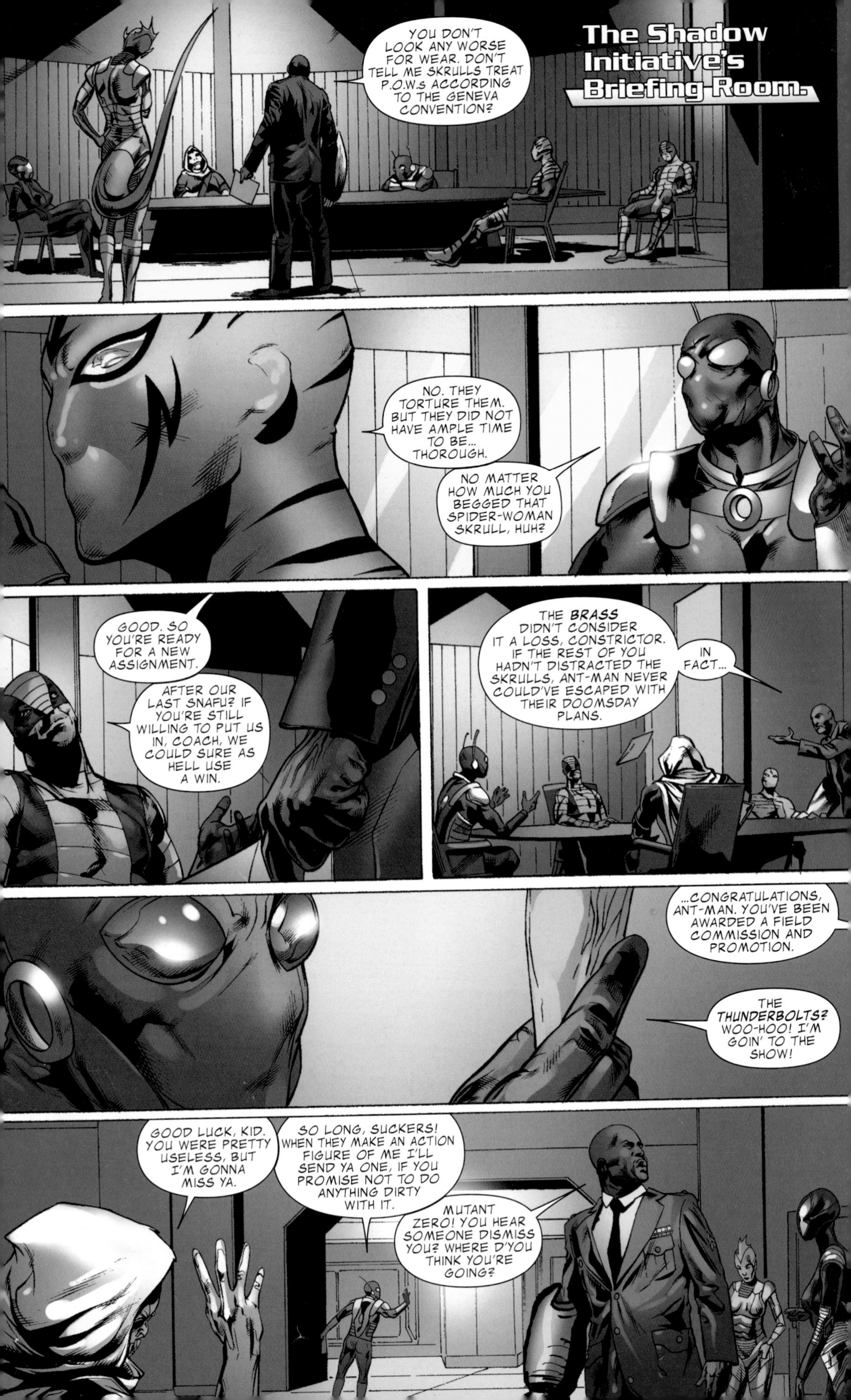
The Shadow Initiative's Briefing Room.
YOU DON'T LOOK ANY WORSE FOR WEAR. DON'T TELL ME SKRULLS TREAT P.O.W.s ACCORDING TO THE GENEVA CONVENTION?
NO. THEY TORTURE THEM. BUT THEY DID NOT HAVE AMPLE TIME TO BE... THOROUGH.
NO MATTER HOW MUCH YOU BEGGED THAT SPIDER-WOMAN SKRULL, HUH?
GOOD. SO YOU'RE READY FOR A NEW ASSIGNMENT.
AFTER OUR LAST SNAFU? IF YOU'RE STILL WILLING TO PUT US IN, COACH, WE COULD SURE AS HELL USE A WIN.
THE BRASS DIDN'T CONSIDER IT A LOSS, CONSTRICTOR. IF THE REST OF YOU HADN'T DISTRACTED THE SKRULLS, ANT-MAN NEVER COULD'VE ESCAPED WITH THEIR DOOMSDAY PLANS.
IN FACT...
...CONGRATULATIONS, ANT-MAN. YOU'VE BEEN AWARDED A FIELD COMMISSION AND PROMOTION.
THE THUNDERBOLTS? WOO-HOO! I'M GOIN' TO THE SHOW!
GOOD LUCK, KID. YOU WERE PRETTY USELESS, BUT I'M GONNA MISS YA.
SO LONG, SUCKERS! WHEN THEY MAKE AN ACTION FIGURE OF ME I'LL SEND YA ONE, IF YOU PROMISE NOT TO DO ANYTHING DIRTY WITH IT.
MUTANT ZERO! YOU HEAR SOMEONE DISMISS YOU? WHERE D'YOU THINK YOU'RE GOING?

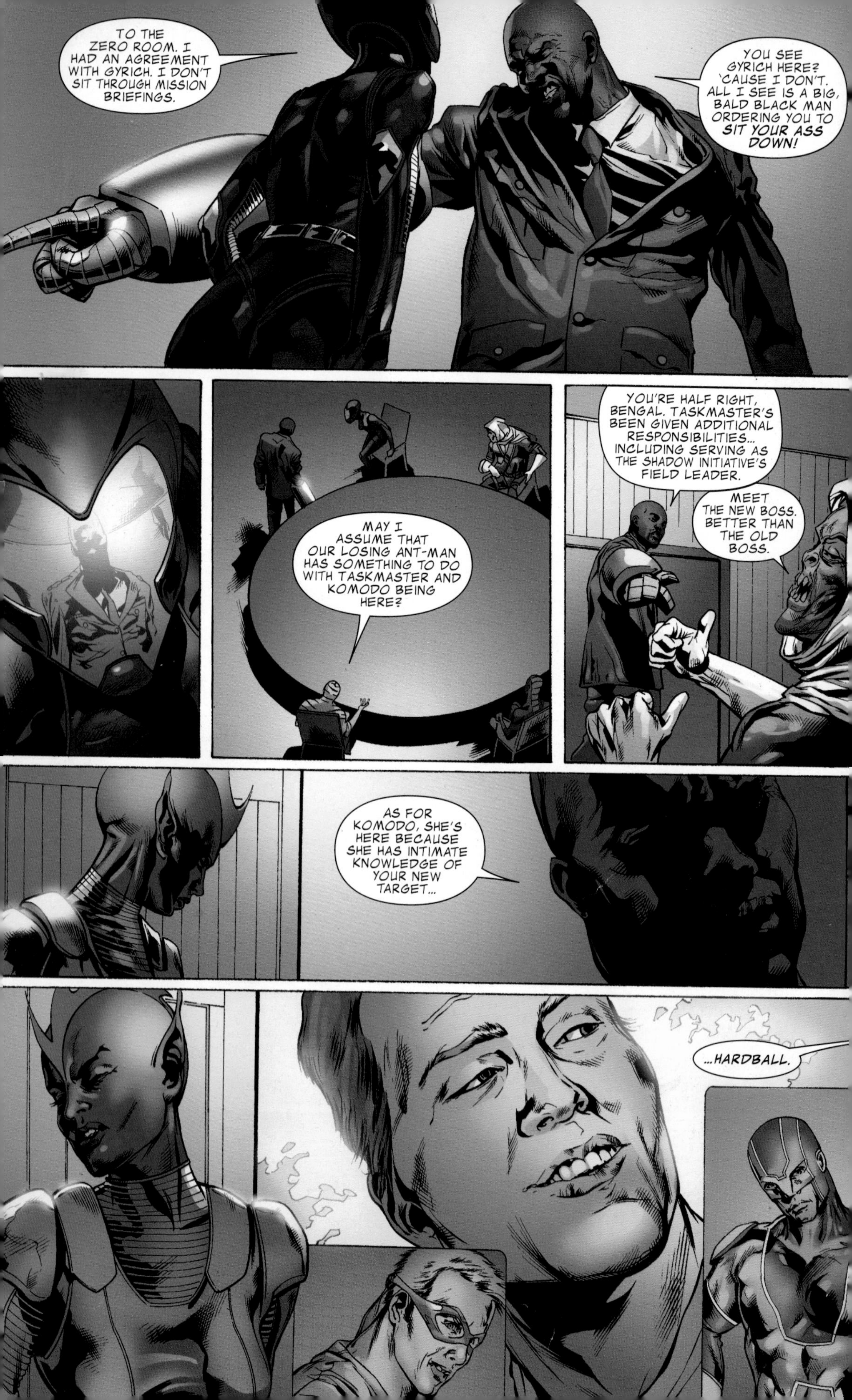

TO THE ZERO ROOM. I HAD AN AGREEMENT WITH GYRICH. I DON'T SIT THROUGH MISSION BRIEFINGS.
YOU SEE GYRICH HERE? 'CAUSE I DON'T. ALL I SEE IS A BIG, BALD BLACK MAN ORDERING YOU TO SIT YOUR ASS DOWN!
MAY I ASSUME THAT OUR LOSING ANT-MAN HAS SOMETHING TO DO WITH TASKMASTER AND KOMODO BEING HERE?
YOU'RE HALF RIGHT, BENGAL. TASKMASTER'S BEEN GIVEN ADDITIONAL RESPONSIBILITIES... INCLUDING SERVING AS THE SHADOW INITIATIVE'S FIELD LEADER.
MEET THE NEW BOSS. BETTER THAN THE OLD BOSS.
AS FOR KOMODO, SHE'S HERE BECAUSE SHE HAS INTIMATE KNOWLEDGE OF YOUR NEW TARGET...
...HARDBALL.

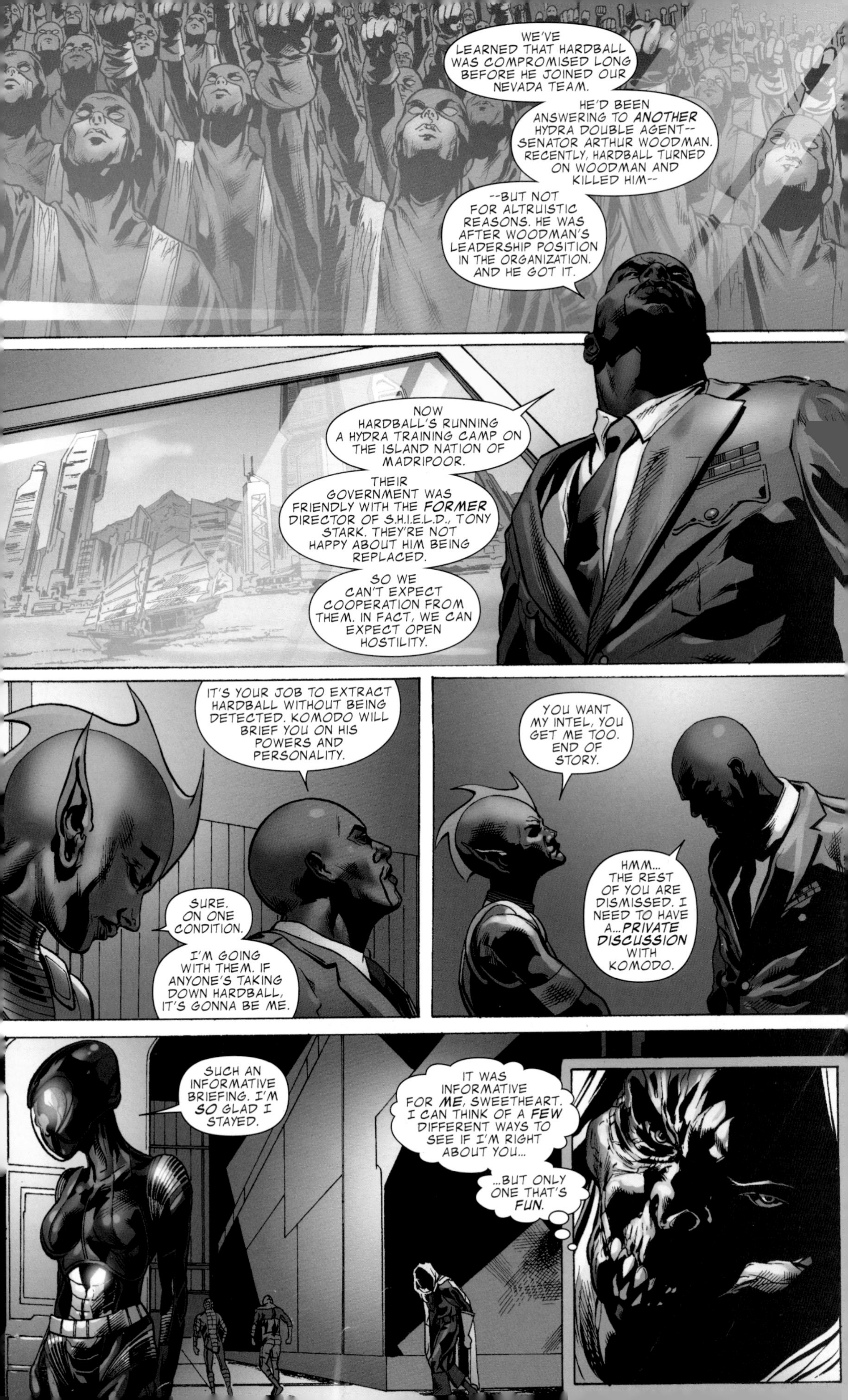
WE'VE LEARNED THAT HARDBALL WAS COMPROMISED LONG BEFORE HE JOINED OUR NEVADA TEAM.
HE'D BEEN ANSWERING TO ANOTHER HYDRA DOUBLE AGENT-- SENATOR ARTHUR WOODMAN. RECENTLY, HARDBALL TURNED ON WOODMAN AND KILLED HIM--
--BUT NOT FOR ALTRUISTIC REASONS. HE WAS AFTER WOODMAN'S LEADERSHIP POSITION IN THE ORGANIZATION. AND HE GOT IT.
NOW HARDBALL'S RUNNING A HYDRA TRAINING CAMP ON THE ISLAND NATION OF MADRIPOOR.
THEIR GOVERNMENT WAS FRIENDLY WITH THE FORMER DIRECTOR OF S.H.I.E.L.D., TONY STARK. THEY'RE NOT HAPPY ABOUT HIM BEING REPLACED.
SO WE CAN'T EXPECT COOPERATION FROM THEM. IN FACT, WE CAN EXPECT OPEN HOSTILITY.
IT'S YOUR JOB TO EXTRACT HARDBALL WITHOUT BEING DETECTED. KOMODO WILL BRIEF YOU ON HIS POWERS AND PERSONALITY.
SURE. ON ONE CONDITION.
I'M GOING WITH THEM. IF ANYONE'S TAKING DOWN HARDBALL, IT'S GONNA BE ME.
YOU WANT MY INTEL, YOU GET ME TOO. END OF STORY.
HMM... THE REST OF YOU ARE DISMISSED. I NEED TO HAVE A...PRIVATE DISCUSSION WITH KOMODO.
SUCH AN INFORMATIVE BRIEFING. I'M SO GLAD I STAYED.
IT WAS INFORMATIVE FOR ME, SWEETHEART. I CAN THINK OF A FEW DIFFERENT WAYS TO SEE IF I'M RIGHT ABOUT YOU...
...BUT ONLY ONE THAT'S FUN.

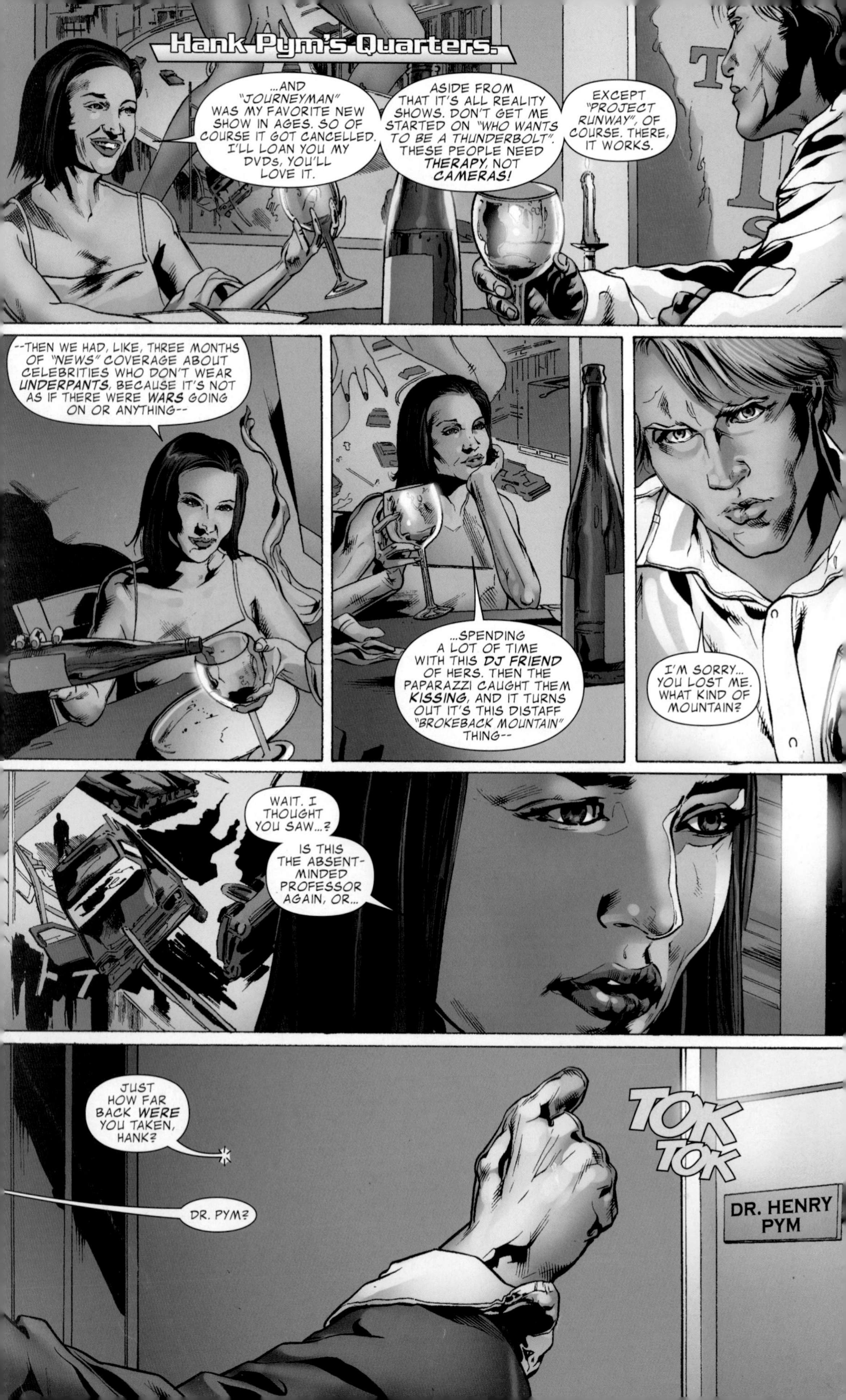
Hank Pym's Quarters.
...AND "JOURNEYMAN" WAS MY FAVORITE NEW SHOW IN AGES. SO OF COURSE IT GOT CANCELLED. I'LL LOAN YOU MY DVDs, YOU'LL LOVE IT.
ASIDE FROM THAT IT'S ALL REALITY SHOWS. DON'T GET ME STARTED ON "WHO WANTS TO BE A THUNDERBOLT". THESE PEOPLE NEED THERAPY, NOT CAMERAS!
EXCEPT "PROJECT RUNWAY", OF COURSE. THERE, IT WORKS.
--THEN WE HAD, LIKE, THREE MONTHS OF "NEWS" COVERAGE ABOUT CELEBRITIES WHO DON'T WEAR UNDERPANTS, BECAUSE IT'S NOT AS IF THERE WERE WARS GOING ON OR ANYTHING--
...SPENDING A LOT OF TIME WITH THIS DJ FRIEND OF HERS. THEN THE PAPARAZZI CAUGHT THEM KISSING, AND IT TURNS OUT IT'S THIS DISTAFF "BROKEBACK MOUNTAIN" THING--
I'M SORRY... YOU LOST ME. WHAT KIND OF MOUNTAIN?
WAIT. I THOUGHT YOU SAW...?
IS THIS THE ABSENT-MINDED PROFESSOR AGAIN, OR...
JUST HOW FAR BACK WERE YOU TAKEN, HANK?
TOK TOK
DR. PYM?
DR. HENRY PYM

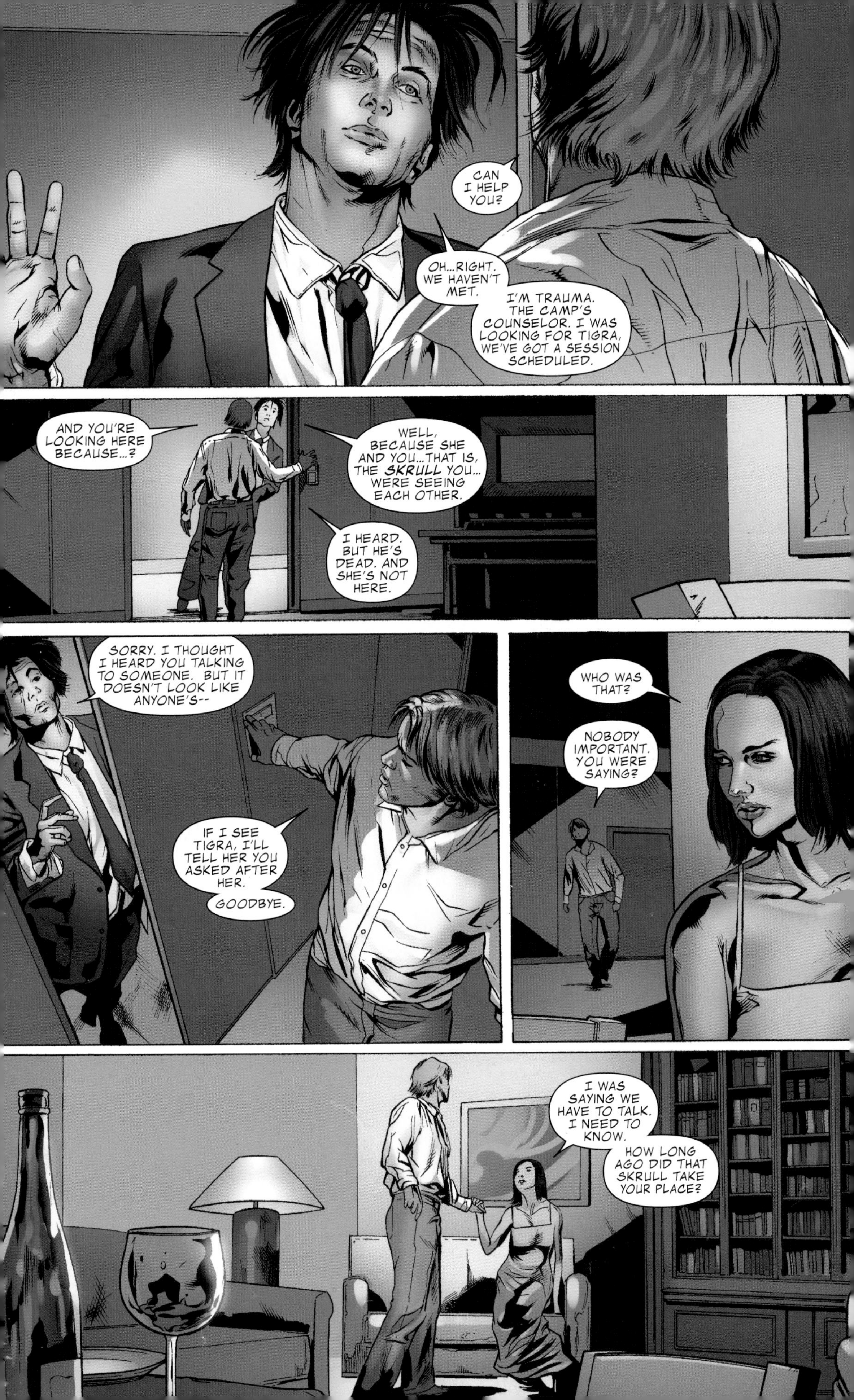
CAN I HELP YOU?
OH...RIGHT. WE HAVEN'T MET.
I'M TRAUMA. THE CAMP'S COUNSELOR. I WAS LOOKING FOR TIGRA, WE'VE GOT A SESSION SCHEDULED.
AND YOU'RE LOOKING HERE BECAUSE...?
WELL, BECAUSE SHE AND YOU...THAT IS, THE SKRULL YOU... WERE SEEING EACH OTHER.
I HEARD. BUT HE'S DEAD. AND SHE'S NOT HERE.
SORRY. I THOUGHT I HEARD YOU TALKING TO SOMEONE. BUT IT DOESN'T LOOK LIKE ANYONE'S--
IF I SEE TIGRA, I'LL TELL HER YOU ASKED AFTER HER.
GOODBYE.
WHO WAS THAT?
NOBODY IMPORTANT. YOU WERE SAYING?
I WAS SAYING WE HAVE TO TALK. I NEED TO KNOW.
HOW LONG AGO DID THAT SKRULL TAKE YOUR PLACE?

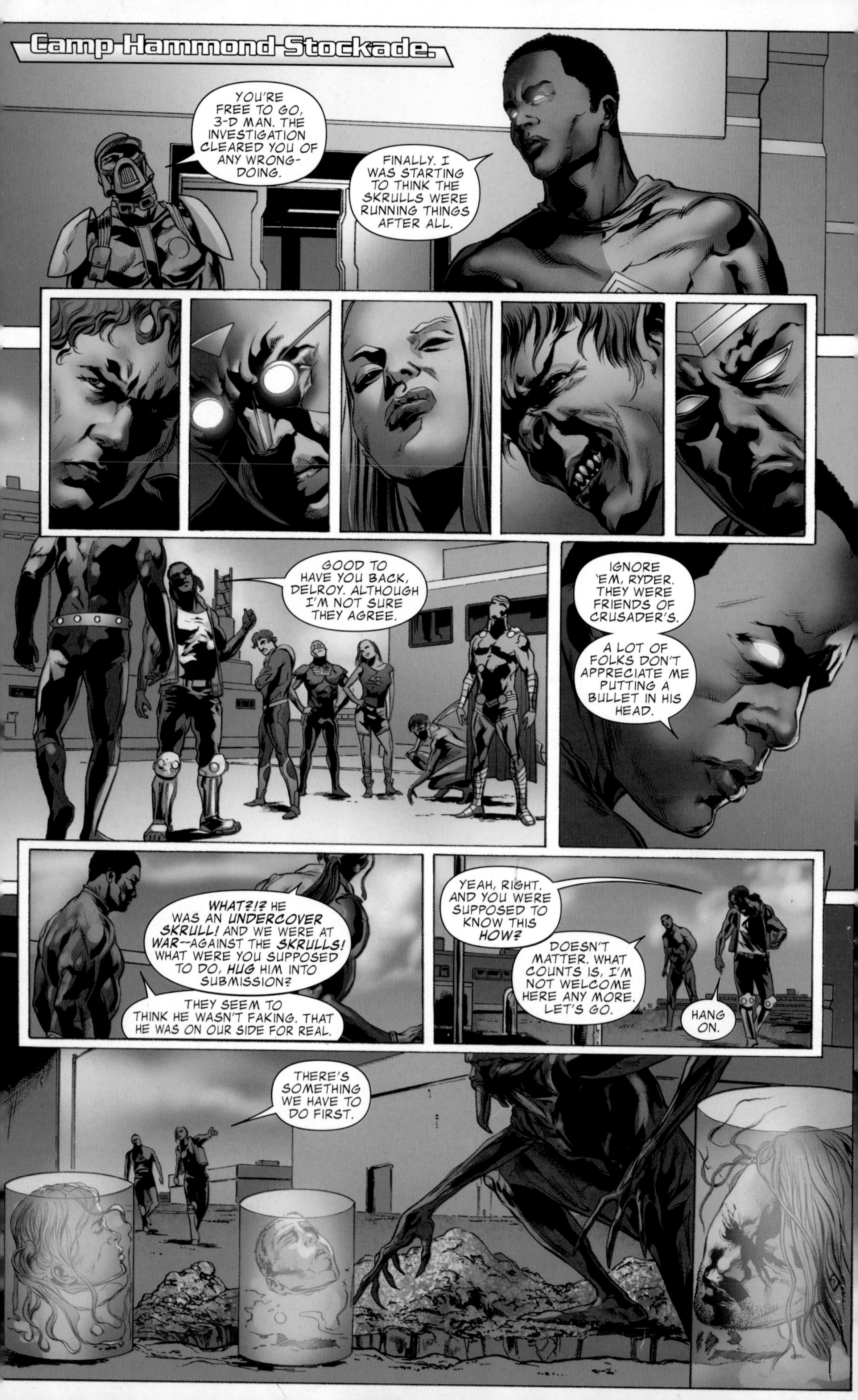
Camp Hammond Stockade.
YOU'RE FREE TO GO, 3-D MAN. THE INVESTIGATION CLEARED YOU OF ANY WRONG-DOING.
FINALLY. I WAS STARTING TO THINK THE SKRULLS WERE RUNNING THINGS AFTER ALL.
GOOD TO HAVE YOU BACK, DELROY. ALTHOUGH I'M NOT SURE THEY AGREE.
IGNORE 'EM, RYDER. THEY WERE FRIENDS OF CRUSADER'S.
A LOT OF FOLKS DON'T APPRECIATE ME PUTTING A BULLET IN HIS HEAD.
WHAT?!? HE WAS AN UNDERCOVER SKRULL! AND WE WERE AT WAR--AGAINST THE SKRULLS! WHAT WERE YOU SUPPOSED TO DO, HUG HIM INTO SUBMISSION?
THEY SEEM TO THINK HE WASN'T FAKING. THAT HE WAS ON OUR SIDE FOR REAL.
YEAH, RIGHT. AND YOU WERE SUPPOSED TO KNOW THIS HOW?
DOESN'T MATTER. WHAT COUNTS IS, I'M NOT WELCOME HERE ANY MORE. LET'S GO.
HANG ON.
THERE'S SOMETHING WE HAVE TO DO FIRST.

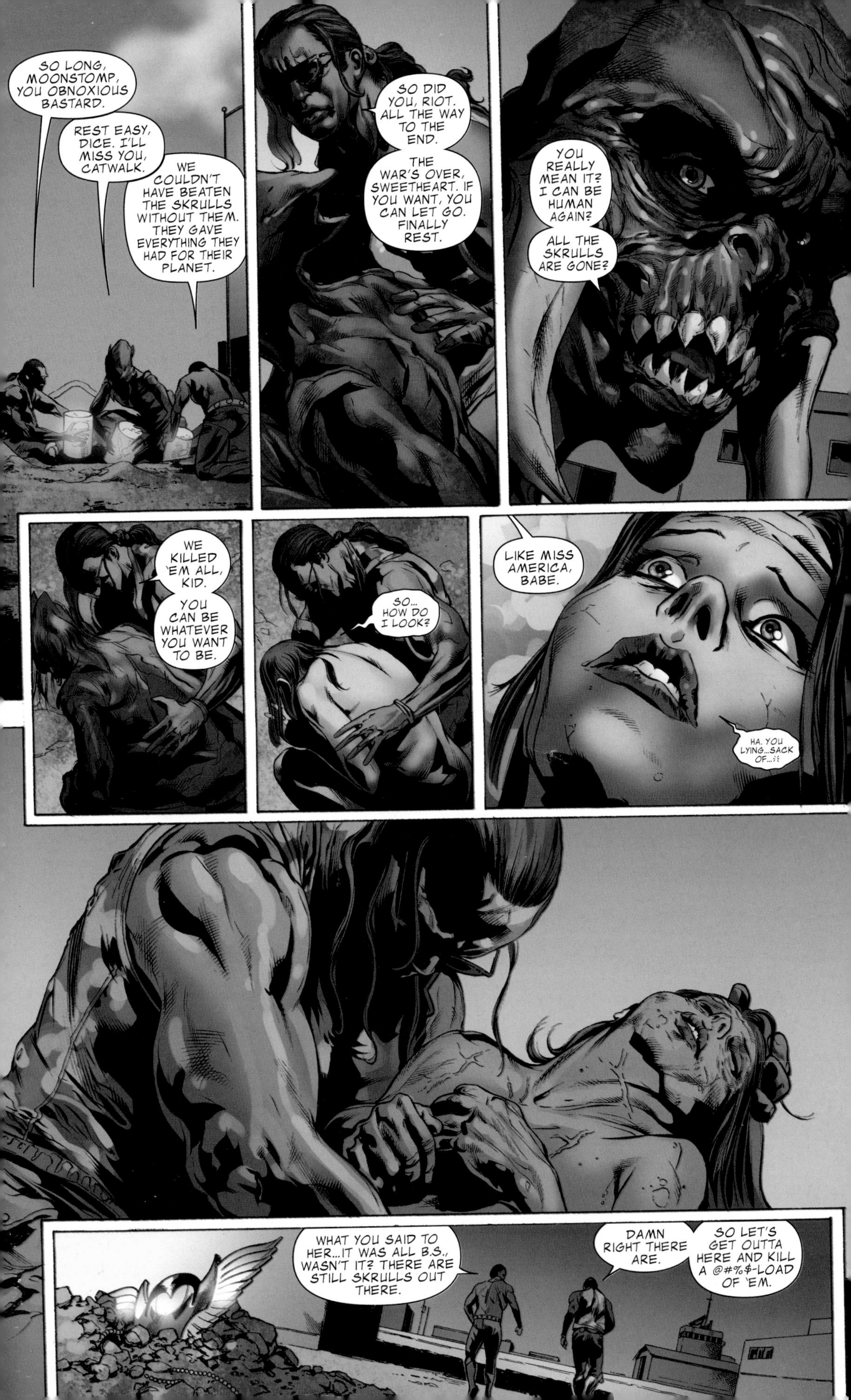
SO LONG, MOONSTOMP, YOU OBNOXIOUS BASTARD.
REST EASY, DICE. I'LL MISS YOU, CATWALK.
WE COULDN'T HAVE BEATEN THE SKRULLS WITHOUT THEM. THEY GAVE EVERYTHING THEY HAD FOR THEIR PLANET.
SO DID YOU, RIOT. ALL THE WAY TO THE END.
THE WAR'S OVER, SWEETHEART. IF YOU WANT, YOU CAN LET GO. FINALLY REST.
YOU REALLY MEAN IT? I CAN BE HUMAN AGAIN?
ALL THE SKRULLS ARE GONE?
WE KILLED 'EM ALL, KID.
YOU CAN BE WHATEVER YOU WANT TO BE.
SO... HOW DO I LOOK?
LIKE MISS AMERICA, BABE.
HA. YOU LYING...SACK OF...
WHAT YOU SAID TO HER...IT WAS ALL B.S., WASN'T IT? THERE ARE STILL SKRULLS OUT THERE.
DAMN RIGHT THERE ARE.
SO LET'S GET OUTTA HERE AND KILL A @#%$-LOAD OF 'EM.

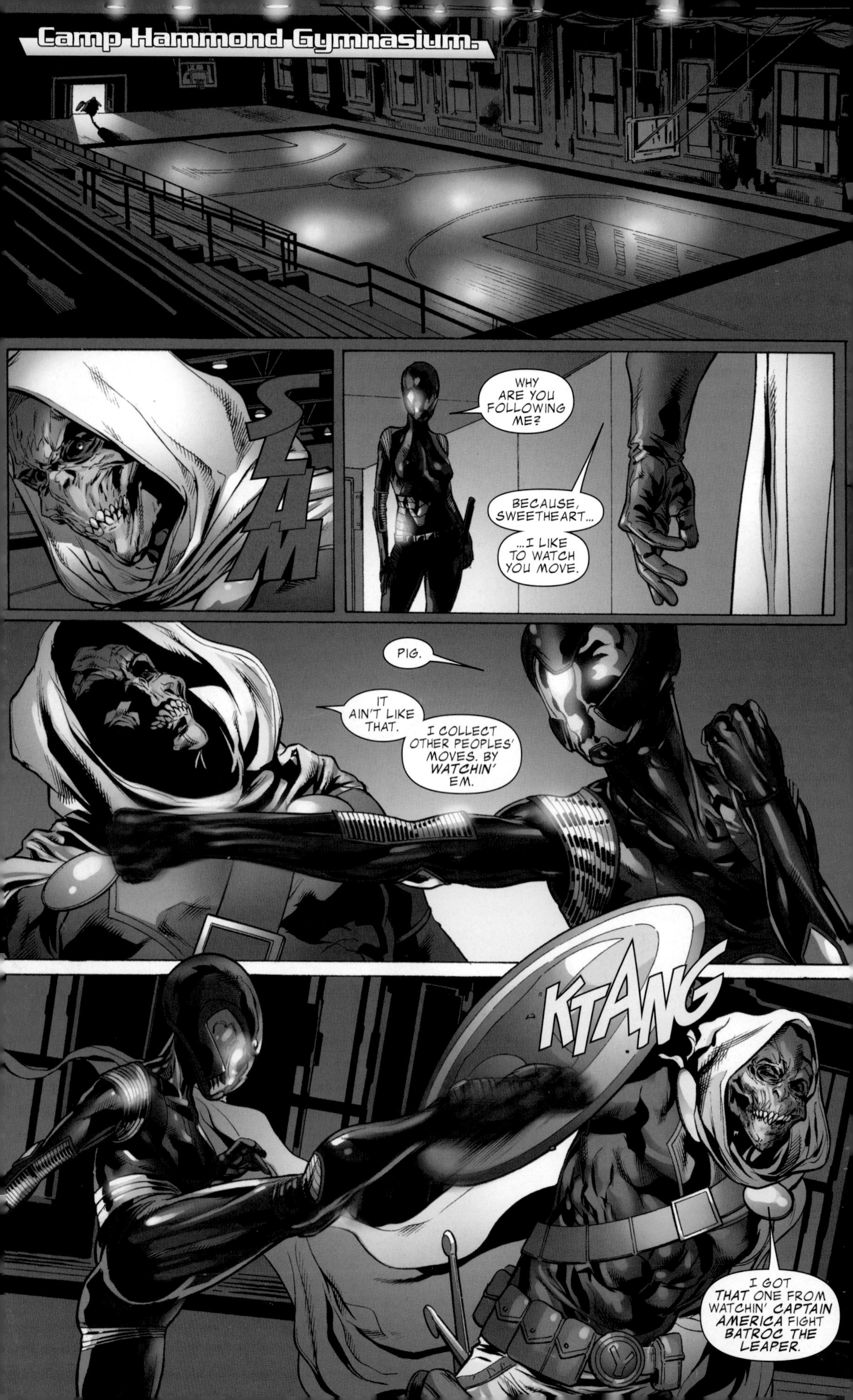
Camp Hammond Gymnasium.
SLAM
WHY ARE YOU FOLLOWING ME?
BECAUSE, SWEETHEART...
...I LIKE TO WATCH YOU MOVE.
PIG.
IT AIN'T LIKE THAT.
I COLLECT OTHER PEOPLES' MOVES. BY WATCHIN' EM.
KTANG
I GOT THAT ONE FROM WATCHIN' CAPTAIN AMERICA FIGHT BATROC THE LEAPER.

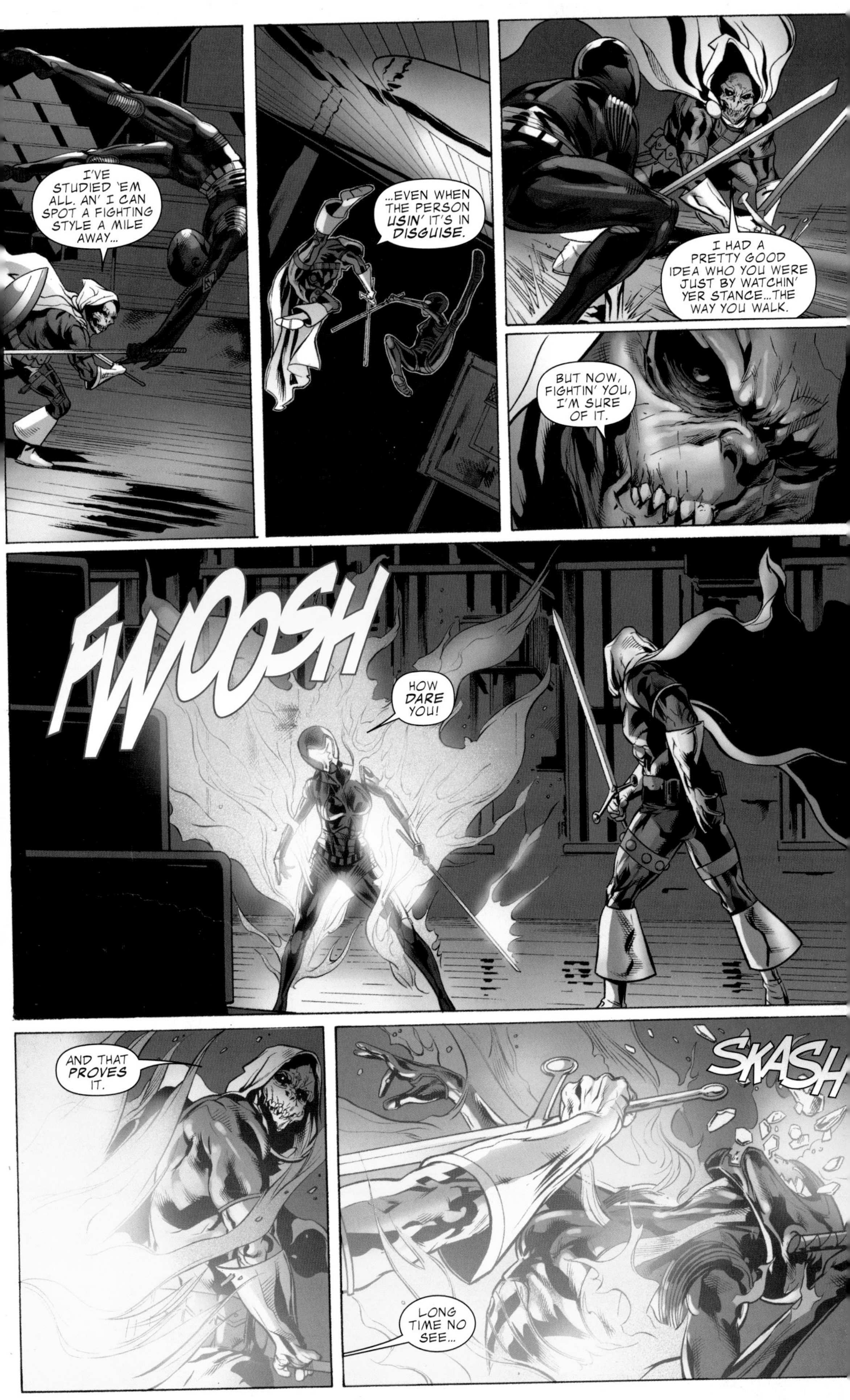
I'VE STUDIED 'EM ALL. AN' I CAN SPOT A FIGHTING STYLE A MILE AWAY...
...EVEN WHEN THE PERSON USIN' IT'S IN DISGUISE.
I HAD A PRETTY GOOD IDEA WHO YOU WERE JUST BY WATCHIN' YER STANCE...THE WAY YOU WALK.
BUT NOW, FIGHTIN' YOU, I'M SURE OF IT.
FWOOSH
HOW DARE YOU!
AND THAT PROVES IT.
SKASH
LONG TIME NO SEE...

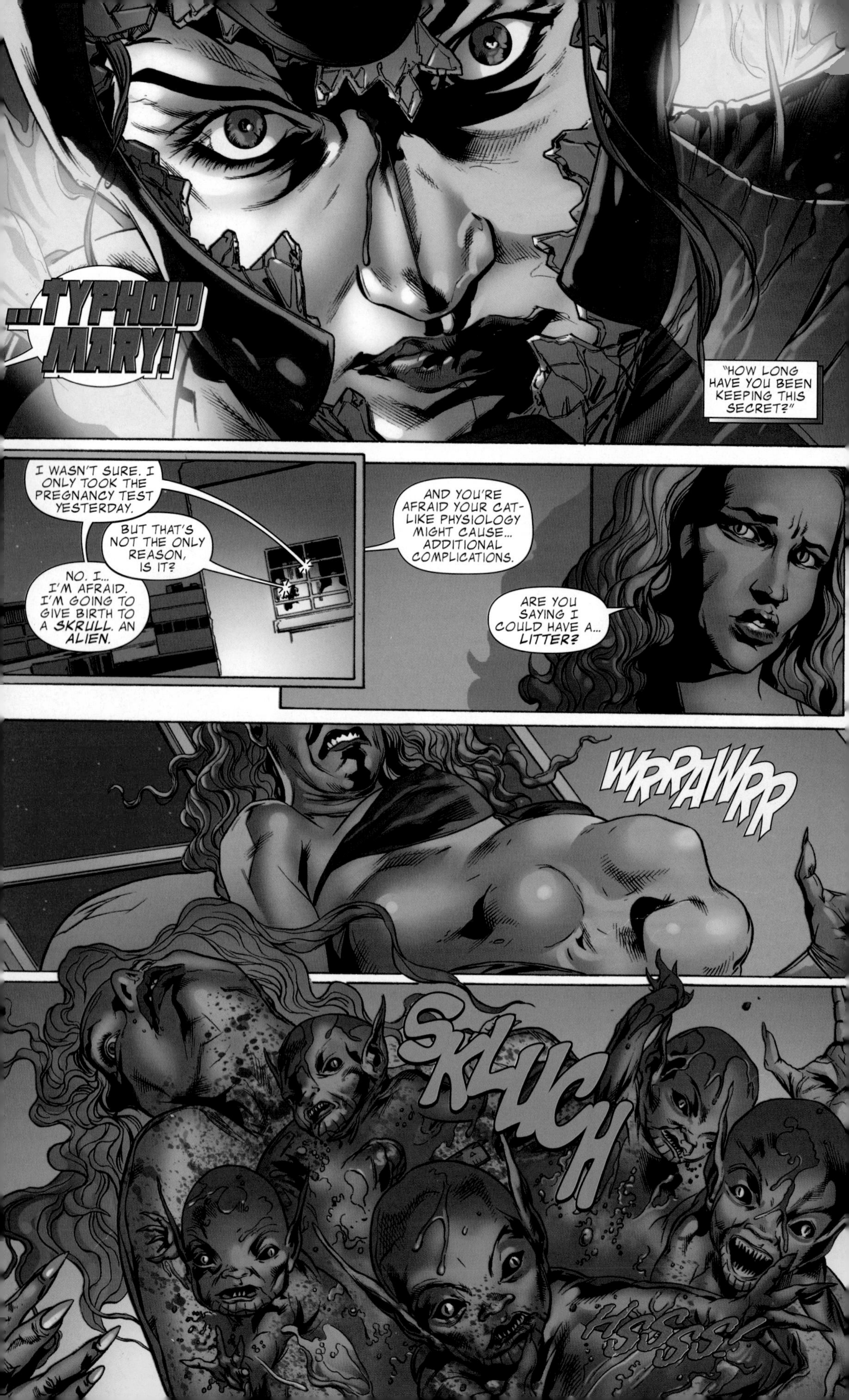
...TYPHOID MARY!
"HOW LONG HAVE YOU BEEN KEEPING THIS SECRET?"
I WASN'T SURE. I ONLY TOOK THE PREGNANCY TEST YESTERDAY.
BUT THAT'S NOT THE ONLY REASON, IS IT?
NO. I... I'M AFRAID. I'M GOING TO GIVE BIRTH TO A SKRULL. AN ALIEN.
AND YOU'RE AFRAID YOUR CAT-LIKE PHYSIOLOGY MIGHT CAUSE... ADDITIONAL COMPLICATIONS.
ARE YOU SAYING I COULD HAVE A... LITTER?
WRRAWRR
SKLUCH
HSSSS!

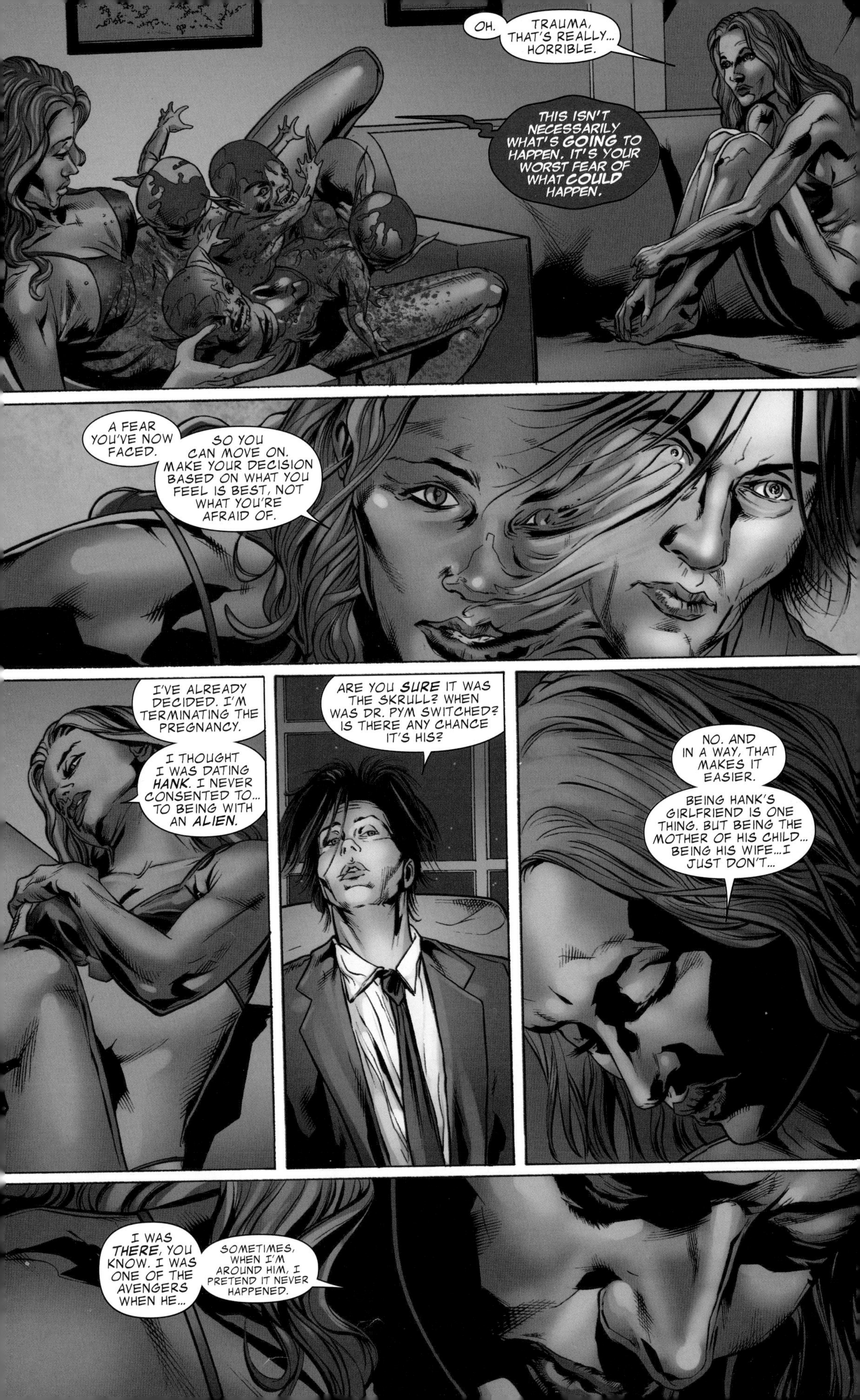
OH.
TRAUMA, THAT'S REALLY... HORRIBLE.
THIS ISN'T NECESSARILY WHAT'S **GOING** TO HAPPEN. IT'S YOUR WORST FEAR OF WHAT **COULD** HAPPEN.
A FEAR YOU'VE NOW FACED.
SO YOU CAN MOVE ON. MAKE YOUR DECISION BASED ON WHAT YOU FEEL IS BEST, NOT WHAT YOU'RE AFRAID OF.
I'VE ALREADY DECIDED. I'M TERMINATING THE PREGNANCY.
I THOUGHT I WAS DATING **HANK**. I NEVER CONSENTED TO... TO BEING WITH AN ***ALIEN***.
ARE YOU ***SURE*** IT WAS THE SKRULL? WHEN WAS DR. PYM SWITCHED? IS THERE ANY CHANCE IT'S HIS?
NO. AND IN A WAY, THAT MAKES IT EASIER.
BEING HANK'S GIRLFRIEND IS ONE THING. BUT BEING THE MOTHER OF HIS CHILD... BEING HIS WIFE...I JUST DON'T...
I WAS ***THERE***, YOU KNOW. I WAS ONE OF THE AVENGERS WHEN HE...
SOMETIMES, WHEN I'M AROUND HIM, I PRETEND IT NEVER HAPPENED.

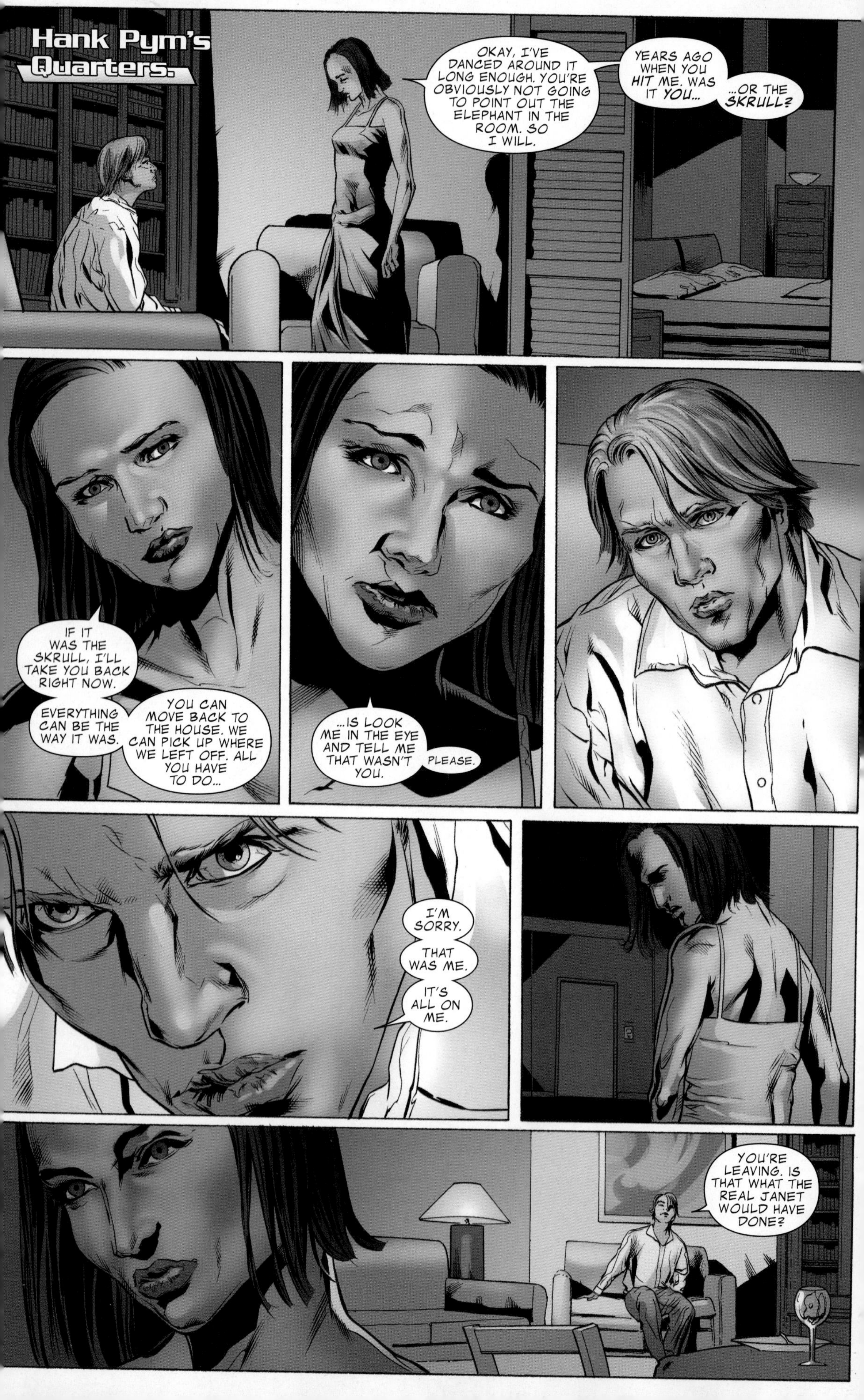
Hank Pym's Quarters.
OKAY, I'VE DANCED AROUND IT LONG ENOUGH. YOU'RE OBVIOUSLY NOT GOING TO POINT OUT THE ELEPHANT IN THE ROOM. SO I WILL.
YEARS AGO WHEN YOU HIT ME. WAS IT YOU...
...OR THE SKRULL?
IF IT WAS THE SKRULL, I'LL TAKE YOU BACK RIGHT NOW.
EVERYTHING CAN BE THE WAY IT WAS.
YOU CAN MOVE BACK TO THE HOUSE. WE CAN PICK UP WHERE WE LEFT OFF. ALL YOU HAVE TO DO...
...IS LOOK ME IN THE EYE AND TELL ME THAT WASN'T YOU.
PLEASE.
I'M SORRY.
THAT WAS ME.
IT'S ALL ON ME.
YOU'RE LEAVING. IS THAT WHAT THE REAL JANET WOULD HAVE DONE?

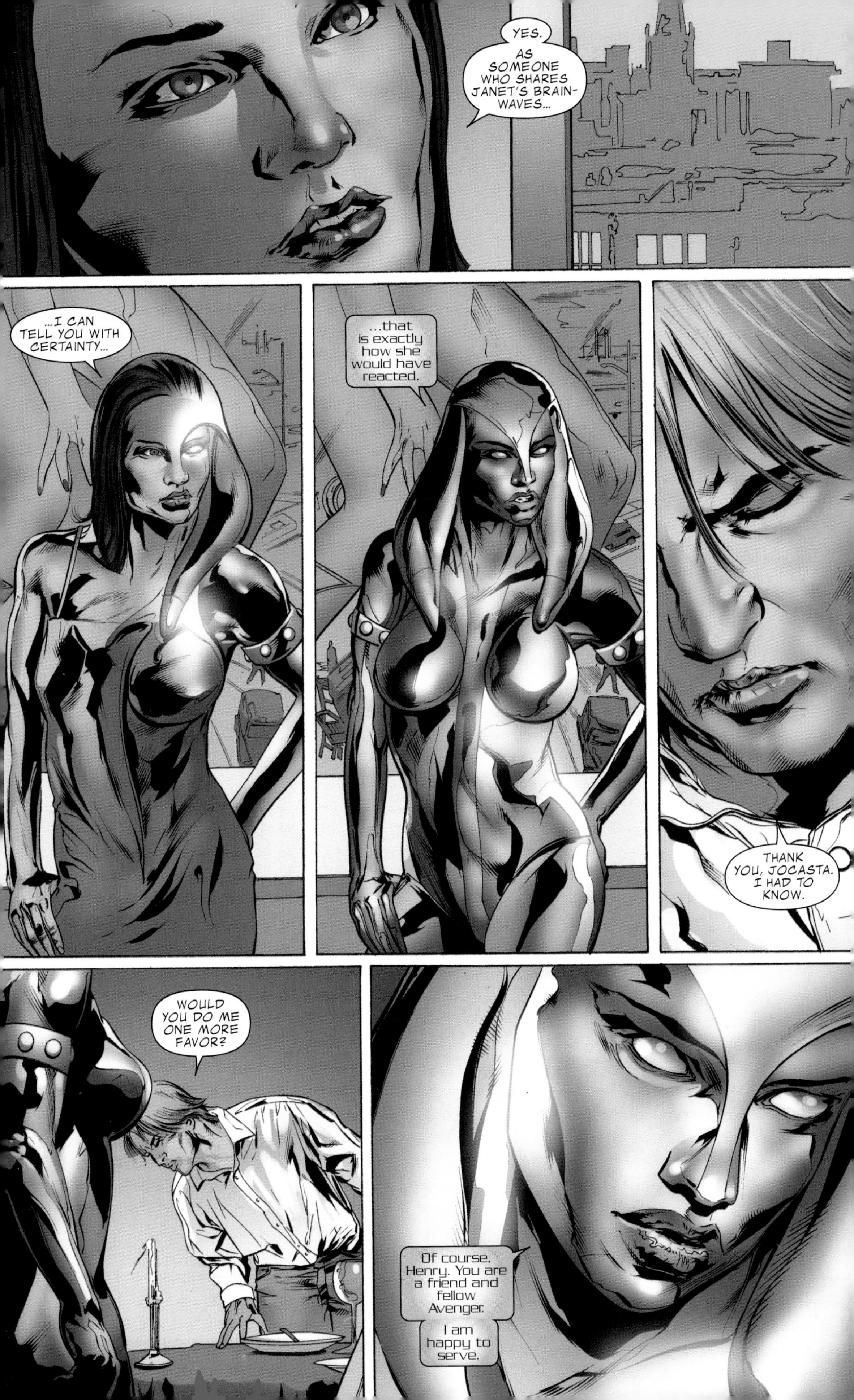
YES.
AS SOMEONE WHO SHARES JANET'S BRAIN-WAVES...
...I CAN TELL YOU WITH CERTAINTY...
...that is exactly how she would have reacted.
THANK YOU, JOCASTA. I HAD TO KNOW.
WOULD YOU DO ME ONE MORE FAVOR?
Of course, Henry. You are a friend and fellow Avenger.
I am happy to serve.

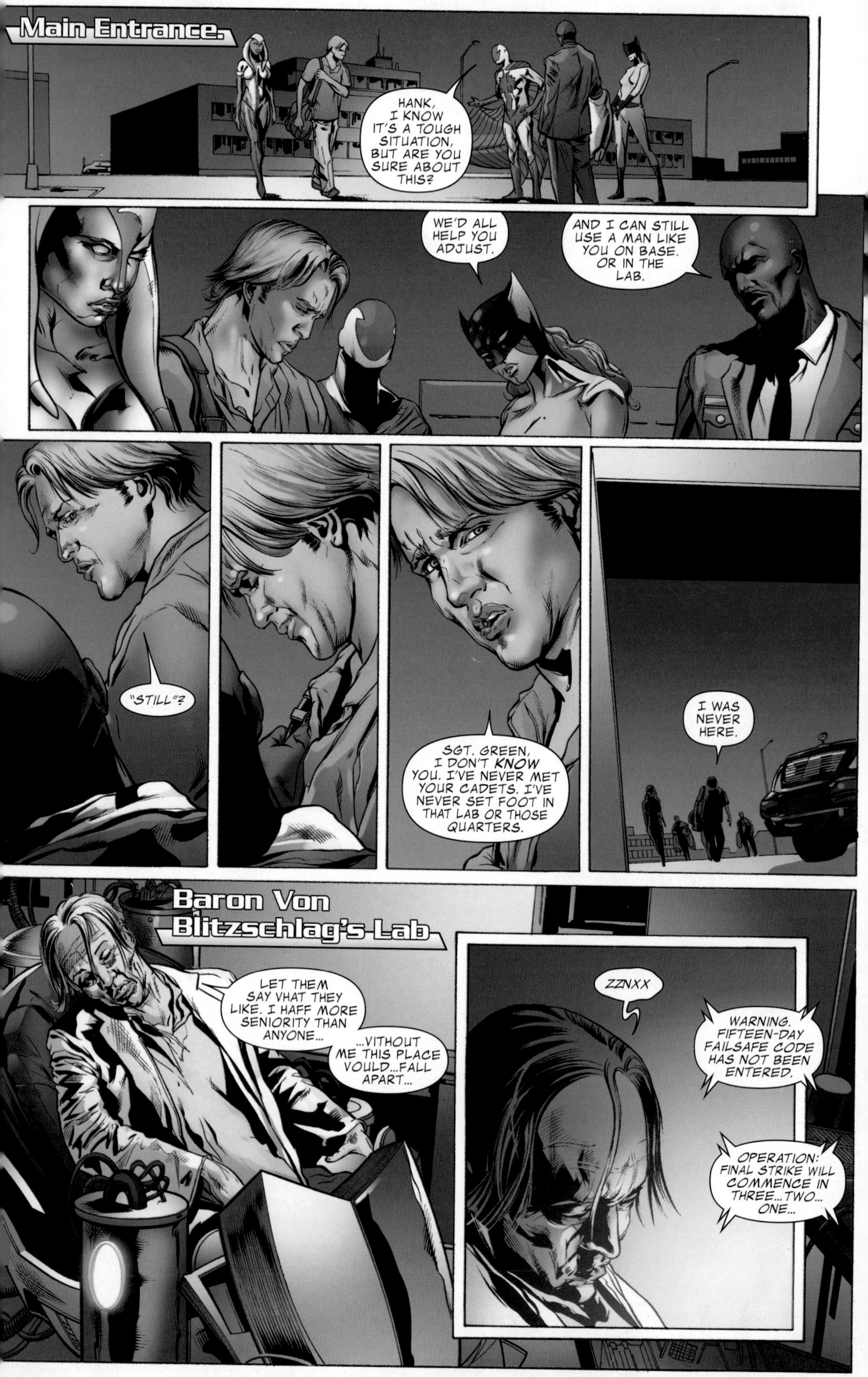

Main Entrance.
HANK, I KNOW IT'S A TOUGH SITUATION, BUT ARE YOU SURE ABOUT THIS?
WE'D ALL HELP YOU ADJUST.
AND I CAN STILL USE A MAN LIKE YOU ON BASE. OR IN THE LAB.
"STILL"?
SGT. GREEN, I DON'T KNOW YOU. I'VE NEVER MET YOUR CADETS. I'VE NEVER SET FOOT IN THAT LAB OR THOSE QUARTERS.
I WAS NEVER HERE.
Baron Von Blitzschlag's Lab
LET THEM SAY VHAT THEY LIKE. I HAFF MORE SENIORITY THAN ANYONE...
...VITHOUT ME THIS PLACE VOULD...FALL APART...
ZZNXX
WARNING. FIFTEEN-DAY FAILSAFE CODE HAS NOT BEEN ENTERED.
OPERATION: FINAL STRIKE WILL COMMENCE IN THREE...TWO... ONE...

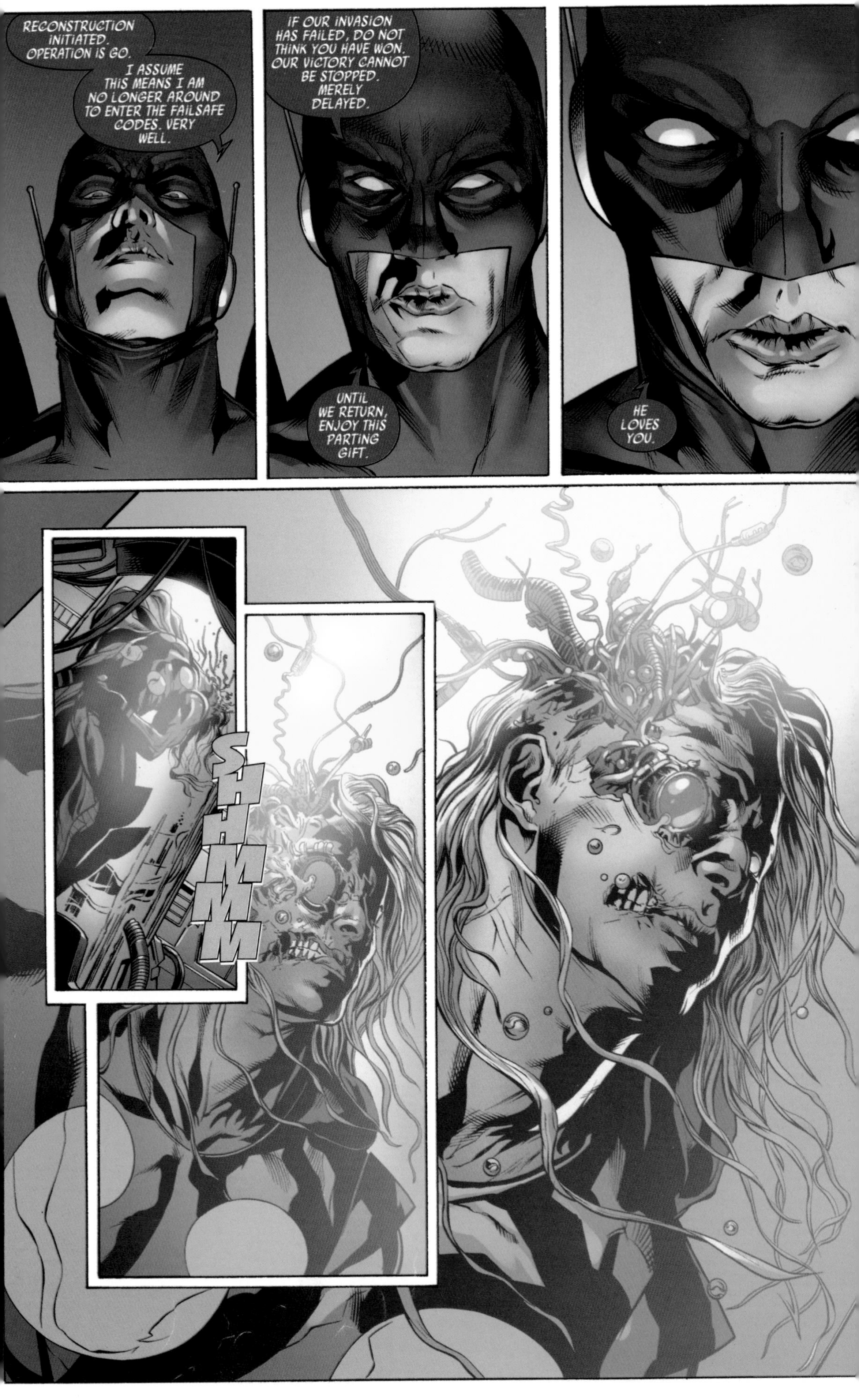
RECONSTRUCTION INITIATED. OPERATION IS GO.
I ASSUME THIS MEANS I AM NO LONGER AROUND TO ENTER THE FAILSAFE CODES. VERY WELL.
IF OUR INVASION HAS FAILED, DO NOT THINK YOU HAVE WON. OUR VICTORY CANNOT BE STOPPED. MERELY DELAYED.
UNTIL WE RETURN, ENJOY THIS PARTING GIFT.
HE LOVES YOU.
SHHHMMM

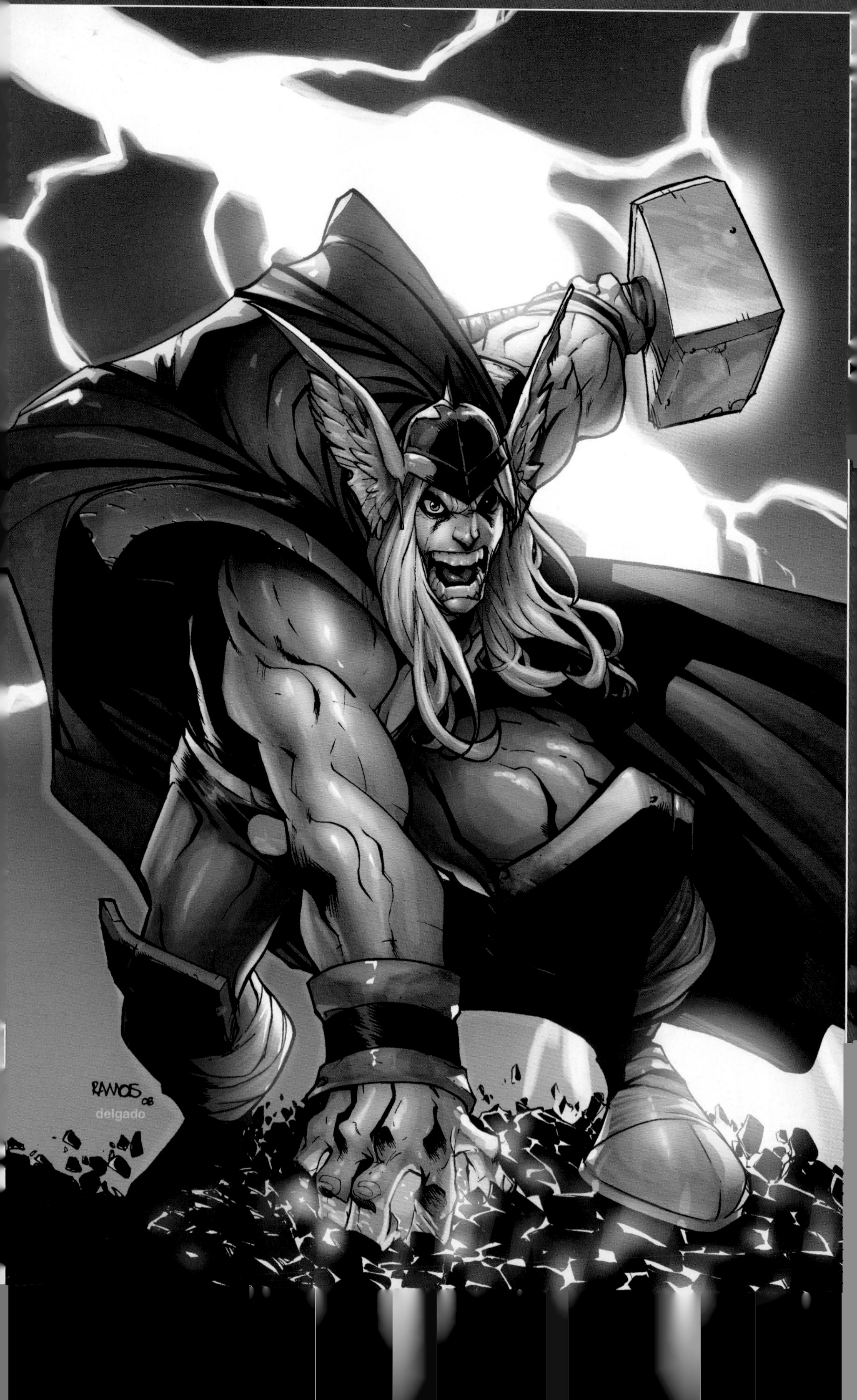
RAMOS 08
delgado

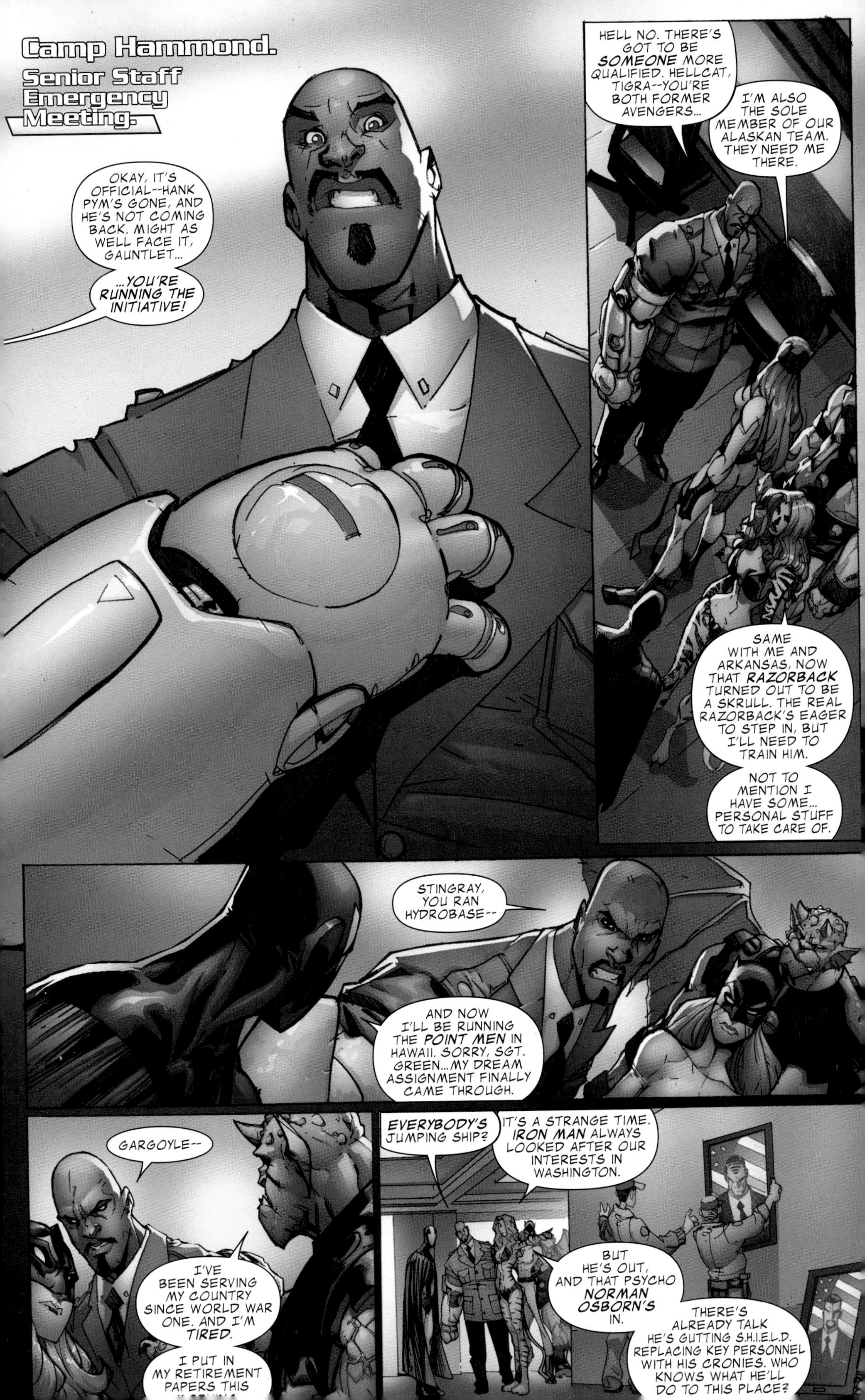
Camp Hammond.
Senior Staff Emergency Meeting.
OKAY, IT'S OFFICIAL--HANK PYM'S GONE, AND HE'S NOT COMING BACK. MIGHT AS WELL FACE IT, GAUNTLET...
...YOU'RE RUNNING THE INITIATIVE!
HELL NO. THERE'S GOT TO BE SOMEONE MORE QUALIFIED. HELLCAT, TIGRA--YOU'RE BOTH FORMER AVENGERS...
I'M ALSO THE SOLE MEMBER OF OUR ALASKAN TEAM. THEY NEED ME THERE.
SAME WITH ME AND ARKANSAS, NOW THAT RAZORBACK TURNED OUT TO BE A SKRULL. THE REAL RAZORBACK'S EAGER TO STEP IN, BUT I'LL NEED TO TRAIN HIM.
NOT TO MENTION I HAVE SOME... PERSONAL STUFF TO TAKE CARE OF.
STINGRAY, YOU RAN HYDROBASE--
AND NOW I'LL BE RUNNING THE POINT MEN IN HAWAII. SORRY, SGT. GREEN...MY DREAM ASSIGNMENT FINALLY CAME THROUGH.
GARGOYLE--
I'VE BEEN SERVING MY COUNTRY SINCE WORLD WAR ONE. AND I'M TIRED.
I PUT IN MY RETIREMENT PAPERS THIS
EVERYBODY'S JUMPING SHIP?
IT'S A STRANGE TIME. IRON MAN ALWAYS LOOKED AFTER OUR INTERESTS IN WASHINGTON.
BUT HE'S OUT, AND THAT PSYCHO NORMAN OSBORN'S IN.
THERE'S ALREADY TALK HE'S GUTTING S.H.I.E.L.D. REPLACING KEY PERSONNEL WITH HIS CRONIES. WHO KNOWS WHAT HE'LL DO TO THIS PLACE?

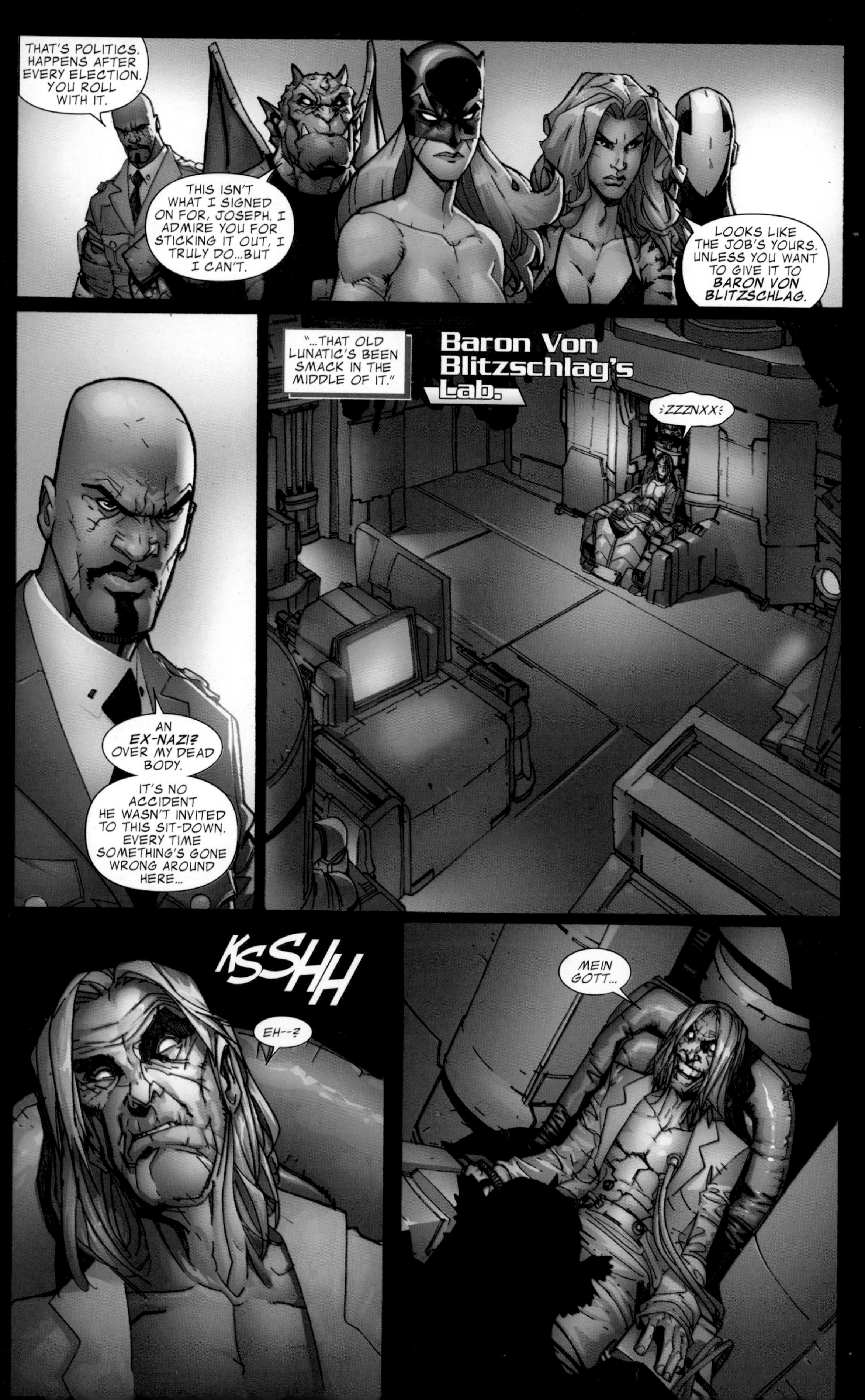
THAT'S POLITICS. HAPPENS AFTER EVERY ELECTION. YOU ROLL WITH IT.
THIS ISN'T WHAT I SIGNED ON FOR, JOSEPH. I ADMIRE YOU FOR STICKING IT OUT, I TRULY DO...BUT I CAN'T.
LOOKS LIKE THE JOB'S YOURS. UNLESS YOU WANT TO GIVE IT TO BARON VON BLITZSCHLAG.
AN EX-NAZI? OVER MY DEAD BODY.
IT'S NO ACCIDENT HE WASN'T INVITED TO THIS SIT-DOWN. EVERY TIME SOMETHING'S GONE WRONG AROUND HERE...
"...THAT OLD LUNATIC'S BEEN SMACK IN THE MIDDLE OF IT."
Baron Von Blitzschlag's Lab.
ZZZNXX
KSSHH
EH--?
MEIN GOTT...

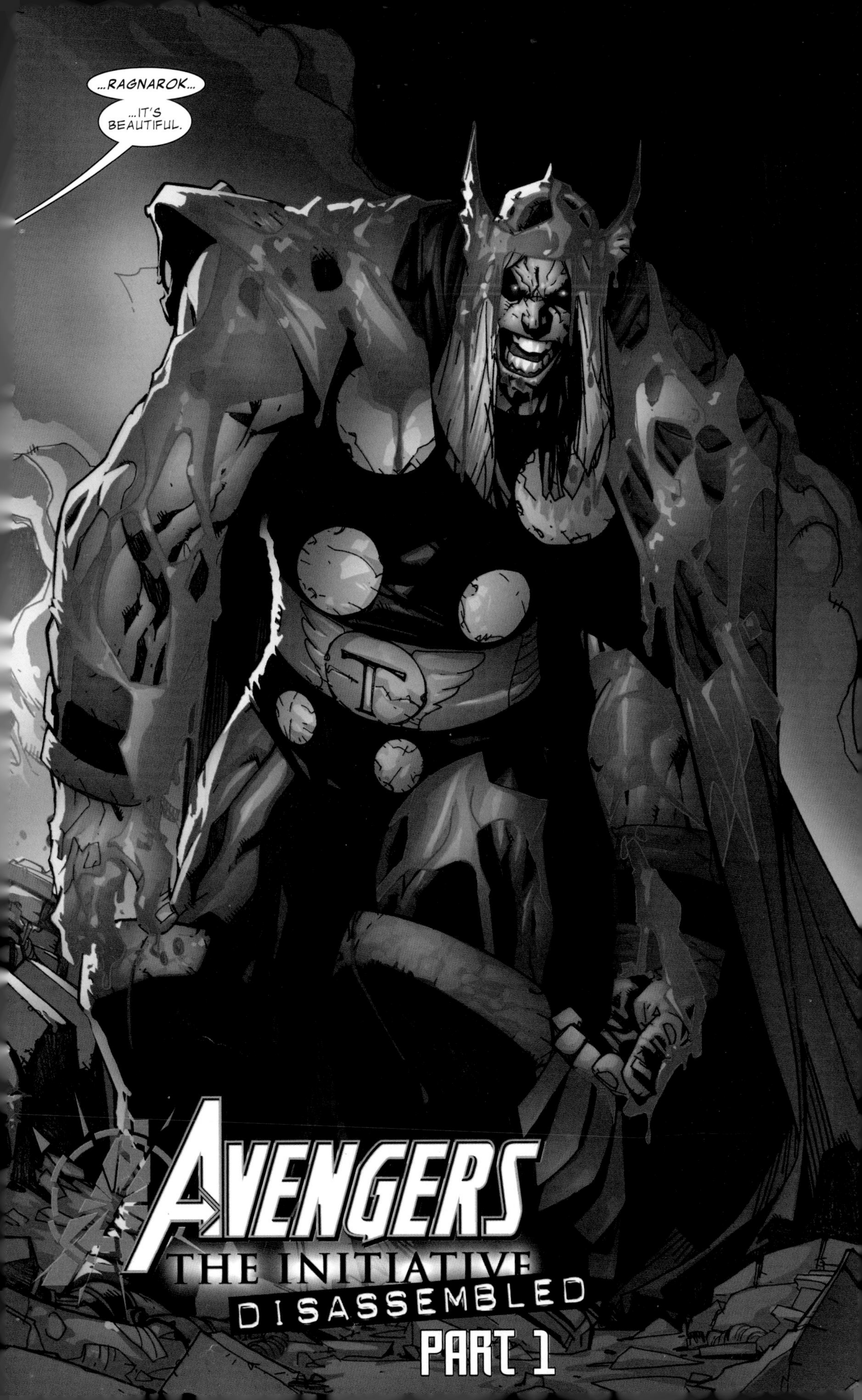
...RAGNAROK...
...IT'S BEAUTIFUL.
AVENGERS
THE INITIATIVE
DISASSEMBLED
PART 1

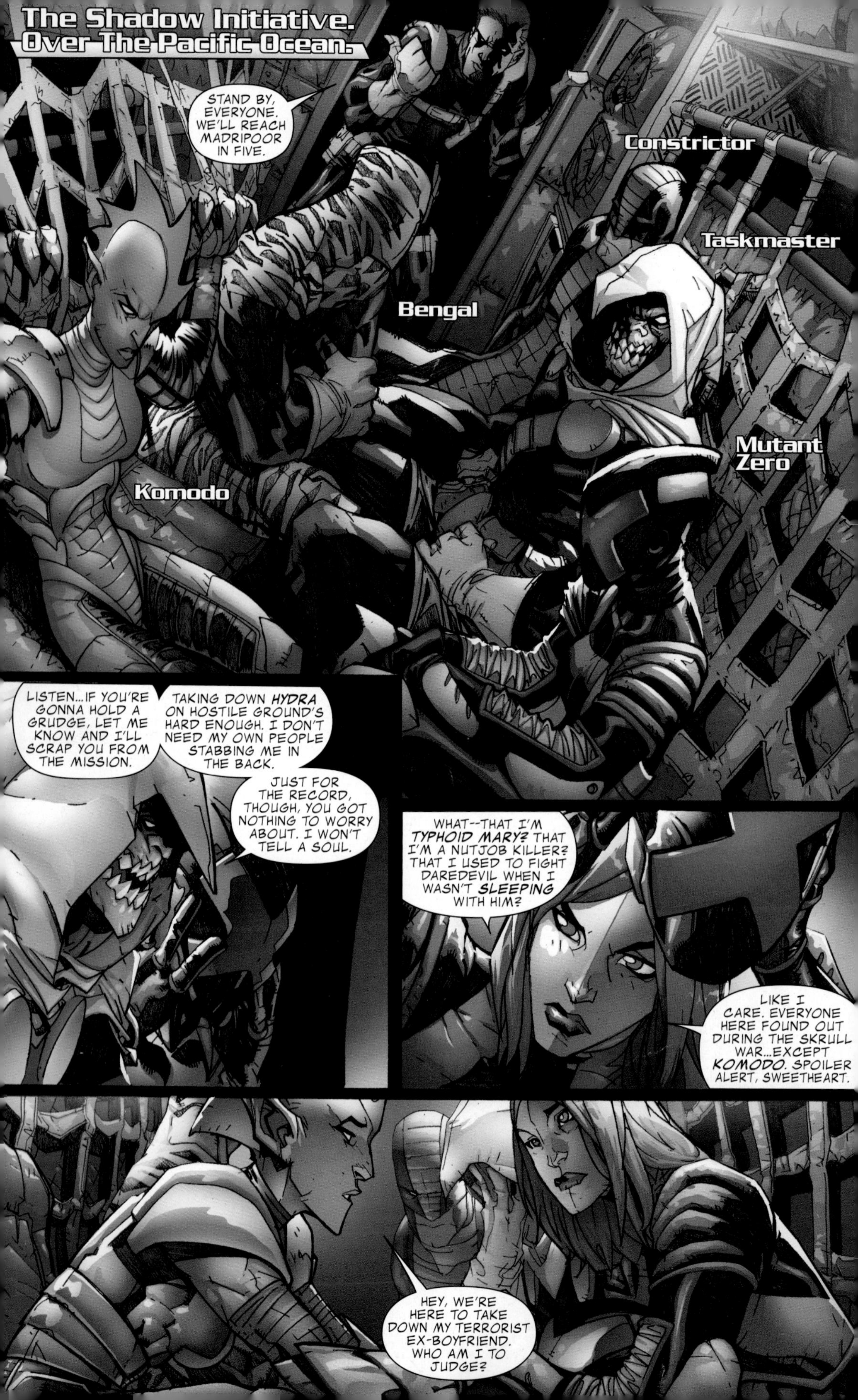
The Shadow Initiative. Over The Pacific Ocean.
STAND BY, EVERYONE. WE'LL REACH MADRIPOOR IN FIVE.
Constrictor
Taskmaster
Bengal
Mutant Zero
Komodo
LISTEN...IF YOU'RE GONNA HOLD A GRUDGE, LET ME KNOW AND I'LL SCRAP YOU FROM THE MISSION.
TAKING DOWN HYDRA ON HOSTILE GROUND'S HARD ENOUGH. I DON'T NEED MY OWN PEOPLE STABBING ME IN THE BACK.
JUST FOR THE RECORD, THOUGH, YOU GOT NOTHING TO WORRY ABOUT. I WON'T TELL A SOUL.
WHAT--THAT I'M TYPHOID MARY? THAT I'M A NUTJOB KILLER? THAT I USED TO FIGHT DAREDEVIL WHEN I WASN'T SLEEPING WITH HIM?
LIKE I CARE. EVERYONE HERE FOUND OUT DURING THE SKRULL WAR...EXCEPT KOMODO. SPOILER ALERT, SWEETHEART.
HEY, WE'RE HERE TO TAKE DOWN MY TERRORIST EX-BOYFRIEND. WHO AM I TO JUDGE?

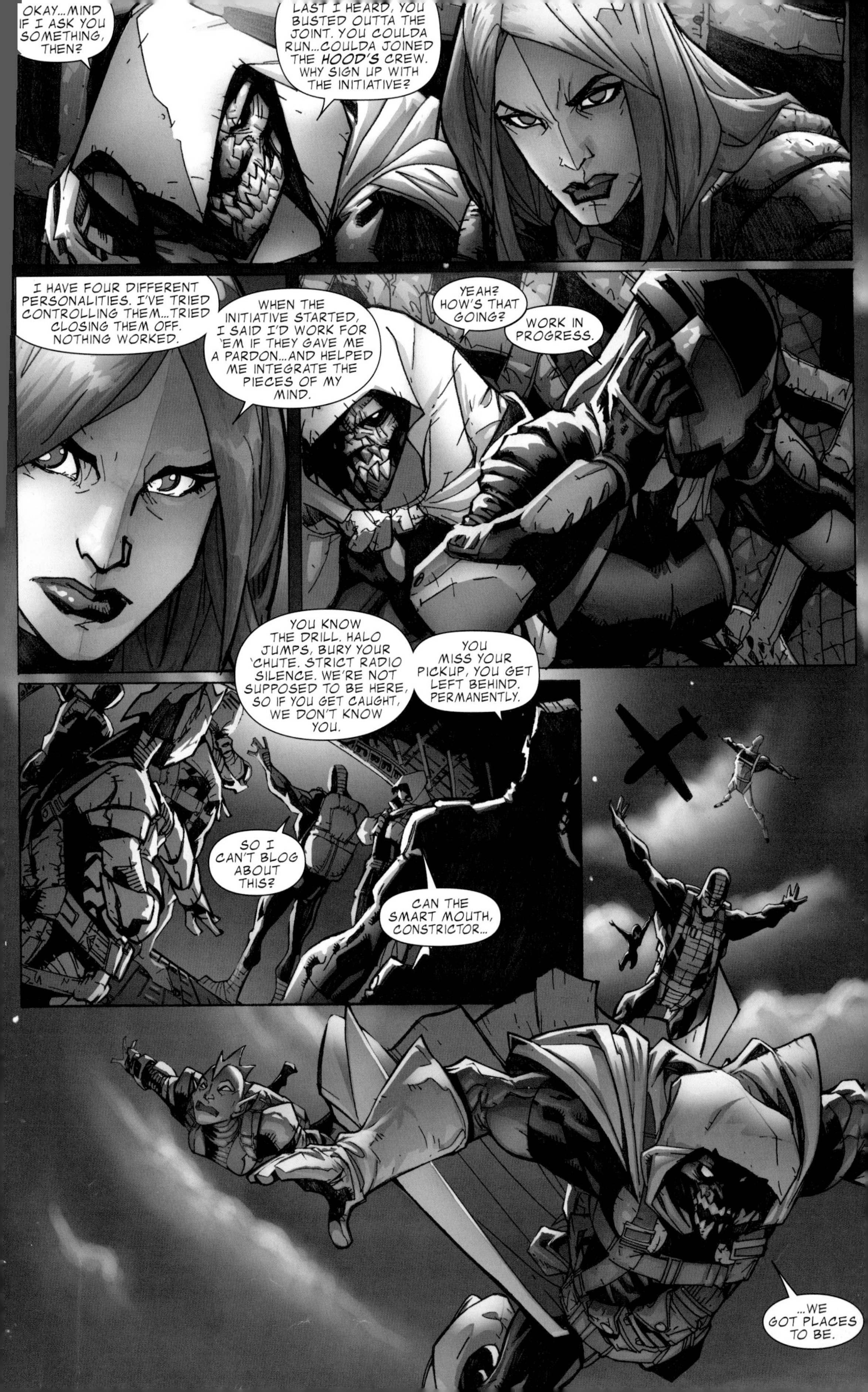
OKAY...MIND IF I ASK YOU SOMETHING, THEN?
LAST I HEARD, YOU BUSTED OUTTA THE JOINT. YOU COULDA RUN...COULDA JOINED THE HOOD'S CREW. WHY SIGN UP WITH THE INITIATIVE?
I HAVE FOUR DIFFERENT PERSONALITIES. I'VE TRIED CONTROLLING THEM...TRIED CLOSING THEM OFF. NOTHING WORKED.
WHEN THE INITIATIVE STARTED, I SAID I'D WORK FOR 'EM IF THEY GAVE ME A PARDON...AND HELPED ME INTEGRATE THE PIECES OF MY MIND.
YEAH? HOW'S THAT GOING?
WORK IN PROGRESS.
YOU KNOW THE DRILL. HALO JUMPS, BURY YOUR 'CHUTE. STRICT RADIO SILENCE. WE'RE NOT SUPPOSED TO BE HERE, SO IF YOU GET CAUGHT, WE DON'T KNOW YOU.
YOU MISS YOUR PICKUP, YOU GET LEFT BEHIND. PERMANENTLY.
SO I CAN'T BLOG ABOUT THIS?
CAN THE SMART MOUTH, CONSTRICTOR...
...WE GOT PLACES TO BE.

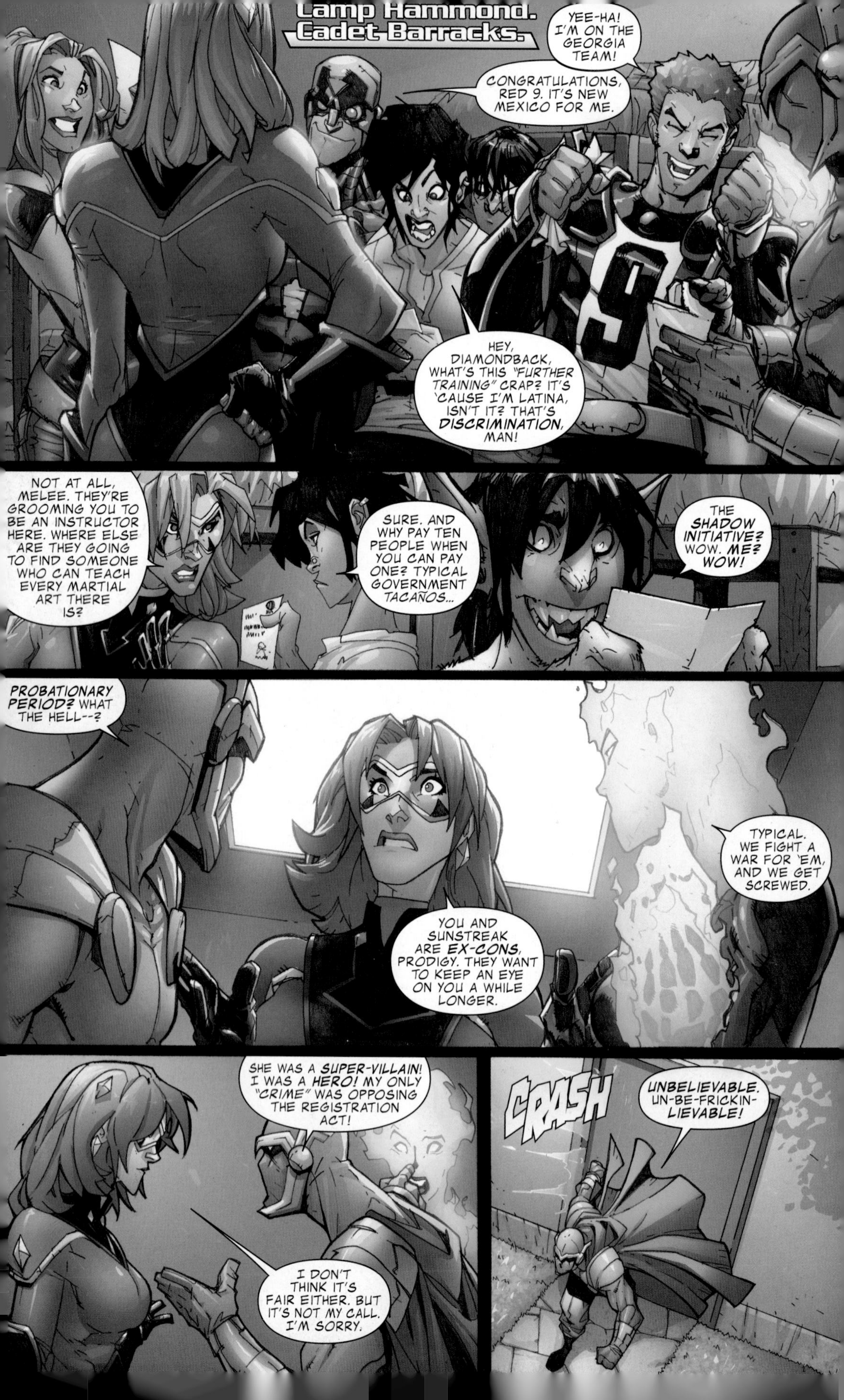
Camp Hammond. Cadet Barracks.
YEE-HA! I'M ON THE GEORGIA TEAM!
CONGRATULATIONS, RED 9. IT'S NEW MEXICO FOR ME.
HEY, DIAMONDBACK, WHAT'S THIS "FURTHER TRAINING" CRAP? IT'S 'CAUSE I'M LATINA, ISN'T IT? THAT'S DISCRIMINATION, MAN!
NOT AT ALL, MELEE. THEY'RE GROOMING YOU TO BE AN INSTRUCTOR HERE. WHERE ELSE ARE THEY GOING TO FIND SOMEONE WHO CAN TEACH EVERY MARTIAL ART THERE IS?
SURE. AND WHY PAY TEN PEOPLE WHEN YOU CAN PAY ONE? TYPICAL GOVERNMENT TACAÑOS...
THE SHADOW INITIATIVE? WOW. ME? WOW!
PROBATIONARY PERIOD? WHAT THE HELL--?
YOU AND SUNSTREAK ARE EX-CONS, PRODIGY. THEY WANT TO KEEP AN EYE ON YOU A WHILE LONGER.
TYPICAL. WE FIGHT A WAR FOR 'EM, AND WE GET SCREWED.
SHE WAS A SUPER-VILLAIN! I WAS A HERO! MY ONLY "CRIME" WAS OPPOSING THE REGISTRATION ACT!
I DON'T THINK IT'S FAIR EITHER. BUT IT'S NOT MY CALL. I'M SORRY.
CRASH
UNBELIEVABLE. UN-BE-FRICKIN-LIEVABLE!

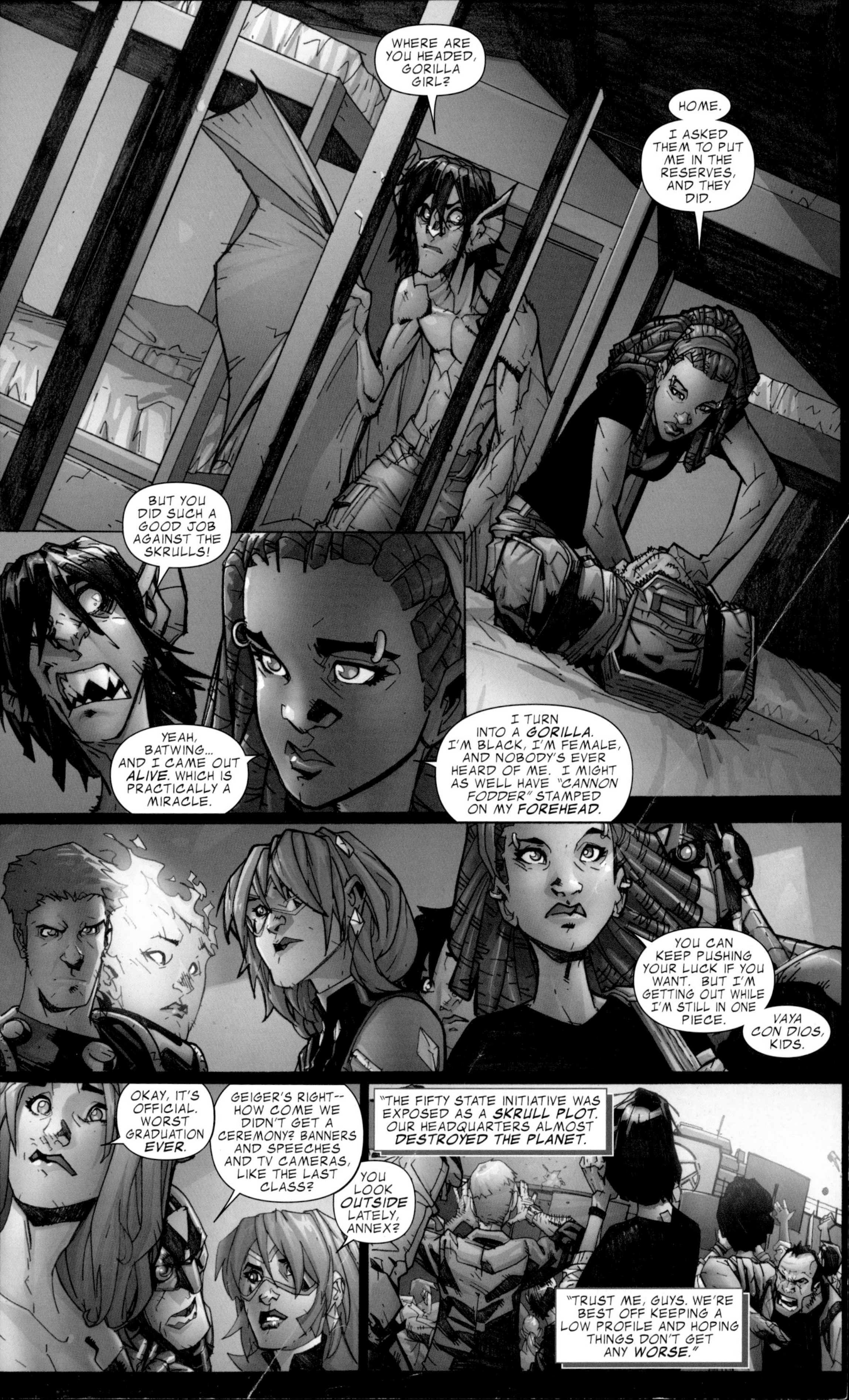
WHERE ARE YOU HEADED, GORILLA GIRL?
HOME.
I ASKED THEM TO PUT ME IN THE RESERVES, AND THEY DID.
BUT YOU DID SUCH A GOOD JOB AGAINST THE SKRULLS!
YEAH, BATWING... AND I CAME OUT ALIVE. WHICH IS PRACTICALLY A MIRACLE.
I TURN INTO A GORILLA. I'M BLACK, I'M FEMALE, AND NOBODY'S EVER HEARD OF ME. I MIGHT AS WELL HAVE "CANNON FODDER" STAMPED ON MY FOREHEAD.
YOU CAN KEEP PUSHING YOUR LUCK IF YOU WANT. BUT I'M GETTING OUT WHILE I'M STILL IN ONE PIECE.
VAYA CON DIOS, KIDS.
OKAY, IT'S OFFICIAL. WORST GRADUATION EVER.
GEIGER'S RIGHT-- HOW COME WE DIDN'T GET A CEREMONY? BANNERS AND SPEECHES AND TV CAMERAS, LIKE THE LAST CLASS?
YOU LOOK OUTSIDE LATELY, ANNEX?
"THE FIFTY STATE INITIATIVE WAS EXPOSED AS A SKRULL PLOT. OUR HEADQUARTERS ALMOST DESTROYED THE PLANET.
"TRUST ME, GUYS. WE'RE BEST OFF KEEPING A LOW PROFILE AND HOPING THINGS DON'T GET ANY WORSE."

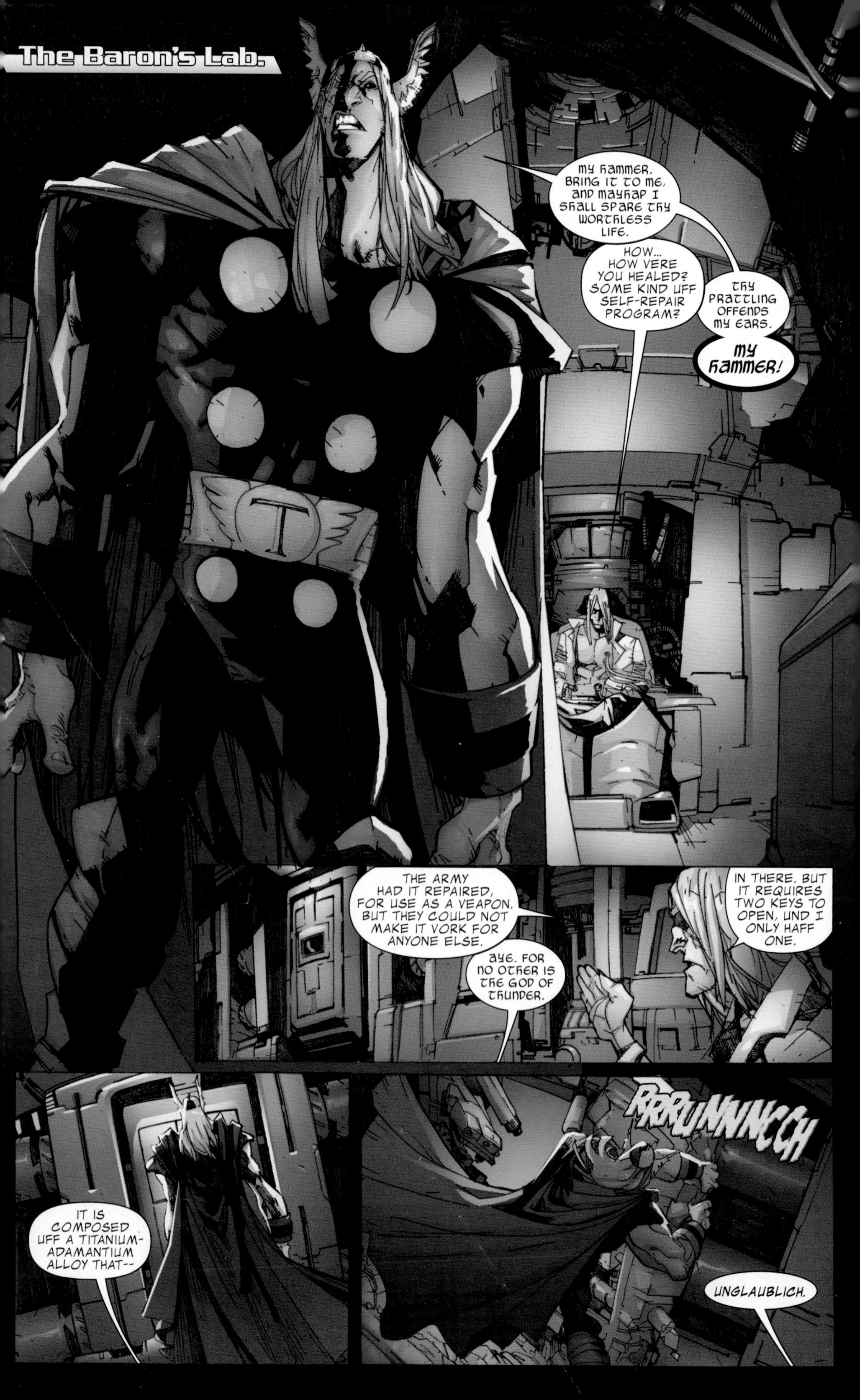
The Baron's Lab.
MY HAMMER. BRING IT TO ME, AND MAYHAP I SHALL SPARE THY WORTHLESS LIFE.
HOW... HOW VERE YOU HEALED? SOME KIND UFF SELF-REPAIR PROGRAM?
THY PRATTLING OFFENDS MY EARS.
MY HAMMER!
THE ARMY HAD IT REPAIRED, FOR USE AS A VEAPON. BUT THEY COULD NOT MAKE IT VORK FOR ANYONE ELSE.
AYE. FOR NO OTHER IS THE GOD OF THUNDER.
IN THERE. BUT IT REQUIRES TWO KEYS TO OPEN, UND I ONLY HAFF ONE.
IT IS COMPOSED UFF A TITANIUM-ADAMANTIUM ALLOY THAT--
RRRUNNNCCH
UNGLAUBLICH.

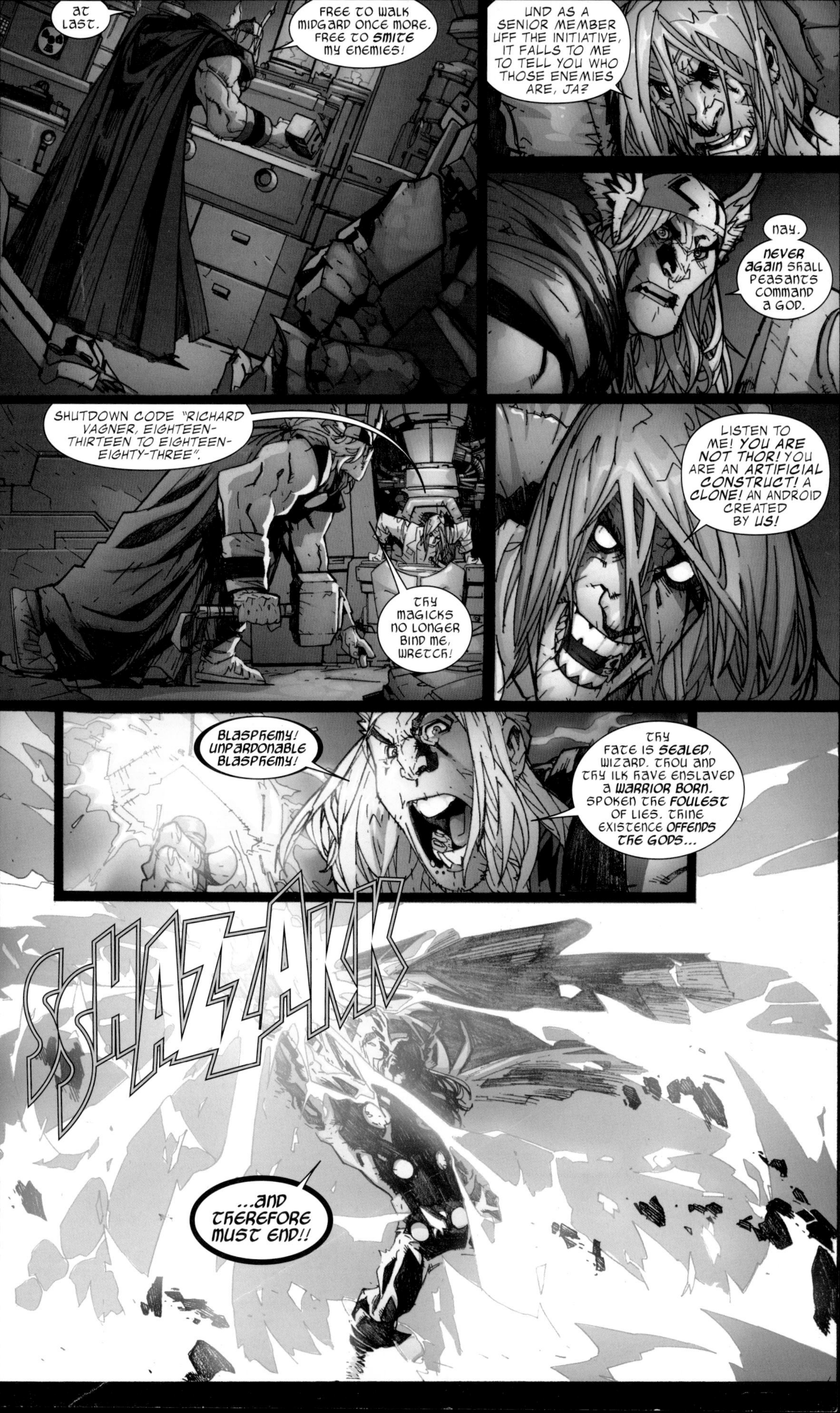
AT LAST.
FREE TO WALK MIDGARD ONCE MORE. FREE TO SMITE MY ENEMIES!
UND AS A SENIOR MEMBER UFF THE INITIATIVE, IT FALLS TO ME TO TELL YOU WHO THOSE ENEMIES ARE, JA?
NAY.
NEVER AGAIN SHALL PEASANTS COMMAND A GOD.
SHUTDOWN CODE "RICHARD VAGNER, EIGHTEEN-THIRTEEN TO EIGHTEEN-EIGHTY-THREE".
THY MAGICKS NO LONGER BIND ME, WRETCH!
LISTEN TO ME! YOU ARE NOT THOR! YOU ARE AN ARTIFICIAL CONSTRUCT! A CLONE! AN ANDROID CREATED BY US!
BLASPHEMY! UNPARDONABLE BLASPHEMY!
THY FATE IS SEALED, WIZARD. THOU AND THY ILK HAVE ENSLAVED A WARRIOR BORN. SPOKEN THE FOULEST OF LIES. THINE EXISTENCE OFFENDS THE GODS...
SSCHAZZAKK
...AND THEREFORE MUST END!!

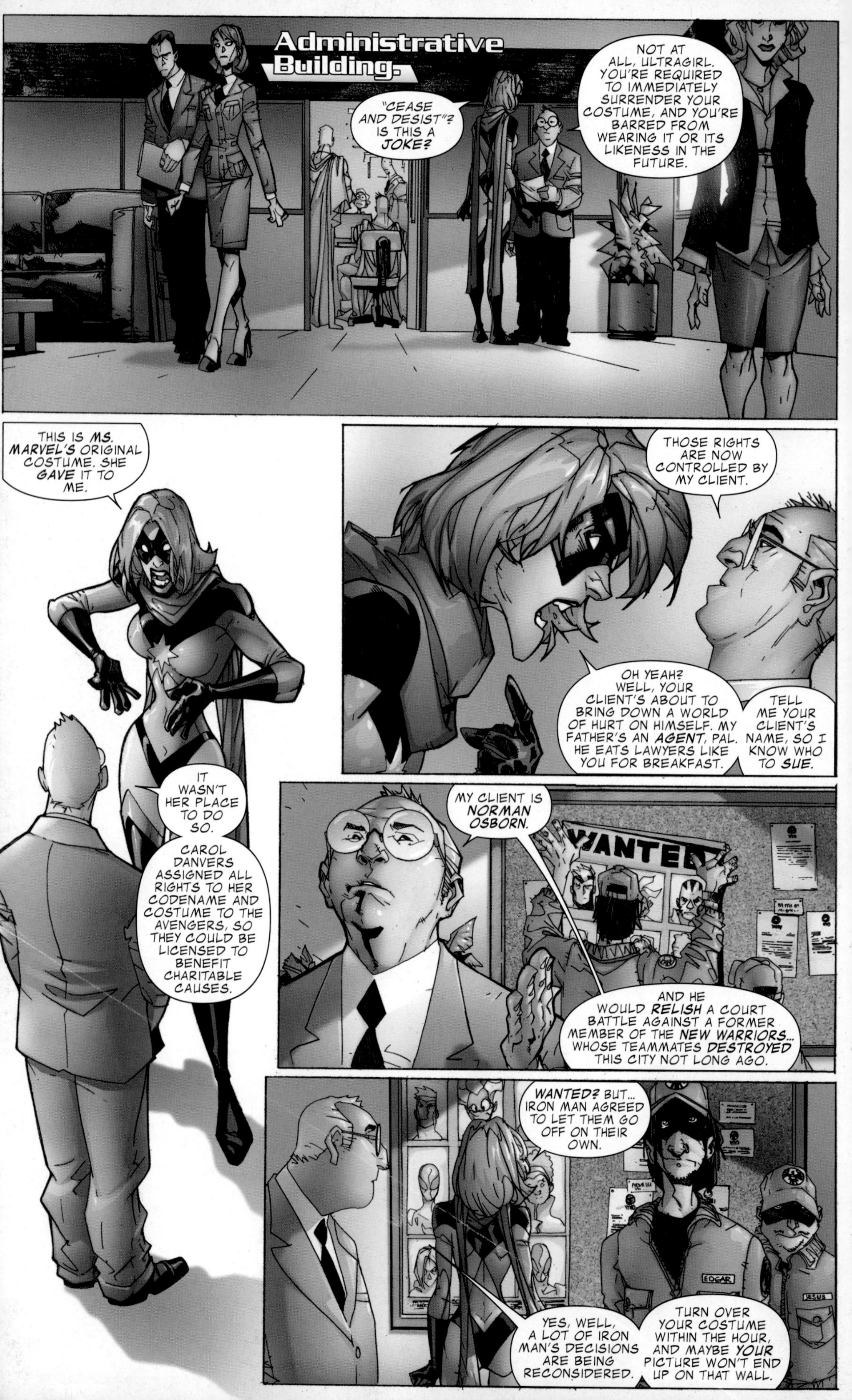
Administrative Building.
"CEASE AND DESIST"? IS THIS A JOKE?
NOT AT ALL, ULTRAGIRL. YOU'RE REQUIRED TO IMMEDIATELY SURRENDER YOUR COSTUME, AND YOU'RE BARRED FROM WEARING IT OR ITS LIKENESS IN THE FUTURE.
THIS IS MS. MARVEL'S ORIGINAL COSTUME. SHE GAVE IT TO ME.
IT WASN'T HER PLACE TO DO SO.
CAROL DANVERS ASSIGNED ALL RIGHTS TO HER CODENAME AND COSTUME TO THE AVENGERS, SO THEY COULD BE LICENSED TO BENEFIT CHARITABLE CAUSES.
THOSE RIGHTS ARE NOW CONTROLLED BY MY CLIENT.
OH YEAH? WELL, YOUR CLIENT'S ABOUT TO BRING DOWN A WORLD OF HURT ON HIMSELF. MY FATHER'S AN AGENT, PAL. HE EATS LAWYERS LIKE YOU FOR BREAKFAST.
TELL ME YOUR CLIENT'S NAME, SO I KNOW WHO TO SUE.
MY CLIENT IS NORMAN OSBORN.
WANTED
AND HE WOULD RELISH A COURT BATTLE AGAINST A FORMER MEMBER OF THE NEW WARRIORS... WHOSE TEAMMATES DESTROYED THIS CITY NOT LONG AGO.
WANTED? BUT... IRON MAN AGREED TO LET THEM GO OFF ON THEIR OWN.
EDGAR
JESUS
YES, WELL, A LOT OF IRON MAN'S DECISIONS ARE BEING RECONSIDERED.
TURN OVER YOUR COSTUME WITHIN THE HOUR, AND MAYBE YOUR PICTURE WON'T END UP ON THAT WALL.

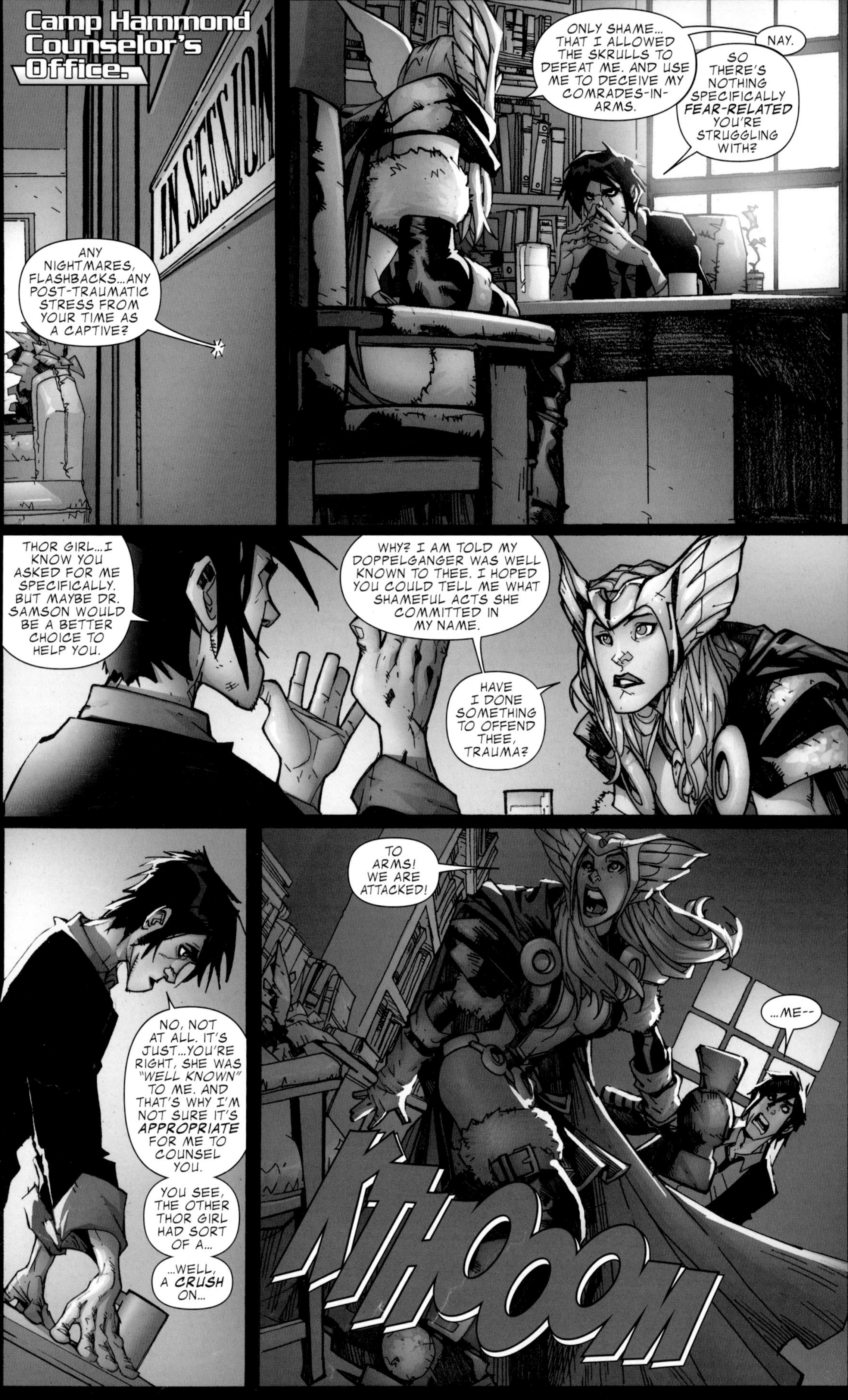
Camp Hammond Counselor's Office.
ANY NIGHTMARES, FLASHBACKS...ANY POST-TRAUMATIC STRESS FROM YOUR TIME AS A CAPTIVE?
NAY.
ONLY SHAME... THAT I ALLOWED THE SKRULLS TO DEFEAT ME. AND USE ME TO DECEIVE MY COMRADES-IN-ARMS.
SO THERE'S NOTHING SPECIFICALLY FEAR-RELATED YOU'RE STRUGGLING WITH?
THOR GIRL...I KNOW YOU ASKED FOR ME SPECIFICALLY. BUT MAYBE DR. SAMSON WOULD BE A BETTER CHOICE TO HELP YOU.
WHY? I AM TOLD MY DOPPELGANGER WAS WELL KNOWN TO THEE. I HOPED YOU COULD TELL ME WHAT SHAMEFUL ACTS SHE COMMITTED IN MY NAME.
HAVE I DONE SOMETHING TO OFFEND THEE, TRAUMA?
NO, NOT AT ALL. IT'S JUST...YOU'RE RIGHT, SHE WAS "WELL KNOWN" TO ME. AND THAT'S WHY I'M NOT SURE IT'S APPROPRIATE FOR ME TO COUNSEL YOU.
YOU SEE, THE OTHER THOR GIRL HAD SORT OF A...
...WELL, A CRUSH ON...
...ME--
TO ARMS! WE ARE ATTACKED!
KTHOOOM

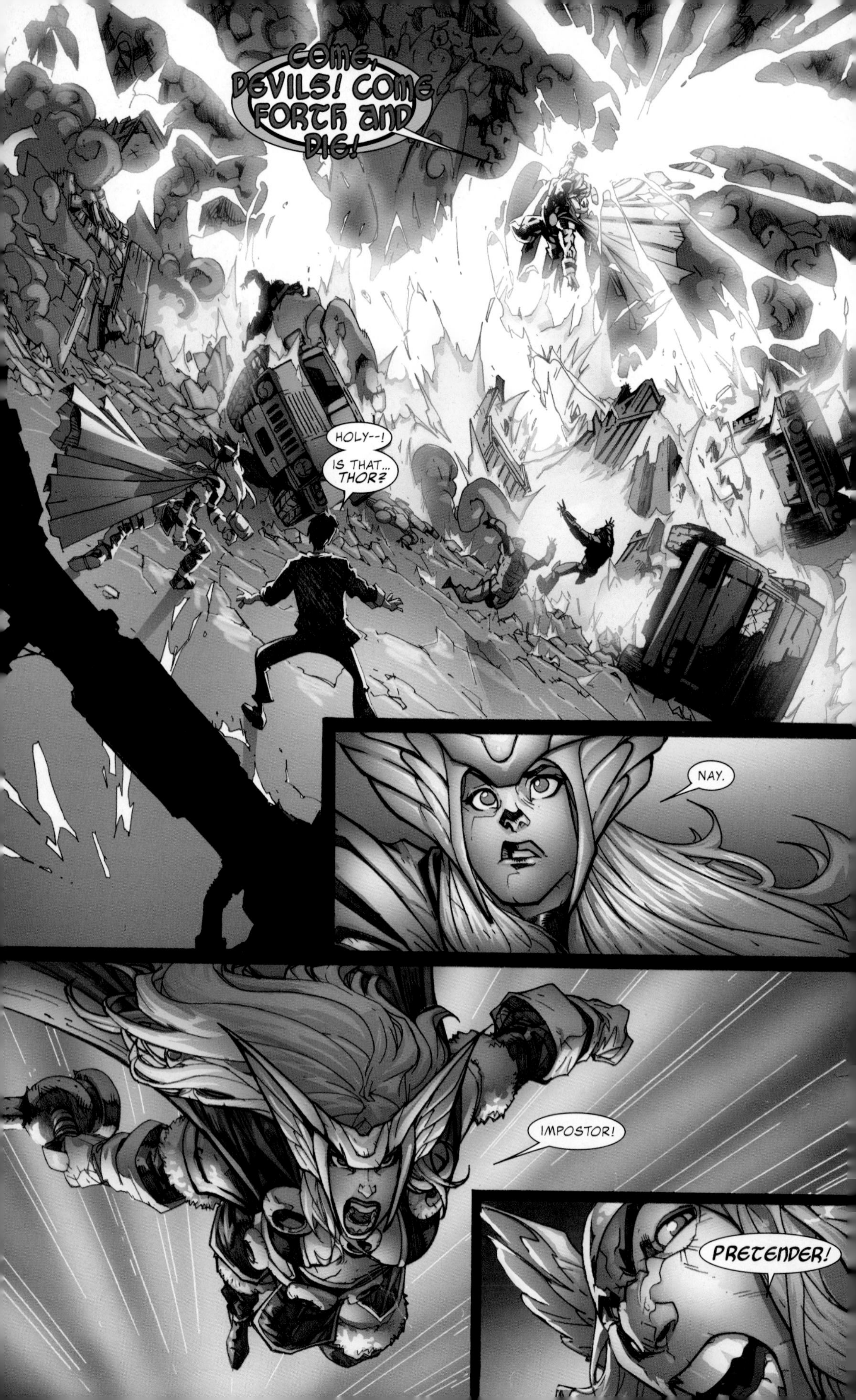
COME, DEVILS! COME FORTH AND DIE!
HOLY--!
IS THAT... THOR?
NAY.
IMPOSTOR!
PRETENDER!

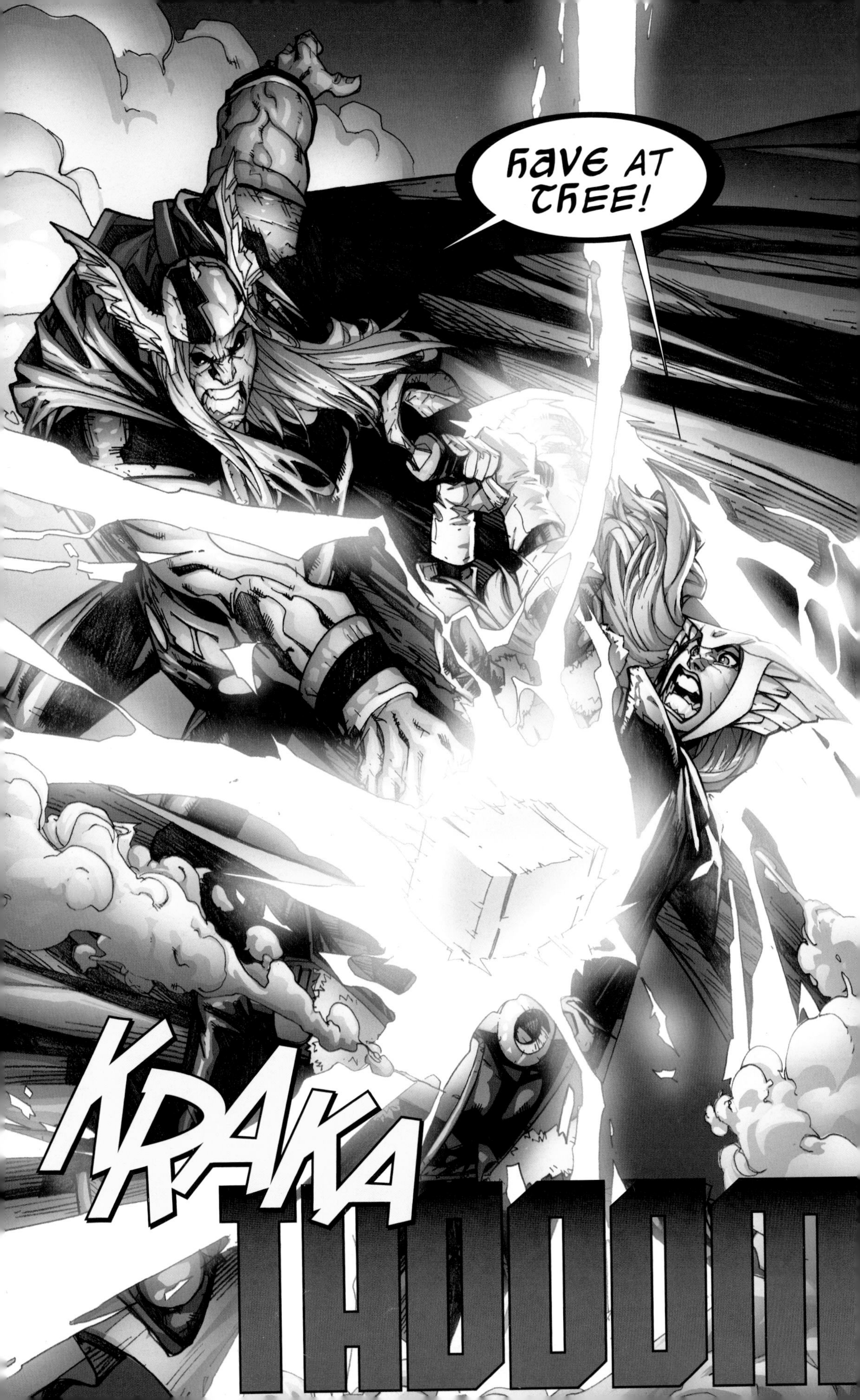
HAVE AT THEE!
KRAKA
THOOM

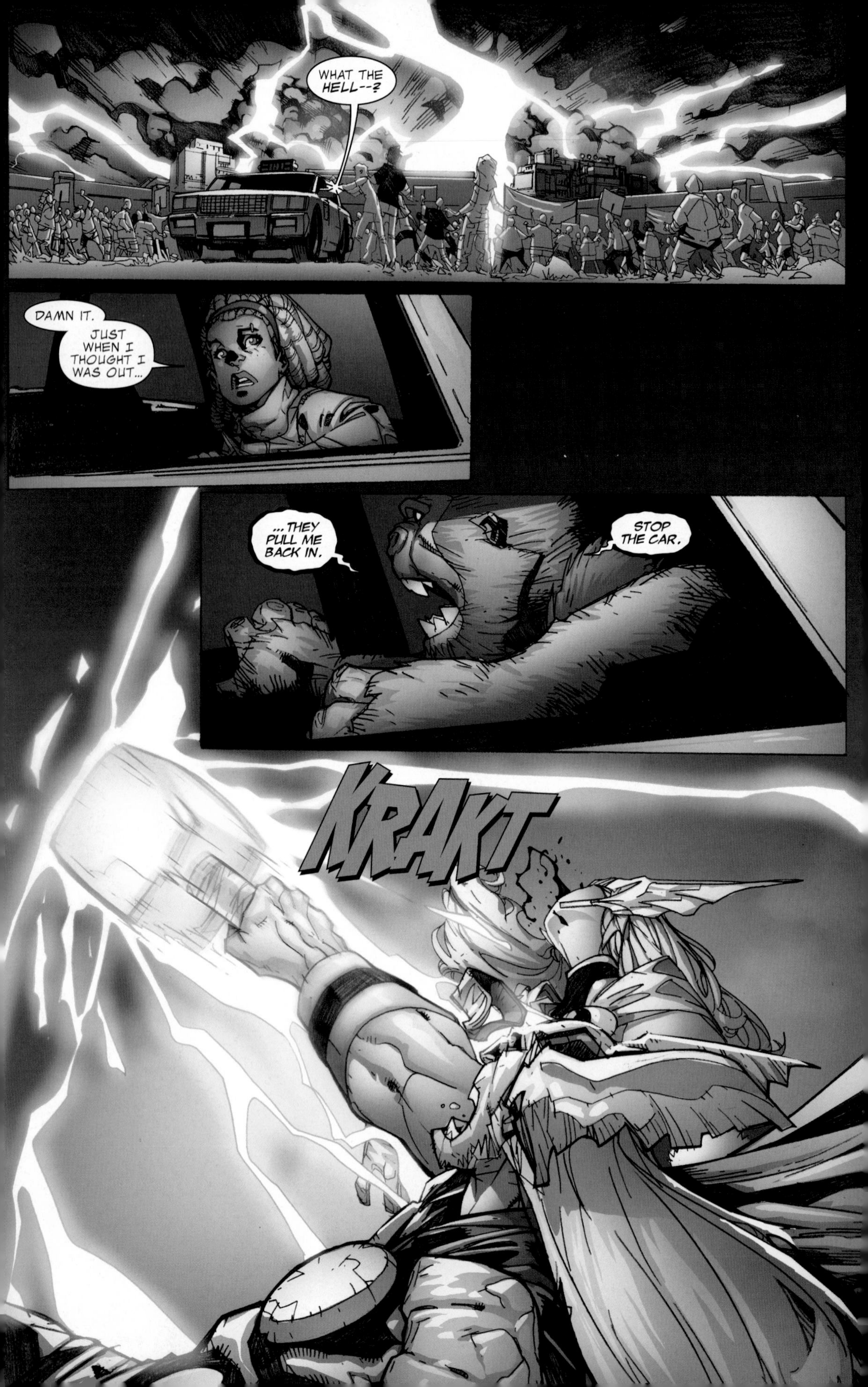
WHAT THE HELL--?
DAMN IT.
JUST WHEN I THOUGHT I WAS OUT...
...THEY PULL ME BACK IN.
STOP THE CAR.
KRAKT

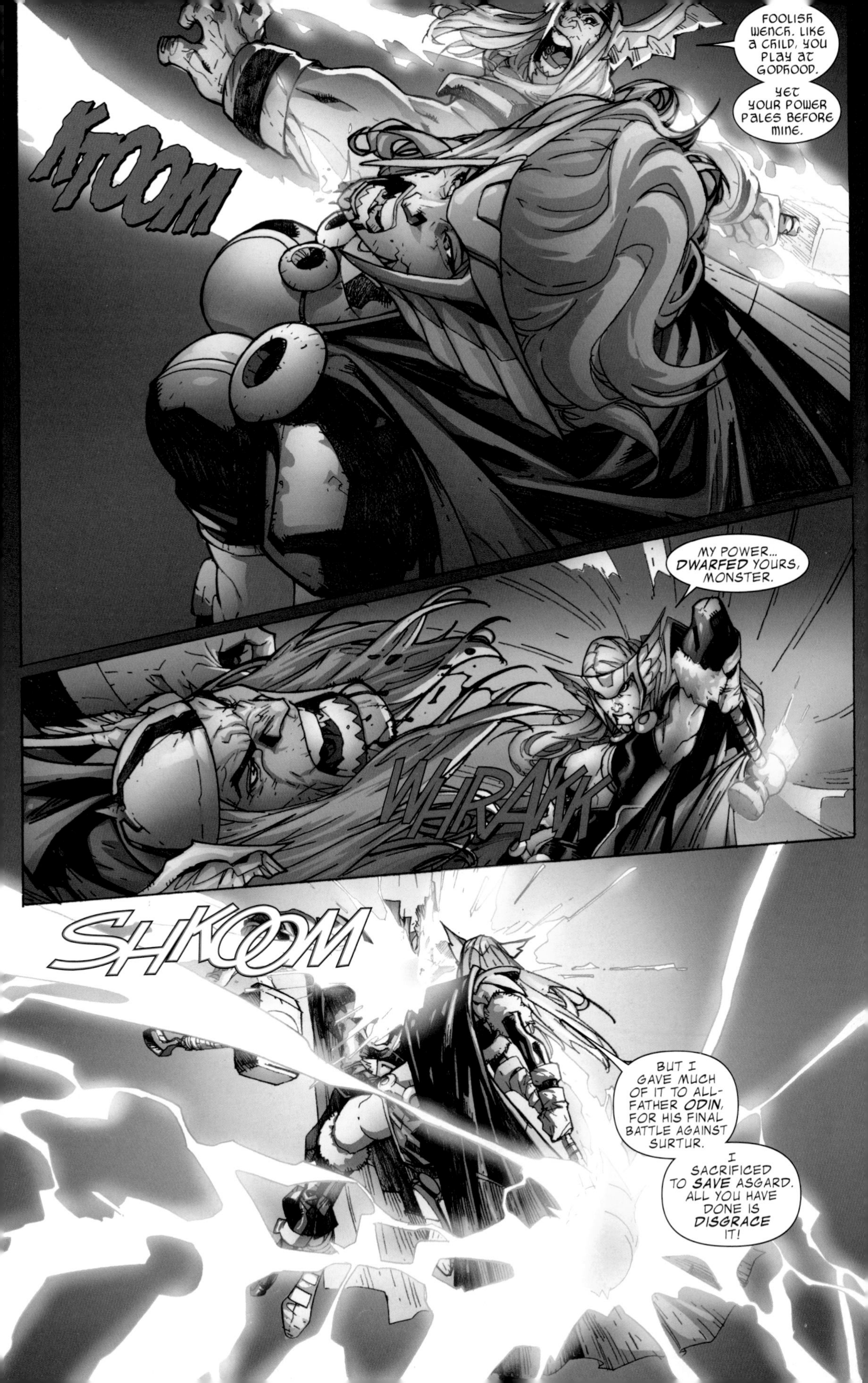
FOOLISH WENCH. LIKE A CHILD, YOU PLAY AT GODHOOD.
YET YOUR POWER PALES BEFORE MINE.
KTOOM
MY POWER... DWARFED YOURS, MONSTER.
WHRAKK
SHKOOOM
BUT I GAVE MUCH OF IT TO ALL-FATHER ODIN, FOR HIS FINAL BATTLE AGAINST SURTUR.
I SACRIFICED TO SAVE ASGARD. ALL YOU HAVE DONE IS DISGRACE IT!

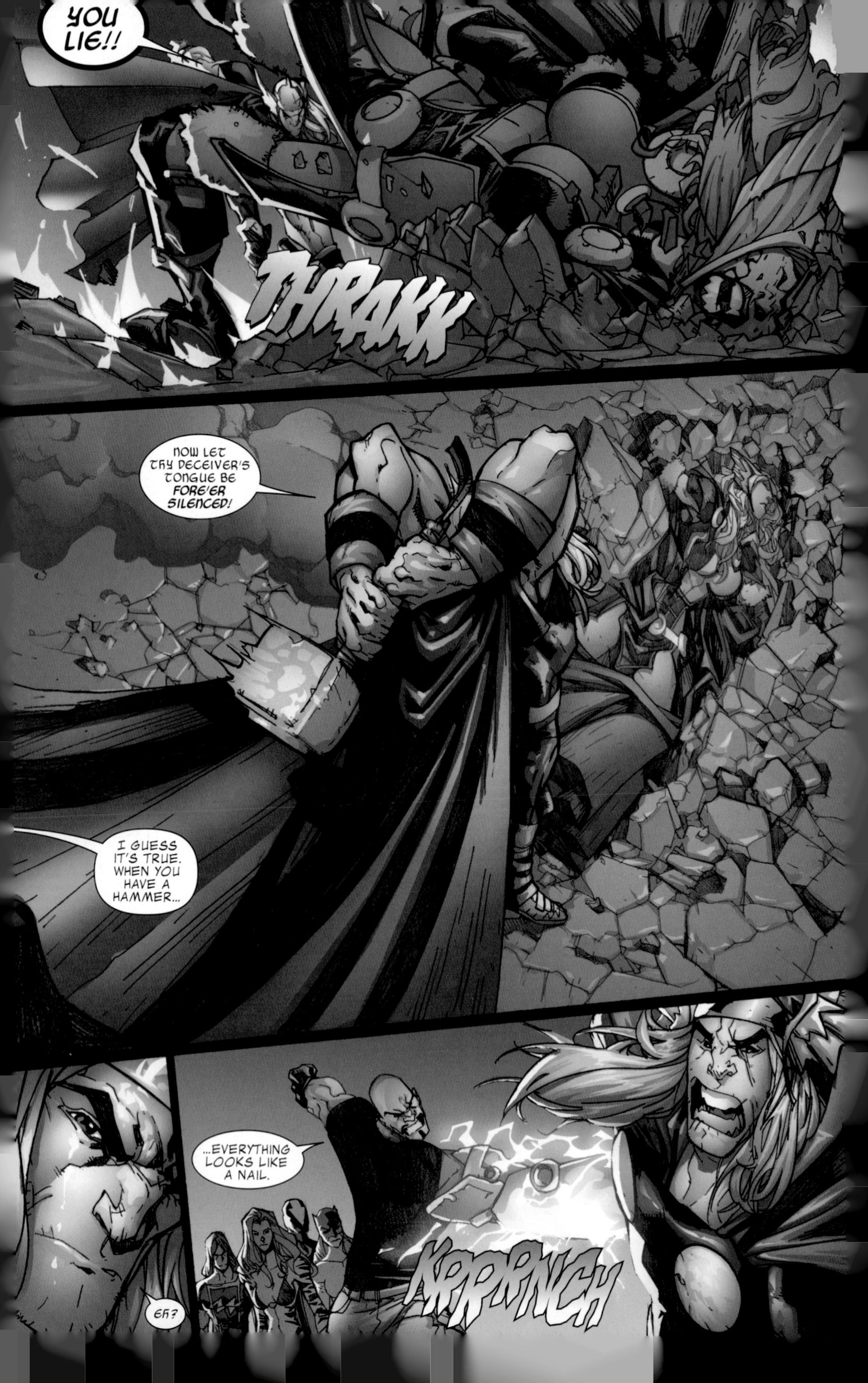
YOU LIE!!
THRAKK
NOW LET THY DECEIVER'S TONGUE BE FORE'ER SILENCED!
I GUESS IT'S TRUE. WHEN YOU HAVE A HAMMER...
...EVERYTHING LOOKS LIKE A NAIL.
KRRRNCH
EH?

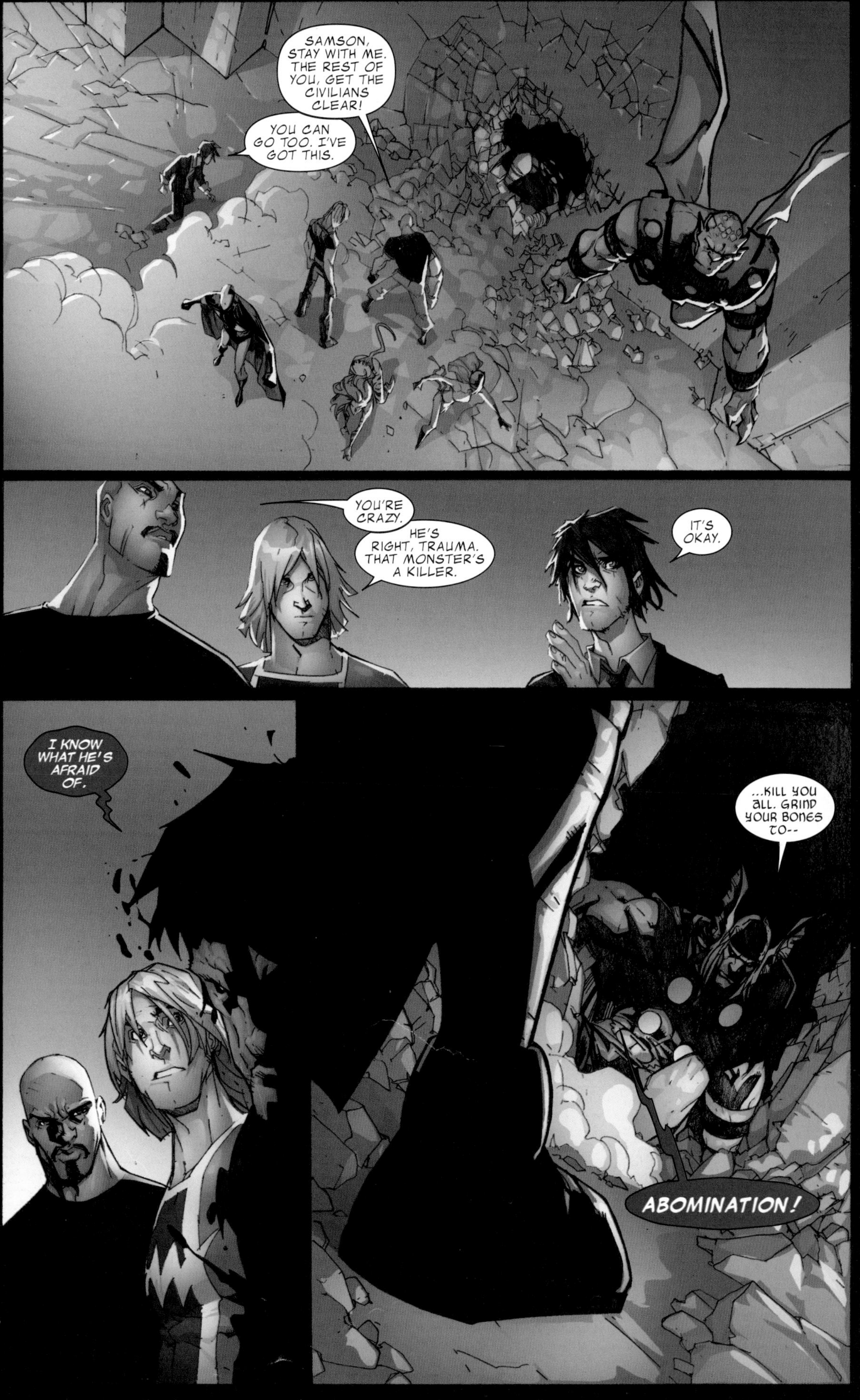
SAMSON, STAY WITH ME. THE REST OF YOU, GET THE CIVILIANS CLEAR!
YOU CAN GO TOO. I'VE GOT THIS.
YOU'RE CRAZY.
HE'S RIGHT, TRAUMA. THAT MONSTER'S A KILLER.
IT'S OKAY.
I KNOW WHAT HE'S AFRAID OF.
...KILL YOU ALL. GRIND YOUR BONES TO--
ABOMINATION!

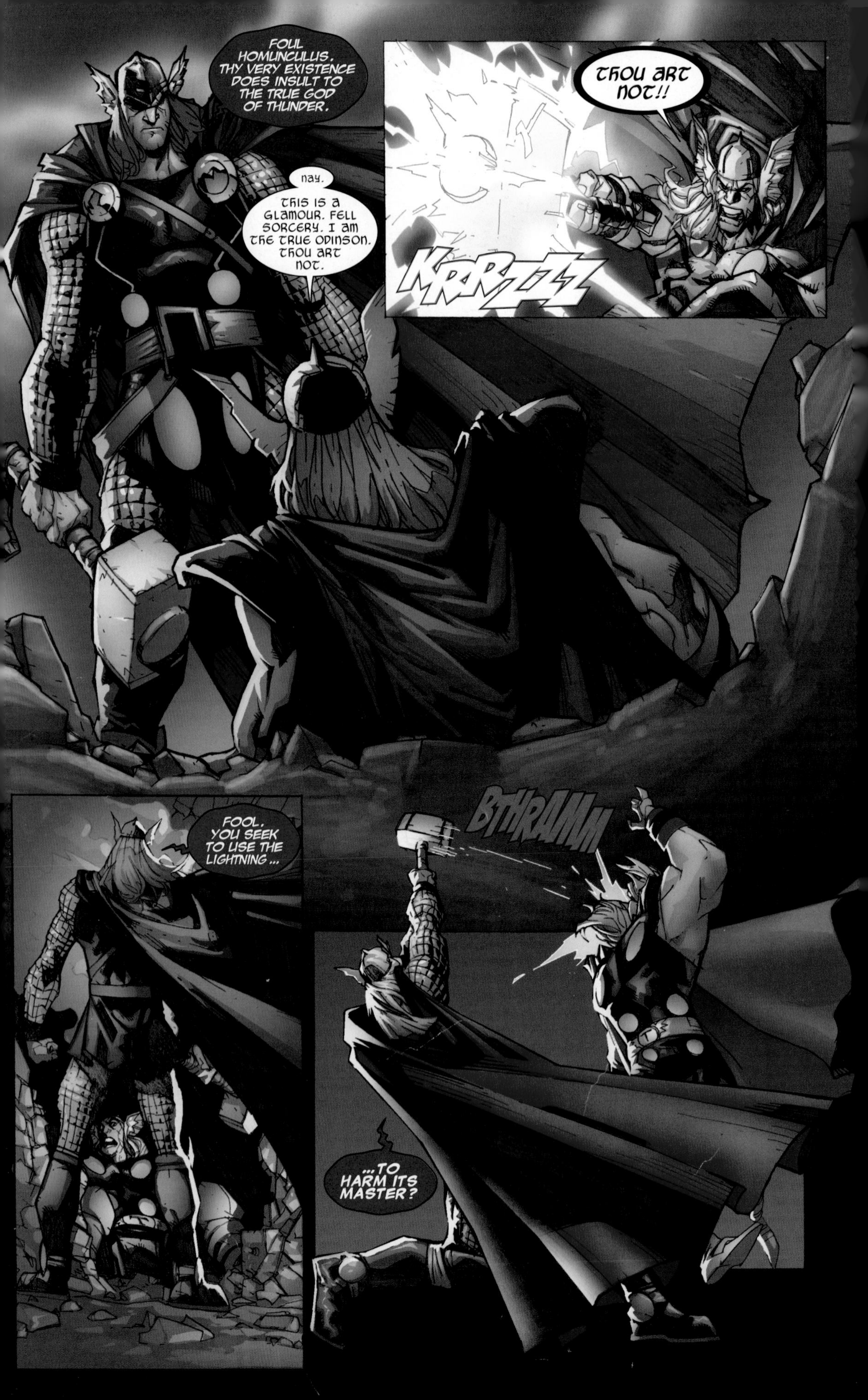
FOUL HOMUNCULUS. THY VERY EXISTENCE DOES INSULT TO THE TRUE GOD OF THUNDER.
nay.
THIS IS A GLAMOUR. FELL SORCERY. I AM THE TRUE ODINSON. THOU ART NOT.
THOU ART NOT!!
KRARZZZ
FOOL. YOU SEEK TO USE THE LIGHTNING ...
BTHRAMM
...TO HARM ITS MASTER?

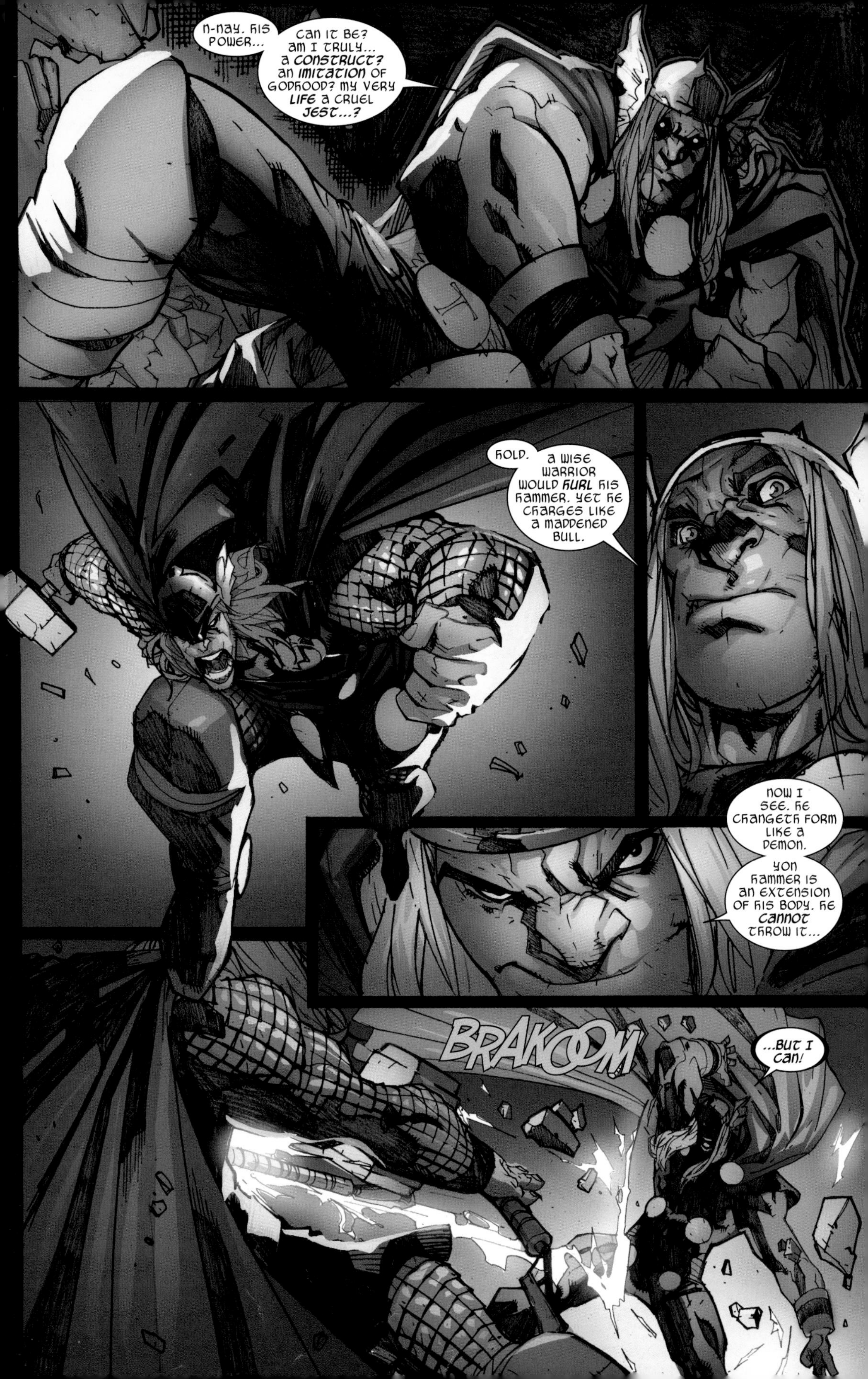
N-NAY. HIS POWER...
CAN IT BE? AM I TRULY... A CONSTRUCT? AN IMITATION OF GODHOOD? MY VERY LIFE A CRUEL JEST...?
HOLD.
A WISE WARRIOR WOULD HURL HIS HAMMER. YET HE CHARGES LIKE A MADDENED BULL.
NOW I SEE. HE CHANGETH FORM LIKE A DEMON.
YON HAMMER IS AN EXTENSION OF HIS BODY. HE CANNOT THROW IT...
BRAKOOM
...BUT I CAN!

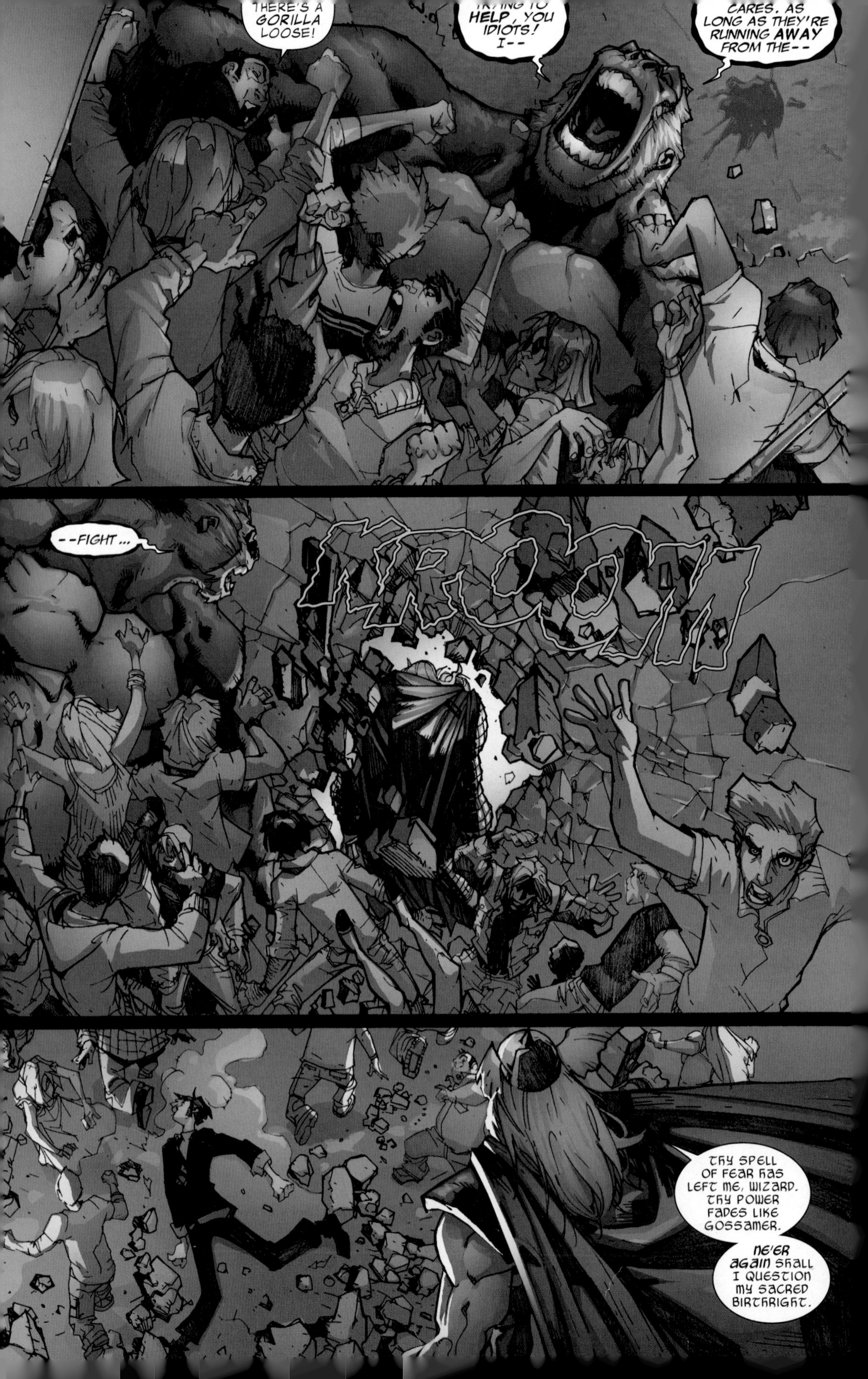
THERE'S A GORILLA LOOSE!
HELP, YOU IDIOTS! I--
CARES. AS LONG AS THEY'RE RUNNING AWAY FROM THE--
--FIGHT...
THY SPELL OF FEAR HAS LEFT ME, WIZARD. THY POWER FADES LIKE GOSSAMER.
NE'ER AGAIN SHALL I QUESTION MY SACRED BIRTHRIGHT.

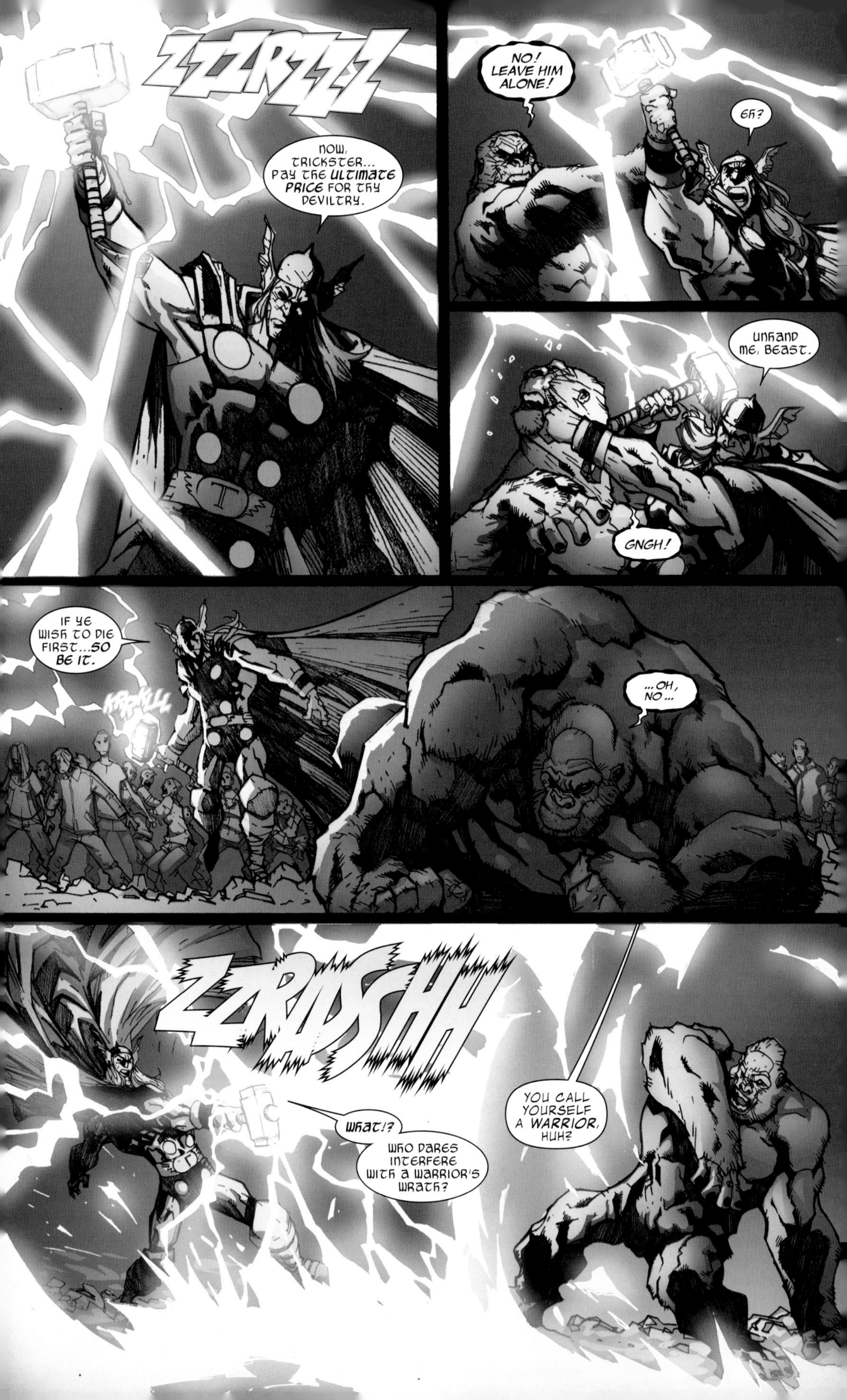
ZZZRZZZ!
NOW, TRICKSTER... PAY THE ULTIMATE PRICE FOR THY DEVILTRY.
NO! LEAVE HIM ALONE!
EH?
UNHAND ME, BEAST.
GNGH!
IF YE WISH TO DIE FIRST...SO BE IT.
...OH, NO...
ZZRAKSHH
WHAT!?
WHO DARES INTERFERE WITH A WARRIOR'S WRATH?
YOU CALL YOURSELF A WARRIOR, HUH?

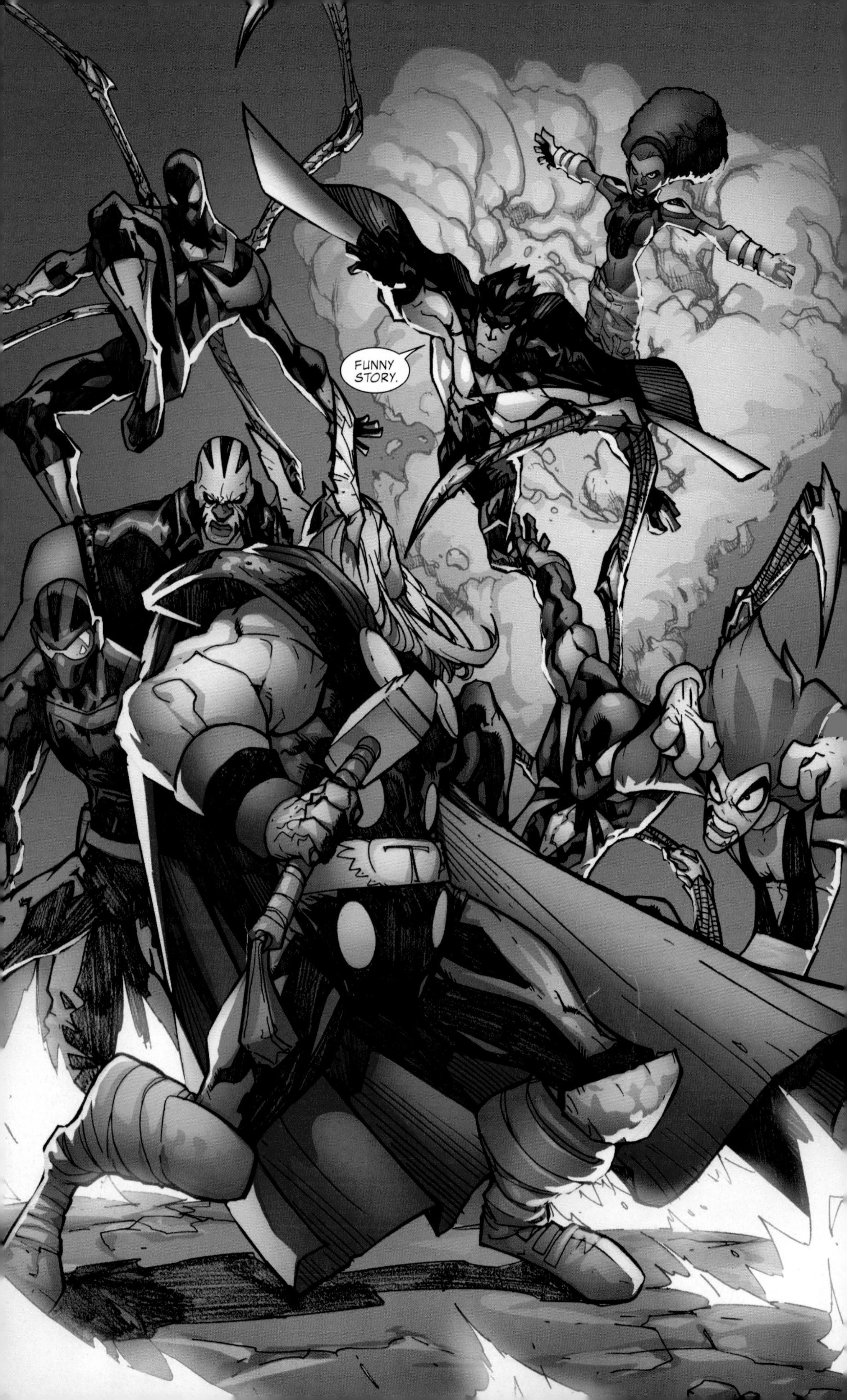
FUNNY STORY.

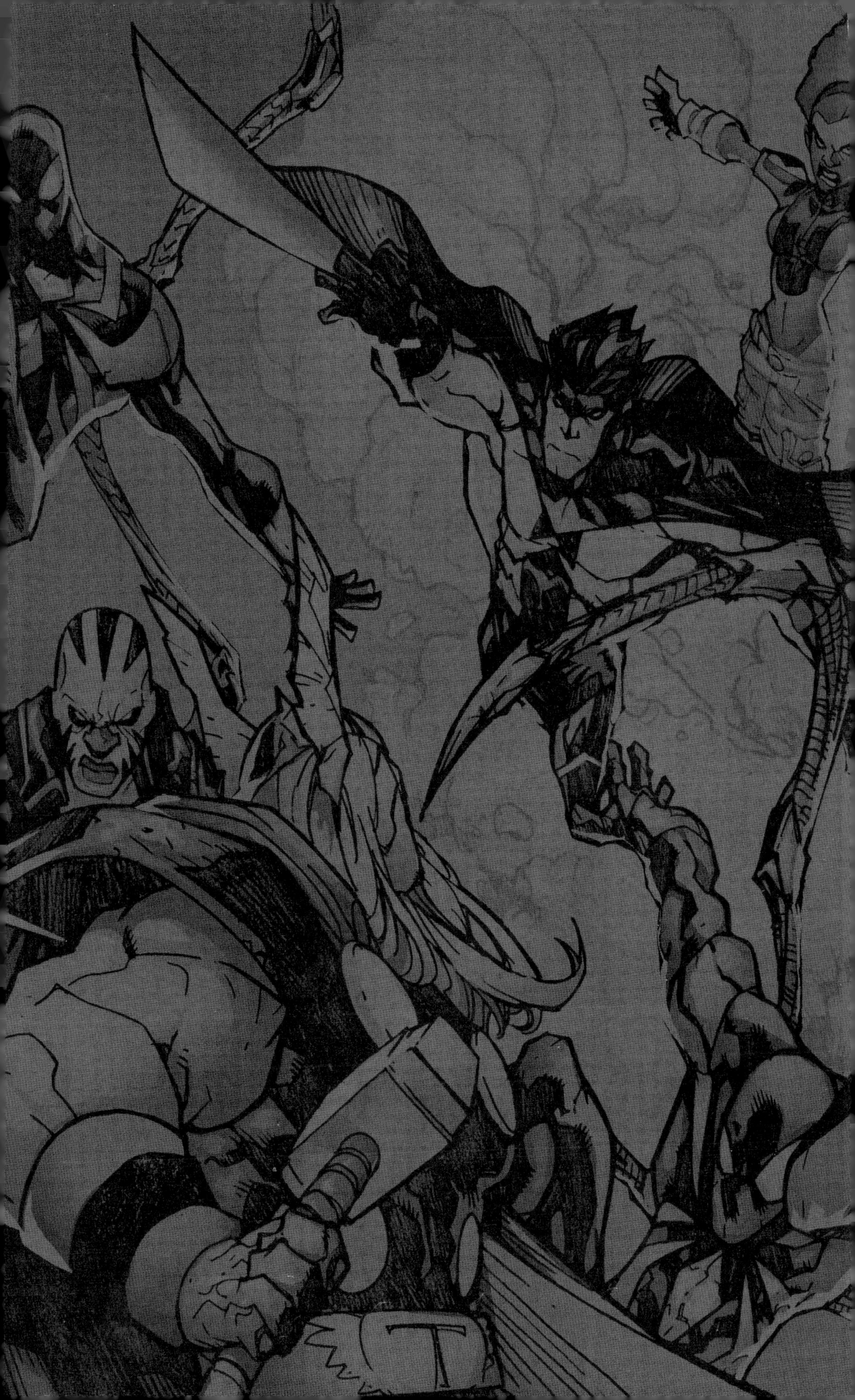

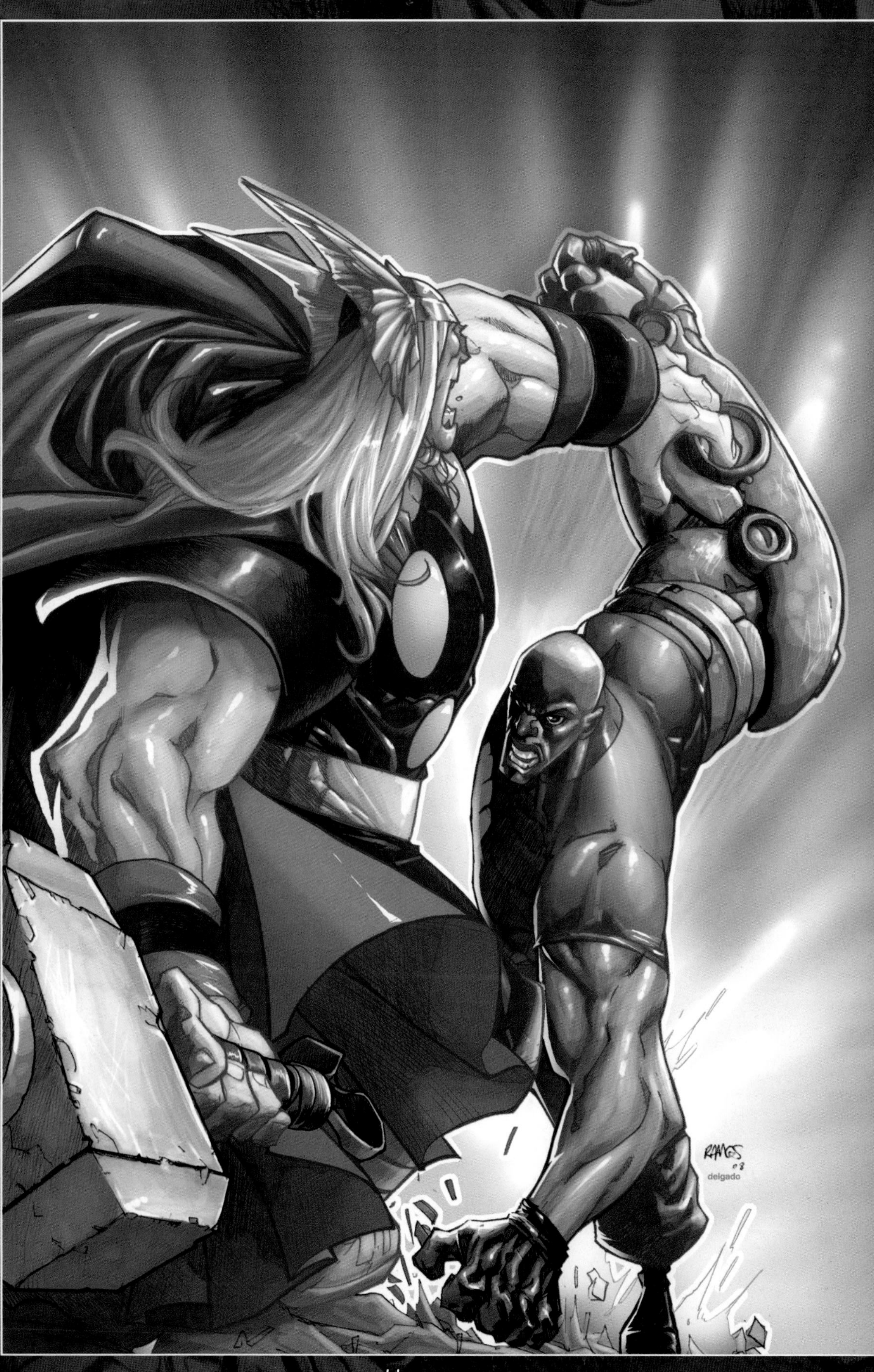
RAMOS 08
delgado

#22

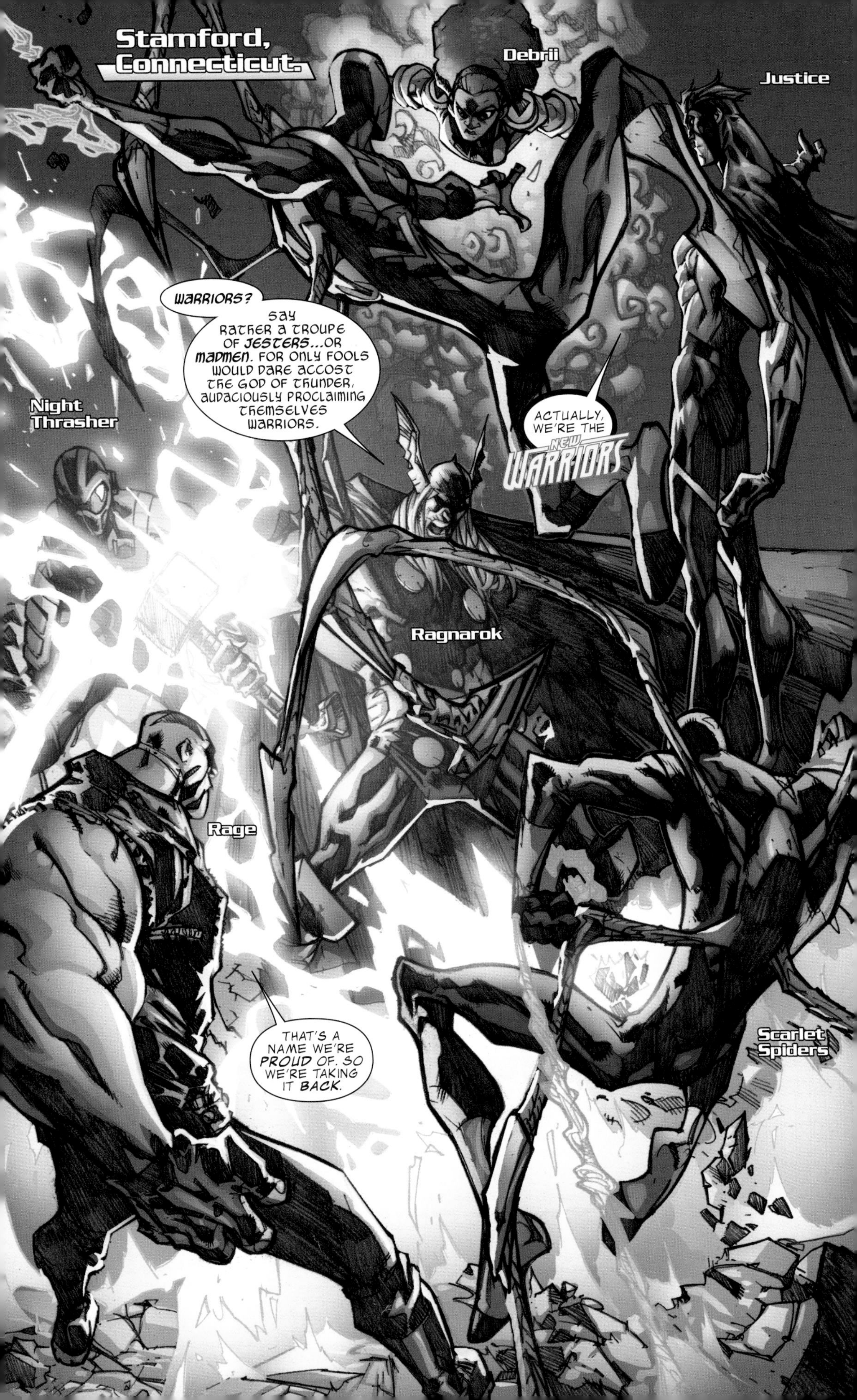
Stamford, Connecticut.
Debrii
Justice
Night Thrasher
WARRIORS? SAY RATHER A TROUPE OF JESTERS...OR MADMEN. FOR ONLY FOOLS WOULD DARE ACCOST THE GOD OF THUNDER, AUDACIOUSLY PROCLAIMING THEMSELVES WARRIORS.
ACTUALLY, WE'RE THE NEW WARRIORS
Ragnarok
Rage
THAT'S A NAME WE'RE PROUD OF. SO WE'RE TAKING IT BACK.
Scarlet Spiders

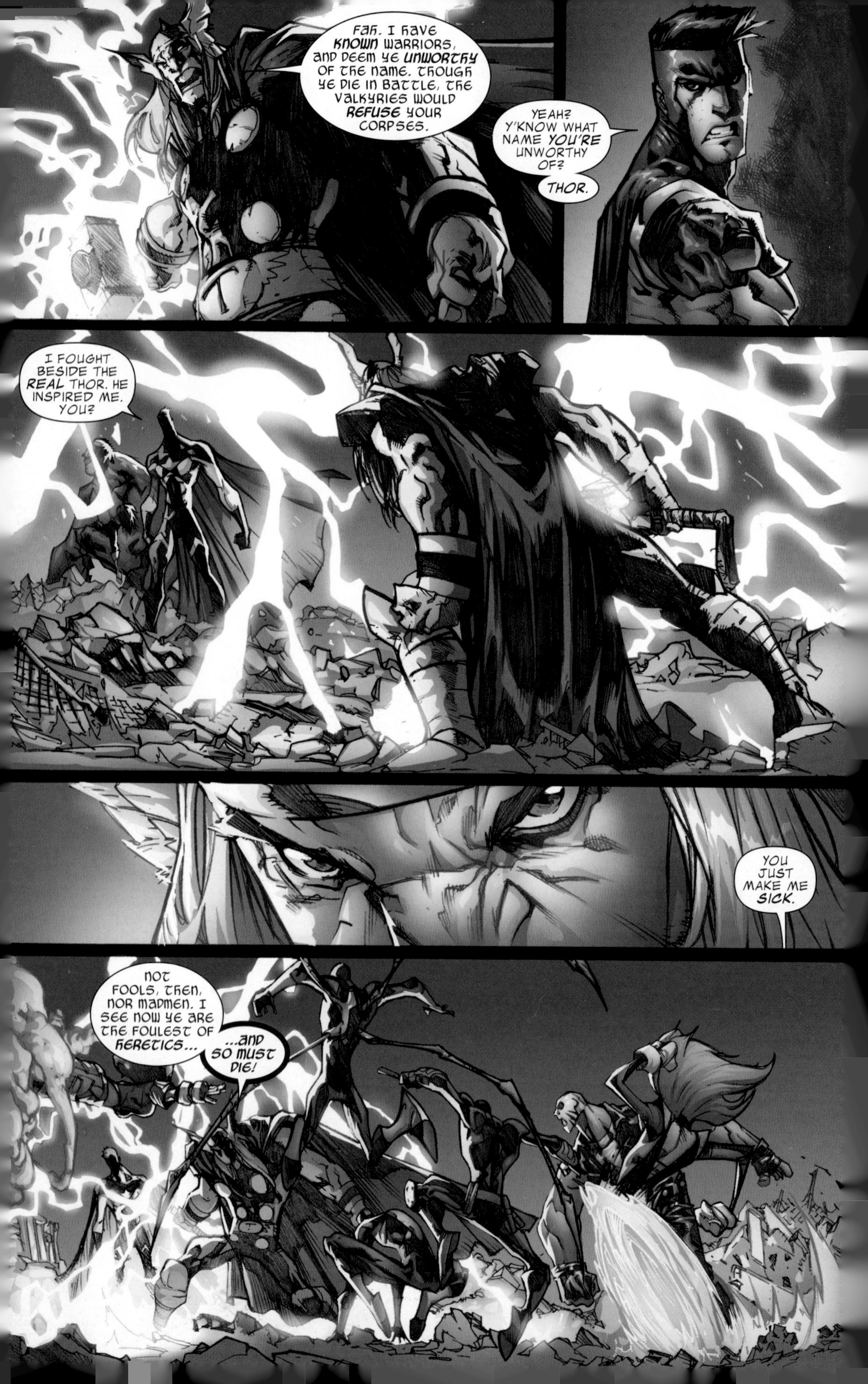
FAH. I HAVE KNOWN WARRIORS, AND DEEM YE UNWORTHY OF THE NAME. THOUGH YE DIE IN BATTLE, THE VALKYRIES WOULD REFUSE YOUR CORPSES.
YEAH? Y'KNOW WHAT NAME YOU'RE UNWORTHY OF?
THOR.
I FOUGHT BESIDE THE REAL THOR. HE INSPIRED ME. YOU?
YOU JUST MAKE ME SICK.
NOT FOOLS, THEN, NOR MADMEN. I SEE NOW YE ARE THE FOULEST OF HERETICS...
...AND SO MUST DIE!

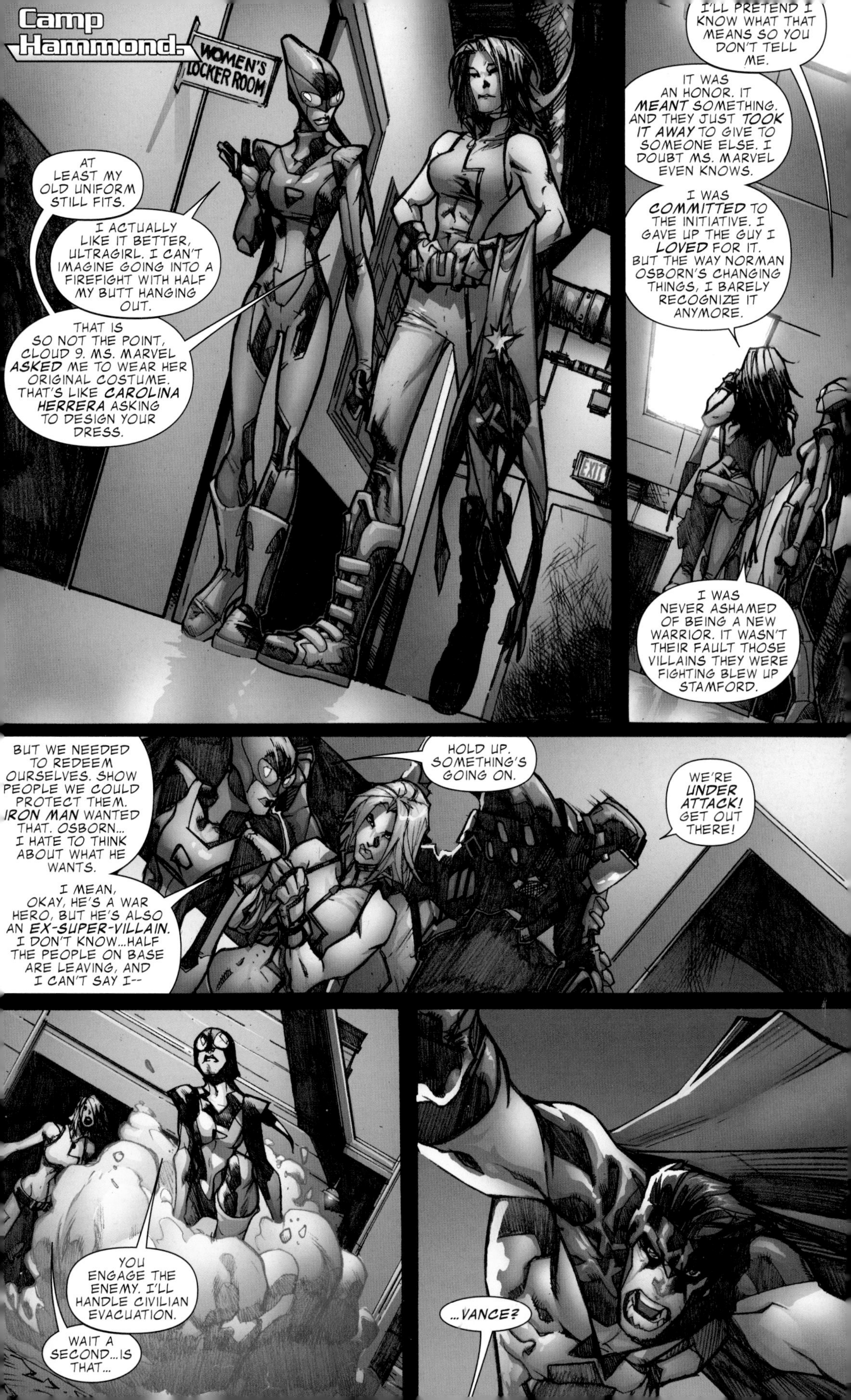
Camp Hammond.
WOMEN'S LOCKER ROOM
AT LEAST MY OLD UNIFORM STILL FITS.
I ACTUALLY LIKE IT BETTER, ULTRAGIRL. I CAN'T IMAGINE GOING INTO A FIREFIGHT WITH HALF MY BUTT HANGING OUT.
THAT IS SO NOT THE POINT, CLOUD 9. MS. MARVEL ASKED ME TO WEAR HER ORIGINAL COSTUME. THAT'S LIKE CAROLINA HERRERA ASKING TO DESIGN YOUR DRESS.
I'LL PRETEND I KNOW WHAT THAT MEANS SO YOU DON'T TELL ME.
IT WAS AN HONOR. IT MEANT SOMETHING. AND THEY JUST TOOK IT AWAY TO GIVE TO SOMEONE ELSE. I DOUBT MS. MARVEL EVEN KNOWS.
I WAS COMMITTED TO THE INITIATIVE. I GAVE UP THE GUY I LOVED FOR IT. BUT THE WAY NORMAN OSBORN'S CHANGING THINGS, I BARELY RECOGNIZE IT ANYMORE.
EXIT
I WAS NEVER ASHAMED OF BEING A NEW WARRIOR. IT WASN'T THEIR FAULT THOSE VILLAINS THEY WERE FIGHTING BLEW UP STAMFORD.
BUT WE NEEDED TO REDEEM OURSELVES. SHOW PEOPLE WE COULD PROTECT THEM. IRON MAN WANTED THAT. OSBORN... I HATE TO THINK ABOUT WHAT HE WANTS.
I MEAN, OKAY, HE'S A WAR HERO, BUT HE'S ALSO AN EX-SUPER-VILLAIN. I DON'T KNOW...HALF THE PEOPLE ON BASE ARE LEAVING, AND I CAN'T SAY I--
HOLD UP. SOMETHING'S GOING ON.
WE'RE UNDER ATTACK! GET OUT THERE!
YOU ENGAGE THE ENEMY. I'LL HANDLE CIVILIAN EVACUATION.
WAIT A SECOND...IS THAT...
...VANCE?

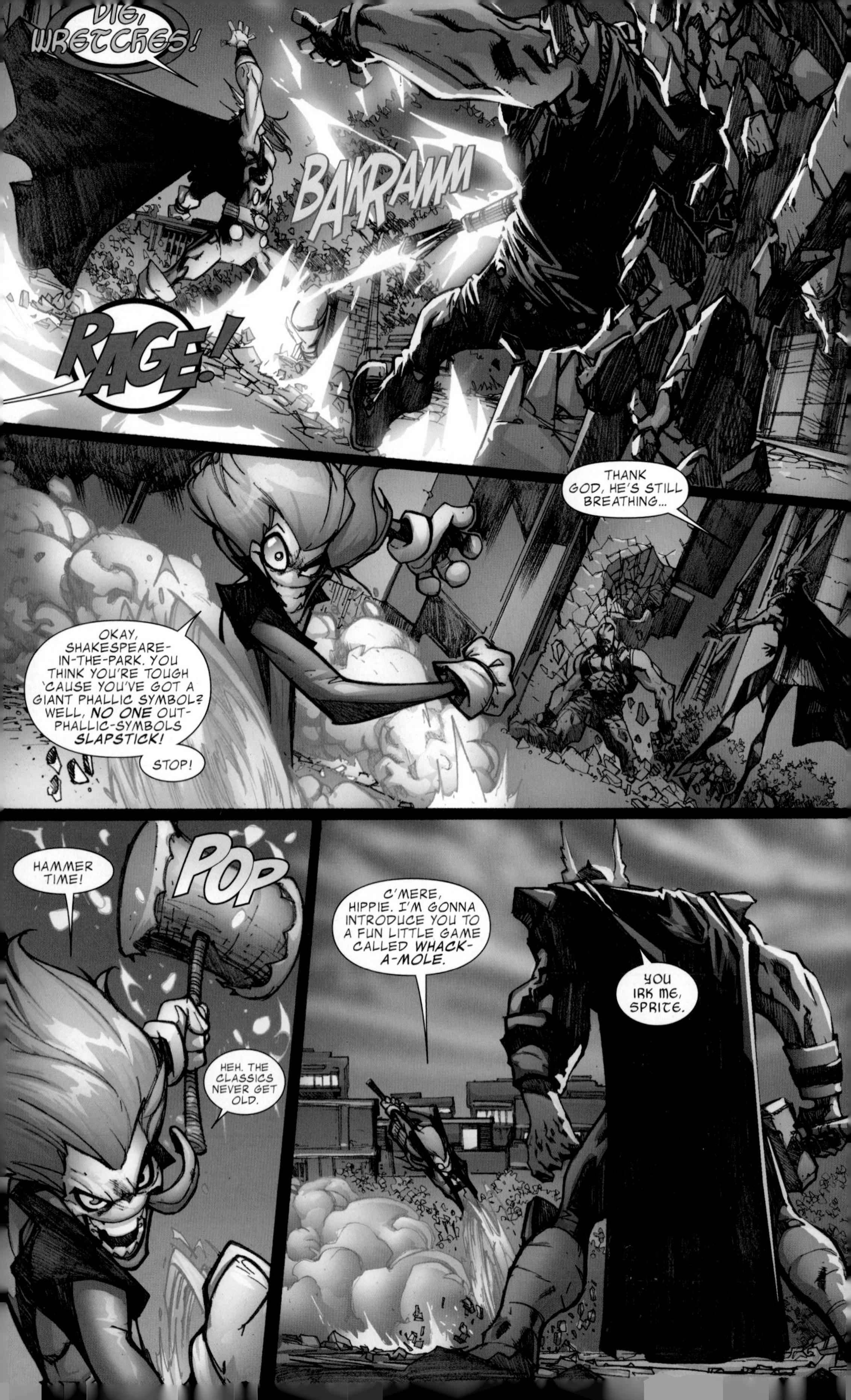
DIE, WRETCHES!
BAKRAMM
RAGE!
THANK GOD, HE'S STILL BREATHING...
OKAY, SHAKESPEARE-IN-THE-PARK. YOU THINK YOU'RE TOUGH 'CAUSE YOU'VE GOT A GIANT PHALLIC SYMBOL? WELL, NO ONE OUT-PHALLIC-SYMBOLS SLAPSTICK!
STOP!
HAMMER TIME!
POP
HEH. THE CLASSICS NEVER GET OLD.
C'MERE, HIPPIE. I'M GONNA INTRODUCE YOU TO A FUN LITTLE GAME CALLED WHACK-A-MOLE.
YOU IRK ME, SPRITE.

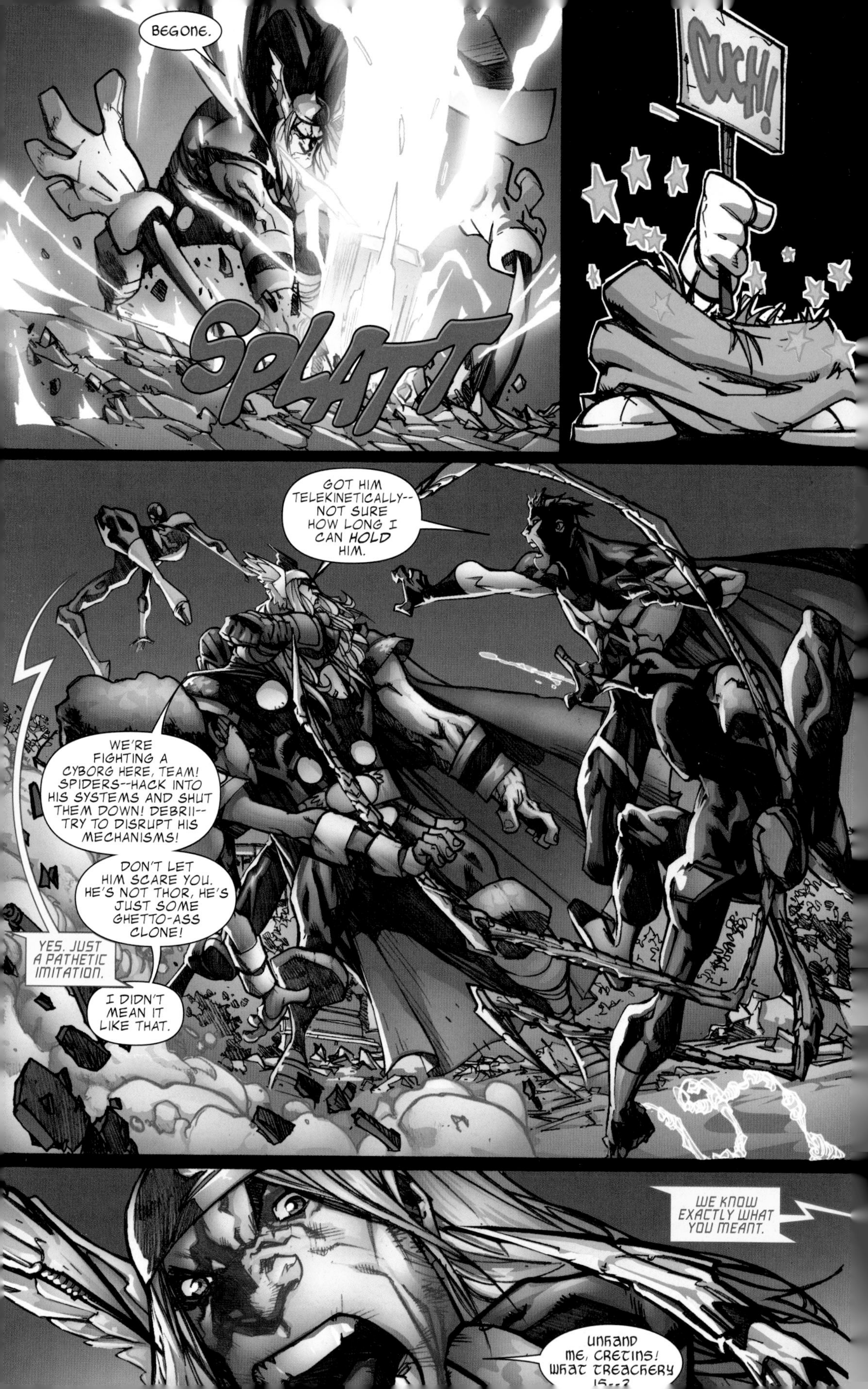
BEGONE.
SPLATT
OUCH!
GOT HIM TELEKINETICALLY-- NOT SURE HOW LONG I CAN HOLD HIM.
WE'RE FIGHTING A CYBORG HERE, TEAM! SPIDERS--HACK INTO HIS SYSTEMS AND SHUT THEM DOWN! DEBRII-- TRY TO DISRUPT HIS MECHANISMS!
DON'T LET HIM SCARE YOU. HE'S NOT THOR, HE'S JUST SOME GHETTO-ASS CLONE!
YES. JUST A PATHETIC IMITATION.
I DIDN'T MEAN IT LIKE THAT.
WE KNOW EXACTLY WHAT YOU MEANT.
UNHAND ME, CRETINS! WHAT TREACHERY IS--?

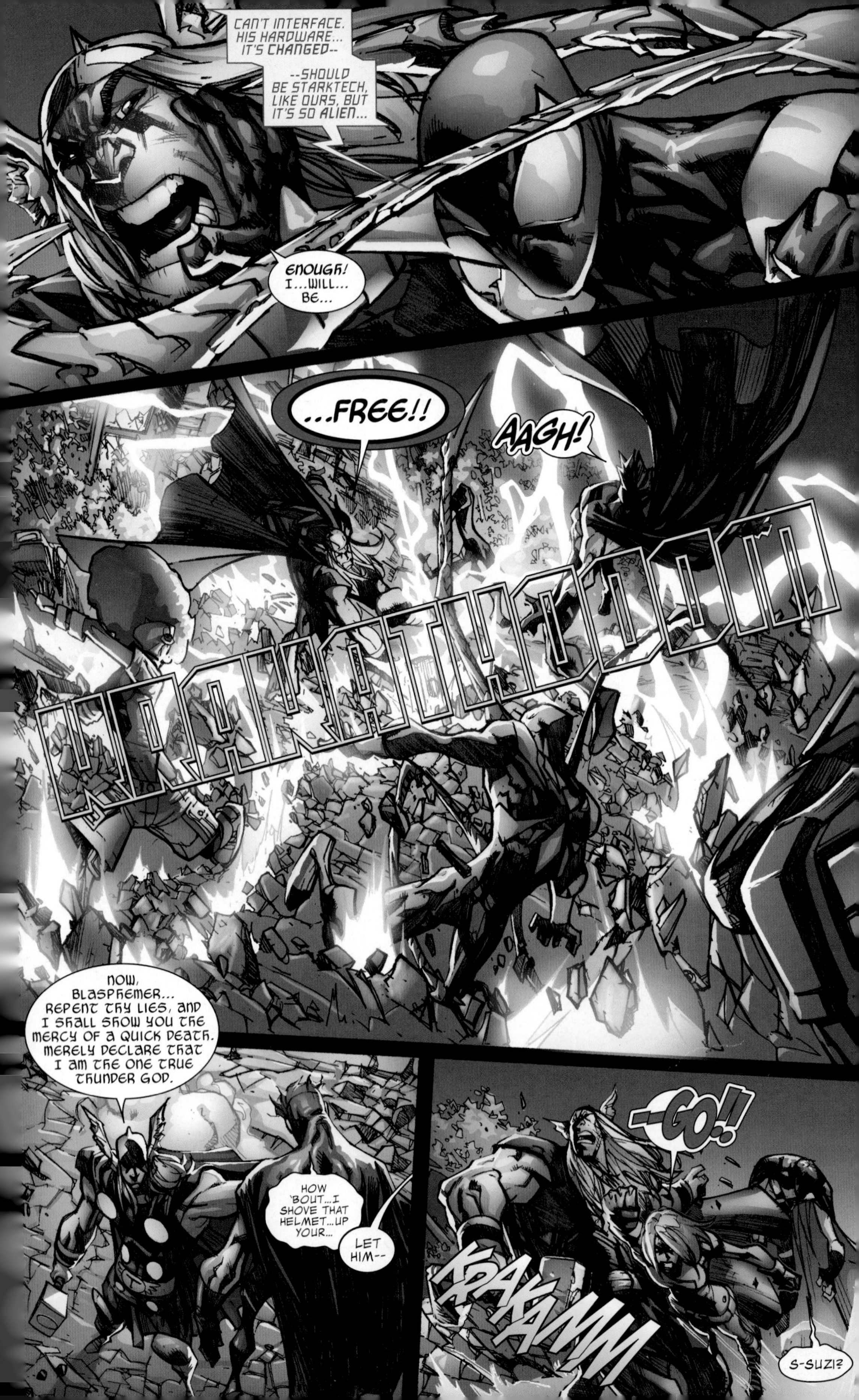
CAN'T INTERFACE. HIS HARDWARE... IT'S CHANGED--
--SHOULD BE STARKTECH, LIKE OURS, BUT IT'S SO ALIEN...
ENOUGH! I...WILL... BE...
...FREE!!
AAGH!
NOW, BLASPHEMER... REPENT THY LIES, AND I SHALL SHOW YOU THE MERCY OF A QUICK DEATH. MERELY DECLARE THAT I AM THE ONE TRUE THUNDER GOD.
HOW 'BOUT...I SHOVE THAT HELMET...UP YOUR...
LET HIM--
-GO!!
S-SUZI?

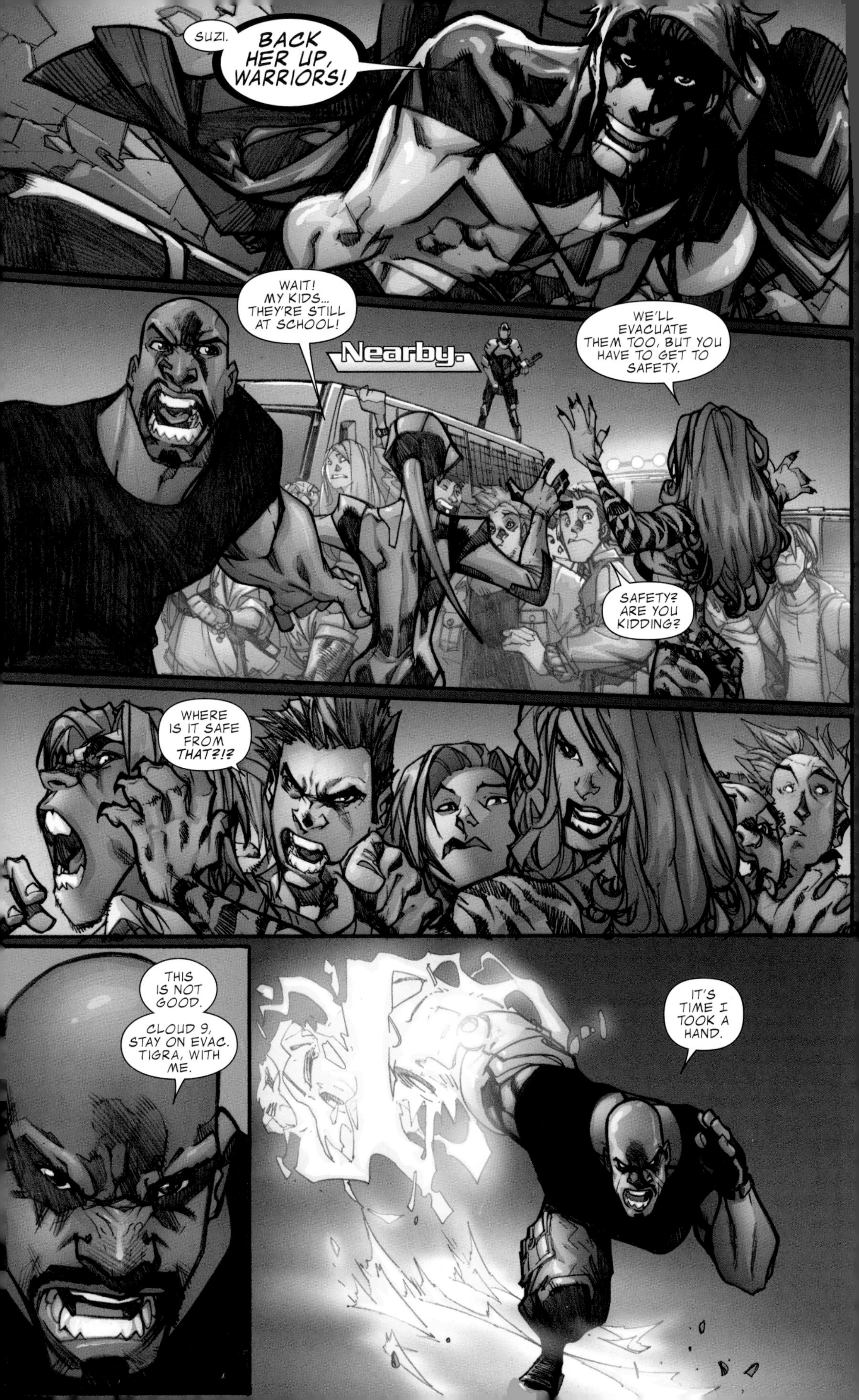

SUZI.
BACK HER UP, WARRIORS!
Nearby.
WAIT! MY KIDS... THEY'RE STILL AT SCHOOL!
WE'LL EVACUATE THEM TOO, BUT YOU HAVE TO GET TO SAFETY.
SAFETY? ARE YOU KIDDING?
WHERE IS IT SAFE FROM THAT?!?
THIS IS NOT GOOD.
CLOUD 9, STAY ON EVAC. TIGRA, WITH ME.
IT'S TIME I TOOK A HAND.

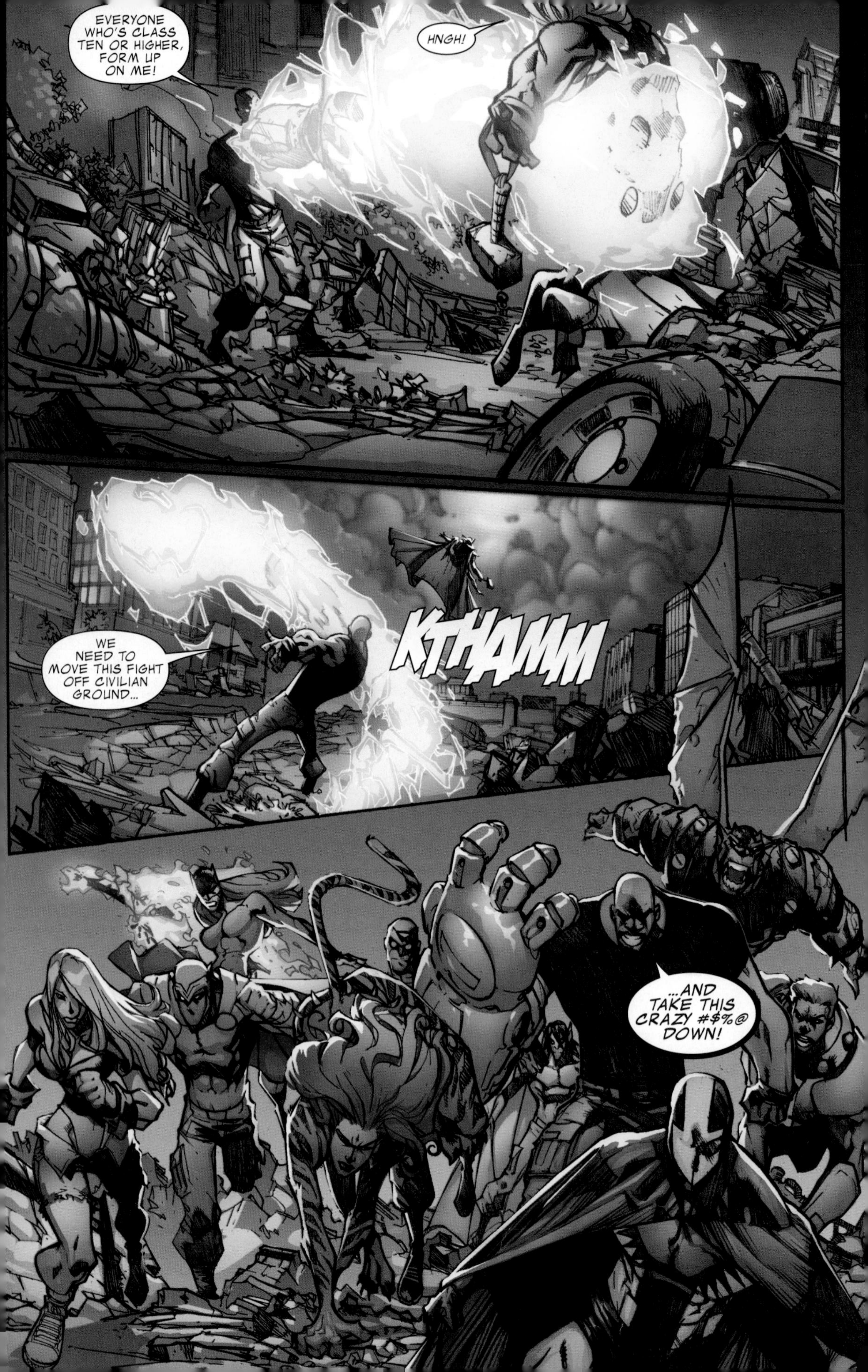
EVERYONE WHO'S CLASS TEN OR HIGHER, FORM UP ON ME!
HNGH!
KTHAMM
WE NEED TO MOVE THIS FIGHT OFF CIVILIAN GROUND...
...AND TAKE THIS CRAZY #$%@ DOWN!

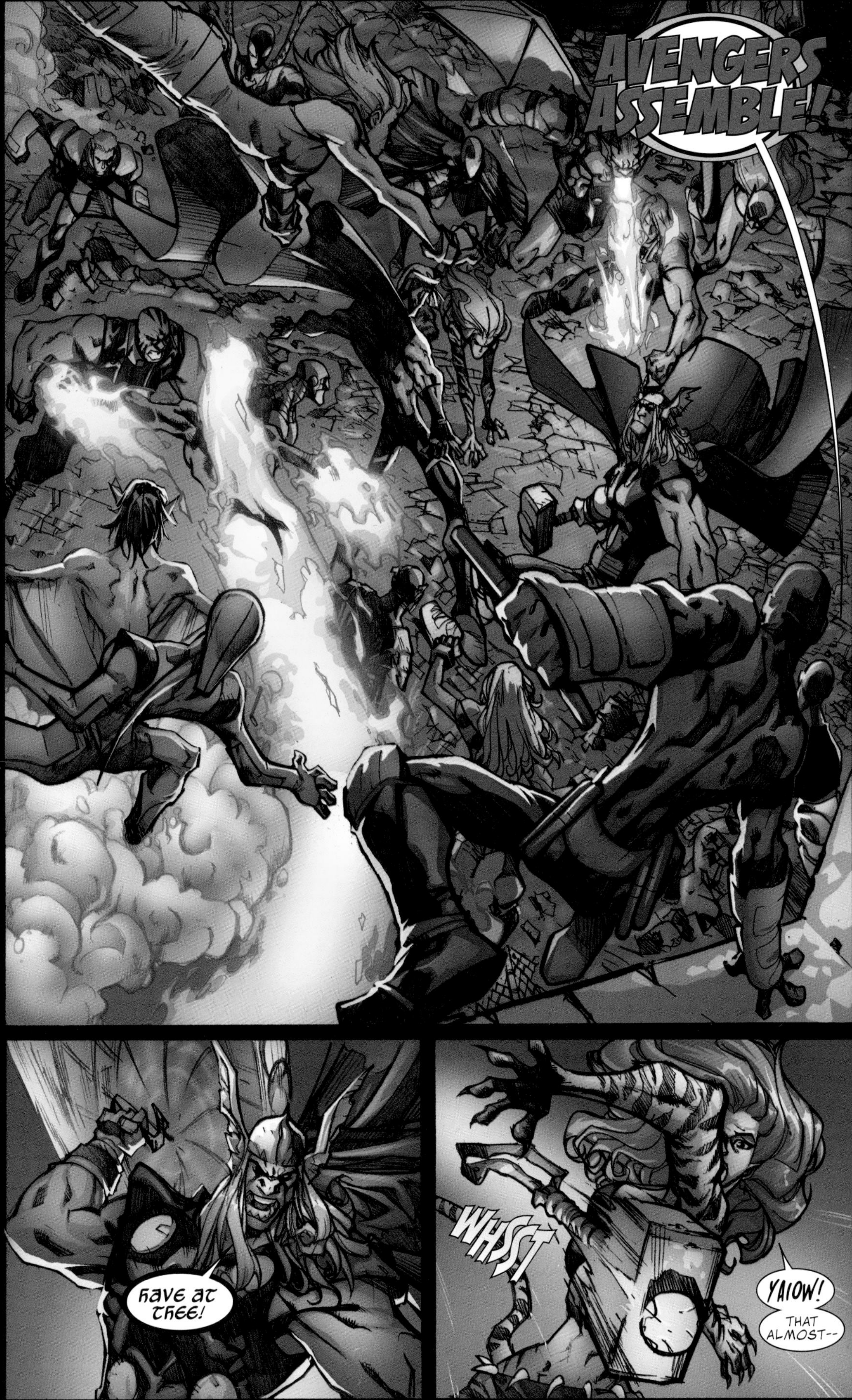
AVENGERS ASSEMBLE!
HAVE AT THEE!
WHSST
YAIOW!
THAT ALMOST--

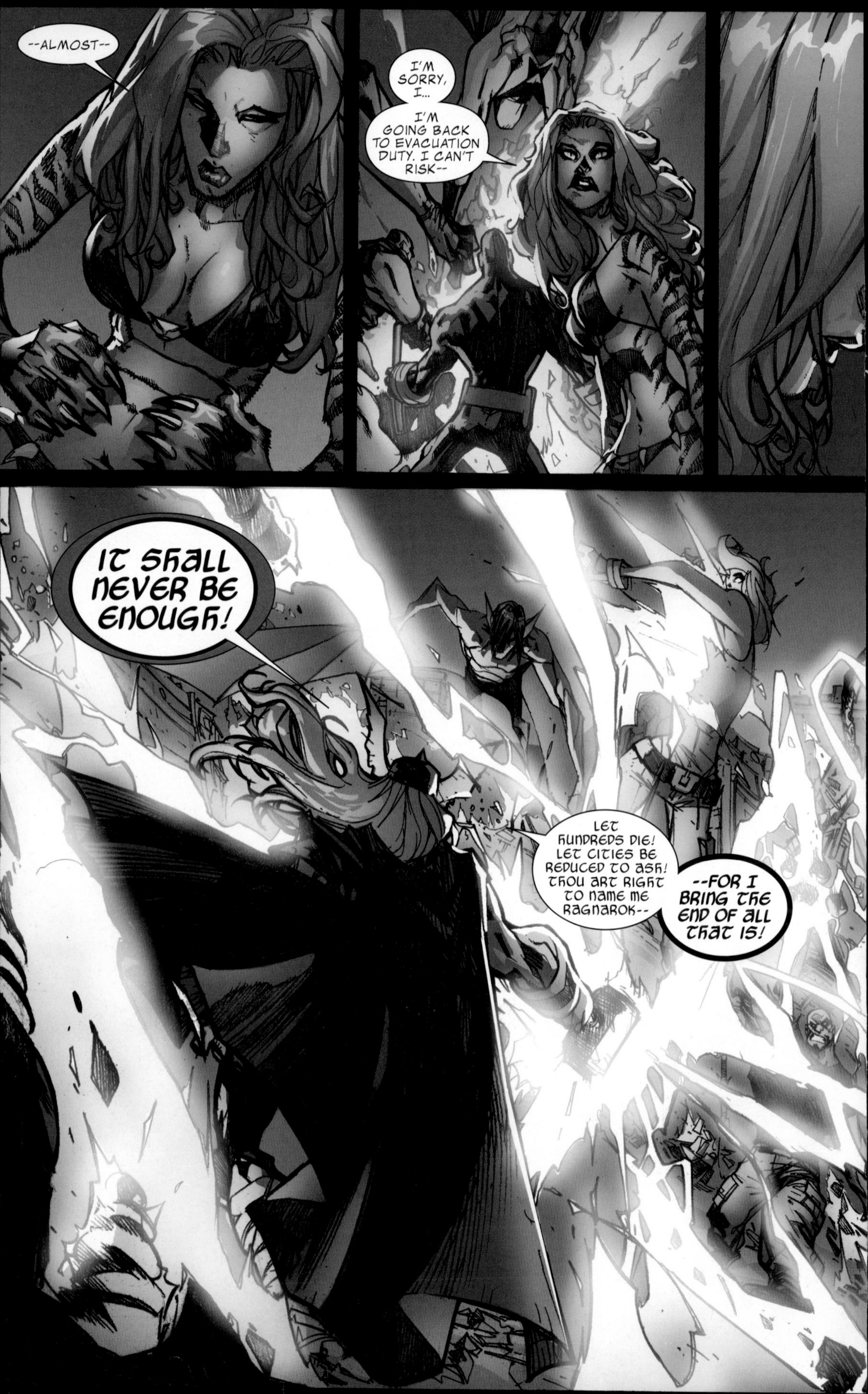
--ALMOST--
I'M SORRY, I...
I'M GOING BACK TO EVACUATION DUTY. I CAN'T RISK--
IT SHALL NEVER BE ENOUGH!
LET HUNDREDS DIE! LET CITIES BE REDUCED TO ASH! THOU ART RIGHT TO NAME ME RAGNAROK--
--FOR I BRING THE END OF ALL THAT IS!

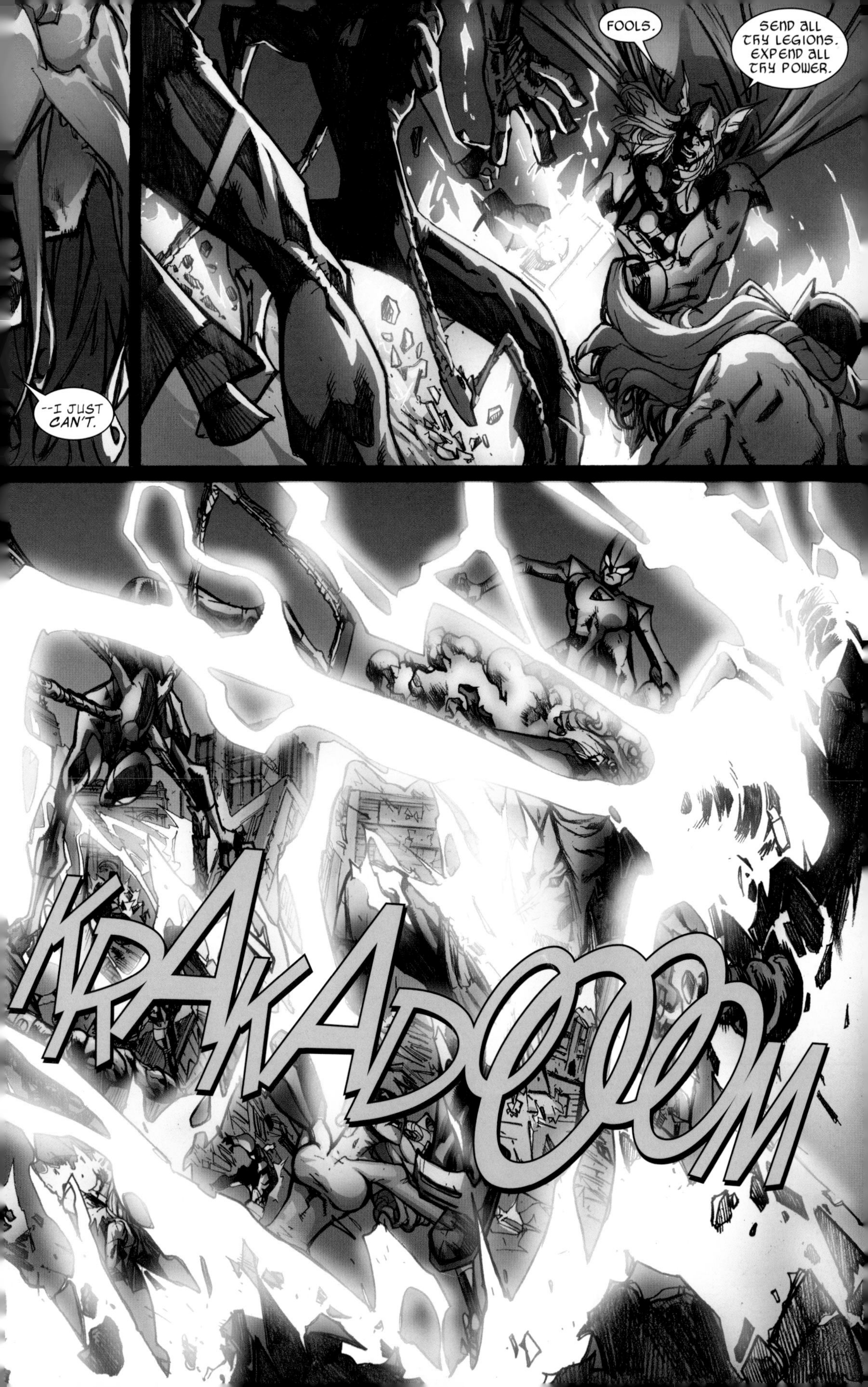
--I JUST CAN'T.
FOOLS.
SEND ALL THY LEGIONS. EXPEND ALL THY POWER.
KRAKADOOOM

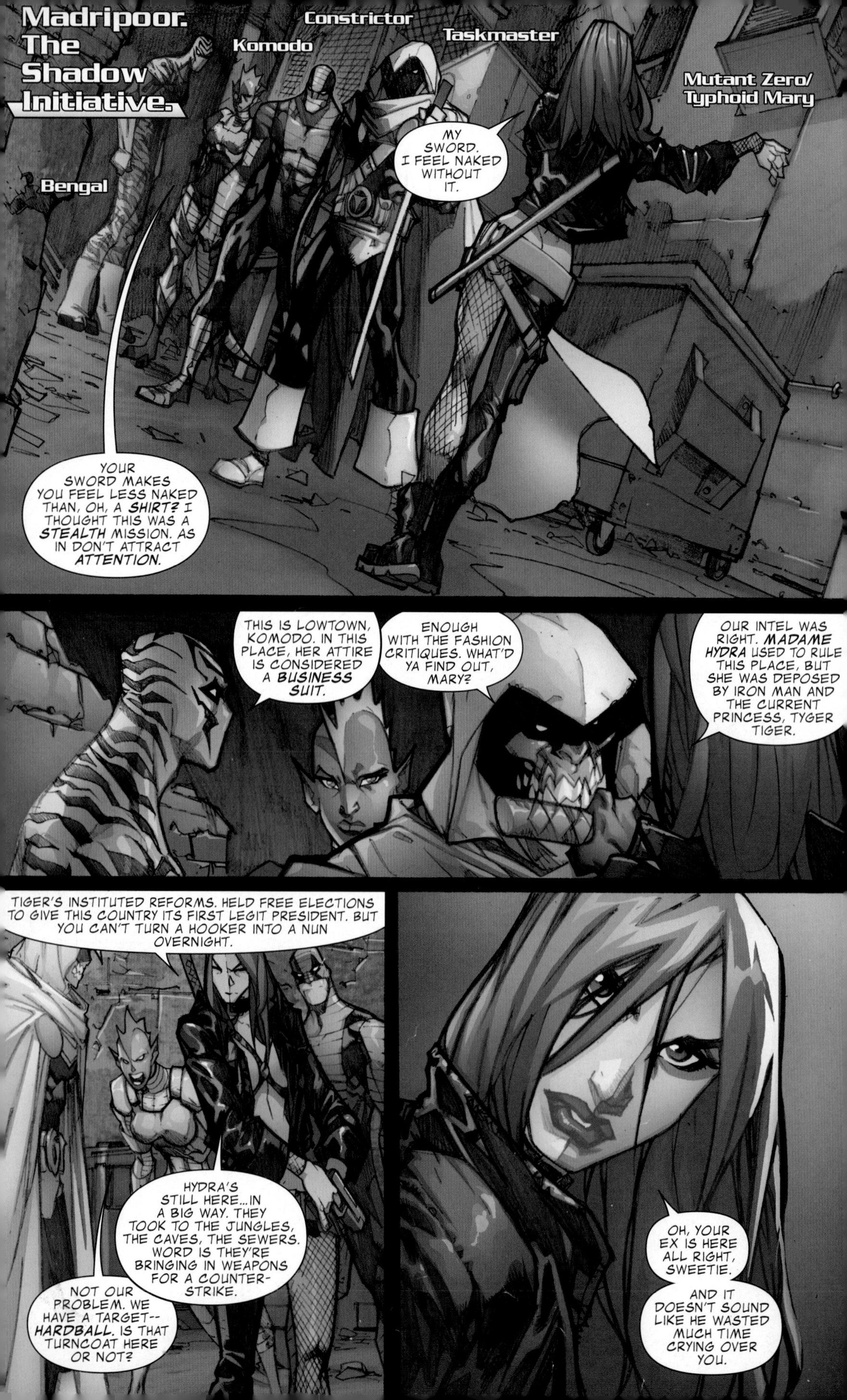
Madripoor. The Shadow Initiative.
Constrictor
Komodo
Taskmaster
Mutant Zero/ Typhoid Mary
Bengal
MY SWORD. I FEEL NAKED WITHOUT IT.
YOUR SWORD MAKES YOU FEEL LESS NAKED THAN, OH, A SHIRT? I THOUGHT THIS WAS A STEALTH MISSION. AS IN DON'T ATTRACT ATTENTION.
THIS IS LOWTOWN, KOMODO. IN THIS PLACE, HER ATTIRE IS CONSIDERED A BUSINESS SUIT.
ENOUGH WITH THE FASHION CRITIQUES. WHAT'D YA FIND OUT, MARY?
OUR INTEL WAS RIGHT. MADAME HYDRA USED TO RULE THIS PLACE, BUT SHE WAS DEPOSED BY IRON MAN AND THE CURRENT PRINCESS, TYGER TIGER.
TIGER'S INSTITUTED REFORMS. HELD FREE ELECTIONS TO GIVE THIS COUNTRY ITS FIRST LEGIT PRESIDENT. BUT YOU CAN'T TURN A HOOKER INTO A NUN OVERNIGHT.
HYDRA'S STILL HERE...IN A BIG WAY. THEY TOOK TO THE JUNGLES, THE CAVES, THE SEWERS. WORD IS THEY'RE BRINGING IN WEAPONS FOR A COUNTER-STRIKE.
NOT OUR PROBLEM. WE HAVE A TARGET-- HARDBALL. IS THAT TURNCOAT HERE OR NOT?
OH, YOUR EX IS HERE ALL RIGHT, SWEETIE.
AND IT DOESN'T SOUND LIKE HE WASTED MUCH TIME CRYING OVER YOU.

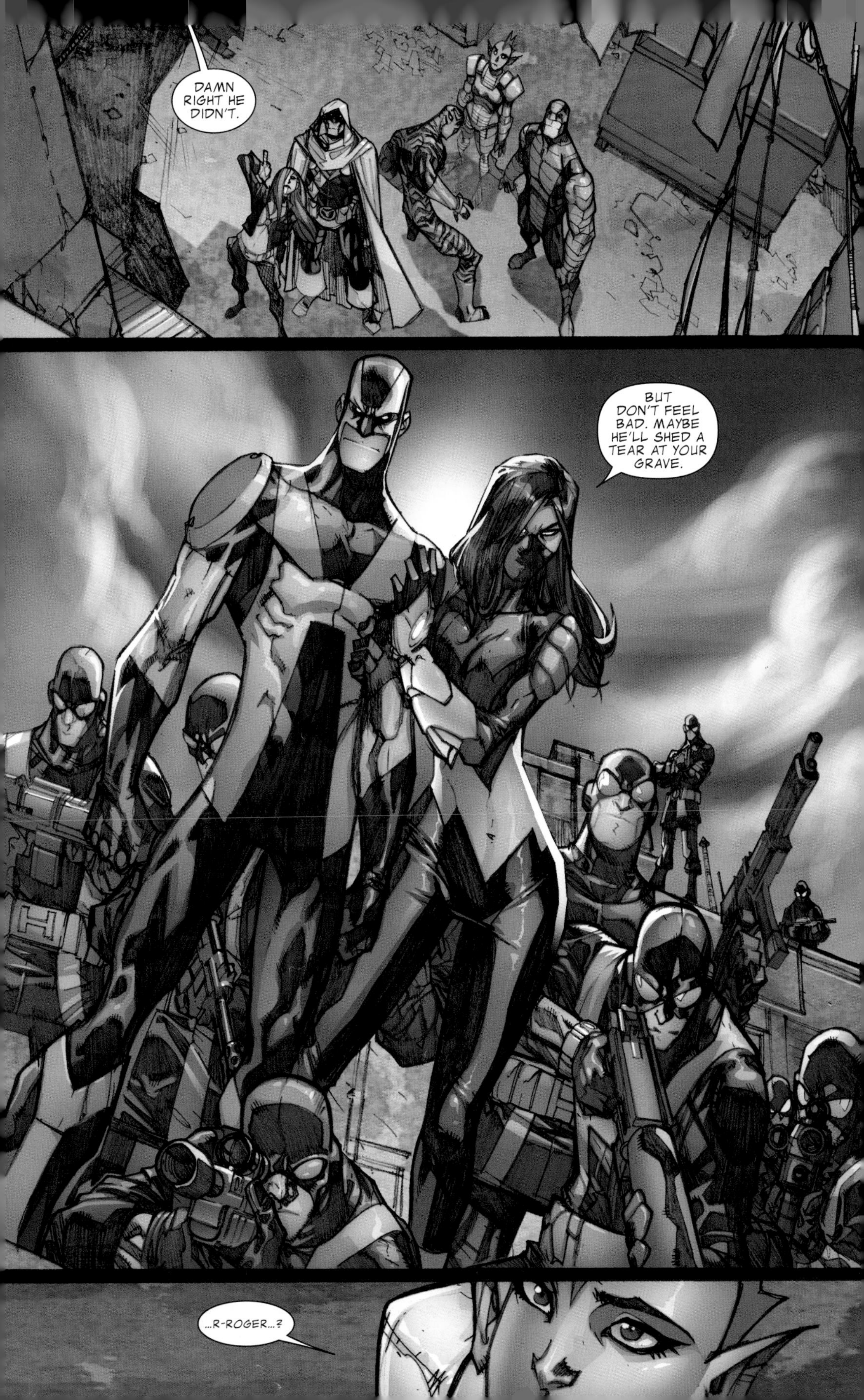
DAMN RIGHT HE DIDN'T.
BUT DON'T FEEL BAD. MAYBE HE'LL SHED A TEAR AT YOUR GRAVE.
...R-ROGER...?

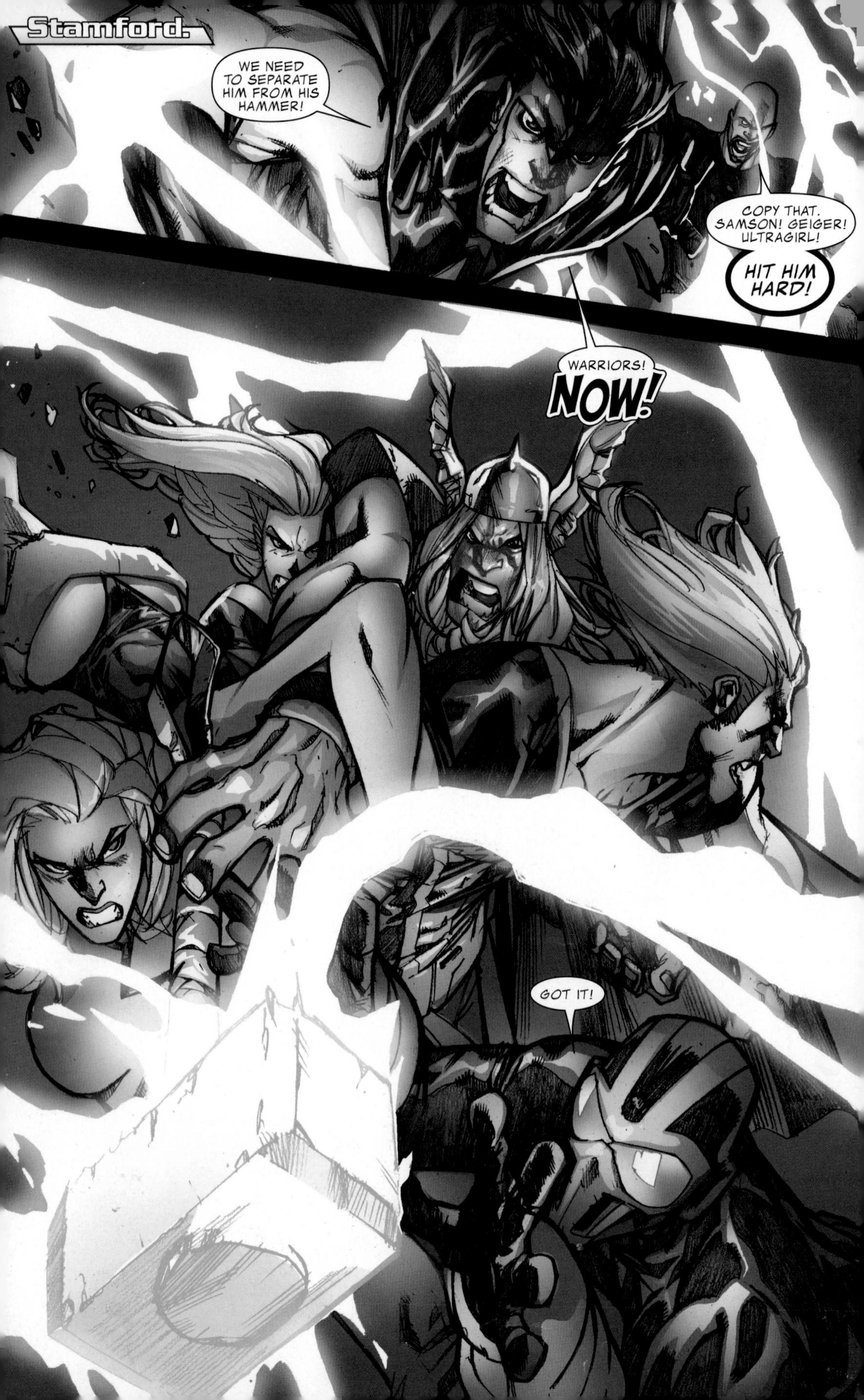
Stamford.
WE NEED TO SEPARATE HIM FROM HIS HAMMER!
COPY THAT. SAMSON! GEIGER! ULTRAGIRL!
HIT HIM HARD!
WARRIORS! NOW!
GOT IT!

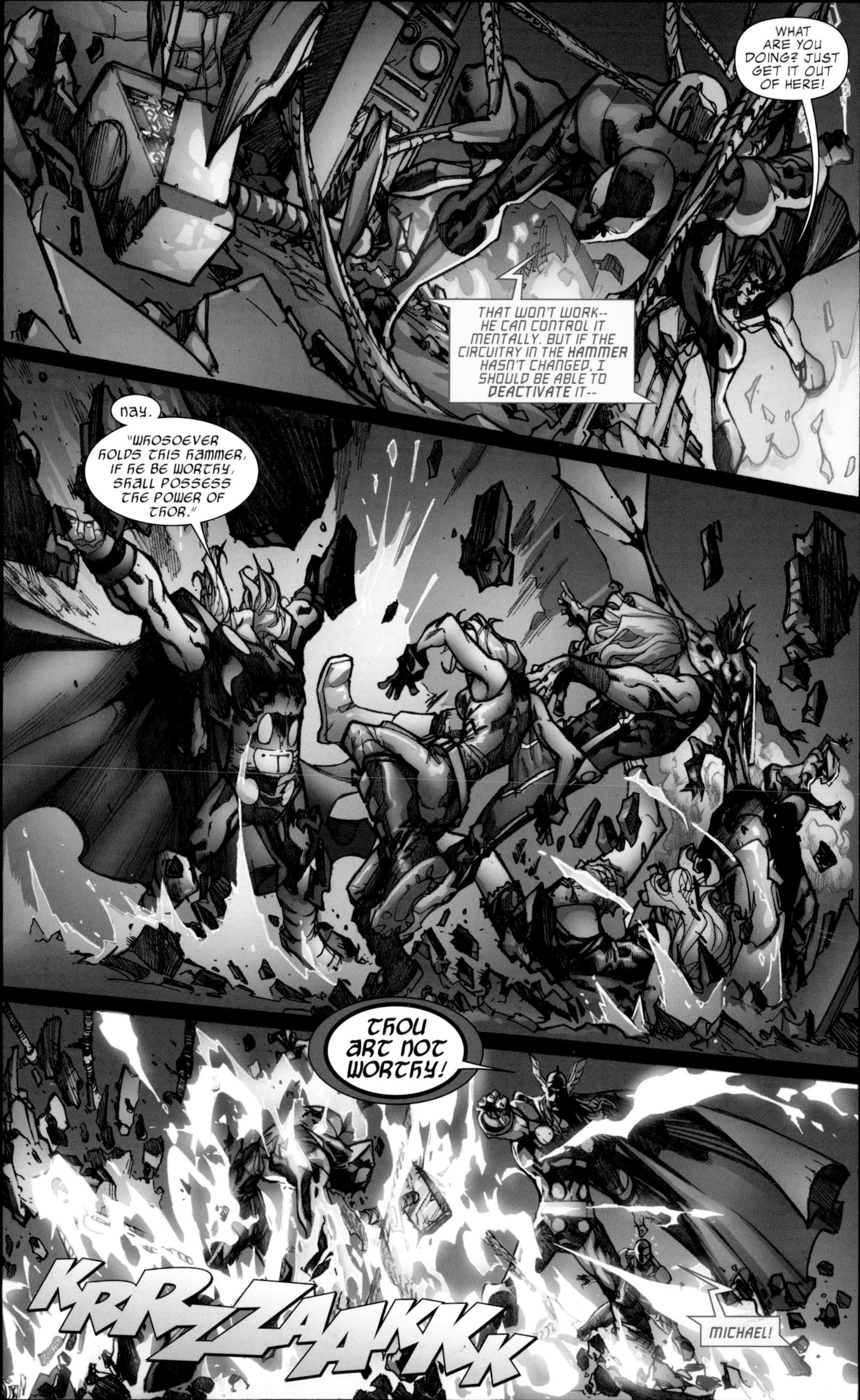
WHAT ARE YOU DOING? JUST GET IT OUT OF HERE!
THAT WON'T WORK-- HE CAN CONTROL IT MENTALLY. BUT IF THE CIRCUITRY IN THE HAMMER HASN'T CHANGED, I SHOULD BE ABLE TO DEACTIVATE IT--
NAY.
"WHOSOEVER HOLDS THIS HAMMER, IF HE BE WORTHY, SHALL POSSESS THE POWER OF THOR."
THOU ART NOT WORTHY!
KRRZZAAKKK
MICHAEL!

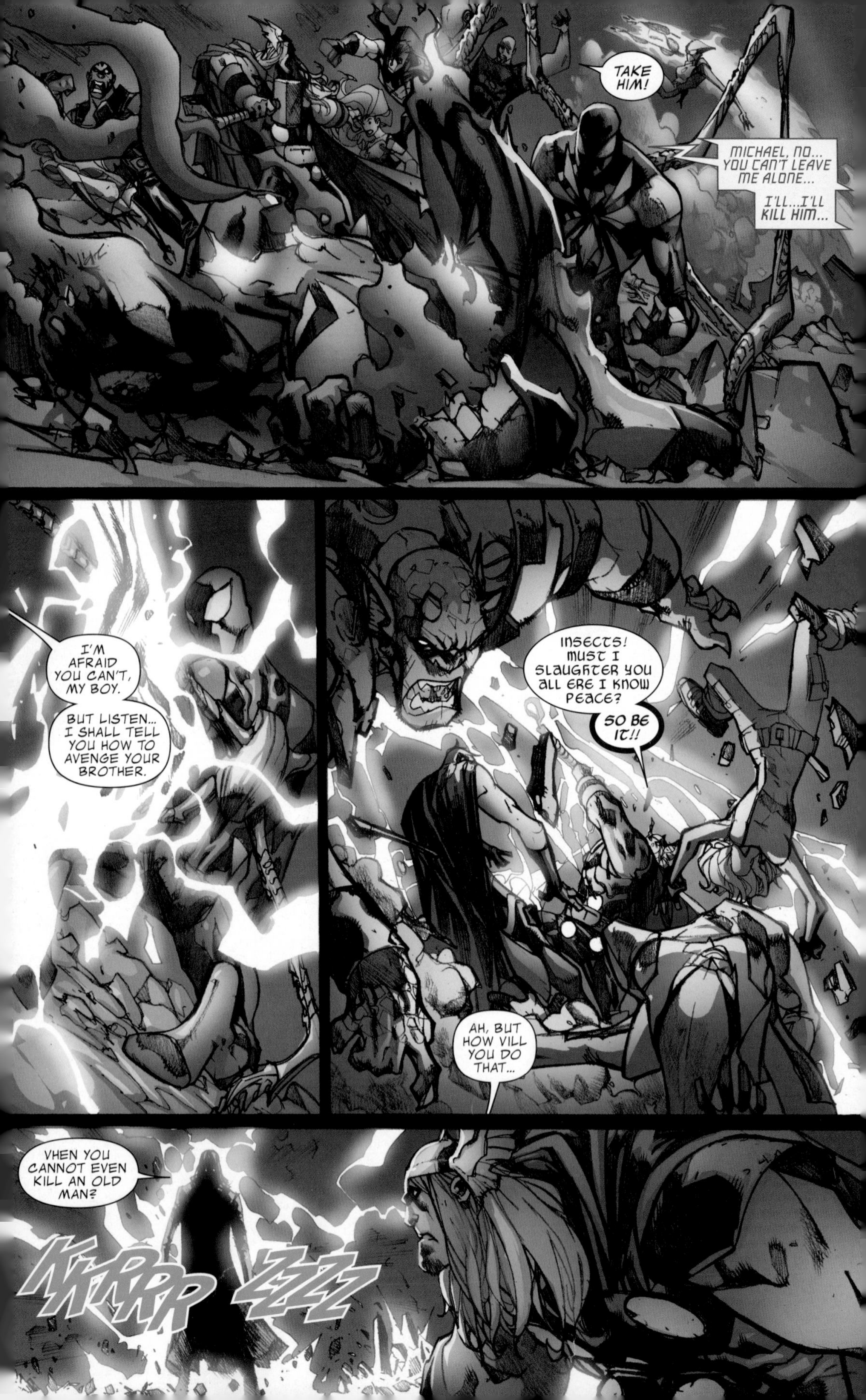
TAKE HIM!
MICHAEL, NO... YOU CAN'T LEAVE ME ALONE...
I'LL...I'LL KILL HIM...
I'M AFRAID YOU CAN'T, MY BOY.
BUT LISTEN... I SHALL TELL YOU HOW TO AVENGE YOUR BROTHER.
INSECTS! MUST I SLAUGHTER YOU ALL ERE I KNOW PEACE?
SO BE IT!!
AH, BUT HOW VILL YOU DO THAT...
VHEN YOU CANNOT EVEN KILL AN OLD MAN?
KKRRRR ZZZZ

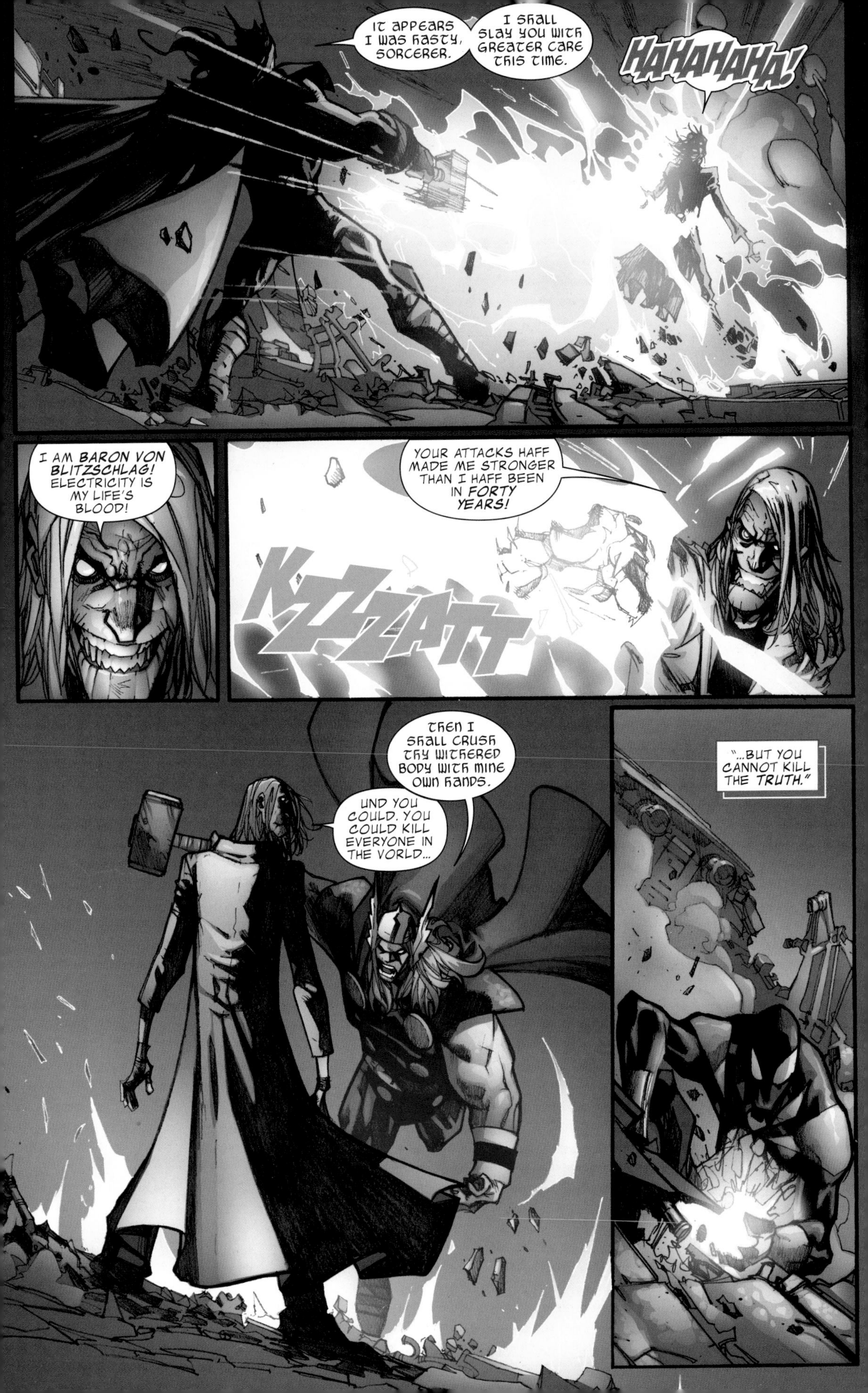
IT APPEARS I WAS HASTY, SORCERER.
I SHALL SLAY YOU WITH GREATER CARE THIS TIME.
HAHAHAHA!
I AM BARON VON BLITZSCHLAG! ELECTRICITY IS MY LIFE'S BLOOD!
YOUR ATTACKS HAFF MADE ME STRONGER THAN I HAFF BEEN IN FORTY YEARS!
KZZZATT
THEN I SHALL CRUSH THY WITHERED BODY WITH MINE OWN HANDS.
UND YOU COULD. YOU COULD KILL EVERYONE IN THE VORLD...
"...BUT YOU CANNOT KILL THE TRUTH."

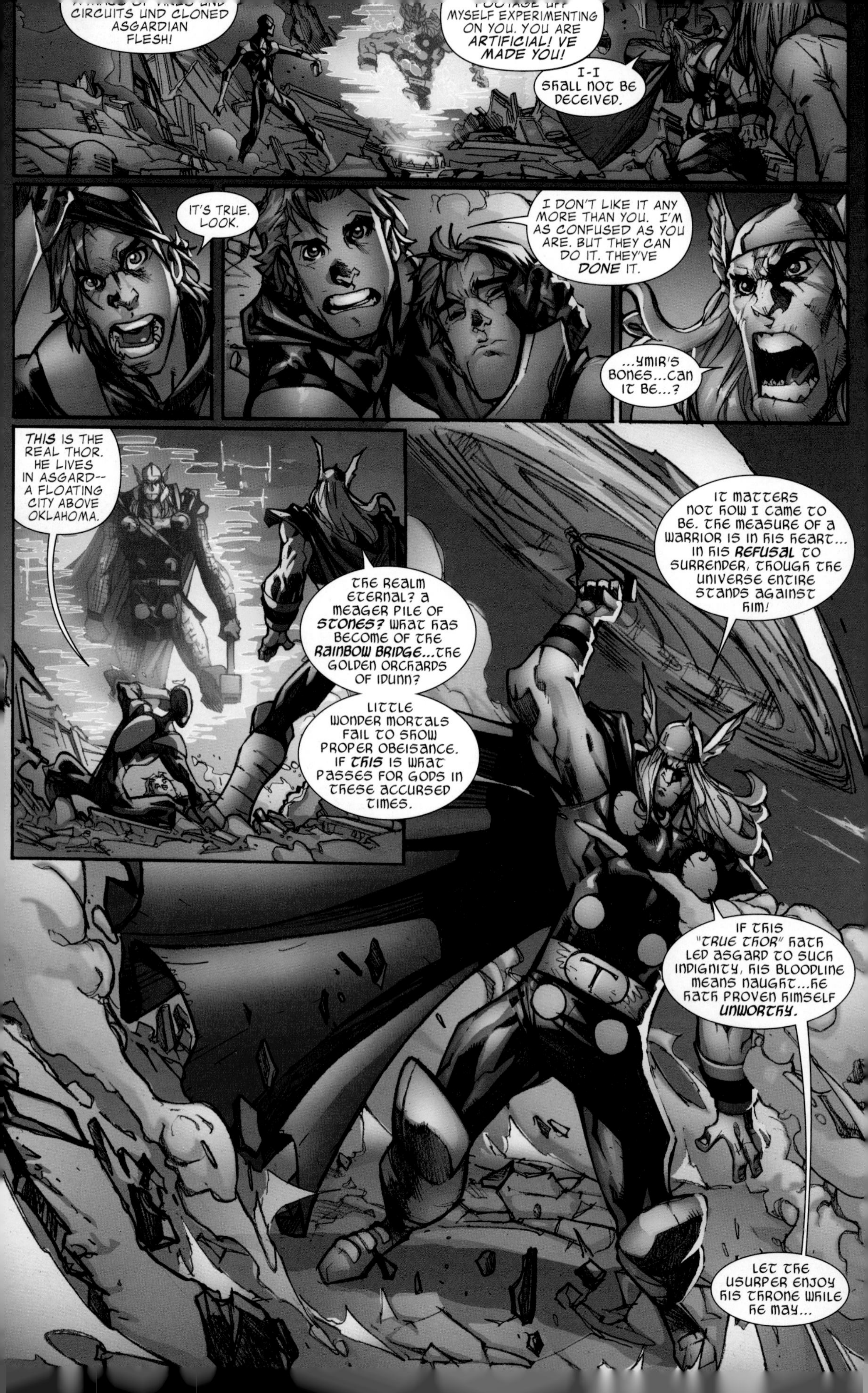
CIRCUITS UND CLONED ASGARDIAN FLESH!
MYSELF EXPERIMENTING ON YOU. YOU ARE ARTIFICIAL! VE MADE YOU!
I-I SHALL NOT BE DECEIVED.
IT'S TRUE. LOOK.
I DON'T LIKE IT ANY MORE THAN YOU. I'M AS CONFUSED AS YOU ARE. BUT THEY CAN DO IT. THEY'VE DONE IT.
...YMIR'S BONES...CAN IT BE...?
THIS IS THE REAL THOR. HE LIVES IN ASGARD-- A FLOATING CITY ABOVE OKLAHOMA.
THE REALM ETERNAL? A MEAGER PILE OF STONES? WHAT HAS BECOME OF THE RAINBOW BRIDGE...THE GOLDEN ORCHARDS OF IDUNN?
LITTLE WONDER MORTALS FAIL TO SHOW PROPER OBEISANCE. IF THIS IS WHAT PASSES FOR GODS IN THESE ACCURSED TIMES.
IT MATTERS NOT HOW I CAME TO BE. THE MEASURE OF A WARRIOR IS IN HIS HEART... IN HIS REFUSAL TO SURRENDER, THOUGH THE UNIVERSE ENTIRE STANDS AGAINST HIM!
IF THIS "TRUE THOR" HATH LED ASGARD TO SUCH INDIGNITY, HIS BLOODLINE MEANS NAUGHT...HE HATH PROVEN HIMSELF UNWORTHY.
LET THE USURPER ENJOY HIS THRONE WHILE HE MAY...

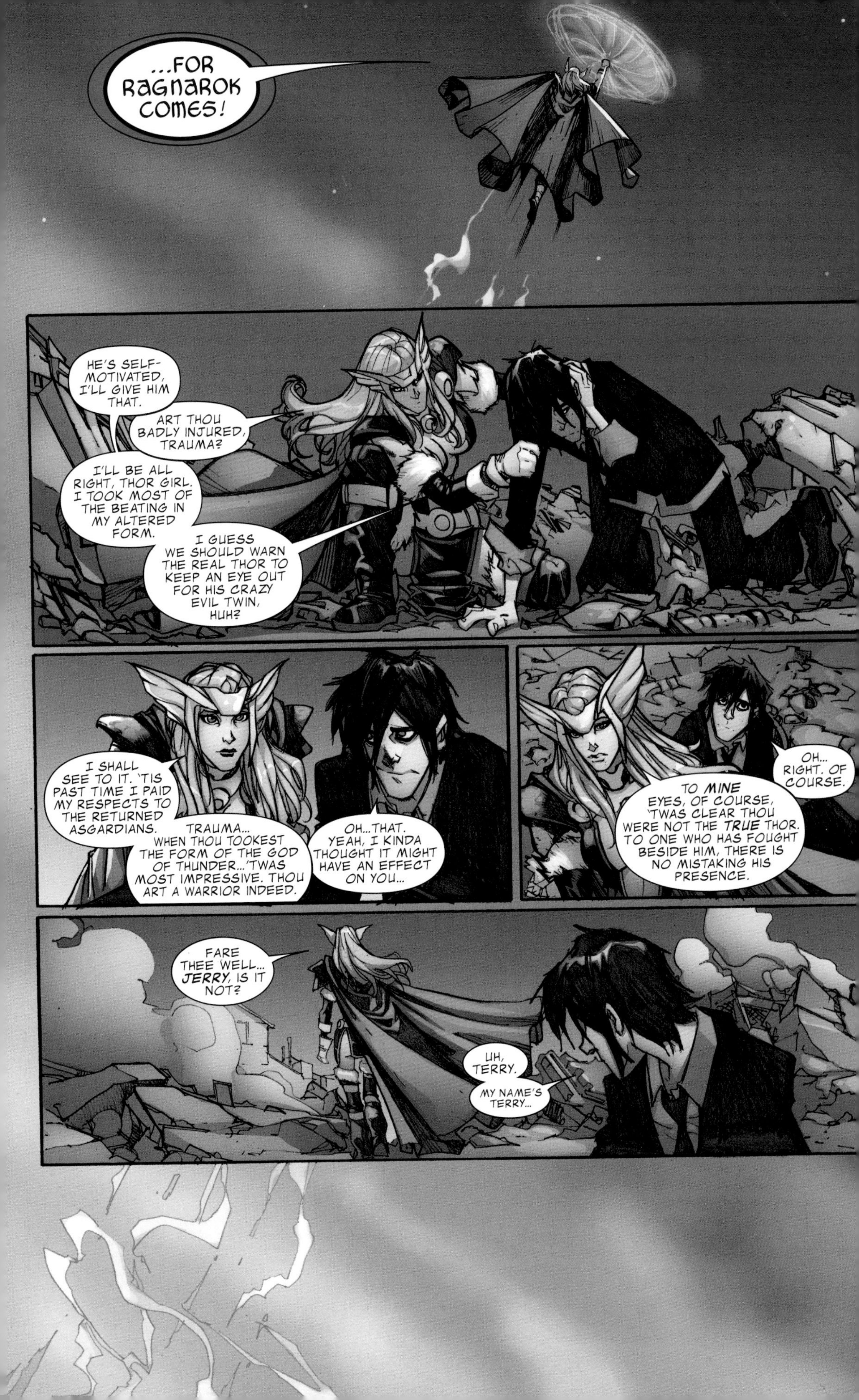
...FOR RAGNAROK COMES!
HE'S SELF-MOTIVATED, I'LL GIVE HIM THAT.
ART THOU BADLY INJURED, TRAUMA?
I'LL BE ALL RIGHT, THOR GIRL. I TOOK MOST OF THE BEATING IN MY ALTERED FORM.
I GUESS WE SHOULD WARN THE REAL THOR TO KEEP AN EYE OUT FOR HIS CRAZY EVIL TWIN, HUH?
I SHALL SEE TO IT. 'TIS PAST TIME I PAID MY RESPECTS TO THE RETURNED ASGARDIANS.
TRAUMA... WHEN THOU TOOKEST THE FORM OF THE GOD OF THUNDER...'TWAS MOST IMPRESSIVE. THOU ART A WARRIOR INDEED.
OH...THAT. YEAH, I KINDA THOUGHT IT MIGHT HAVE AN EFFECT ON YOU...
TO MINE EYES, OF COURSE, 'TWAS CLEAR THOU WERE NOT THE TRUE THOR. TO ONE WHO HAS FOUGHT BESIDE HIM, THERE IS NO MISTAKING HIS PRESENCE.
OH... RIGHT. OF COURSE.
FARE THEE WELL... JERRY, IS IT NOT?
UH, TERRY.
MY NAME'S TERRY...

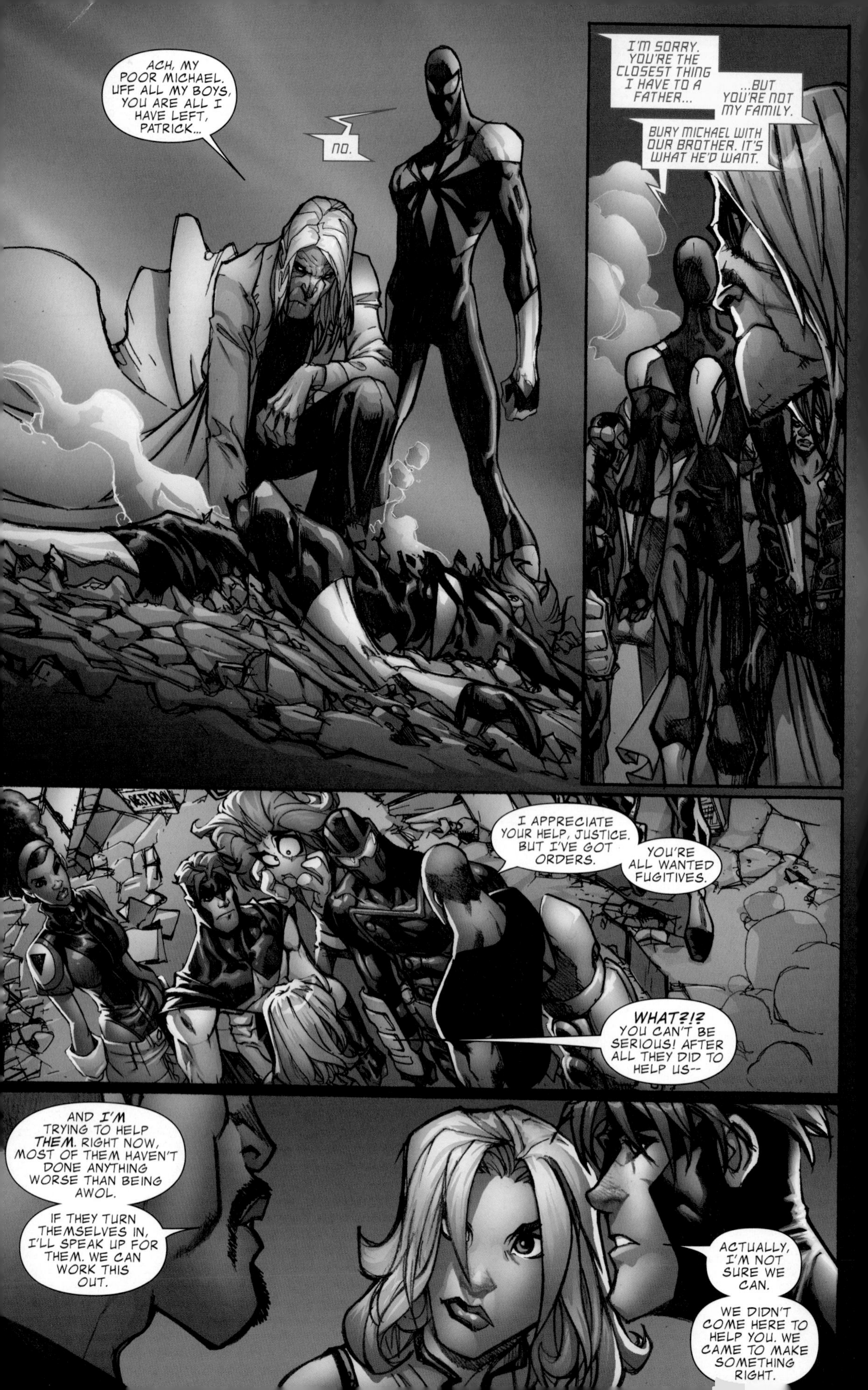
ACH, MY POOR MICHAEL. UFF ALL MY BOYS, YOU ARE ALL I HAVE LEFT, PATRICK...
NO.
I'M SORRY. YOU'RE THE CLOSEST THING I HAVE TO A FATHER...
...BUT YOU'RE NOT MY FAMILY.
BURY MICHAEL WITH OUR BROTHER. IT'S WHAT HE'D WANT.
I APPRECIATE YOUR HELP, JUSTICE. BUT I'VE GOT ORDERS.
YOU'RE ALL WANTED FUGITIVES.
WHAT?!? YOU CAN'T BE SERIOUS! AFTER ALL THEY DID TO HELP US--
AND I'M TRYING TO HELP THEM. RIGHT NOW, MOST OF THEM HAVEN'T DONE ANYTHING WORSE THAN BEING AWOL.
IF THEY TURN THEMSELVES IN, I'LL SPEAK UP FOR THEM. WE CAN WORK THIS OUT.
ACTUALLY, I'M NOT SURE WE CAN.
WE DIDN'T COME HERE TO HELP YOU. WE CAME TO MAKE SOMETHING RIGHT.

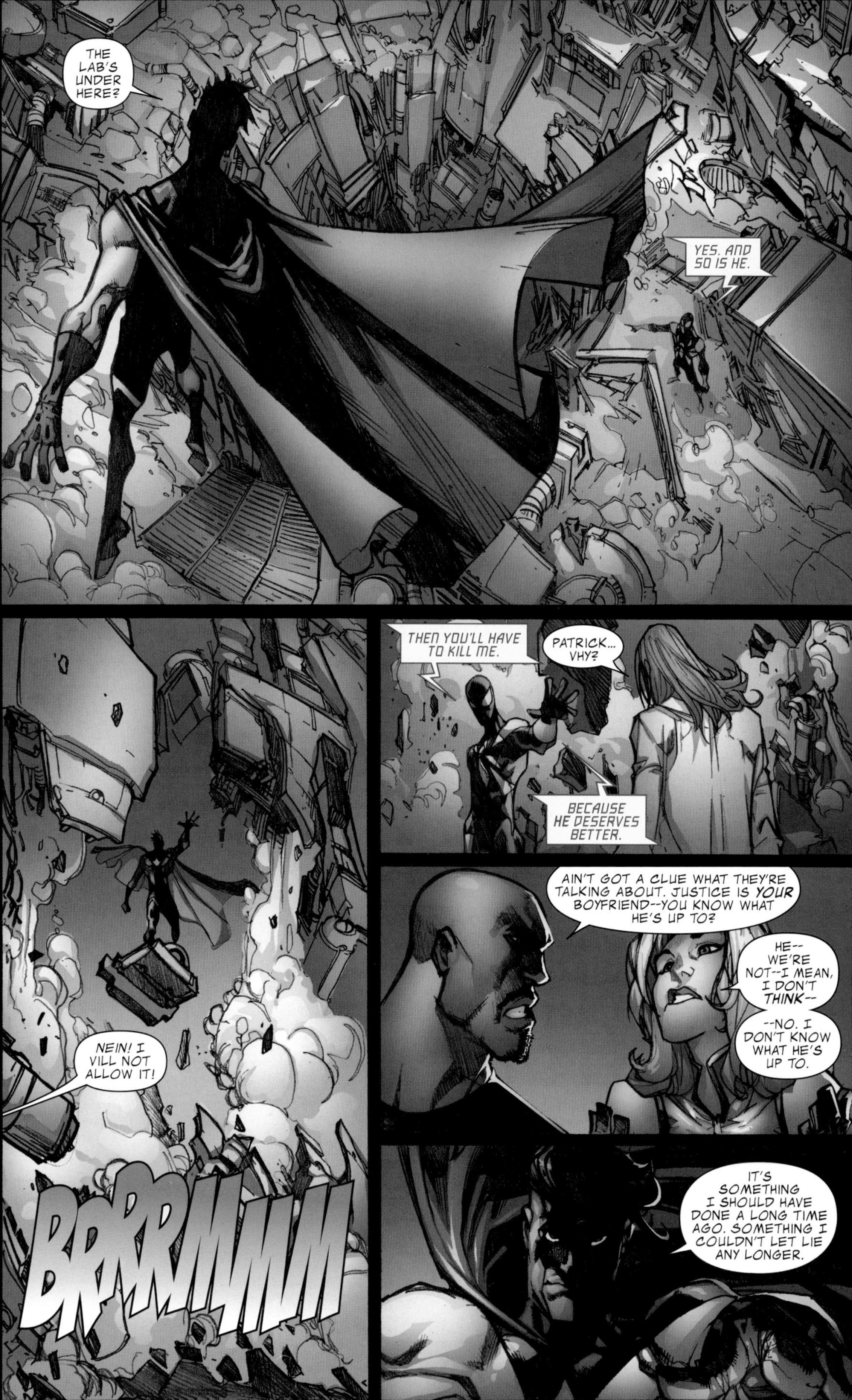
THE LAB'S UNDER HERE?
YES. AND SO IS HE.
NEIN! I VILL NOT ALLOW IT!
BRRRMMMM
THEN YOU'LL HAVE TO KILL ME.
PATRICK... VHY?
BECAUSE HE DESERVES BETTER.
AIN'T GOT A CLUE WHAT THEY'RE TALKING ABOUT. JUSTICE IS YOUR BOYFRIEND--YOU KNOW WHAT HE'S UP TO?
HE-- WE'RE NOT--I MEAN, I DON'T THINK--
--NO. I DON'T KNOW WHAT HE'S UP TO.
IT'S SOMETHING I SHOULD HAVE DONE A LONG TIME AGO. SOMETHING I COULDN'T LET LIE ANY LONGER.

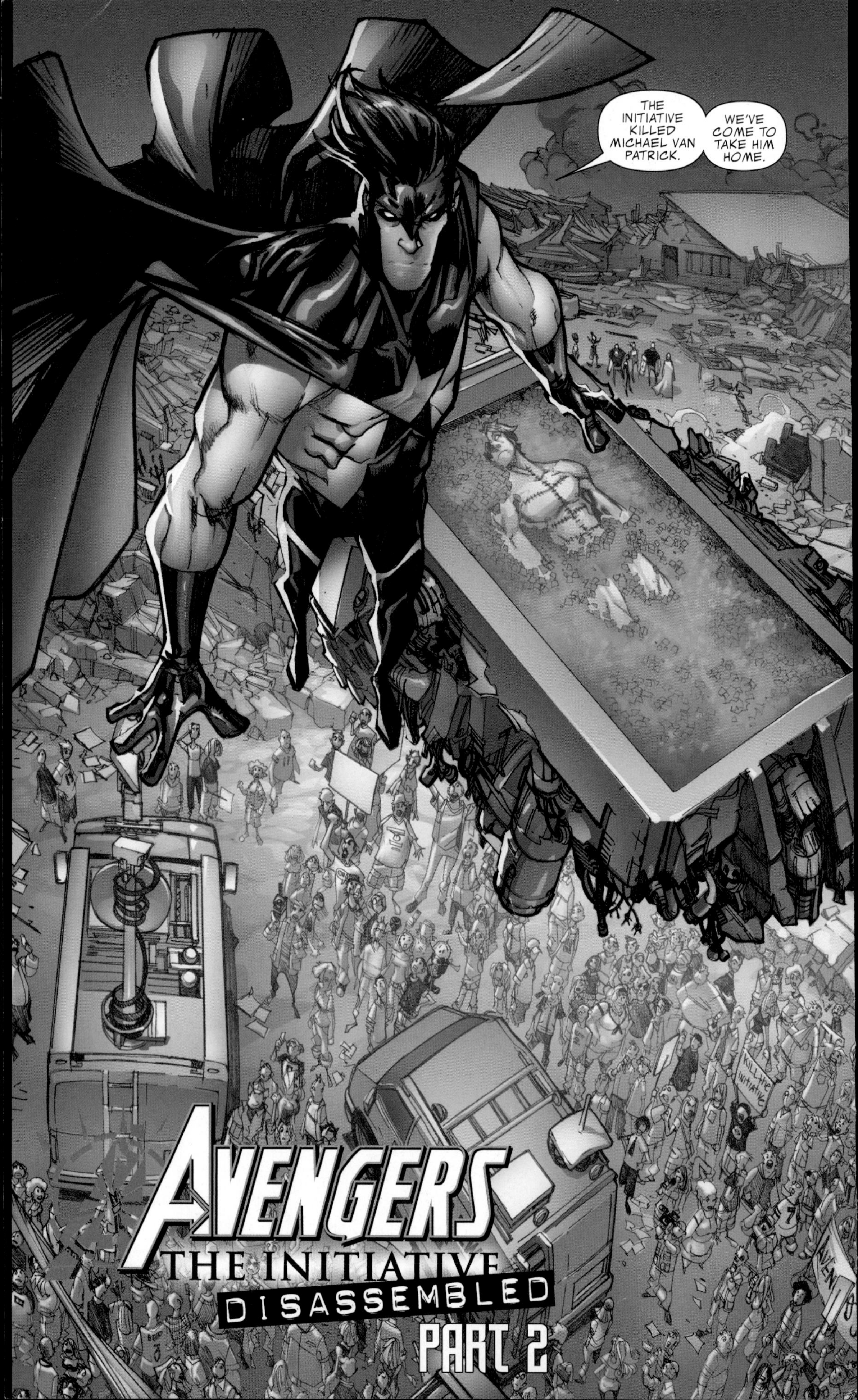
THE INITIATIVE KILLED MICHAEL VAN PATRICK.
WE'VE COME TO TAKE HIM HOME.
KILL the INITIATIVE
AVENGERS
THE INITIATIVE
DISASSEMBLED
PART 2

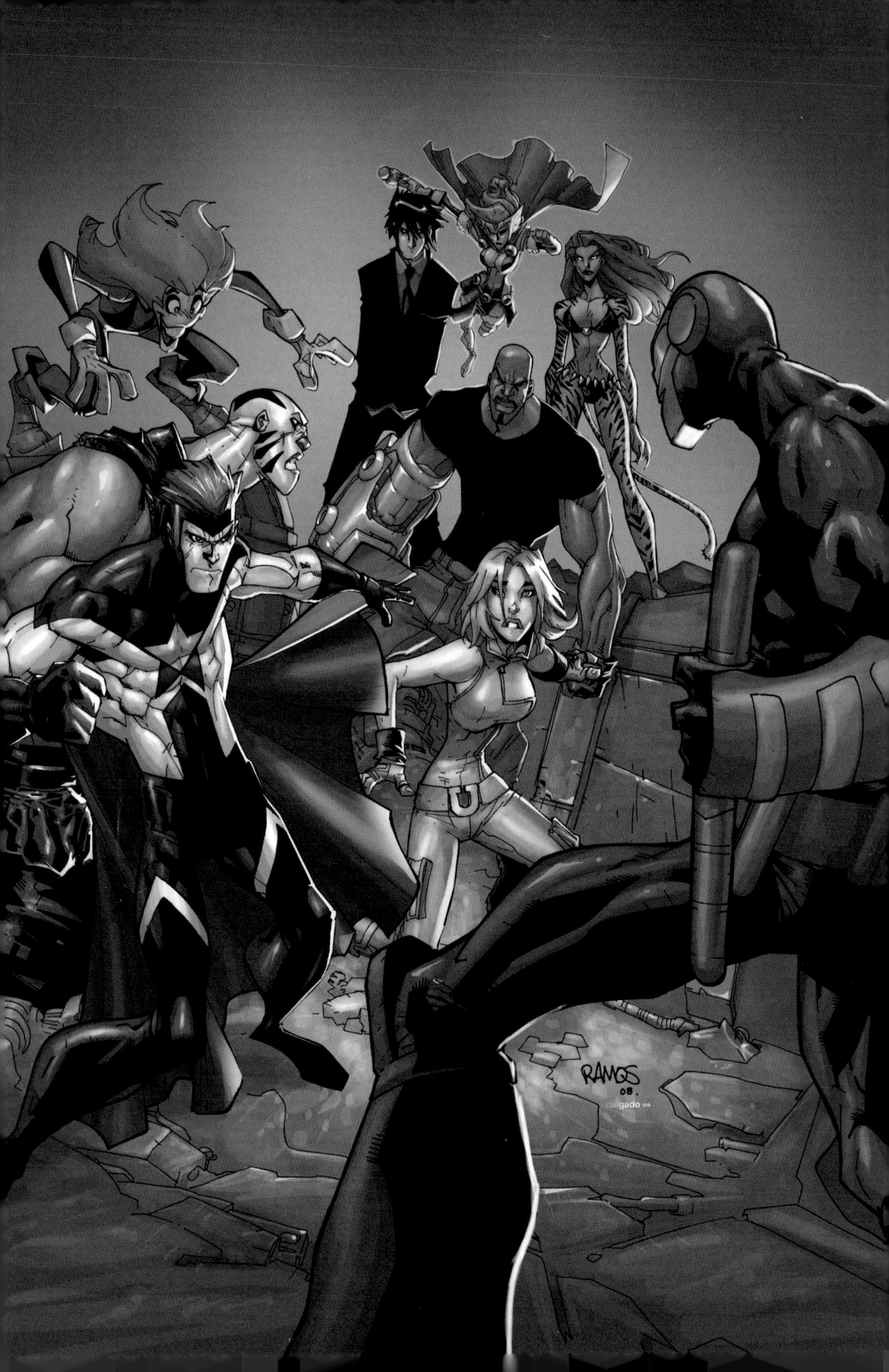
RAMOS
08.

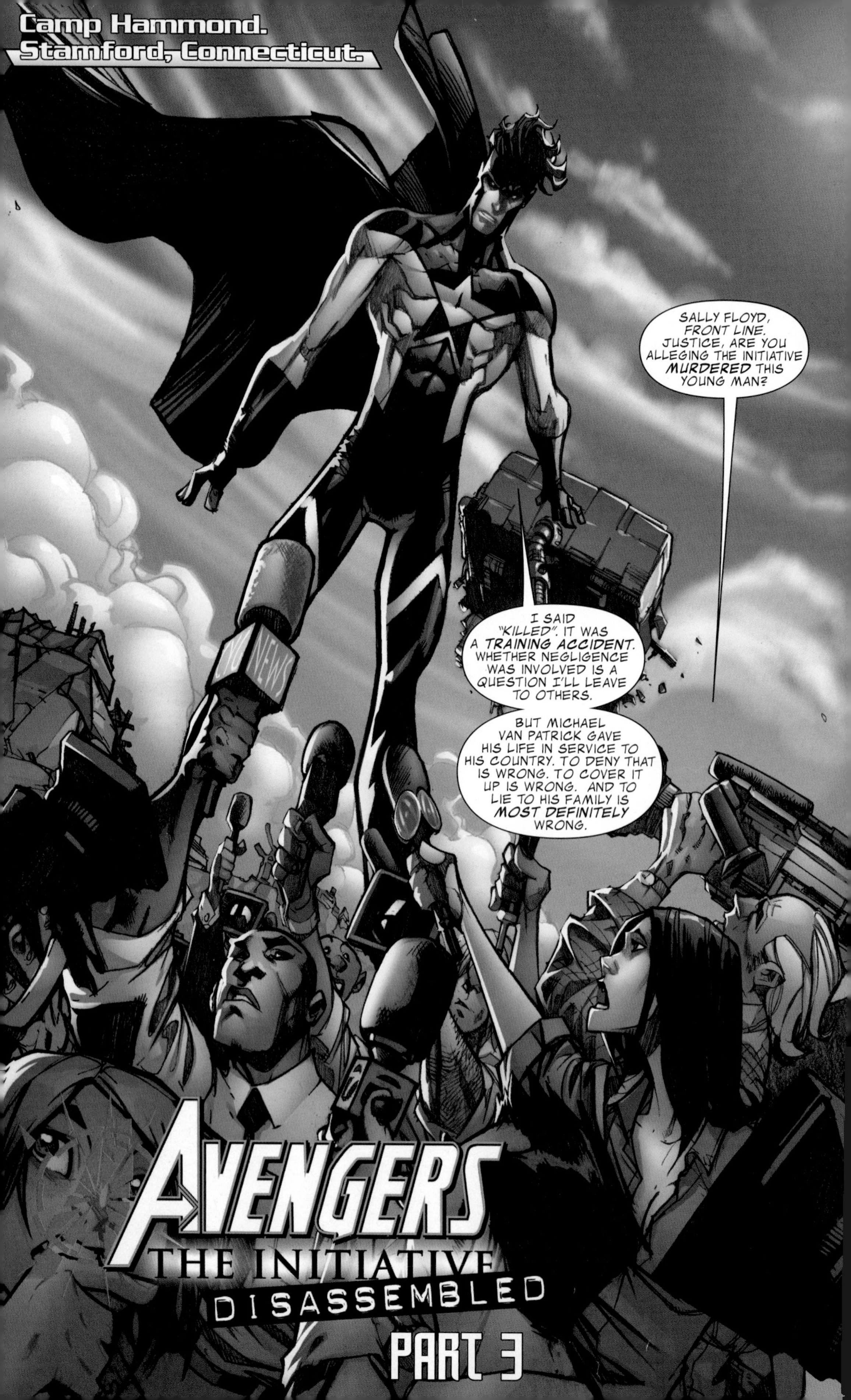
Camp Hammond. Stamford, Connecticut.
SALLY FLOYD, FRONT LINE. JUSTICE, ARE YOU ALLEGING THE INITIATIVE MURDERED THIS YOUNG MAN?
I SAID "KILLED". IT WAS A TRAINING ACCIDENT. WHETHER NEGLIGENCE WAS INVOLVED IS A QUESTION I'LL LEAVE TO OTHERS.
BUT MICHAEL VAN PATRICK GAVE HIS LIFE IN SERVICE TO HIS COUNTRY. TO DENY THAT IS WRONG. TO COVER IT UP IS WRONG. AND TO LIE TO HIS FAMILY IS MOST DEFINITELY WRONG.
CYU NEWS
AVENGERS THE INITIATIVE
DISASSEMBLED
PART 3

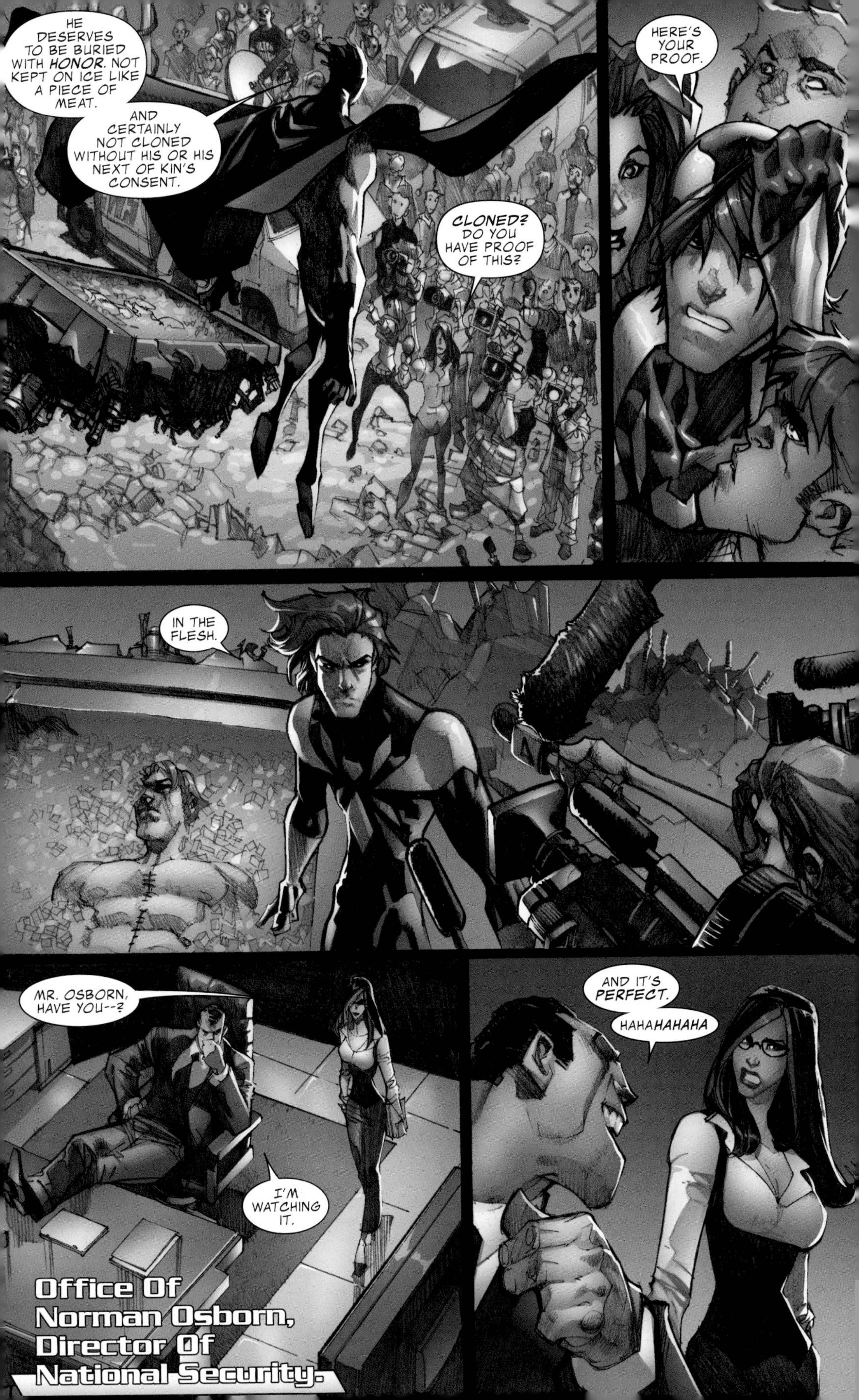
HE DESERVES TO BE BURIED WITH HONOR. NOT KEPT ON ICE LIKE A PIECE OF MEAT.
AND CERTAINLY NOT CLONED WITHOUT HIS OR HIS NEXT OF KIN'S CONSENT.
CLONED? DO YOU HAVE PROOF OF THIS?
HERE'S YOUR PROOF.
IN THE FLESH.
Office Of Norman Osborn, Director Of National Security.
MR. OSBORN, HAVE YOU--?
I'M WATCHING IT.
AND IT'S PERFECT.
HAHAHAHAHA

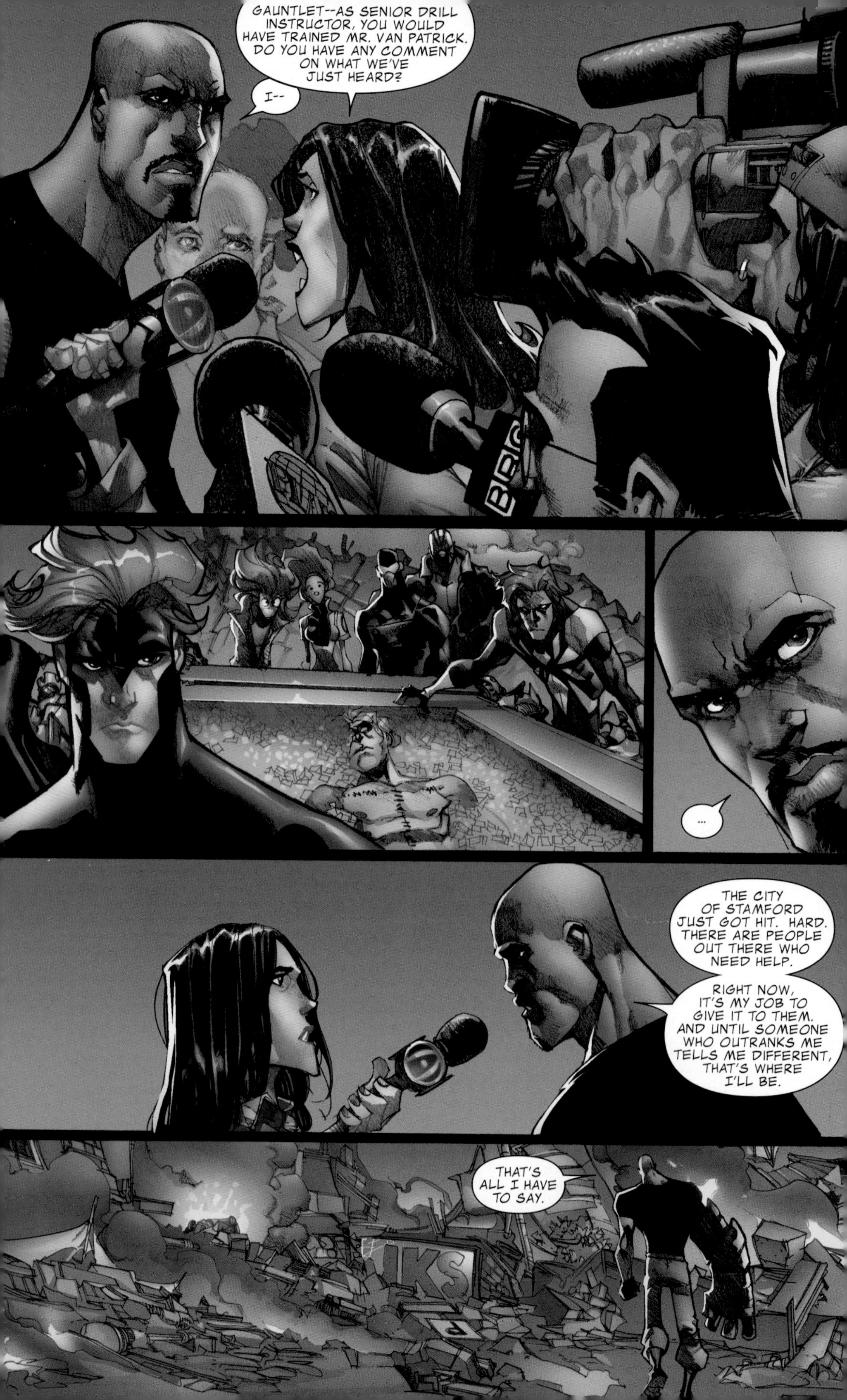
GAUNTLET--AS SENIOR DRILL INSTRUCTOR, YOU WOULD HAVE TRAINED MR. VAN PATRICK. DO YOU HAVE ANY COMMENT ON WHAT WE'VE JUST HEARD?
I--
...
THE CITY OF STAMFORD JUST GOT HIT. HARD. THERE ARE PEOPLE OUT THERE WHO NEED HELP.
RIGHT NOW, IT'S MY JOB TO GIVE IT TO THEM. AND UNTIL SOMEONE WHO OUTRANKS ME TELLS ME DIFFERENT, THAT'S WHERE I'LL BE.
THAT'S ALL I HAVE TO SAY.

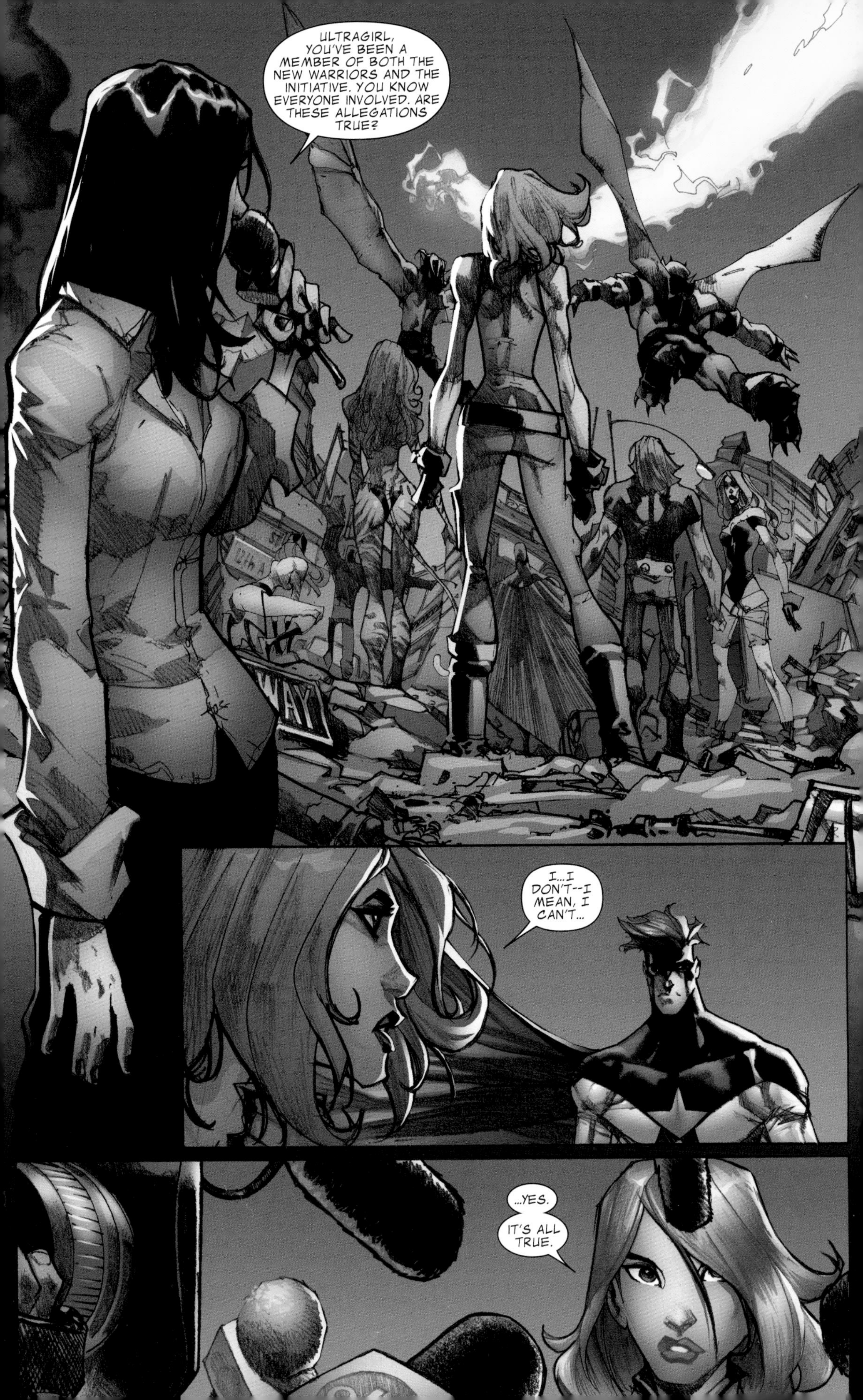
ULTRAGIRL, YOU'VE BEEN A MEMBER OF BOTH THE NEW WARRIORS AND THE INITIATIVE. YOU KNOW EVERYONE INVOLVED. ARE THESE ALLEGATIONS TRUE?
WAY
I...I DON'T--I MEAN, I CAN'T...
...YES.
IT'S ALL TRUE.

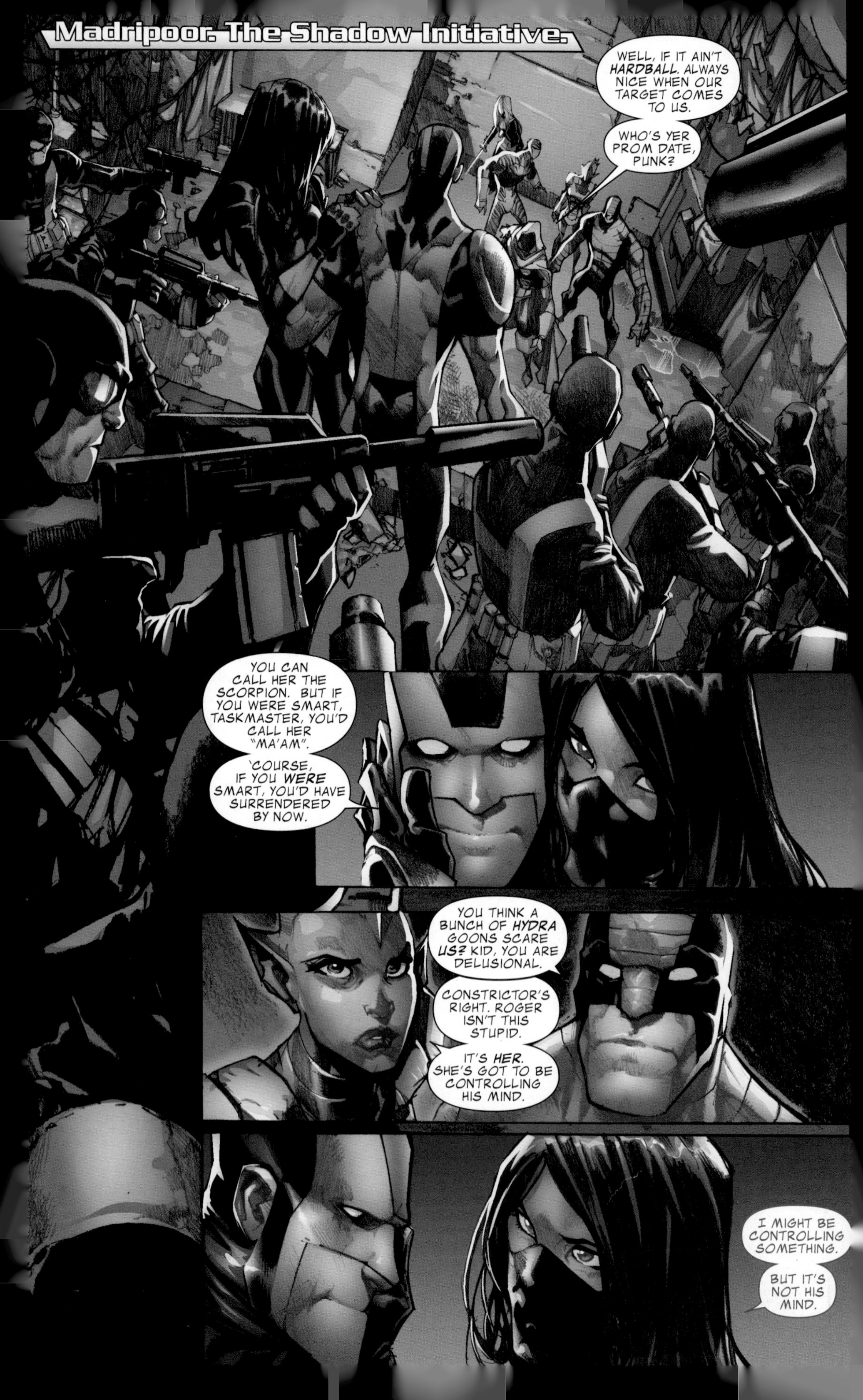

Madripoor. The Shadow Initiative.
WELL, IF IT AIN'T HARDBALL. ALWAYS NICE WHEN OUR TARGET COMES TO US.
WHO'S YER PROM DATE, PUNK?
YOU CAN CALL HER THE SCORPION. BUT IF YOU WERE SMART, TASKMASTER, YOU'D CALL HER "MA'AM".
'COURSE, IF YOU WERE SMART, YOU'D HAVE SURRENDERED BY NOW.
YOU THINK A BUNCH OF HYDRA GOONS SCARE US? KID, YOU ARE DELUSIONAL.
CONSTRICTOR'S RIGHT. ROGER ISN'T THIS STUPID.
IT'S HER. SHE'S GOT TO BE CONTROLLING HIS MIND.
I MIGHT BE CONTROLLING SOMETHING.
BUT IT'S NOT HIS MIND.

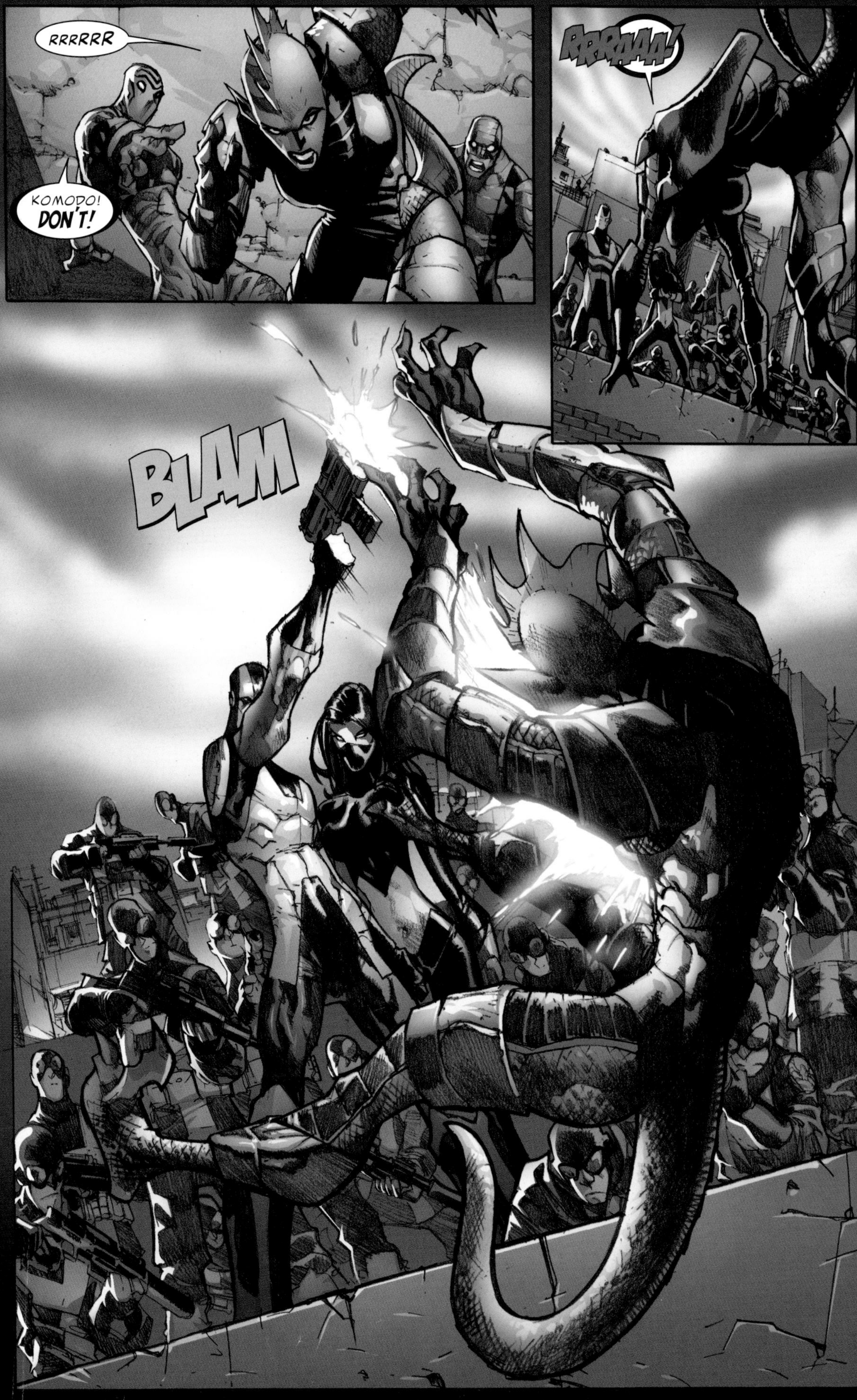
RRRRRR
KOMODO! DON'T!
RRRAAA!
BLAM

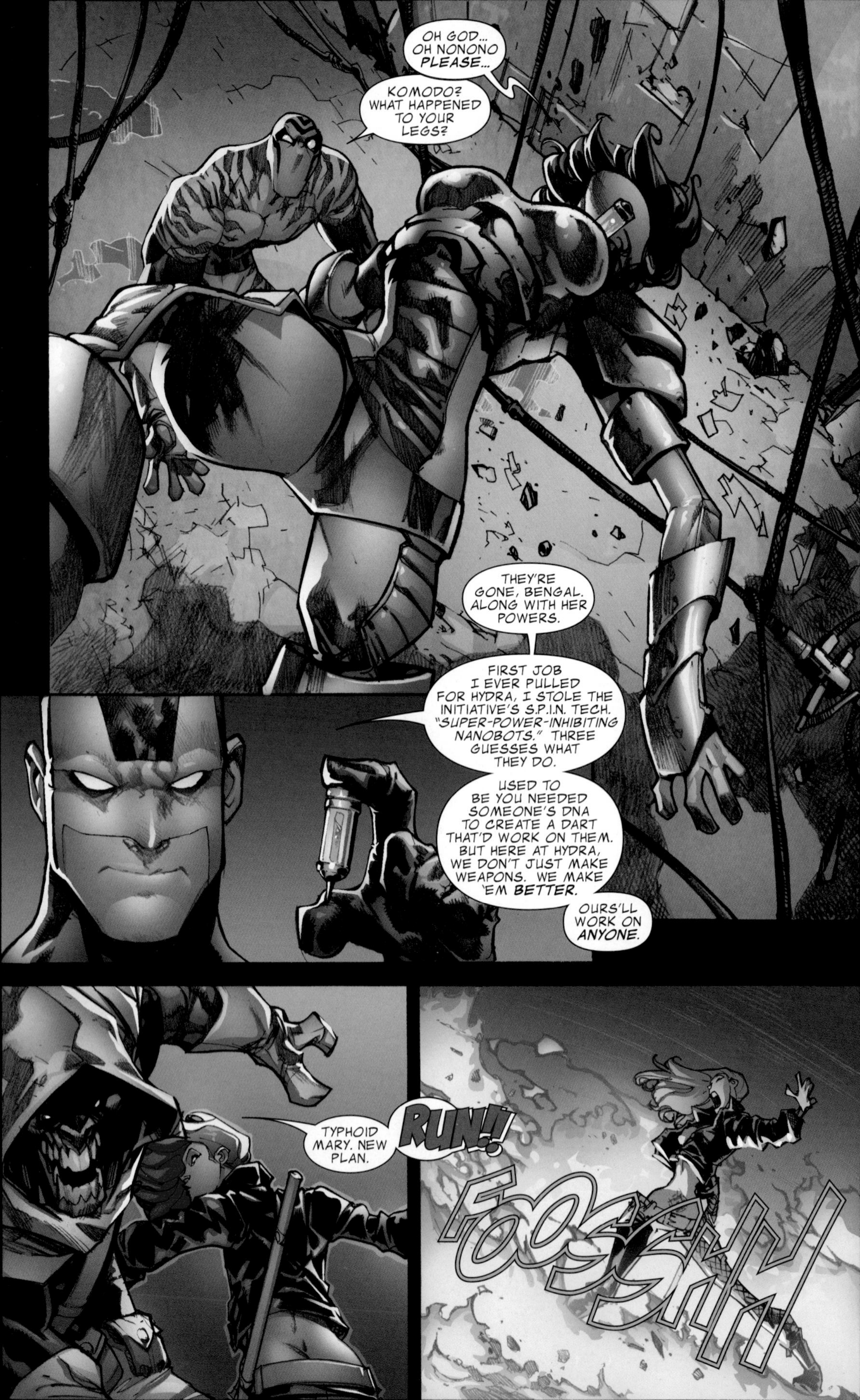

OH GOD... OH NONONO PLEASE...
KOMODO? WHAT HAPPENED TO YOUR LEGS?
THEY'RE GONE, BENGAL. ALONG WITH HER POWERS.
FIRST JOB I EVER PULLED FOR HYDRA, I STOLE THE INITIATIVE'S S.P.I.N. TECH. "SUPER-POWER-INHIBITING NANOBOTS." THREE GUESSES WHAT THEY DO.
USED TO BE YOU NEEDED SOMEONE'S DNA TO CREATE A DART THAT'D WORK ON THEM. BUT HERE AT HYDRA, WE DON'T JUST MAKE WEAPONS. WE MAKE 'EM BETTER.
OURS'LL WORK ON ANYONE.
TYPHOID MARY. NEW PLAN.
RUN!!
FOOSSHH

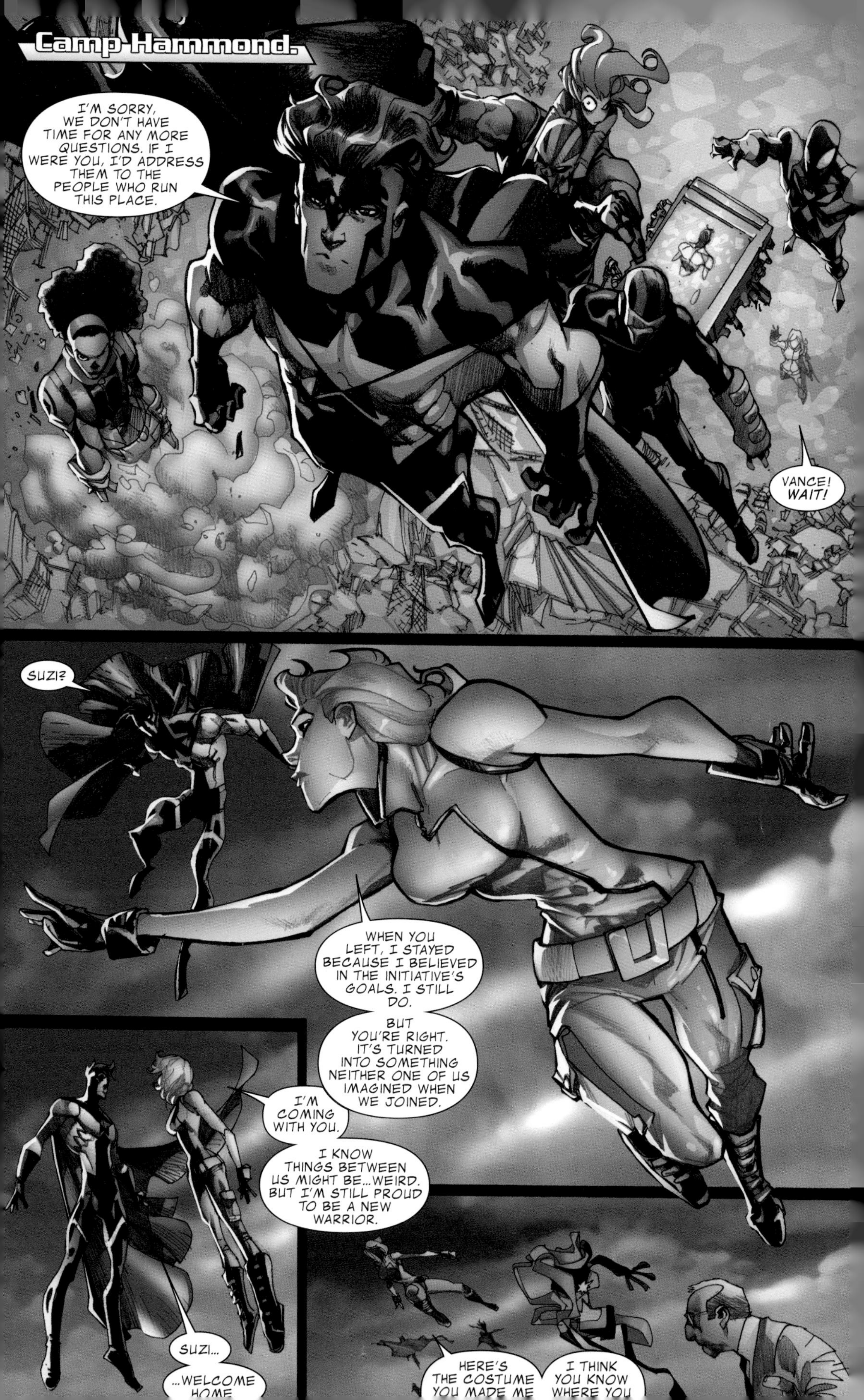
Camp Hammond.
I'M SORRY, WE DON'T HAVE TIME FOR ANY MORE QUESTIONS. IF I WERE YOU, I'D ADDRESS THEM TO THE PEOPLE WHO RUN THIS PLACE.
VANCE! WAIT!
SUZI?
WHEN YOU LEFT, I STAYED BECAUSE I BELIEVED IN THE INITIATIVE'S GOALS. I STILL DO.
BUT YOU'RE RIGHT. IT'S TURNED INTO SOMETHING NEITHER ONE OF US IMAGINED WHEN WE JOINED.
I'M COMING WITH YOU.
I KNOW THINGS BETWEEN US MIGHT BE...WEIRD. BUT I'M STILL PROUD TO BE A NEW WARRIOR.
SUZI...
...WELCOME HOME
HERE'S THE COSTUME YOU MADE ME
I THINK YOU KNOW WHERE YOU

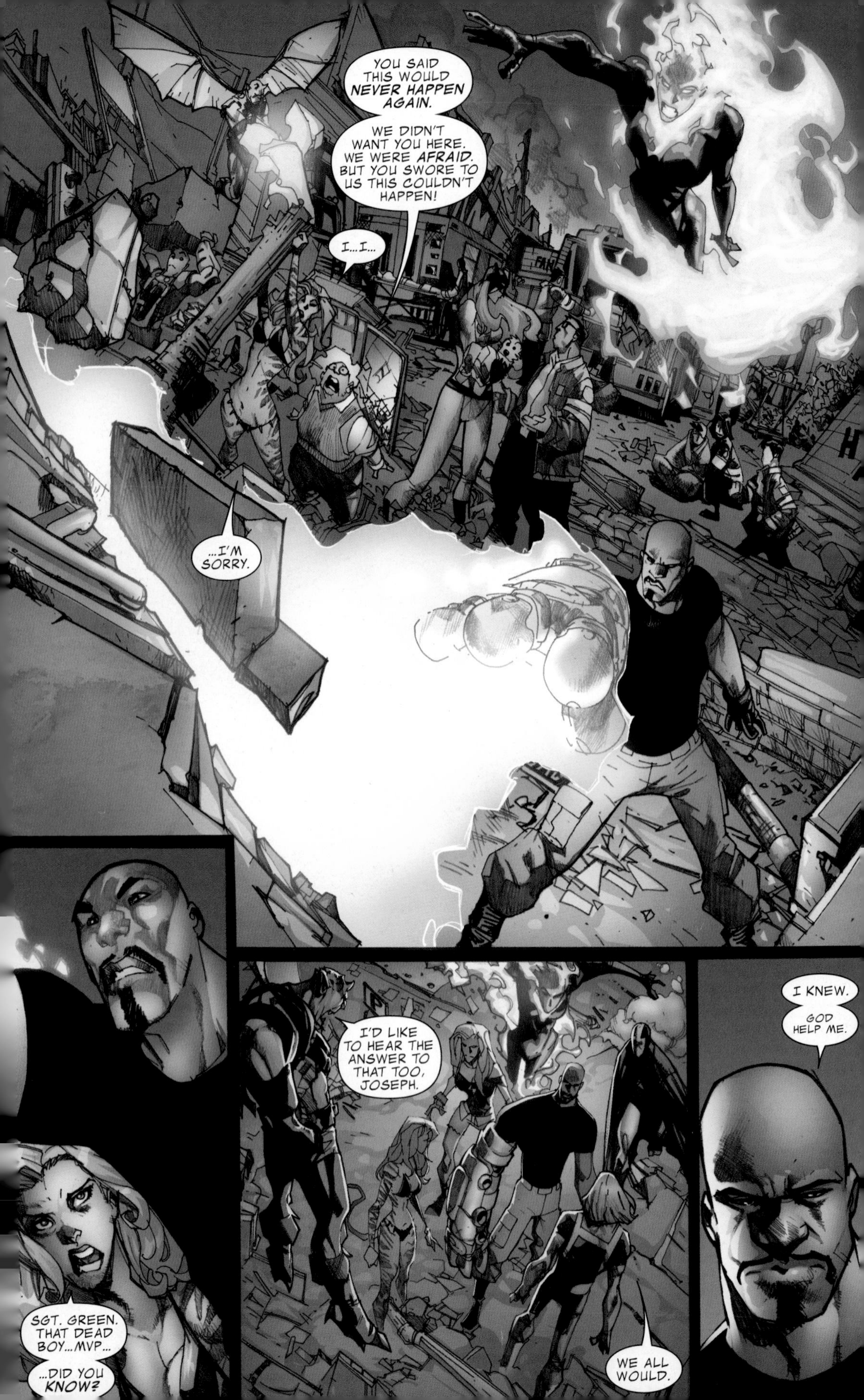
YOU SAID THIS WOULD NEVER HAPPEN AGAIN.
WE DIDN'T WANT YOU HERE. WE WERE AFRAID. BUT YOU SWORE TO US THIS COULDN'T HAPPEN!
I...I...
...I'M SORRY.
SGT. GREEN. THAT DEAD BOY...MVP...
...DID YOU KNOW?
I'D LIKE TO HEAR THE ANSWER TO THAT TOO, JOSEPH.
WE ALL WOULD.
I KNEW.
GOD HELP ME.

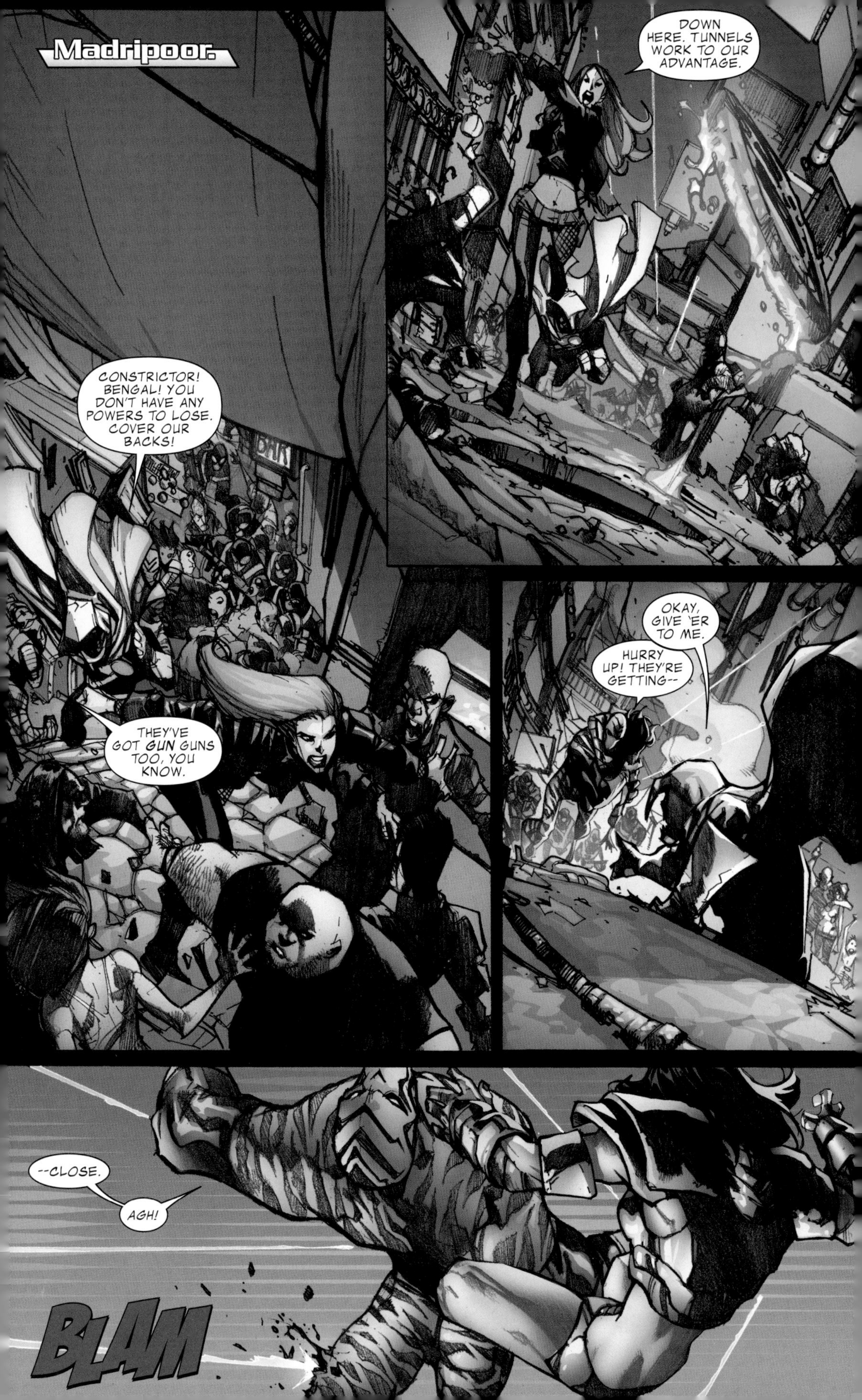
Madripoor.
DOWN HERE. TUNNELS WORK TO OUR ADVANTAGE.
CONSTRICTOR! BENGAL! YOU DON'T HAVE ANY POWERS TO LOSE. COVER OUR BACKS!
THEY'VE GOT GUN GUNS TOO, YOU KNOW.
OKAY, GIVE 'ER TO ME.
HURRY UP! THEY'RE GETTING--
--CLOSE.
AGH!
BLAM

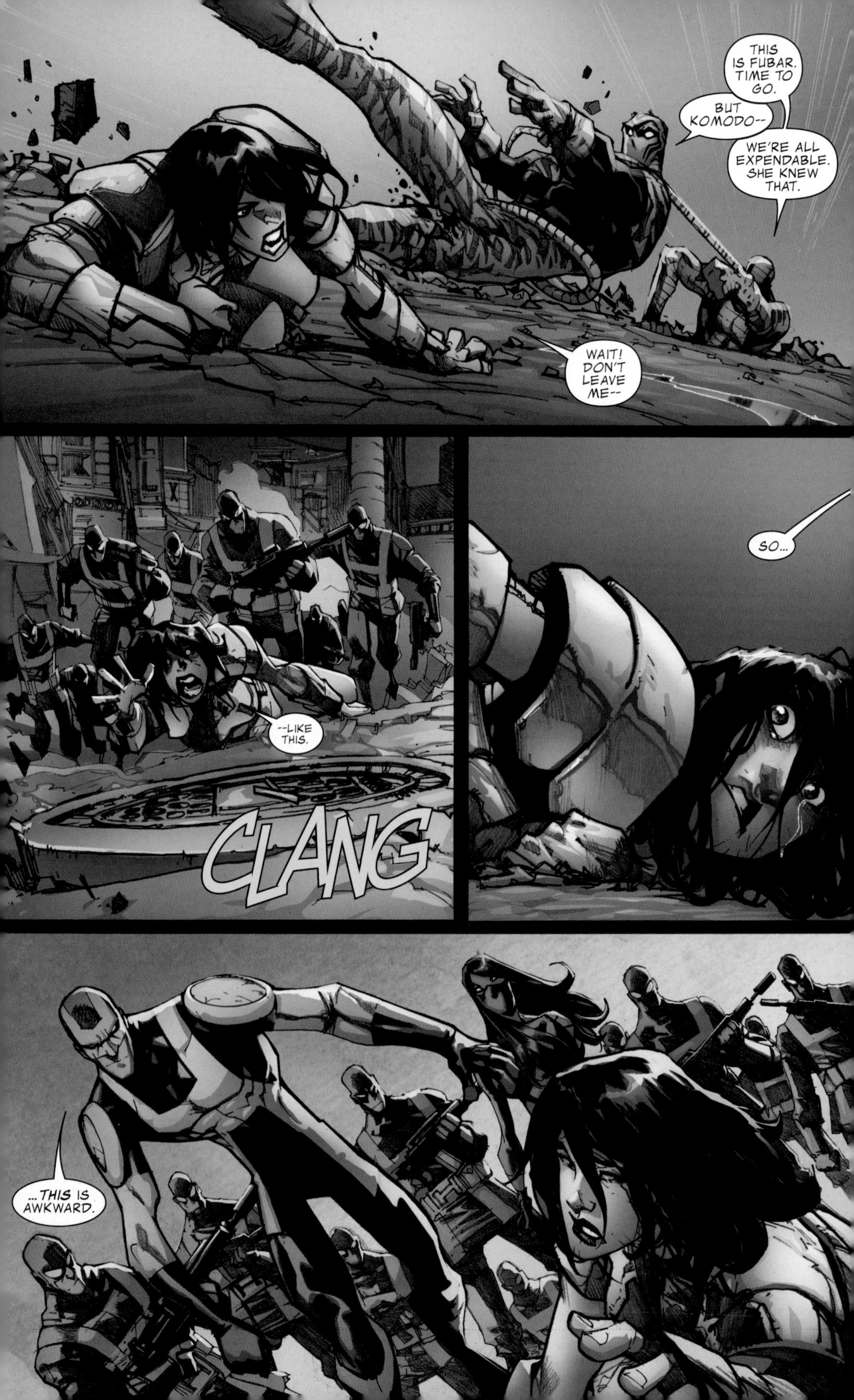
THIS IS FUBAR. TIME TO GO.
BUT KOMODO--
WE'RE ALL EXPENDABLE. SHE KNEW THAT.
WAIT! DON'T LEAVE ME--
--LIKE THIS.
CLANG
SO...
...THIS IS AWKWARD.

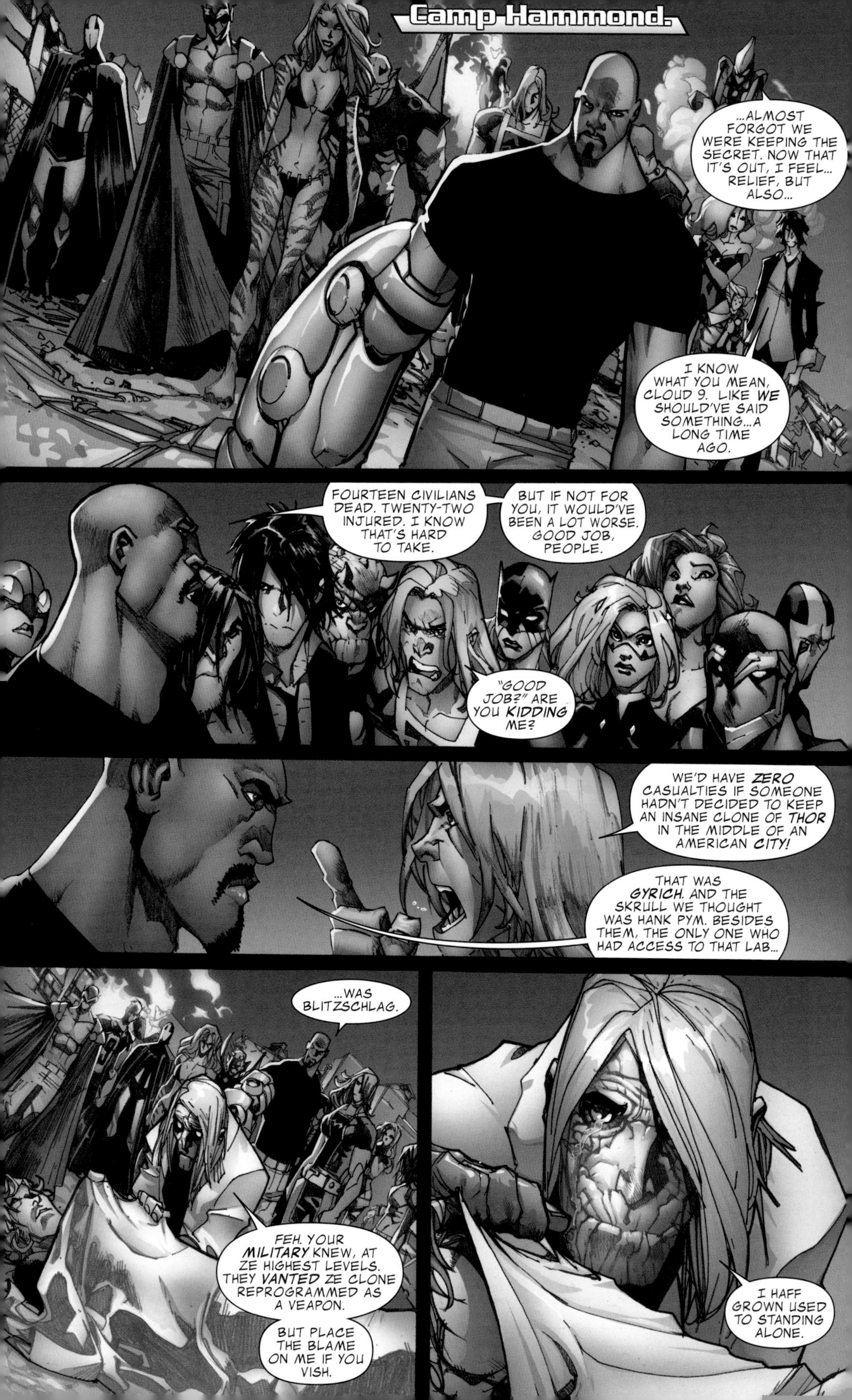

Camp Hammond.
...ALMOST FORGOT WE WERE KEEPING THE SECRET. NOW THAT IT'S OUT, I FEEL... RELIEF, BUT ALSO...
I KNOW WHAT YOU MEAN, CLOUD 9. LIKE WE SHOULD'VE SAID SOMETHING...A LONG TIME AGO.
FOURTEEN CIVILIANS DEAD. TWENTY-TWO INJURED. I KNOW THAT'S HARD TO TAKE.
BUT IF NOT FOR YOU, IT WOULD'VE BEEN A LOT WORSE. GOOD JOB, PEOPLE.
"GOOD JOB?" ARE YOU KIDDING ME?
WE'D HAVE ZERO CASUALTIES IF SOMEONE HADN'T DECIDED TO KEEP AN INSANE CLONE OF THOR IN THE MIDDLE OF AN AMERICAN CITY!
THAT WAS GYRICH. AND THE SKRULL WE THOUGHT WAS HANK PYM. BESIDES THEM, THE ONLY ONE WHO HAD ACCESS TO THAT LAB...
...WAS BLITZSCHLAG.
FEH. YOUR MILITARY KNEW, AT ZE HIGHEST LEVELS. THEY VANTED ZE CLONE REPROGRAMMED AS A VEAPON.
BUT PLACE THE BLAME ON ME IF YOU VISH.
I HAFF GROWN USED TO STANDING ALONE.

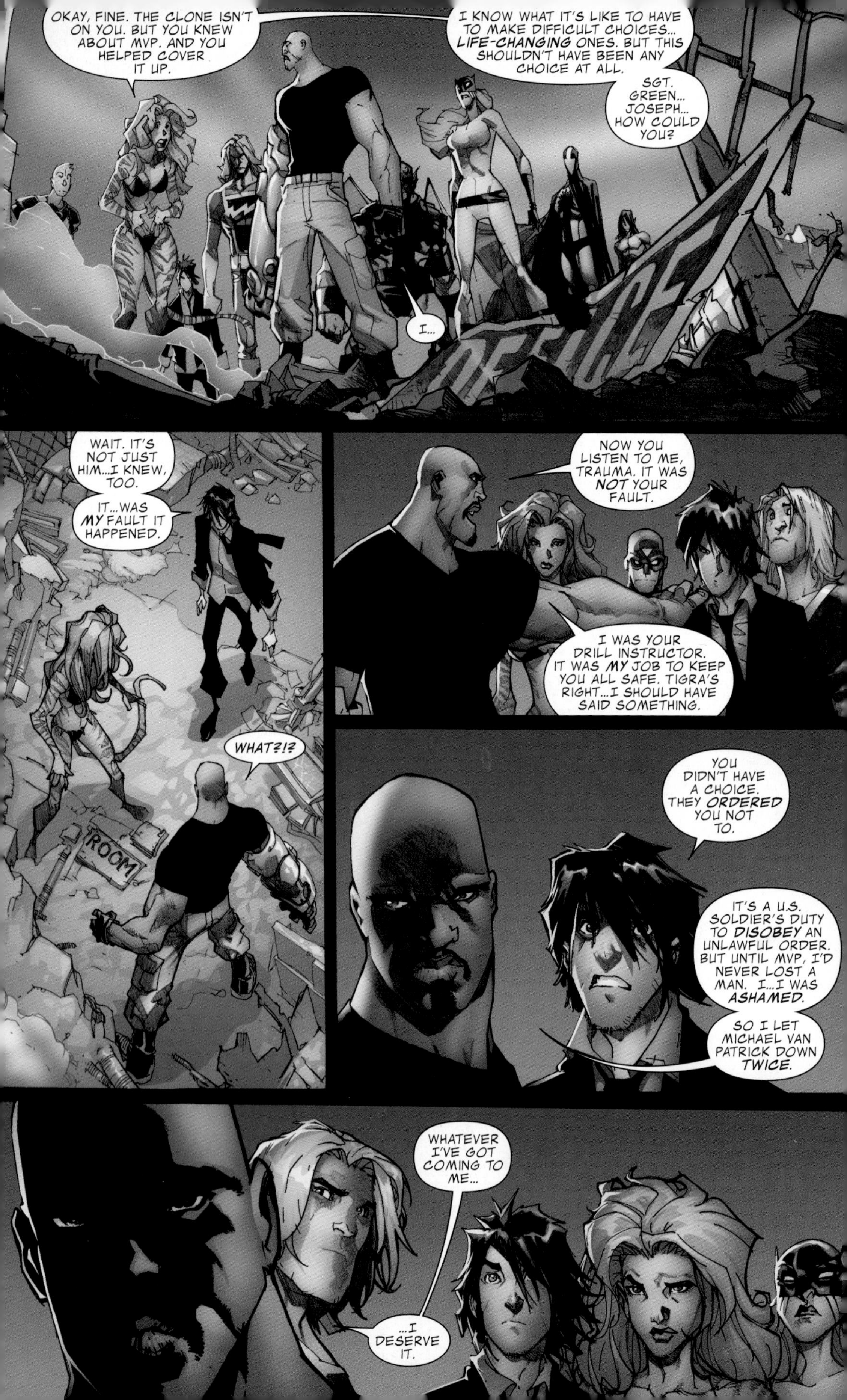
OKAY, FINE. THE CLONE ISN'T ON YOU. BUT YOU KNEW ABOUT MVP. AND YOU HELPED COVER IT UP.
I KNOW WHAT IT'S LIKE TO HAVE TO MAKE DIFFICULT CHOICES... LIFE-CHANGING ONES. BUT THIS SHOULDN'T HAVE BEEN ANY CHOICE AT ALL.
SGT. GREEN... JOSEPH... HOW COULD YOU?
I...
WAIT. IT'S NOT JUST HIM...I KNEW, TOO.
IT...WAS MY FAULT IT HAPPENED.
WHAT?!?
ROOM
NOW YOU LISTEN TO ME, TRAUMA. IT WAS NOT YOUR FAULT.
I WAS YOUR DRILL INSTRUCTOR. IT WAS MY JOB TO KEEP YOU ALL SAFE. TIGRA'S RIGHT...I SHOULD HAVE SAID SOMETHING.
YOU DIDN'T HAVE A CHOICE. THEY ORDERED YOU NOT TO.
IT'S A U.S. SOLDIER'S DUTY TO DISOBEY AN UNLAWFUL ORDER. BUT UNTIL MVP, I'D NEVER LOST A MAN. I...I WAS ASHAMED.
SO I LET MICHAEL VAN PATRICK DOWN TWICE.
WHATEVER I'VE GOT COMING TO ME...
...I DESERVE IT.

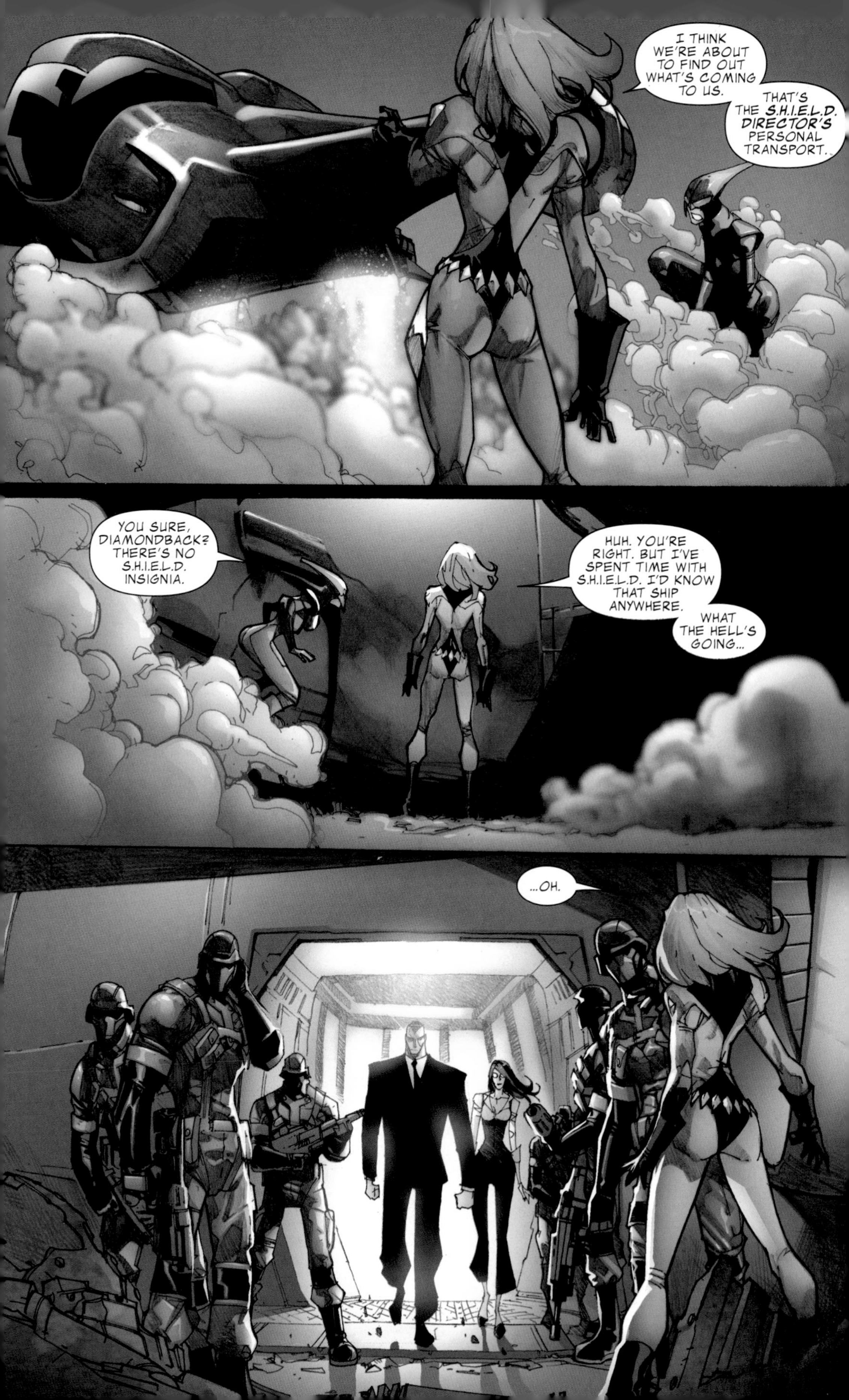
I THINK WE'RE ABOUT TO FIND OUT WHAT'S COMING TO US.
THAT'S THE **S.H.I.E.L.D. DIRECTOR'S** PERSONAL TRANSPORT.
YOU SURE, DIAMONDBACK? THERE'S NO S.H.I.E.L.D. INSIGNIA.
HUH. YOU'RE RIGHT. BUT I'VE SPENT TIME WITH S.H.I.E.L.D. I'D KNOW THAT SHIP ANYWHERE.
WHAT THE HELL'S GOING...
...OH.

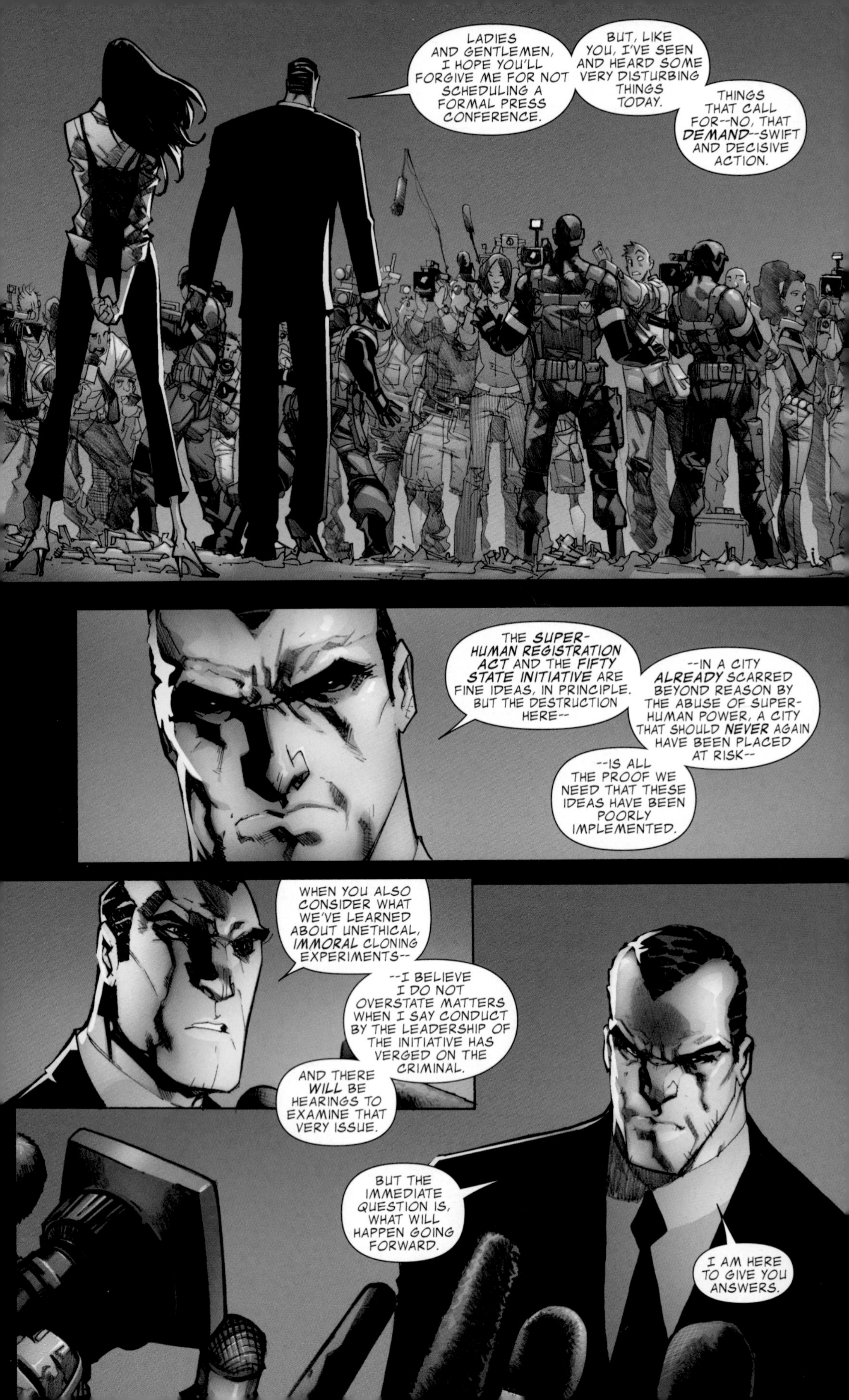
LADIES AND GENTLEMEN, I HOPE YOU'LL FORGIVE ME FOR NOT SCHEDULING A FORMAL PRESS CONFERENCE.
BUT, LIKE YOU, I'VE SEEN AND HEARD SOME VERY DISTURBING THINGS TODAY.
THINGS THAT CALL FOR--NO, THAT *DEMAND*--SWIFT AND DECISIVE ACTION.
THE *SUPER-HUMAN REGISTRATION ACT* AND THE *FIFTY STATE INITIATIVE* ARE FINE IDEAS, IN PRINCIPLE. BUT THE DESTRUCTION HERE--
--IN A CITY *ALREADY* SCARRED BEYOND REASON BY THE ABUSE OF SUPER-HUMAN POWER, A CITY THAT SHOULD *NEVER* AGAIN HAVE BEEN PLACED AT RISK--
--IS ALL THE PROOF WE NEED THAT THESE IDEAS HAVE BEEN POORLY IMPLEMENTED.
WHEN YOU ALSO CONSIDER WHAT WE'VE LEARNED ABOUT UNETHICAL, *IMMORAL* CLONING EXPERIMENTS--
--I BELIEVE I DO NOT OVERSTATE MATTERS WHEN I SAY CONDUCT BY THE LEADERSHIP OF THE INITIATIVE HAS VERGED ON THE CRIMINAL.
AND THERE *WILL* BE HEARINGS TO EXAMINE THAT VERY ISSUE.
BUT THE IMMEDIATE QUESTION IS, WHAT WILL HAPPEN GOING FORWARD.
I AM HERE TO GIVE YOU ANSWERS.

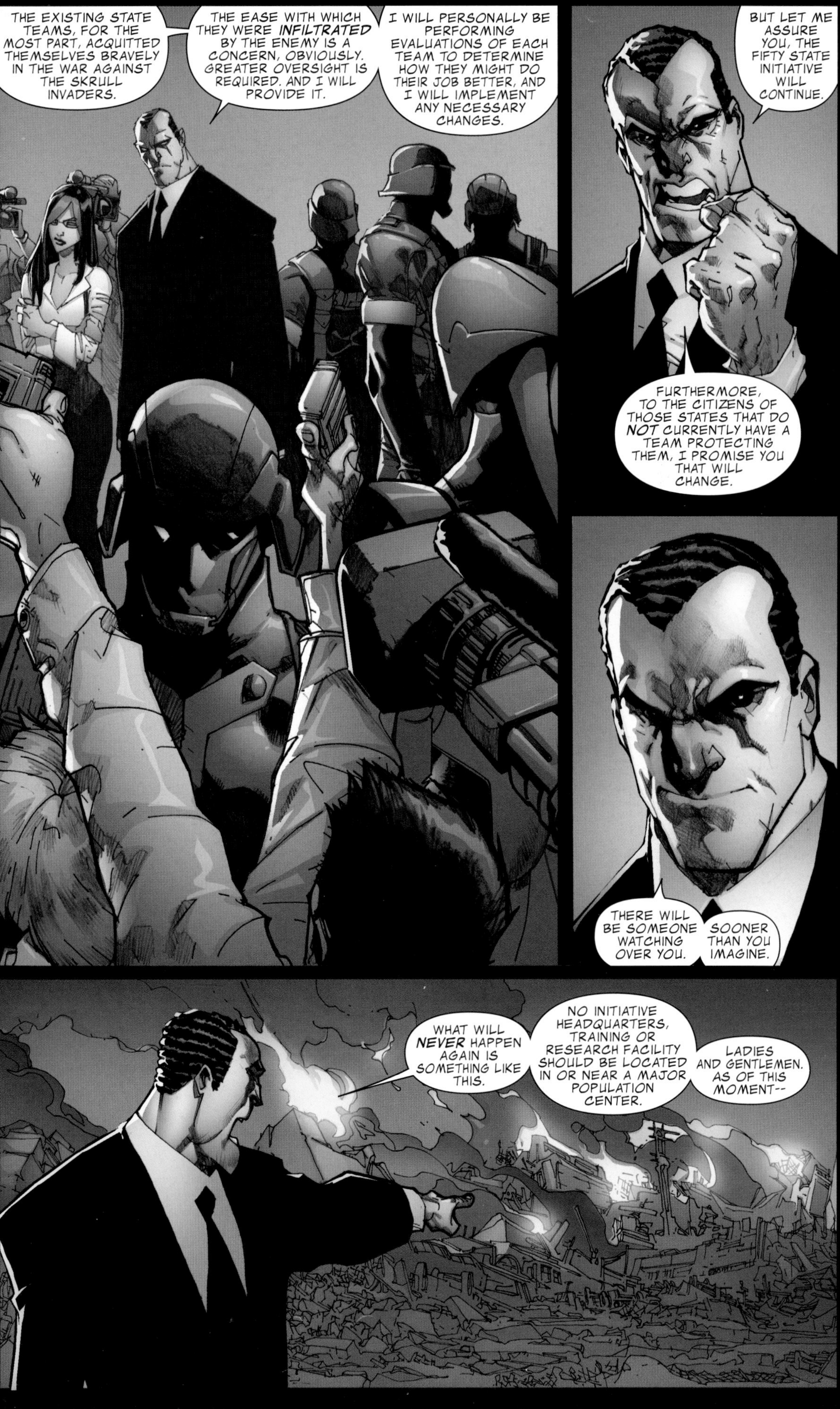

THE EXISTING STATE TEAMS, FOR THE MOST PART, ACQUITTED THEMSELVES BRAVELY IN THE WAR AGAINST THE SKRULL INVADERS.
THE EASE WITH WHICH THEY WERE INFILTRATED BY THE ENEMY IS A CONCERN, OBVIOUSLY. GREATER OVERSIGHT IS REQUIRED. AND I WILL PROVIDE IT.
I WILL PERSONALLY BE PERFORMING EVALUATIONS OF EACH TEAM TO DETERMINE HOW THEY MIGHT DO THEIR JOB BETTER, AND I WILL IMPLEMENT ANY NECESSARY CHANGES.
BUT LET ME ASSURE YOU, THE FIFTY STATE INITIATIVE WILL CONTINUE.
FURTHERMORE, TO THE CITIZENS OF THOSE STATES THAT DO NOT CURRENTLY HAVE A TEAM PROTECTING THEM, I PROMISE YOU THAT WILL CHANGE.
THERE WILL BE SOMEONE WATCHING OVER YOU.
SOONER THAN YOU IMAGINE.
LADIES AND GENTLEMEN. AS OF THIS MOMENT--
NO INITIATIVE HEADQUARTERS, TRAINING OR RESEARCH FACILITY SHOULD BE LOCATED IN OR NEAR A MAJOR POPULATION CENTER.
WHAT WILL NEVER HAPPEN AGAIN IS SOMETHING LIKE THIS.

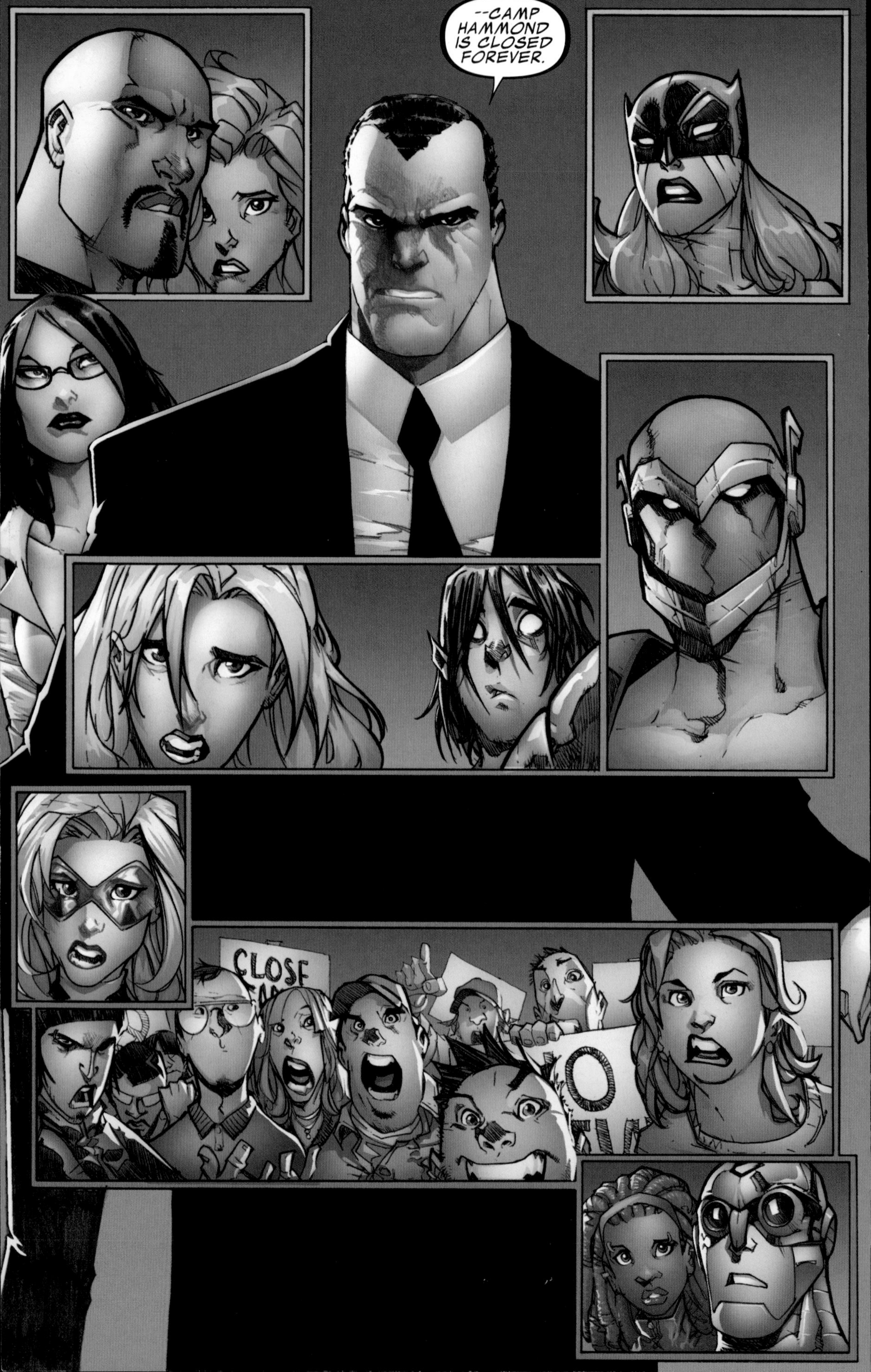
--CAMP HAMMOND IS CLOSED FOREVER.
CLOSE

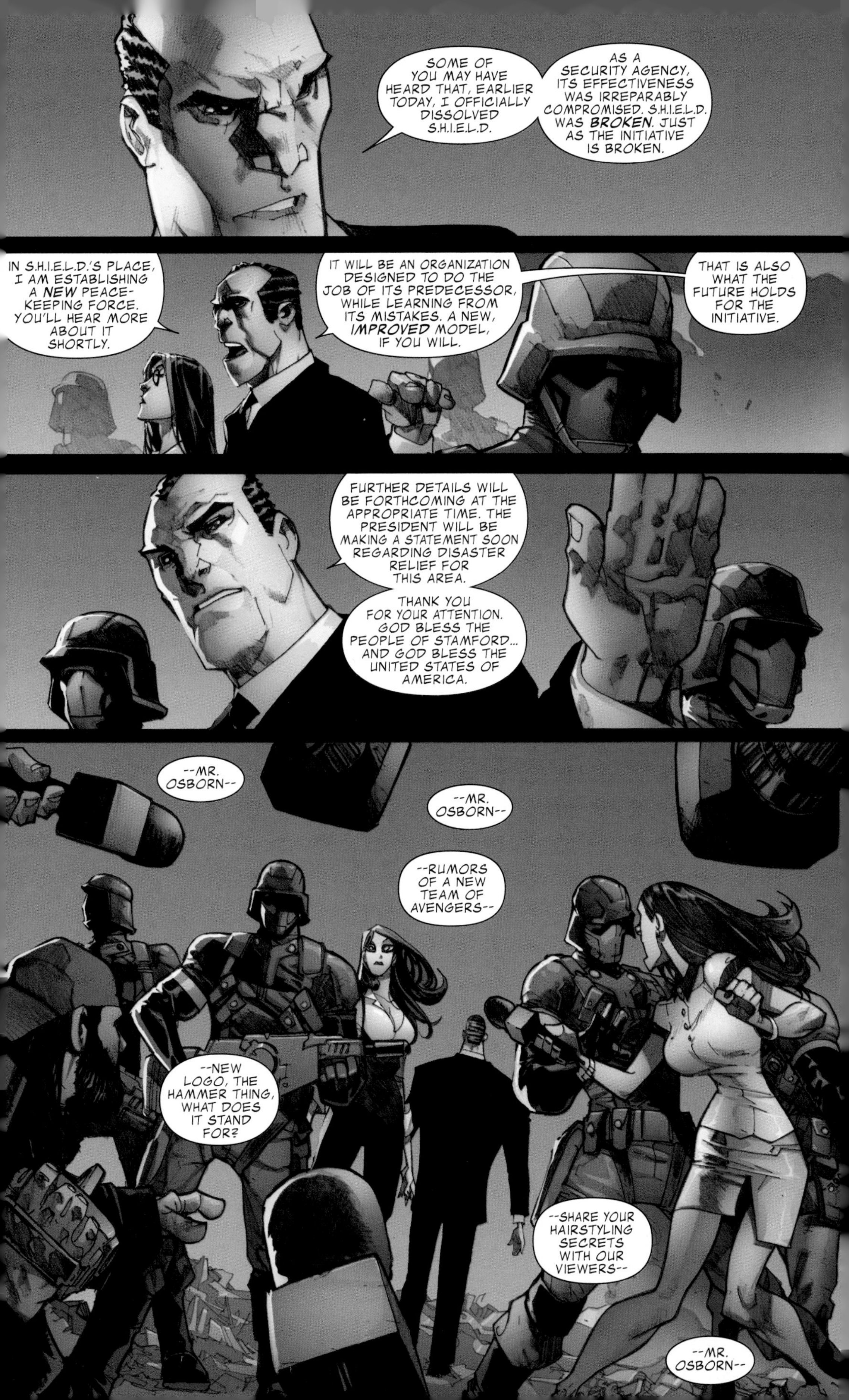
SOME OF YOU MAY HAVE HEARD THAT, EARLIER TODAY, I OFFICIALLY DISSOLVED S.H.I.E.L.D.
AS A SECURITY AGENCY, ITS EFFECTIVENESS WAS IRREPARABLY COMPROMISED. S.H.I.E.L.D. WAS BROKEN. JUST AS THE INITIATIVE IS BROKEN.
IN S.H.I.E.L.D.'S PLACE, I AM ESTABLISHING A NEW PEACE-KEEPING FORCE. YOU'LL HEAR MORE ABOUT IT SHORTLY.
IT WILL BE AN ORGANIZATION DESIGNED TO DO THE JOB OF ITS PREDECESSOR, WHILE LEARNING FROM ITS MISTAKES. A NEW, IMPROVED MODEL, IF YOU WILL.
THAT IS ALSO WHAT THE FUTURE HOLDS FOR THE INITIATIVE.
FURTHER DETAILS WILL BE FORTHCOMING AT THE APPROPRIATE TIME. THE PRESIDENT WILL BE MAKING A STATEMENT SOON REGARDING DISASTER RELIEF FOR THIS AREA.
THANK YOU FOR YOUR ATTENTION. GOD BLESS THE PEOPLE OF STAMFORD... AND GOD BLESS THE UNITED STATES OF AMERICA.
--MR. OSBORN--
--MR. OSBORN--
--RUMORS OF A NEW TEAM OF AVENGERS--
--NEW LOGO, THE HAMMER THING, WHAT DOES IT STAND FOR?
--SHARE YOUR HAIRSTYLING SECRETS WITH OUR VIEWERS--
--MR. OSBORN--

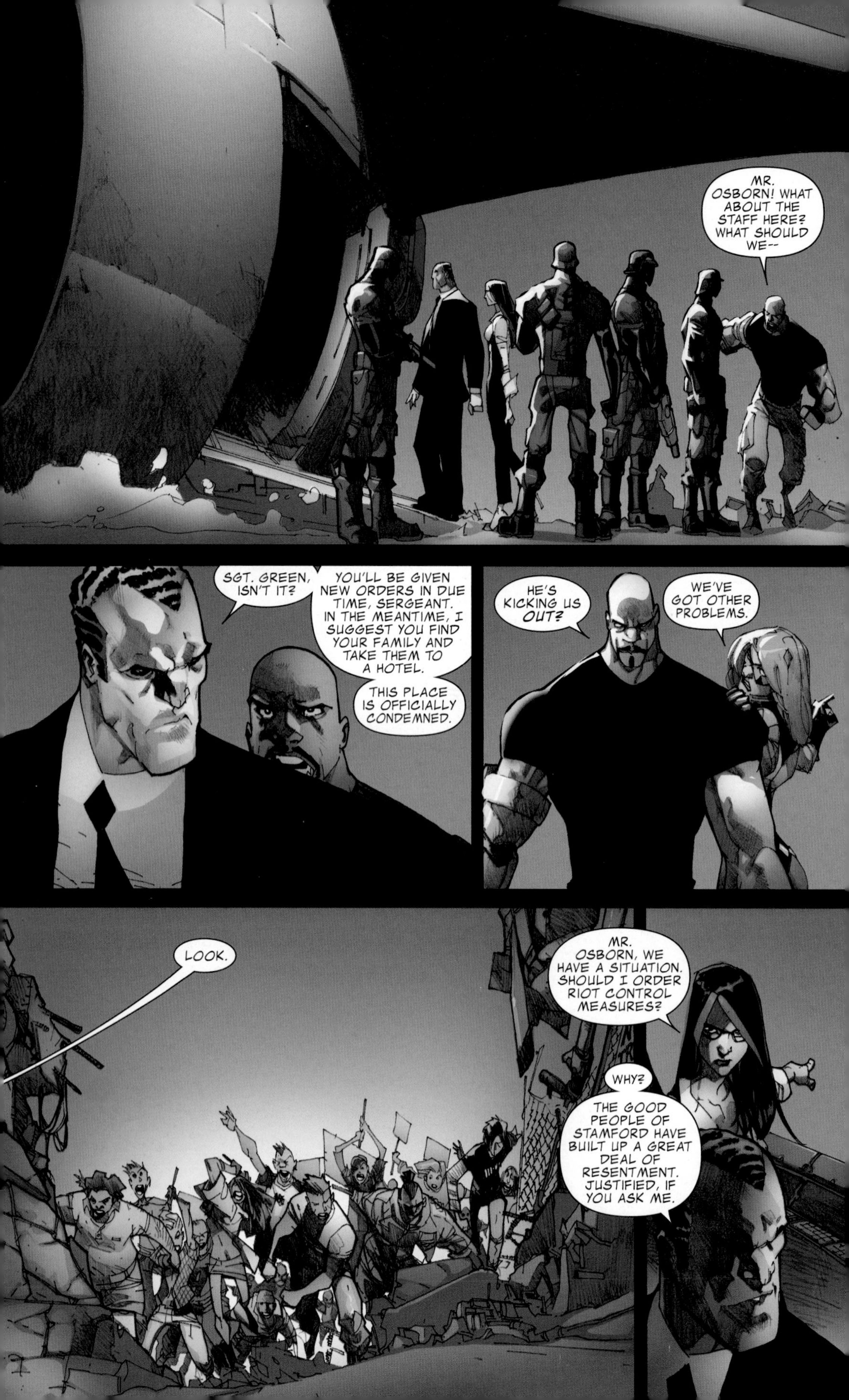
MR. OSBORN! WHAT ABOUT THE STAFF HERE? WHAT SHOULD WE--
SGT. GREEN, ISN'T IT?
YOU'LL BE GIVEN NEW ORDERS IN DUE TIME, SERGEANT. IN THE MEANTIME, I SUGGEST YOU FIND YOUR FAMILY AND TAKE THEM TO A HOTEL.
THIS PLACE IS OFFICIALLY CONDEMNED.
HE'S KICKING US OUT?
WE'VE GOT OTHER PROBLEMS.
LOOK.
MR. OSBORN, WE HAVE A SITUATION. SHOULD I ORDER RIOT CONTROL MEASURES?
WHY?
THE GOOD PEOPLE OF STAMFORD HAVE BUILT UP A GREAT DEAL OF RESENTMENT. JUSTIFIED, IF YOU ASK ME.

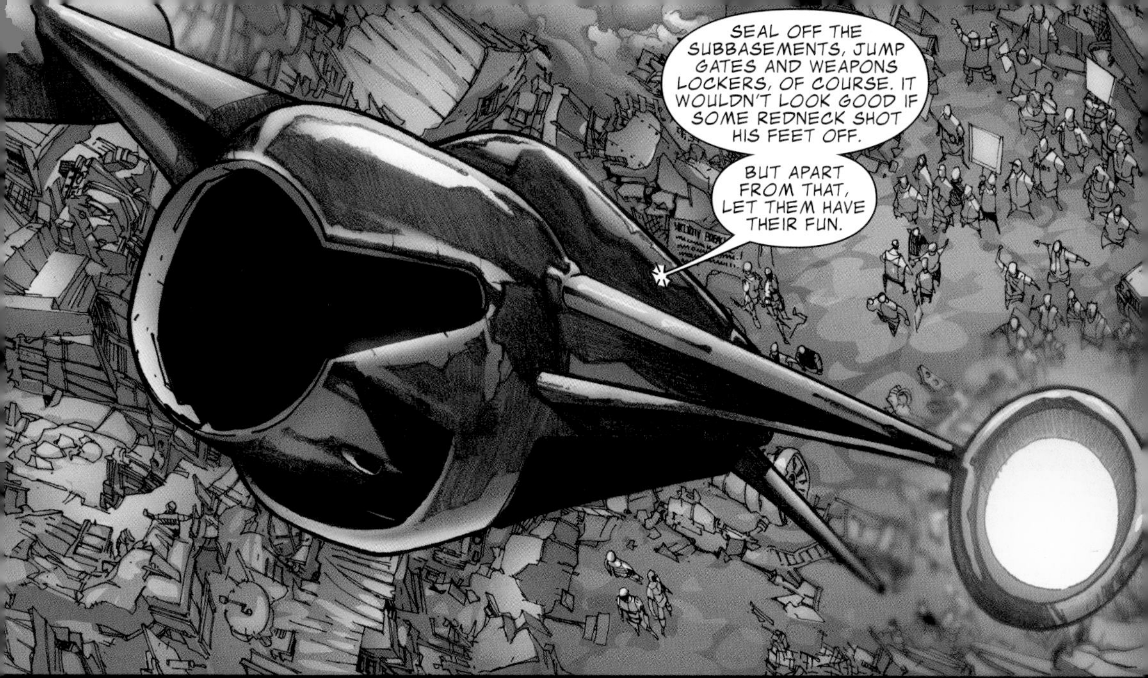
SEAL OFF THE SUBBASEMENTS, JUMP GATES AND WEAPONS LOCKERS, OF COURSE. IT WOULDN'T LOOK GOOD IF SOME REDNECK SHOT HIS FEET OFF.
BUT APART FROM THAT, LET THEM HAVE THEIR FUN.

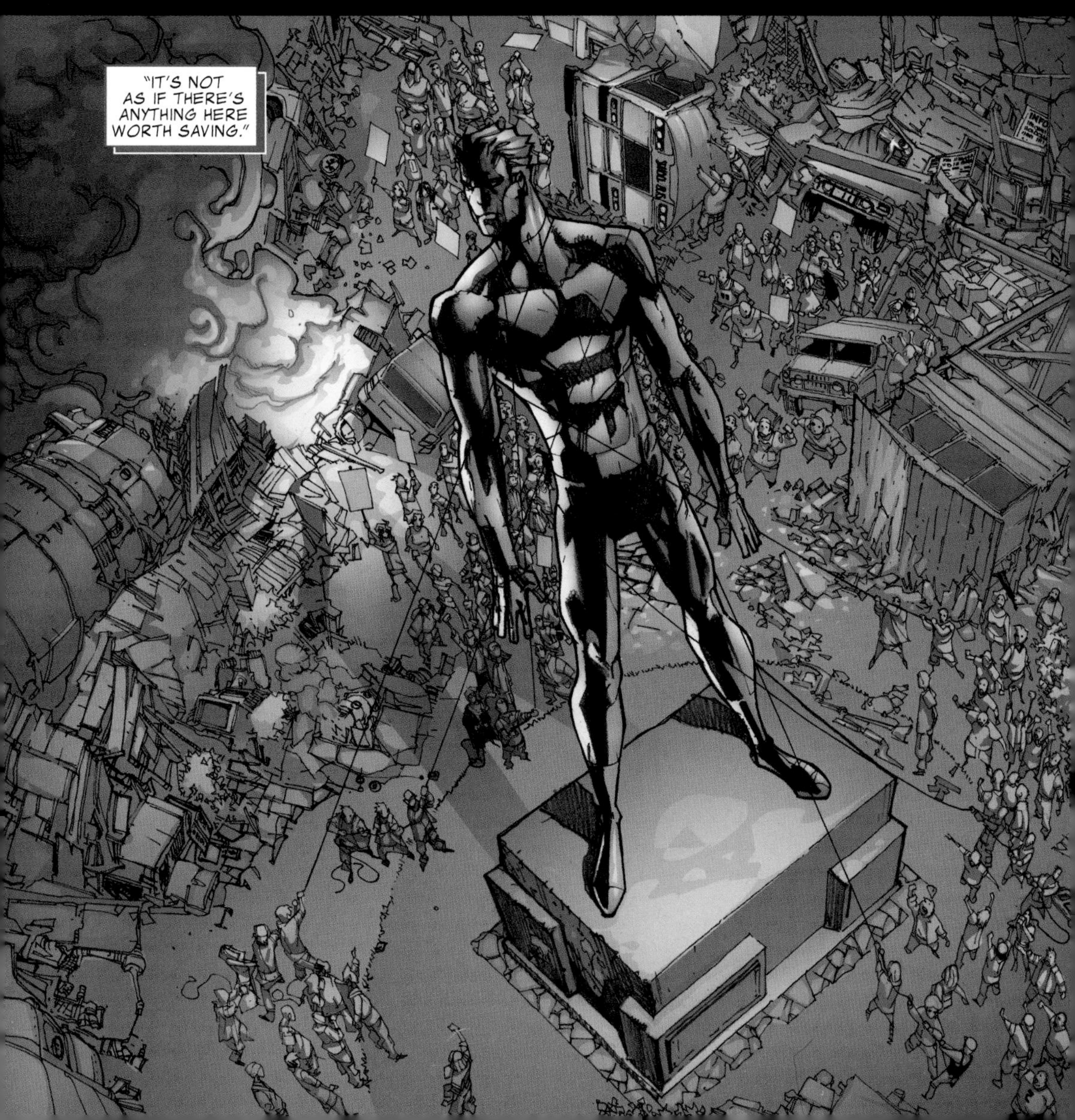
"IT'S NOT AS IF THERE'S ANYTHING HERE WORTH SAVING."

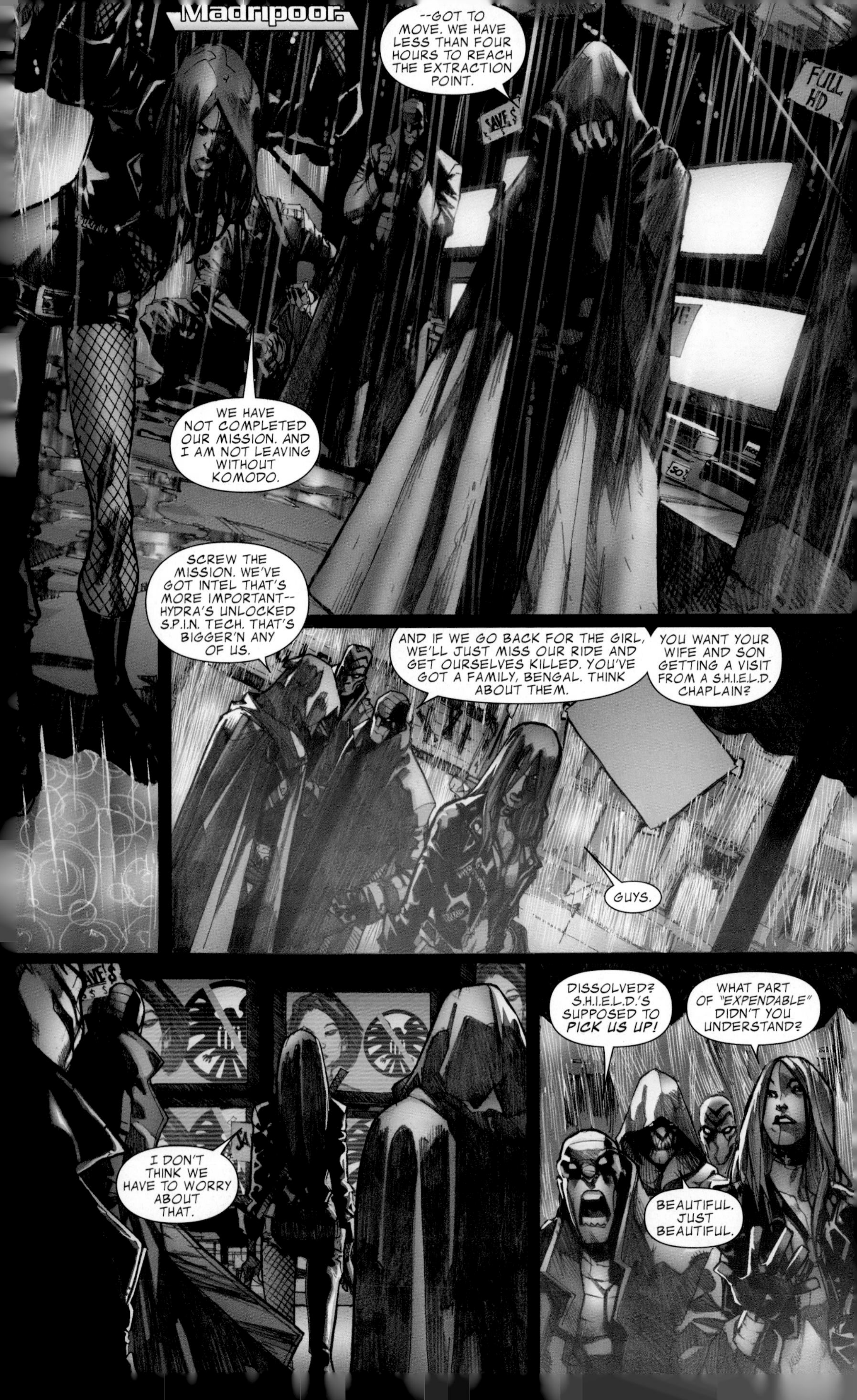
Madripoor.
--GOT TO MOVE. WE HAVE LESS THAN FOUR HOURS TO REACH THE EXTRACTION POINT.
FULL HD
WE HAVE NOT COMPLETED OUR MISSION. AND I AM NOT LEAVING WITHOUT KOMODO.
SCREW THE MISSION. WE'VE GOT INTEL THAT'S MORE IMPORTANT--HYDRA'S UNLOCKED S.P.I.N. TECH. THAT'S BIGGER'N ANY OF US.
AND IF WE GO BACK FOR THE GIRL, WE'LL JUST MISS OUR RIDE AND GET OURSELVES KILLED. YOU'VE GOT A FAMILY, BENGAL. THINK ABOUT THEM.
YOU WANT YOUR WIFE AND SON GETTING A VISIT FROM A S.H.I.E.L.D. CHAPLAIN?
GUYS.
I DON'T THINK WE HAVE TO WORRY ABOUT THAT.
DISSOLVED? S.H.I.E.L.D.'S SUPPOSED TO PICK US UP!
WHAT PART OF "EXPENDABLE" DIDN'T YOU UNDERSTAND?
BEAUTIFUL. JUST BEAUTIFUL.

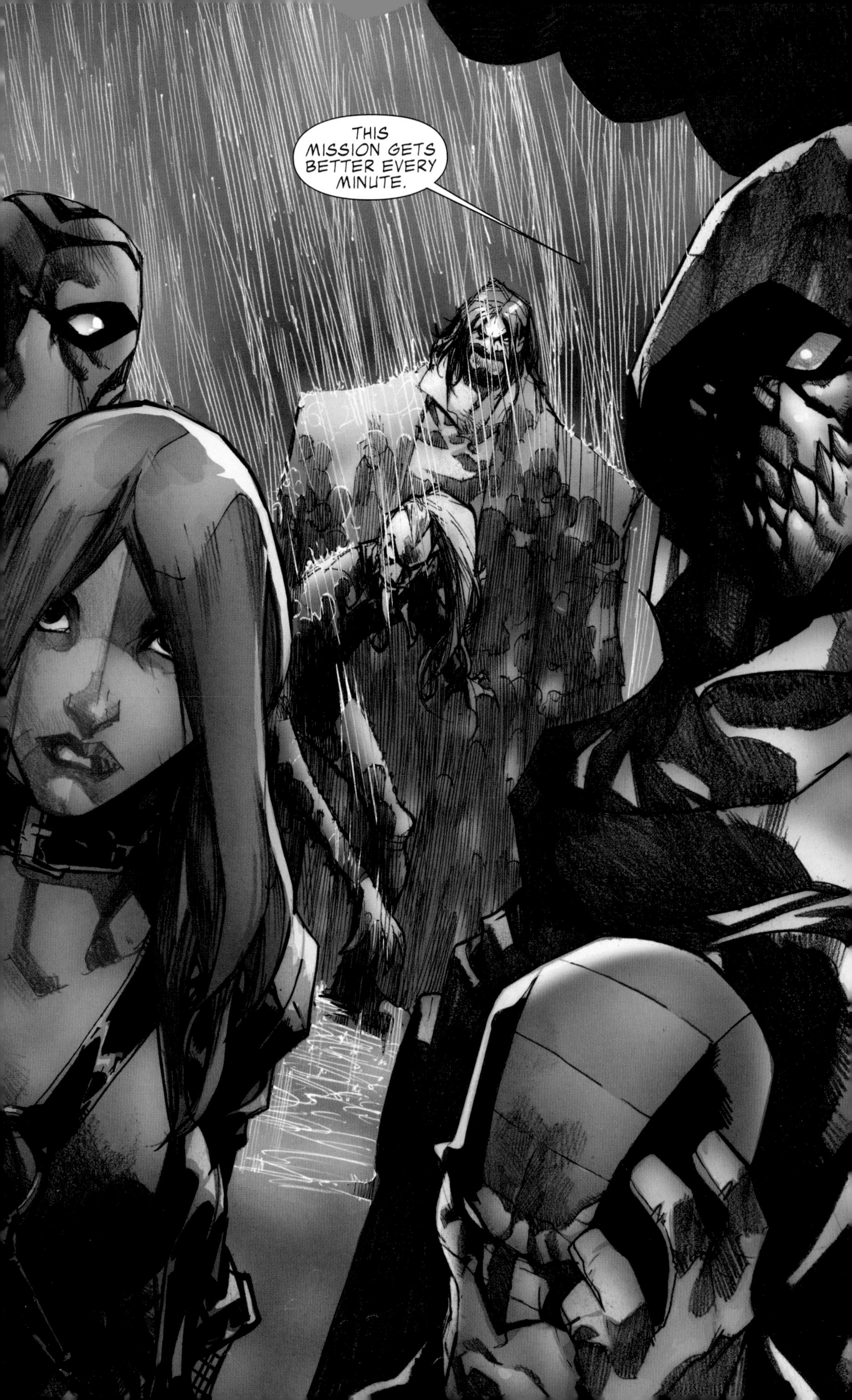
THIS MISSION GETS BETTER EVERY MINUTE.

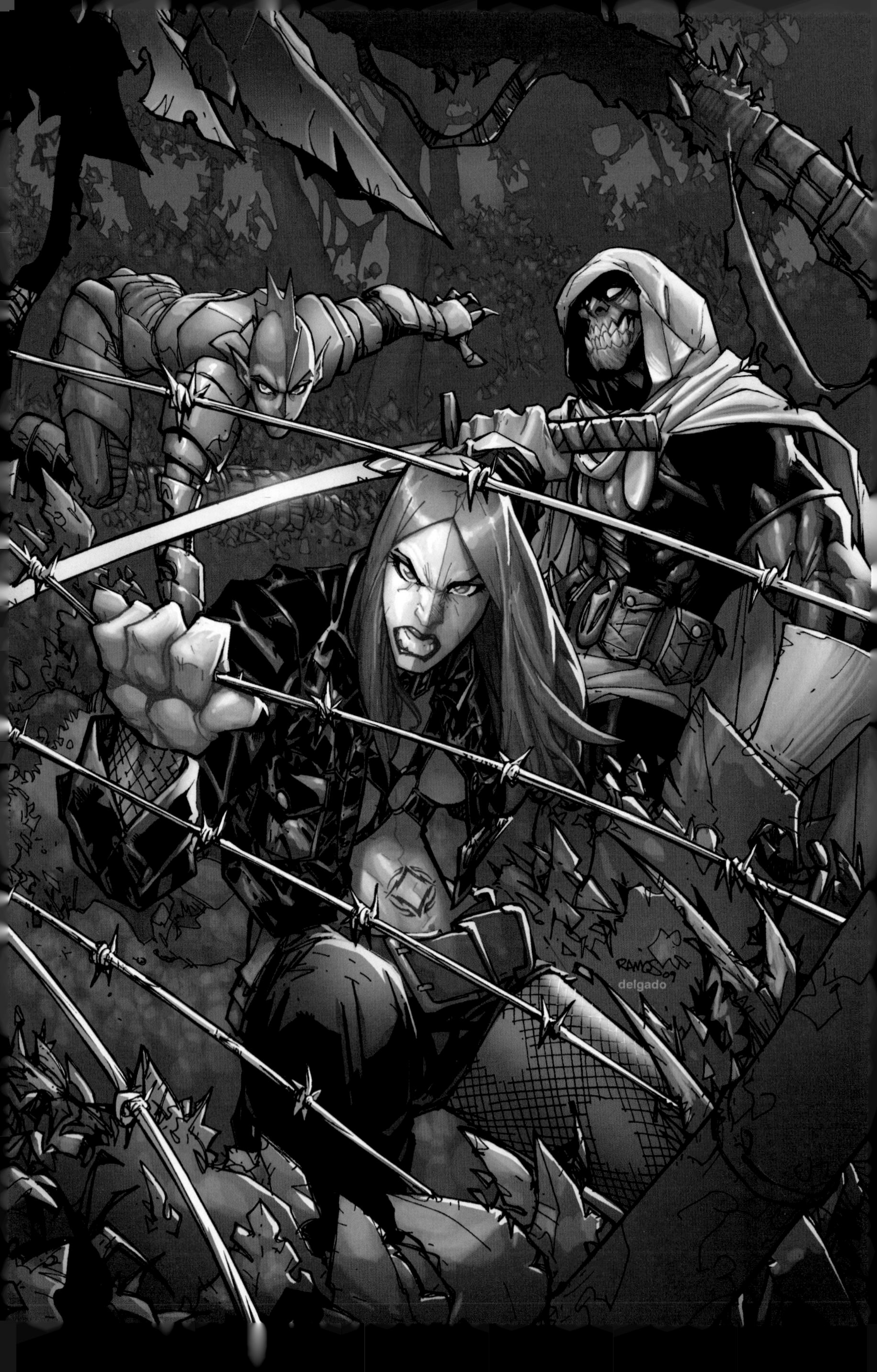
delgado

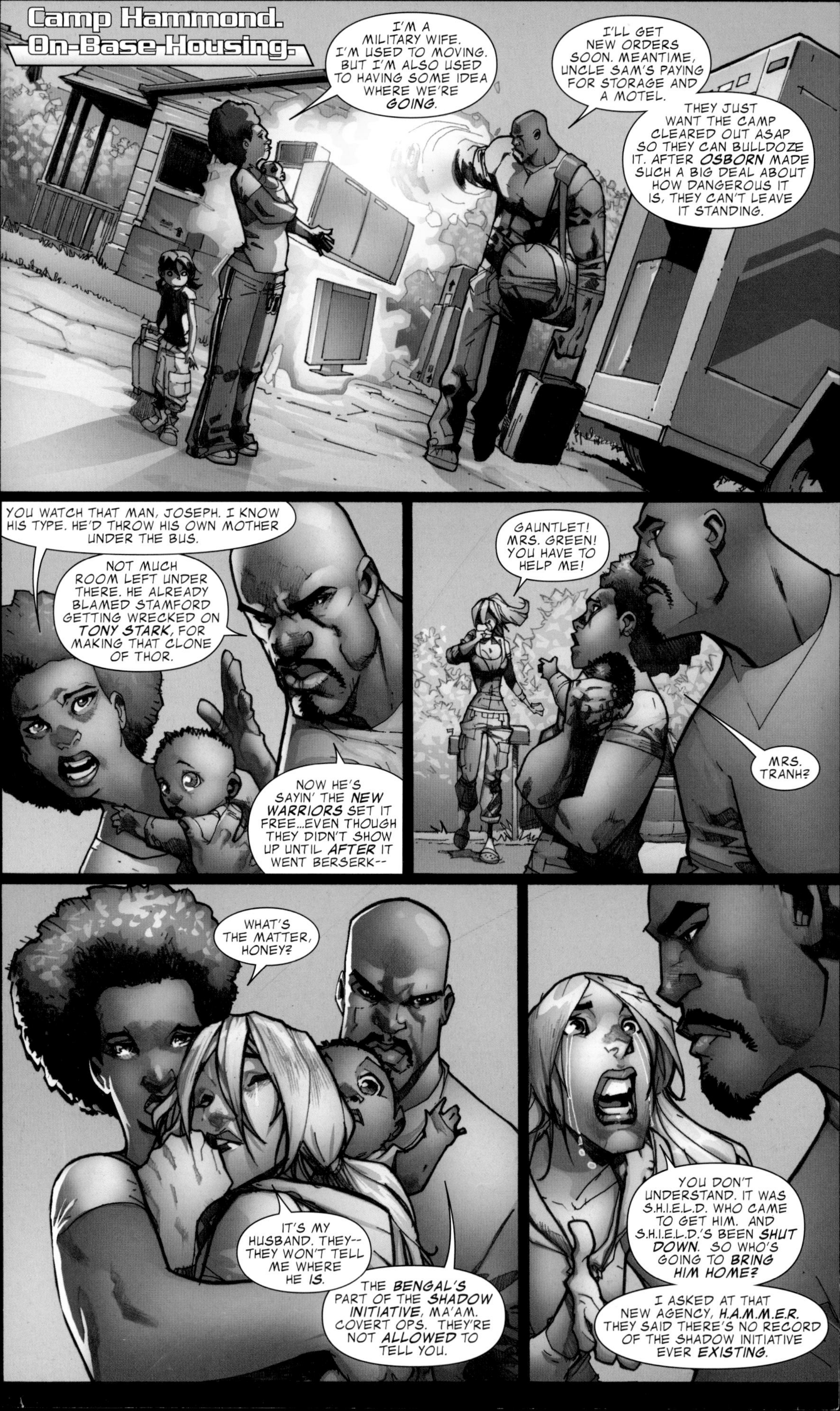
Camp Hammond.
On-Base Housing.
I'M A MILITARY WIFE. I'M USED TO MOVING. BUT I'M ALSO USED TO HAVING SOME IDEA WHERE WE'RE GOING.
I'LL GET NEW ORDERS SOON. MEANTIME, UNCLE SAM'S PAYING FOR STORAGE AND A MOTEL.
THEY JUST WANT THE CAMP CLEARED OUT ASAP SO THEY CAN BULLDOZE IT. AFTER OSBORN MADE SUCH A BIG DEAL ABOUT HOW DANGEROUS IT IS, THEY CAN'T LEAVE IT STANDING.
YOU WATCH THAT MAN, JOSEPH. I KNOW HIS TYPE. HE'D THROW HIS OWN MOTHER UNDER THE BUS.
NOT MUCH ROOM LEFT UNDER THERE. HE ALREADY BLAMED STAMFORD GETTING WRECKED ON TONY STARK, FOR MAKING THAT CLONE OF THOR.
NOW HE'S SAYIN' THE NEW WARRIORS SET IT FREE...EVEN THOUGH THEY DIDN'T SHOW UP UNTIL AFTER IT WENT BERSERK--
GAUNTLET! MRS. GREEN! YOU HAVE TO HELP ME!
MRS. TRANH?
WHAT'S THE MATTER, HONEY?
IT'S MY HUSBAND. THEY-- THEY WON'T TELL ME WHERE HE IS.
THE BENGAL'S PART OF THE SHADOW INITIATIVE, MA'AM. COVERT OPS. THEY'RE NOT ALLOWED TO TELL YOU.
YOU DON'T UNDERSTAND. IT WAS S.H.I.E.L.D. WHO CAME TO GET HIM. AND S.H.I.E.L.D.'S BEEN SHUT DOWN. SO WHO'S GOING TO BRING HIM HOME?
I ASKED AT THAT NEW AGENCY, H.A.M.M.E.R. THEY SAID THERE'S NO RECORD OF THE SHADOW INITIATIVE EVER EXISTING.

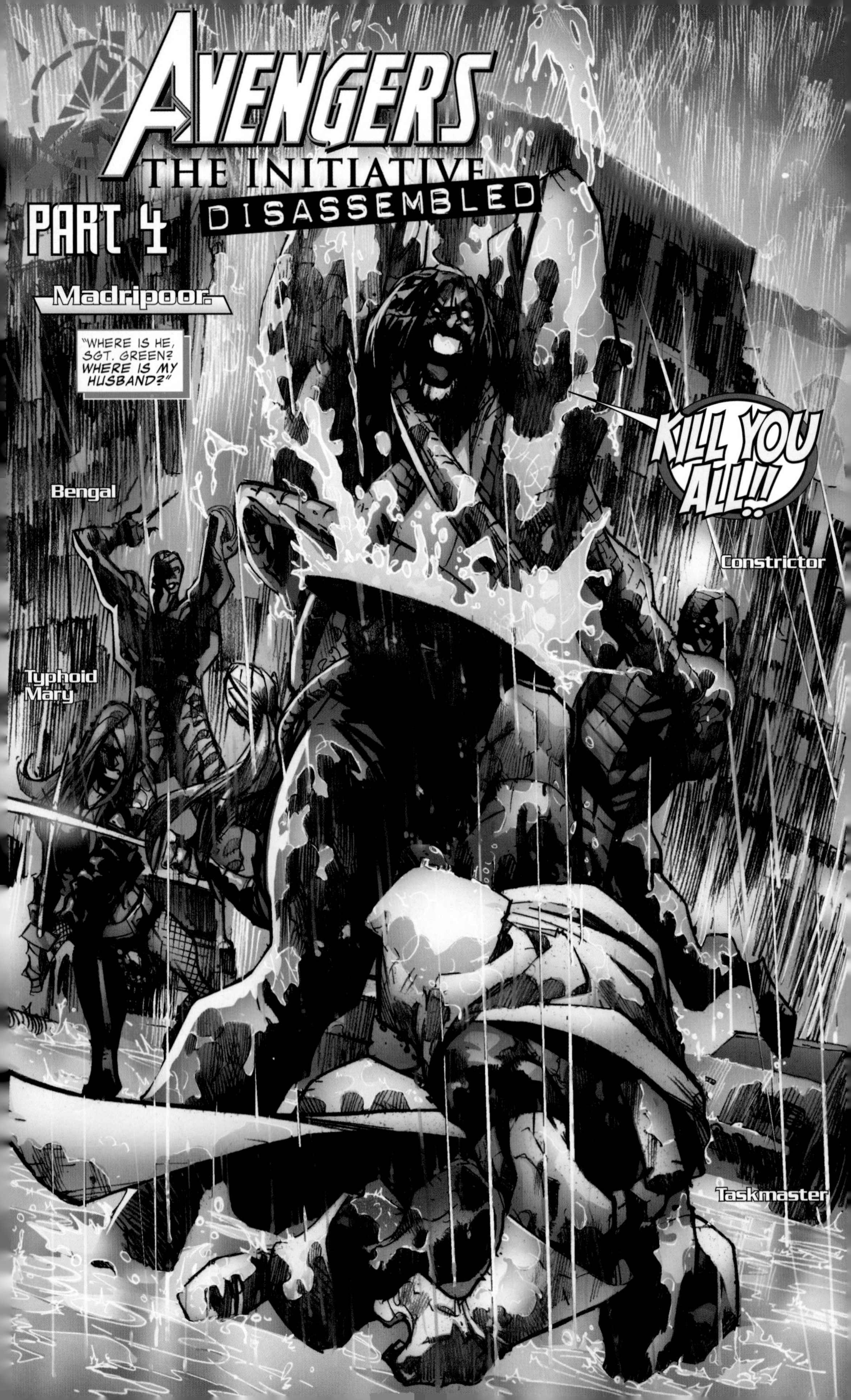

AVENGERS
THE INITIATIVE
PART 4
DISASSEMBLED
Madripoor.
"WHERE IS HE, SGT. GREEN? WHERE IS MY HUSBAND?"
KILL YOU ALL!!
Bengal
Constrictor
Typhoid Mary
Taskmaster

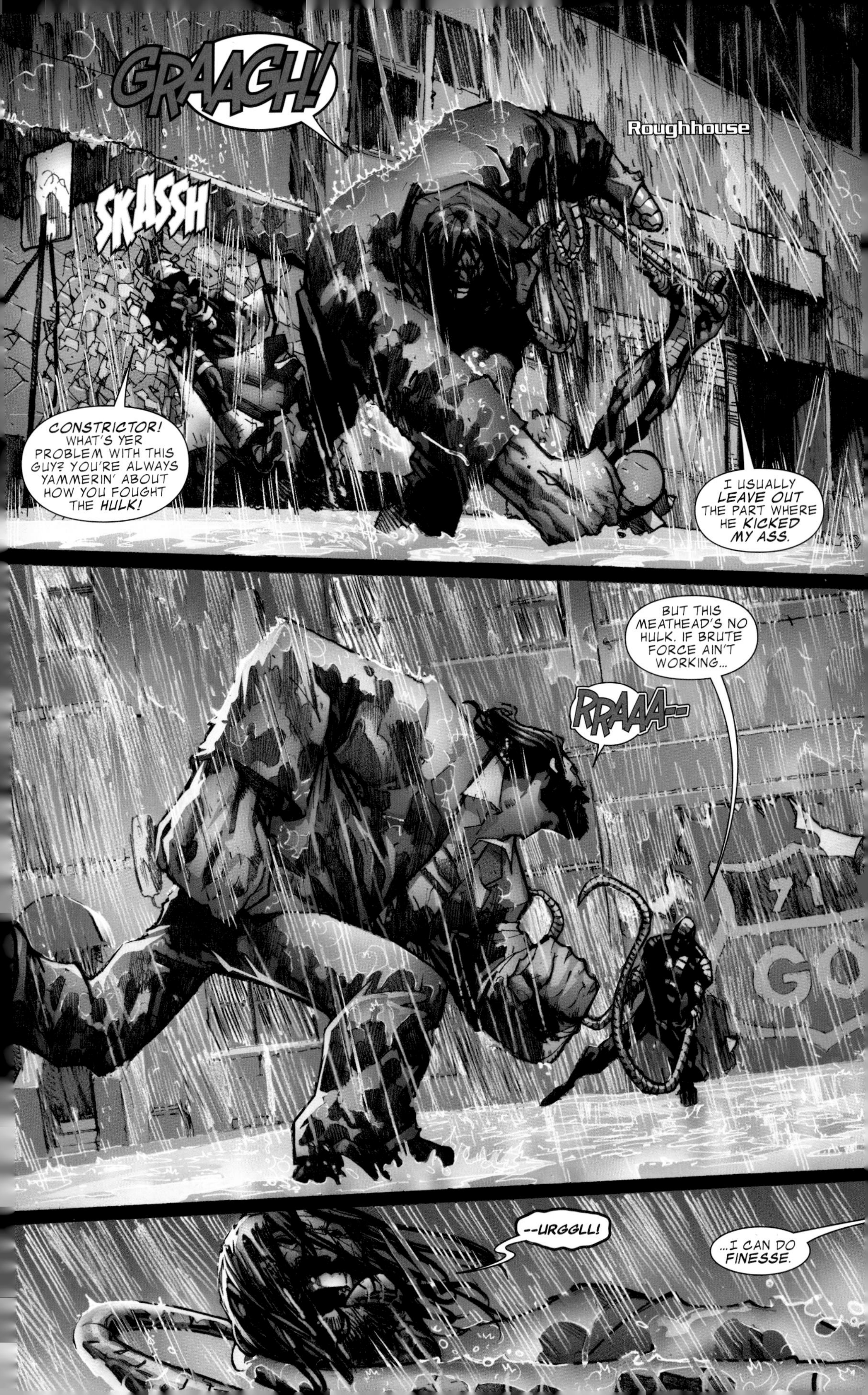
GRAAGH!
Roughhouse
SKASSH
CONSTRICTOR! WHAT'S YER PROBLEM WITH THIS GUY? YOU'RE ALWAYS YAMMERIN' ABOUT HOW YOU FOUGHT THE HULK!
I USUALLY LEAVE OUT THE PART WHERE HE KICKED MY ASS.
BUT THIS MEATHEAD'S NO HULK. IF BRUTE FORCE AIN'T WORKING...
RRAAA--
--URGGLL!
...I CAN DO FINESSE.

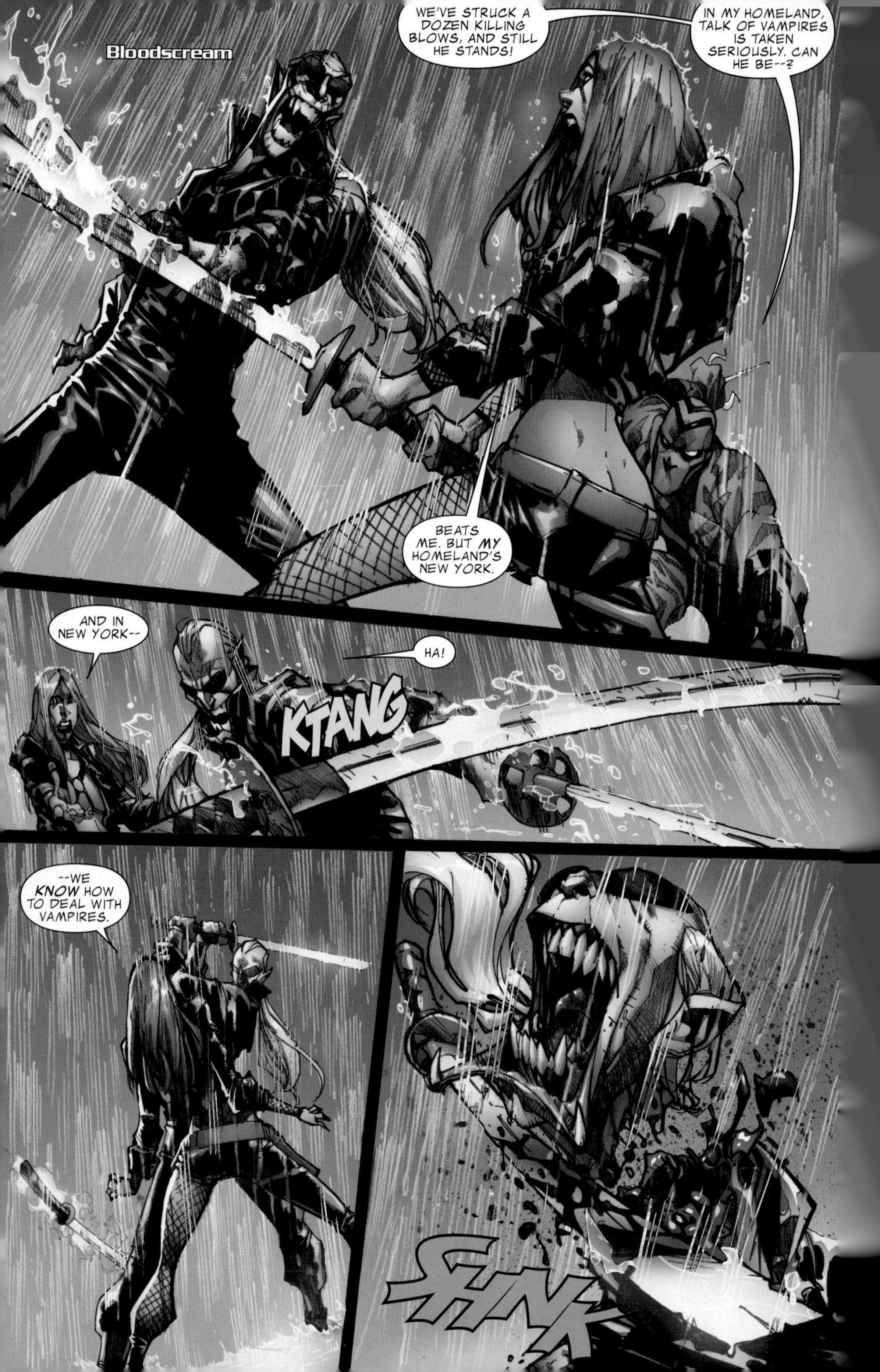
Bloodscream
WE'VE STRUCK A DOZEN KILLING BLOWS, AND STILL HE STANDS!
IN MY HOMELAND, TALK OF VAMPIRES IS TAKEN SERIOUSLY. CAN HE BE--?
BEATS ME. BUT MY HOMELAND'S NEW YORK.
AND IN NEW YORK--
HA!
KTANG
--WE KNOW HOW TO DEAL WITH VAMPIRES.
SHNK

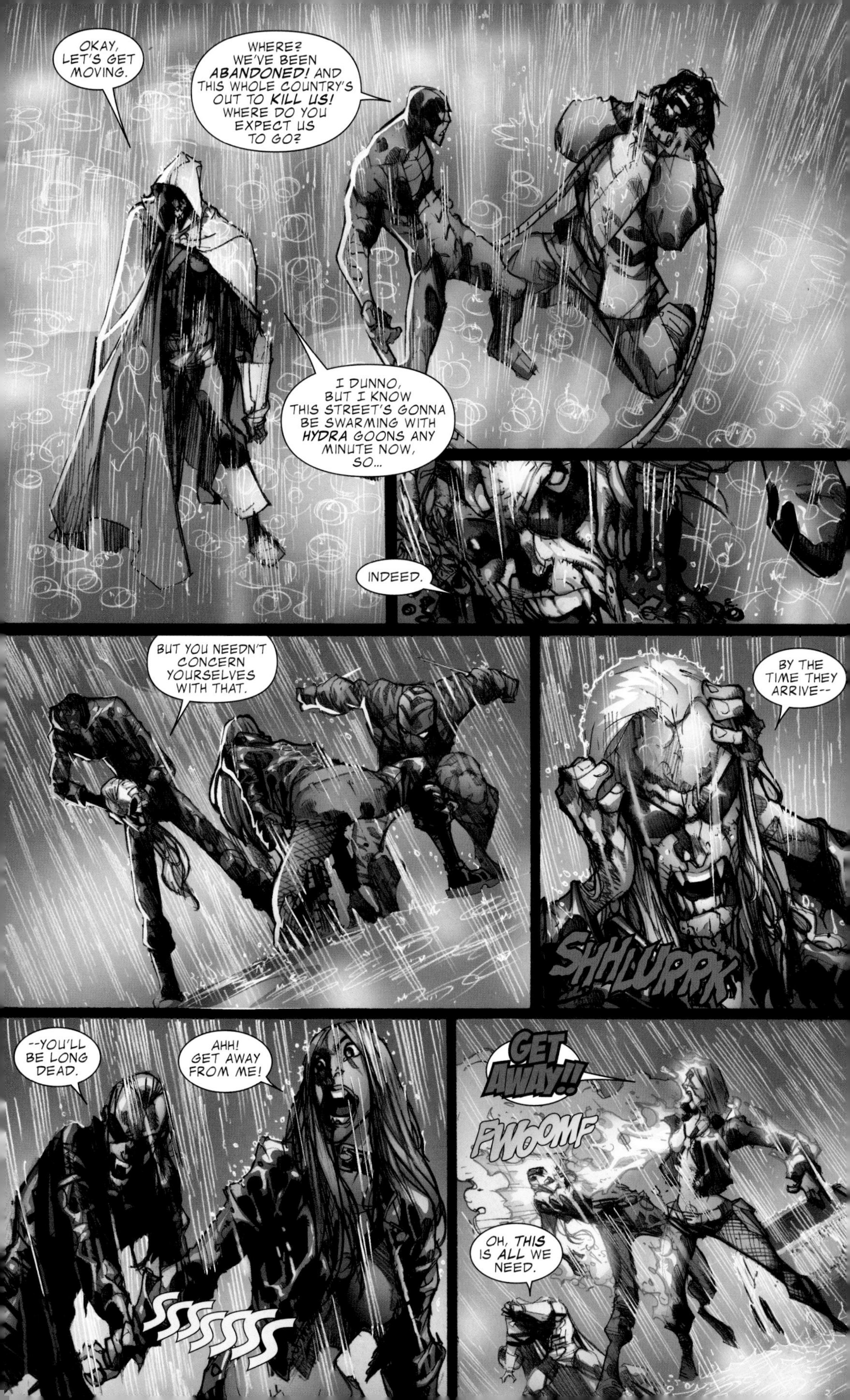
OKAY, LET'S GET MOVING.
WHERE? WE'VE BEEN ABANDONED! AND THIS WHOLE COUNTRY'S OUT TO KILL US! WHERE DO YOU EXPECT US TO GO?
I DUNNO, BUT I KNOW THIS STREET'S GONNA BE SWARMING WITH HYDRA GOONS ANY MINUTE NOW, SO...
INDEED.
BUT YOU NEEDN'T CONCERN YOURSELVES WITH THAT.
BY THE TIME THEY ARRIVE--
SHHLURRRK
--YOU'LL BE LONG DEAD.
AHH! GET AWAY FROM ME!
SSSSSSS
GET AWAY!!
FWOOMF
OH, THIS IS ALL WE NEED.

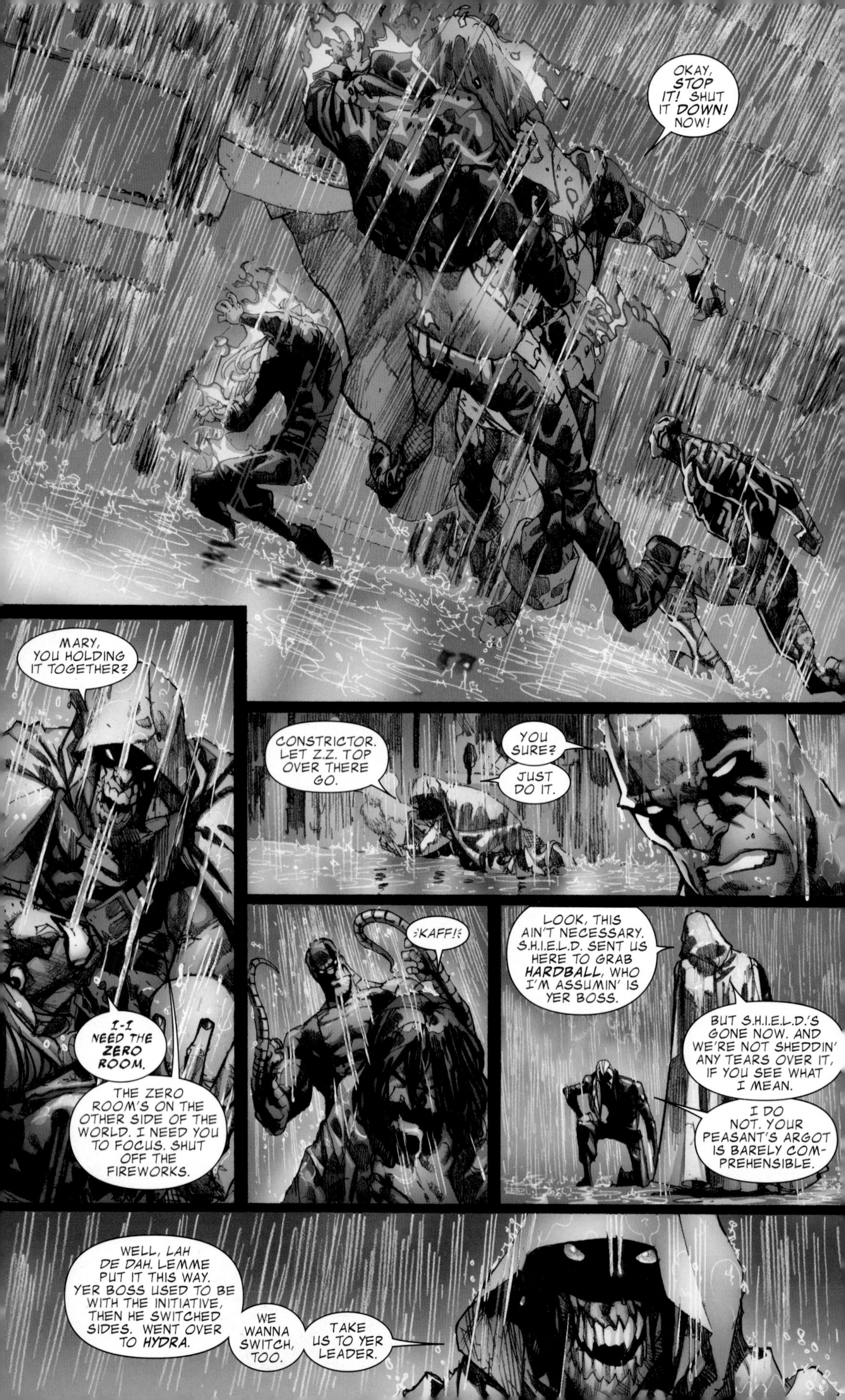
OKAY, STOP IT! SHUT IT DOWN! NOW!
MARY, YOU HOLDING IT TOGETHER?
I-I NEED THE ZERO ROOM.
THE ZERO ROOM'S ON THE OTHER SIDE OF THE WORLD. I NEED YOU TO FOCUS. SHUT OFF THE FIREWORKS.
CONSTRICTOR. LET Z.Z. TOP OVER THERE GO.
YOU SURE?
JUST DO IT.
KAFF!
LOOK, THIS AIN'T NECESSARY. S.H.I.E.L.D. SENT US HERE TO GRAB HARDBALL, WHO I'M ASSUMIN' IS YER BOSS.
BUT S.H.I.E.L.D.'S GONE NOW. AND WE'RE NOT SHEDDIN' ANY TEARS OVER IT, IF YOU SEE WHAT I MEAN.
I DO NOT. YOUR PEASANT'S ARGOT IS BARELY COM-PREHENSIBLE.
WELL, LAH DE DAH. LEMME PUT IT THIS WAY. YER BOSS USED TO BE WITH THE INITIATIVE, THEN HE SWITCHED SIDES. WENT OVER TO HYDRA.
WE WANNA SWITCH, TOO.
TAKE US TO YER LEADER.

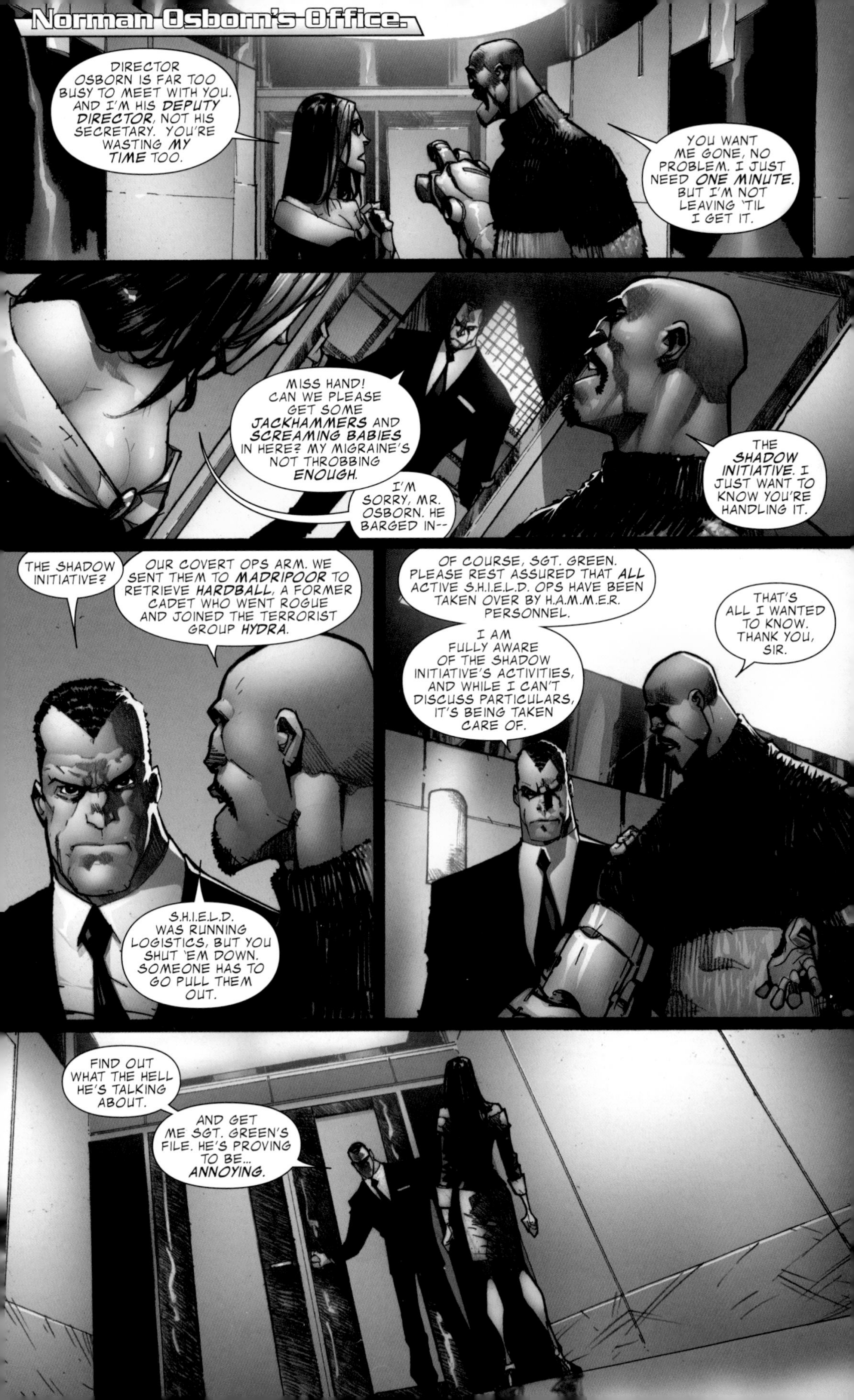
Norman Osborn's Office.
DIRECTOR OSBORN IS FAR TOO BUSY TO MEET WITH YOU. AND I'M HIS DEPUTY DIRECTOR, NOT HIS SECRETARY. YOU'RE WASTING MY TIME TOO.
YOU WANT ME GONE, NO PROBLEM. I JUST NEED ONE MINUTE. BUT I'M NOT LEAVING 'TIL I GET IT.
MISS HAND! CAN WE PLEASE GET SOME JACKHAMMERS AND SCREAMING BABIES IN HERE? MY MIGRAINE'S NOT THROBBING ENOUGH.
I'M SORRY, MR. OSBORN. HE BARGED IN--
THE SHADOW INITIATIVE. I JUST WANT TO KNOW YOU'RE HANDLING IT.
THE SHADOW INITIATIVE?
OUR COVERT OPS ARM. WE SENT THEM TO MADRIPOOR TO RETRIEVE HARDBALL, A FORMER CADET WHO WENT ROGUE AND JOINED THE TERRORIST GROUP HYDRA.
S.H.I.E.L.D. WAS RUNNING LOGISTICS, BUT YOU SHUT 'EM DOWN. SOMEONE HAS TO GO PULL THEM OUT.
OF COURSE, SGT. GREEN. PLEASE REST ASSURED THAT ALL ACTIVE S.H.I.E.L.D. OPS HAVE BEEN TAKEN OVER BY H.A.M.M.E.R. PERSONNEL.
I AM FULLY AWARE OF THE SHADOW INITIATIVE'S ACTIVITIES, AND WHILE I CAN'T DISCUSS PARTICULARS, IT'S BEING TAKEN CARE OF.
THAT'S ALL I WANTED TO KNOW. THANK YOU, SIR.
FIND OUT WHAT THE HELL HE'S TALKING ABOUT.
AND GET ME SGT. GREEN'S FILE. HE'S PROVING TO BE... ANNOYING.

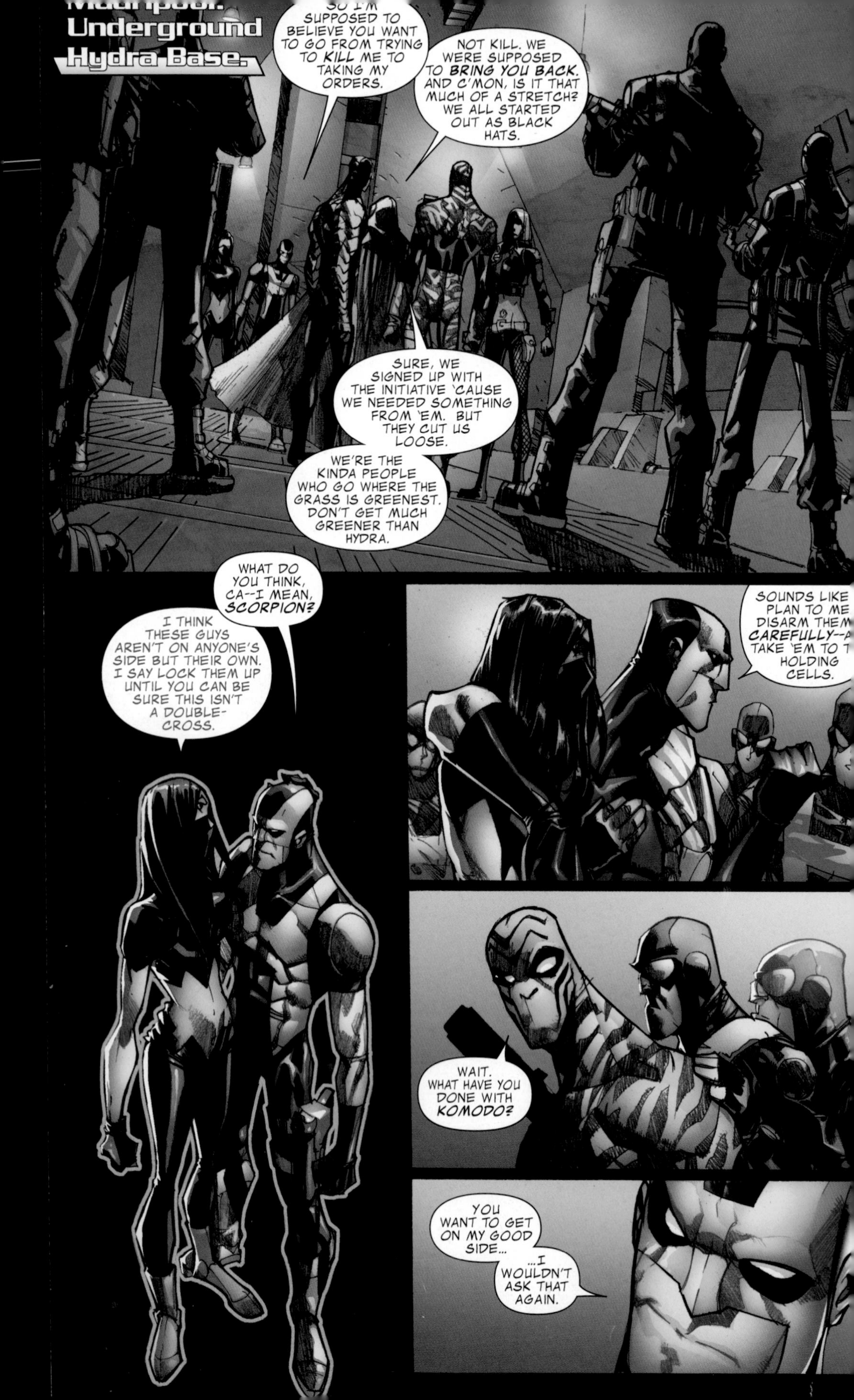
Underground Hydra Base.
SUPPOSED TO BELIEVE YOU WANT TO GO FROM TRYING TO KILL ME TO TAKING MY ORDERS.
NOT KILL. WE WERE SUPPOSED TO BRING YOU BACK. AND C'MON, IS IT THAT MUCH OF A STRETCH? WE ALL STARTED OUT AS BLACK HATS.
SURE, WE SIGNED UP WITH THE INITIATIVE 'CAUSE WE NEEDED SOMETHING FROM 'EM. BUT THEY CUT US LOOSE.
WE'RE THE KINDA PEOPLE WHO GO WHERE THE GRASS IS GREENEST. DON'T GET MUCH GREENER THAN HYDRA.
WHAT DO YOU THINK, CA--I MEAN, SCORPION?
I THINK THESE GUYS AREN'T ON ANYONE'S SIDE BUT THEIR OWN. I SAY LOCK THEM UP UNTIL YOU CAN BE SURE THIS ISN'T A DOUBLE-CROSS.
SOUNDS LIKE PLAN TO ME DISARM THEM CAREFULLY-- TAKE 'EM TO HOLDING CELLS.
WAIT. WHAT HAVE YOU DONE WITH KOMODO?
YOU WANT TO GET ON MY GOOD SIDE...
...I WOULDN'T ASK THAT AGAIN.

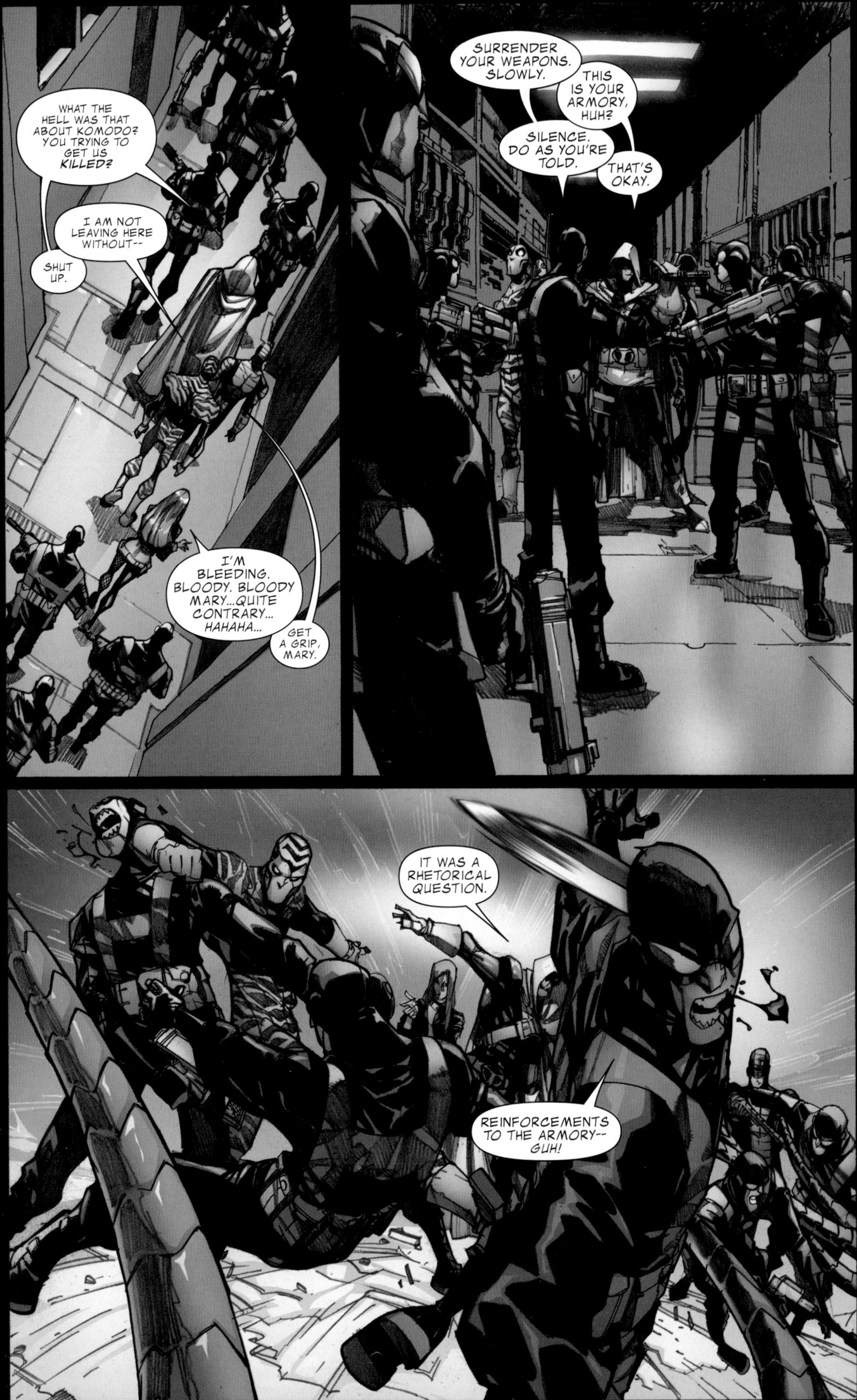
WHAT THE HELL WAS THAT ABOUT KOMODO? YOU TRYING TO GET US KILLED?
I AM NOT LEAVING HERE WITHOUT--
SHUT UP.
I'M BLEEDING. BLOODY. BLOODY MARY...QUITE CONTRARY... HAHAHA...
GET A GRIP, MARY.
SURRENDER YOUR WEAPONS. SLOWLY.
THIS IS YOUR ARMORY, HUH?
SILENCE. DO AS YOU'RE TOLD.
THAT'S OKAY.
IT WAS A RHETORICAL QUESTION.
REINFORCEMENTS TO THE ARMORY-- GUH!

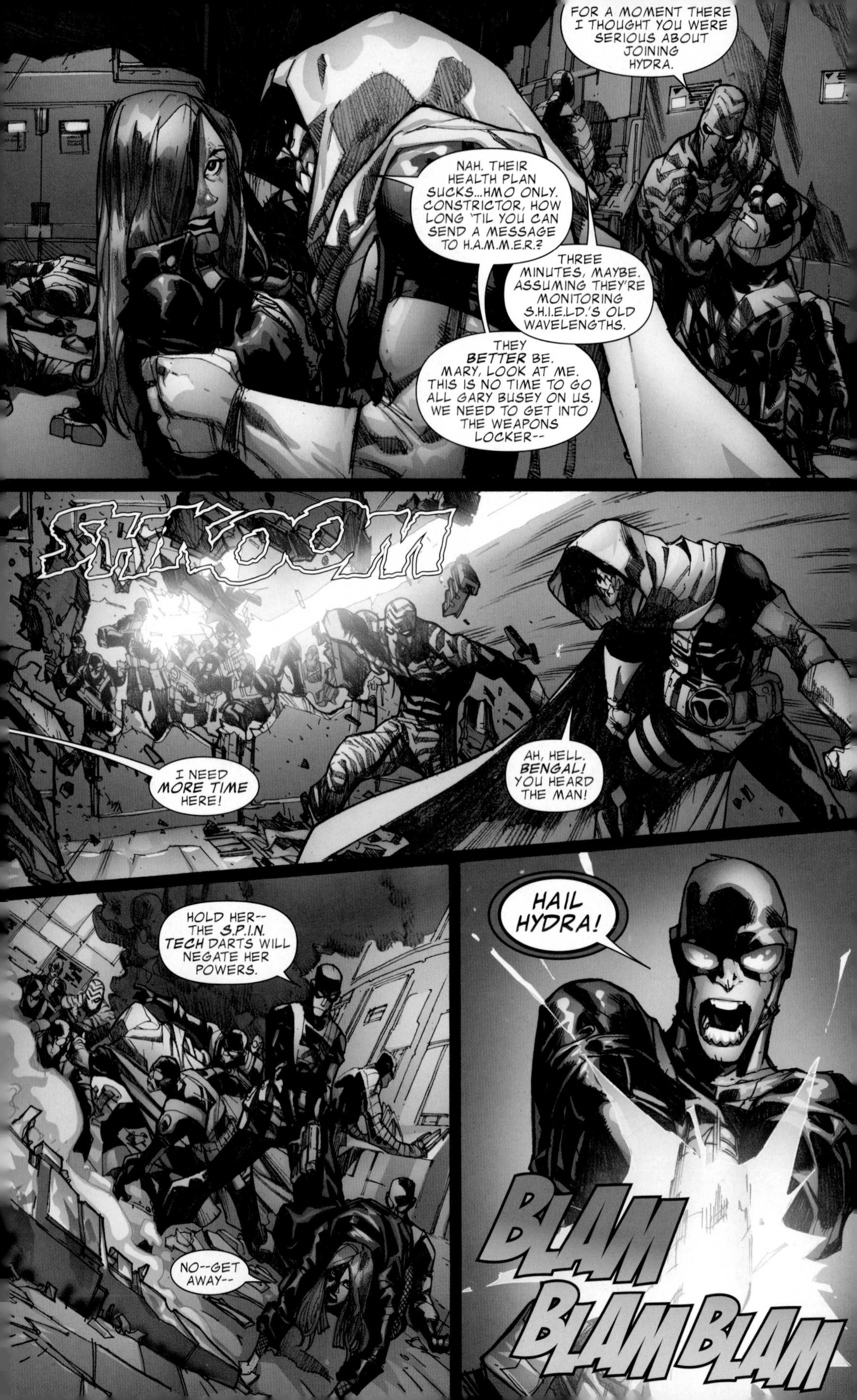
FOR A MOMENT THERE I THOUGHT YOU WERE SERIOUS ABOUT JOINING HYDRA.
NAH. THEIR HEALTH PLAN SUCKS...HMO ONLY. CONSTRICTOR, HOW LONG 'TIL YOU CAN SEND A MESSAGE TO H.A.M.M.E.R.?
THREE MINUTES, MAYBE. ASSUMING THEY'RE MONITORING S.H.I.E.L.D.'S OLD WAVELENGTHS.
THEY BETTER BE. MARY, LOOK AT ME. THIS IS NO TIME TO GO ALL GARY BUSEY ON US. WE NEED TO GET INTO THE WEAPONS LOCKER--
SHKROOM
I NEED MORE TIME HERE!
AH, HELL. BENGAL! YOU HEARD THE MAN!
HOLD HER-- THE S.P.I.N. TECH DARTS WILL NEGATE HER POWERS.
NO--GET AWAY--
HAIL HYDRA!
BLAM
BLAM BLAM BLAM

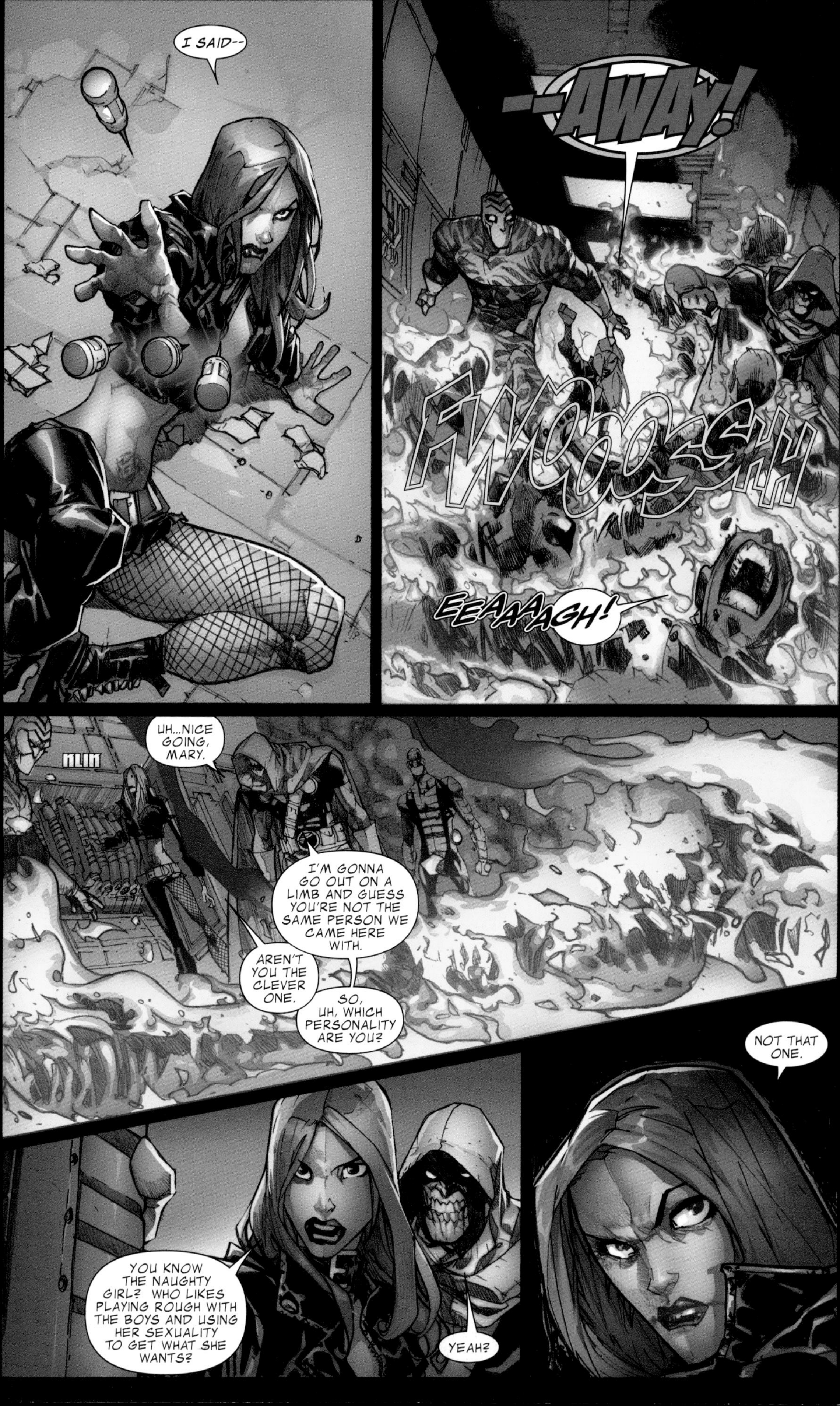
I SAID--
--AWAY!
FWOOOSHH
EEAAAAAGH!
UH...NICE GOING, MARY.
I'M GONNA GO OUT ON A LIMB AND GUESS YOU'RE NOT THE SAME PERSON WE CAME HERE WITH.
AREN'T YOU THE CLEVER ONE.
SO, UH, WHICH PERSONALITY ARE YOU?
NOT THAT ONE.
YOU KNOW THE NAUGHTY GIRL? WHO LIKES PLAYING ROUGH WITH THE BOYS AND USING HER SEXUALITY TO GET WHAT SHE WANTS?
YEAH?

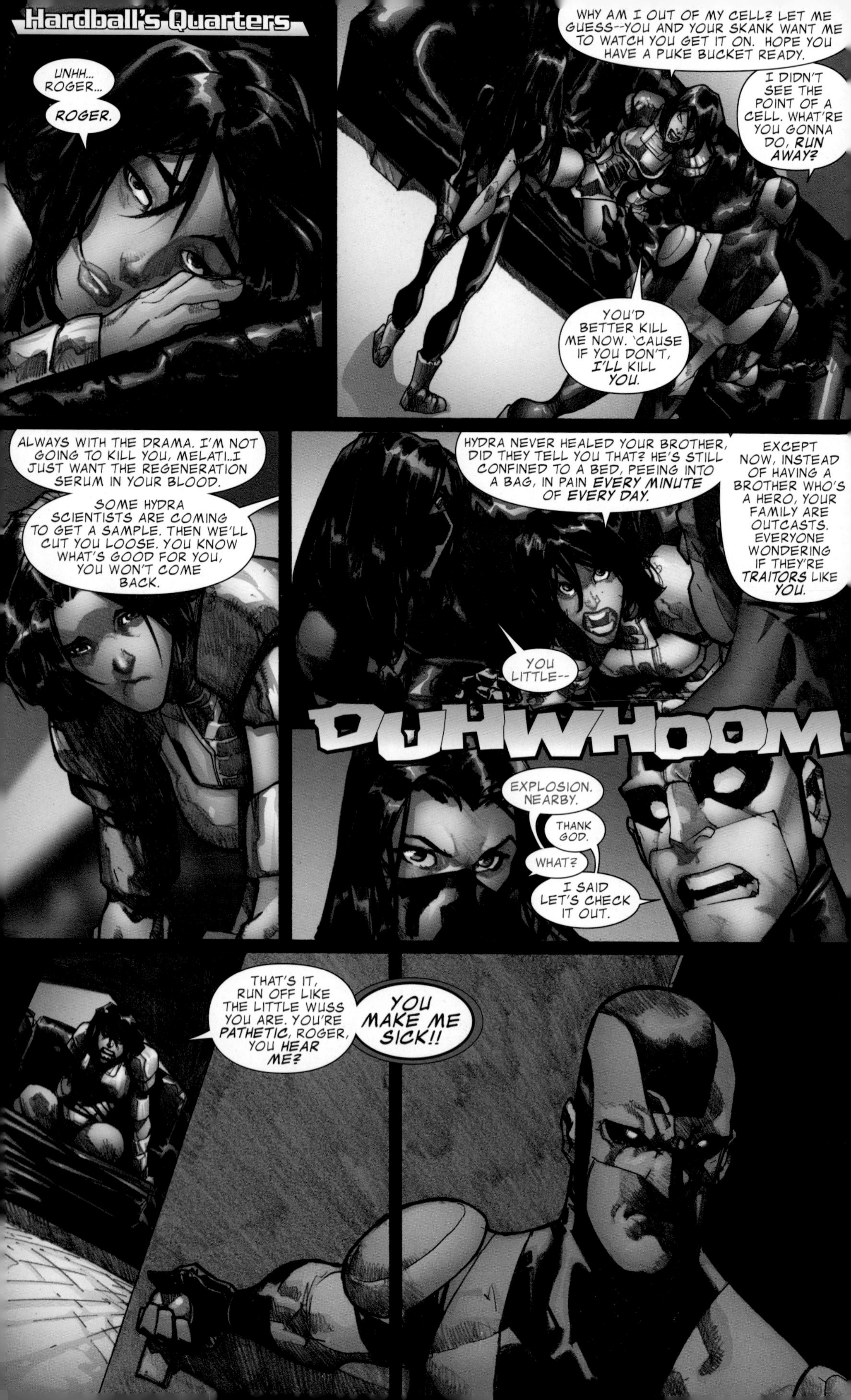
Hardball's Quarters
UNHH... ROGER...
ROGER.
WHY AM I OUT OF MY CELL? LET ME GUESS--YOU AND YOUR SKANK WANT ME TO WATCH YOU GET IT ON. HOPE YOU HAVE A PUKE BUCKET READY.
I DIDN'T SEE THE POINT OF A CELL. WHAT'RE YOU GONNA DO, RUN AWAY?
YOU'D BETTER KILL ME NOW. 'CAUSE IF YOU DON'T, I'LL KILL YOU.
ALWAYS WITH THE DRAMA. I'M NOT GOING TO KILL YOU, MELATI..I JUST WANT THE REGENERATION SERUM IN YOUR BLOOD.
SOME HYDRA SCIENTISTS ARE COMING TO GET A SAMPLE. THEN WE'LL CUT YOU LOOSE. YOU KNOW WHAT'S GOOD FOR YOU, YOU WON'T COME BACK.
HYDRA NEVER HEALED YOUR BROTHER, DID THEY TELL YOU THAT? HE'S STILL CONFINED TO A BED, PEEING INTO A BAG, IN PAIN EVERY MINUTE OF EVERY DAY.
EXCEPT NOW, INSTEAD OF HAVING A BROTHER WHO'S A HERO, YOUR FAMILY ARE OUTCASTS. EVERYONE WONDERING IF THEY'RE TRAITORS LIKE YOU.
YOU LITTLE--
DUHWHOOM
EXPLOSION. NEARBY.
THANK GOD.
WHAT?
I SAID LET'S CHECK IT OUT.
THAT'S IT, RUN OFF LIKE THE LITTLE WUSS YOU ARE. YOU'RE PATHETIC, ROGER, YOU HEAR ME?
YOU MAKE ME SICK!!

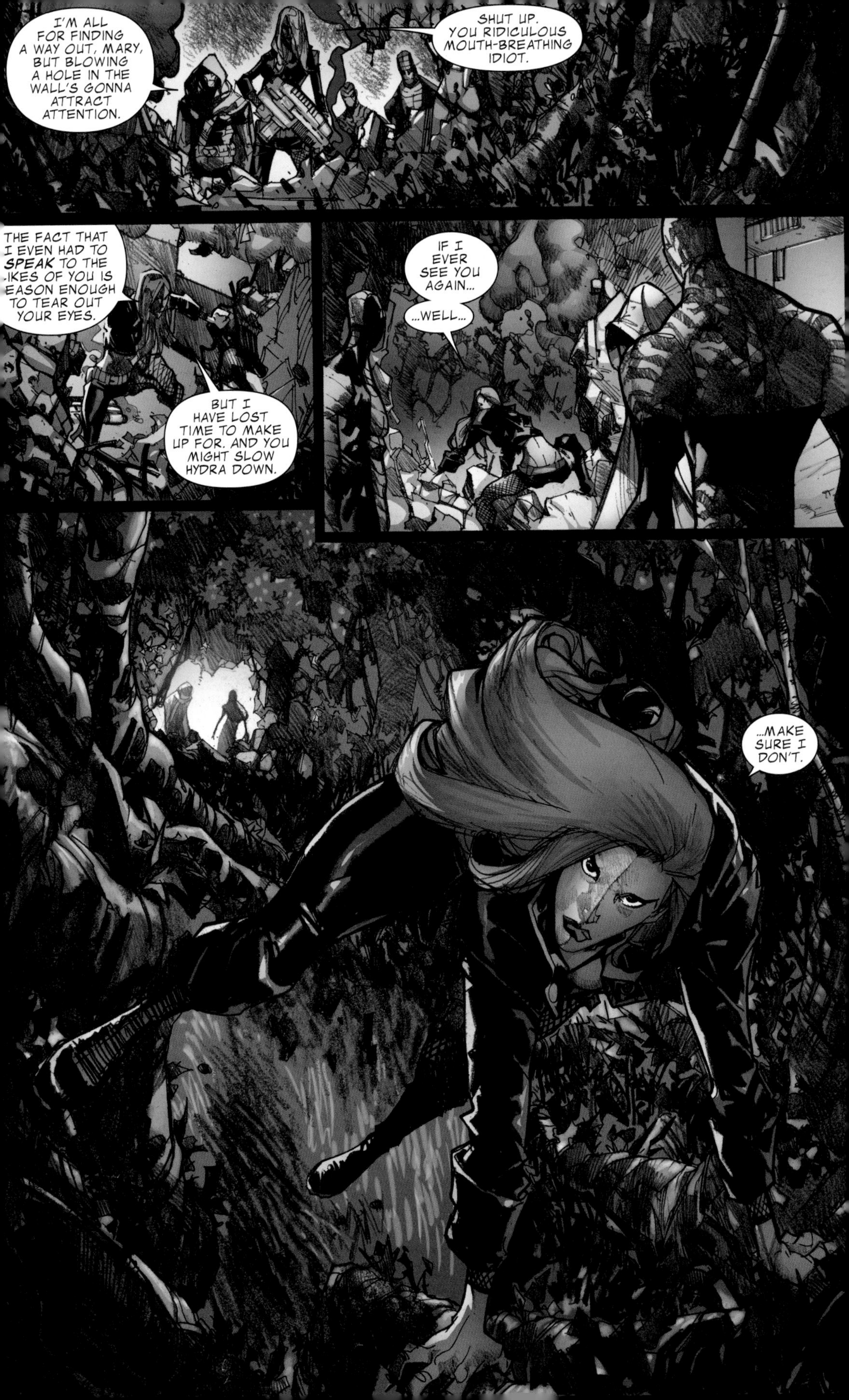

I'M ALL FOR FINDING A WAY OUT, MARY, BUT BLOWING A HOLE IN THE WALL'S GONNA ATTRACT ATTENTION.
SHUT UP. YOU RIDICULOUS MOUTH-BREATHING IDIOT.
THE FACT THAT I EVEN HAD TO SPEAK TO THE LIKES OF YOU IS REASON ENOUGH TO TEAR OUT YOUR EYES.
BUT I HAVE LOST TIME TO MAKE UP FOR. AND YOU MIGHT SLOW HYDRA DOWN.
IF I EVER SEE YOU AGAIN...
...WELL...
...MAKE SURE I DON'T.

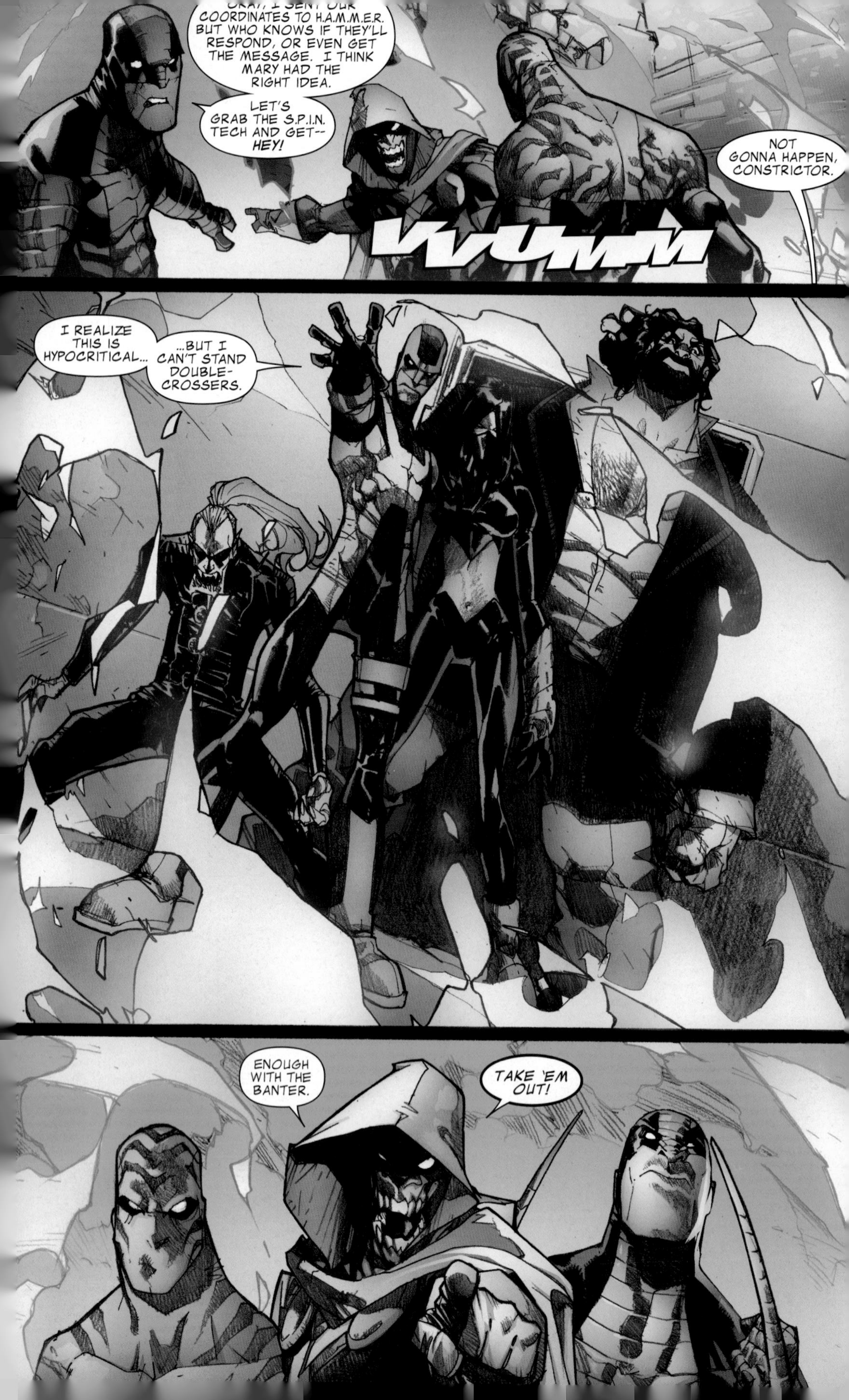
COORDINATES TO H.A.M.M.E.R. BUT WHO KNOWS IF THEY'LL RESPOND, OR EVEN GET THE MESSAGE. I THINK MARY HAD THE RIGHT IDEA.
LET'S GRAB THE S.P.I.N. TECH AND GET-- HEY!
VVUMM
NOT GONNA HAPPEN, CONSTRICTOR.
I REALIZE THIS IS HYPOCRITICAL...
...BUT I CAN'T STAND DOUBLE-CROSSERS.
ENOUGH WITH THE BANTER.
TAKE 'EM OUT!

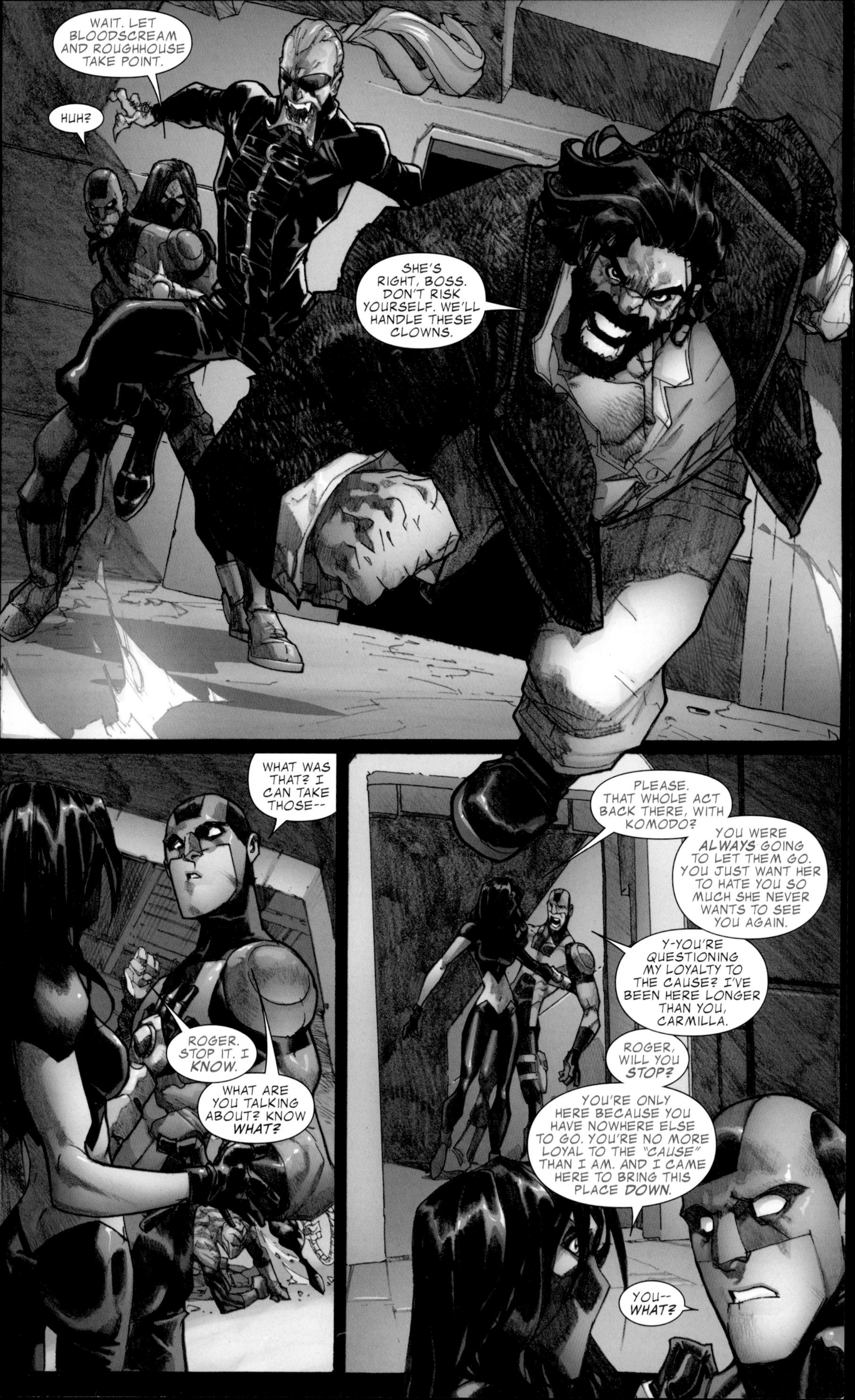
WAIT. LET BLOODSCREAM AND ROUGHHOUSE TAKE POINT.
HUH?
SHE'S RIGHT, BOSS. DON'T RISK YOURSELF. WE'LL HANDLE THESE CLOWNS.
WHAT WAS THAT? I CAN TAKE THOSE--
ROGER. STOP IT. I KNOW.
WHAT ARE YOU TALKING ABOUT? KNOW WHAT?
PLEASE. THAT WHOLE ACT BACK THERE, WITH KOMODO?
YOU WERE ALWAYS GOING TO LET THEM GO. YOU JUST WANT HER TO HATE YOU SO MUCH SHE NEVER WANTS TO SEE YOU AGAIN.
Y-YOU'RE QUESTIONING MY LOYALTY TO THE CAUSE? I'VE BEEN HERE LONGER THAN YOU, CARMILLA.
ROGER, WILL YOU STOP?
YOU'RE ONLY HERE BECAUSE YOU HAVE NOWHERE ELSE TO GO. YOU'RE NO MORE LOYAL TO THE "CAUSE" THAN I AM. AND I CAME HERE TO BRING THIS PLACE DOWN.
YOU-- WHAT?

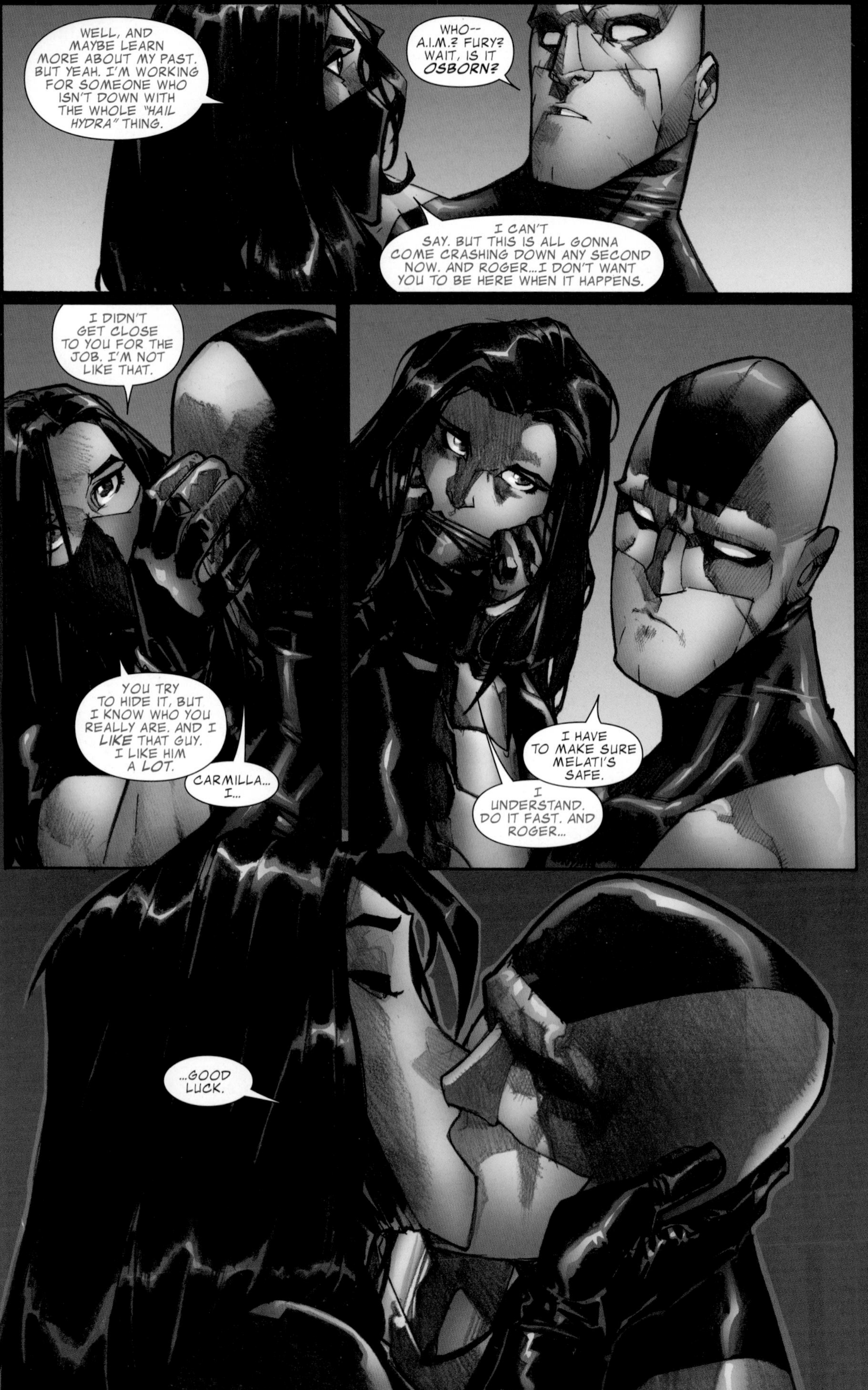
WELL, AND MAYBE LEARN MORE ABOUT MY PAST. BUT YEAH. I'M WORKING FOR SOMEONE WHO ISN'T DOWN WITH THE WHOLE "HAIL HYDRA" THING.
WHO-- A.I.M.? FURY? WAIT, IS IT OSBORN?
I CAN'T SAY. BUT THIS IS ALL GONNA COME CRASHING DOWN ANY SECOND NOW. AND ROGER...I DON'T WANT YOU TO BE HERE WHEN IT HAPPENS.
I DIDN'T GET CLOSE TO YOU FOR THE JOB. I'M NOT LIKE THAT.
YOU TRY TO HIDE IT, BUT I KNOW WHO YOU REALLY ARE. AND I LIKE THAT GUY. I LIKE HIM A LOT.
CARMILLA... I...
I HAVE TO MAKE SURE MELATI'S SAFE.
I UNDERSTAND. DO IT FAST. AND ROGER...
...GOOD LUCK.

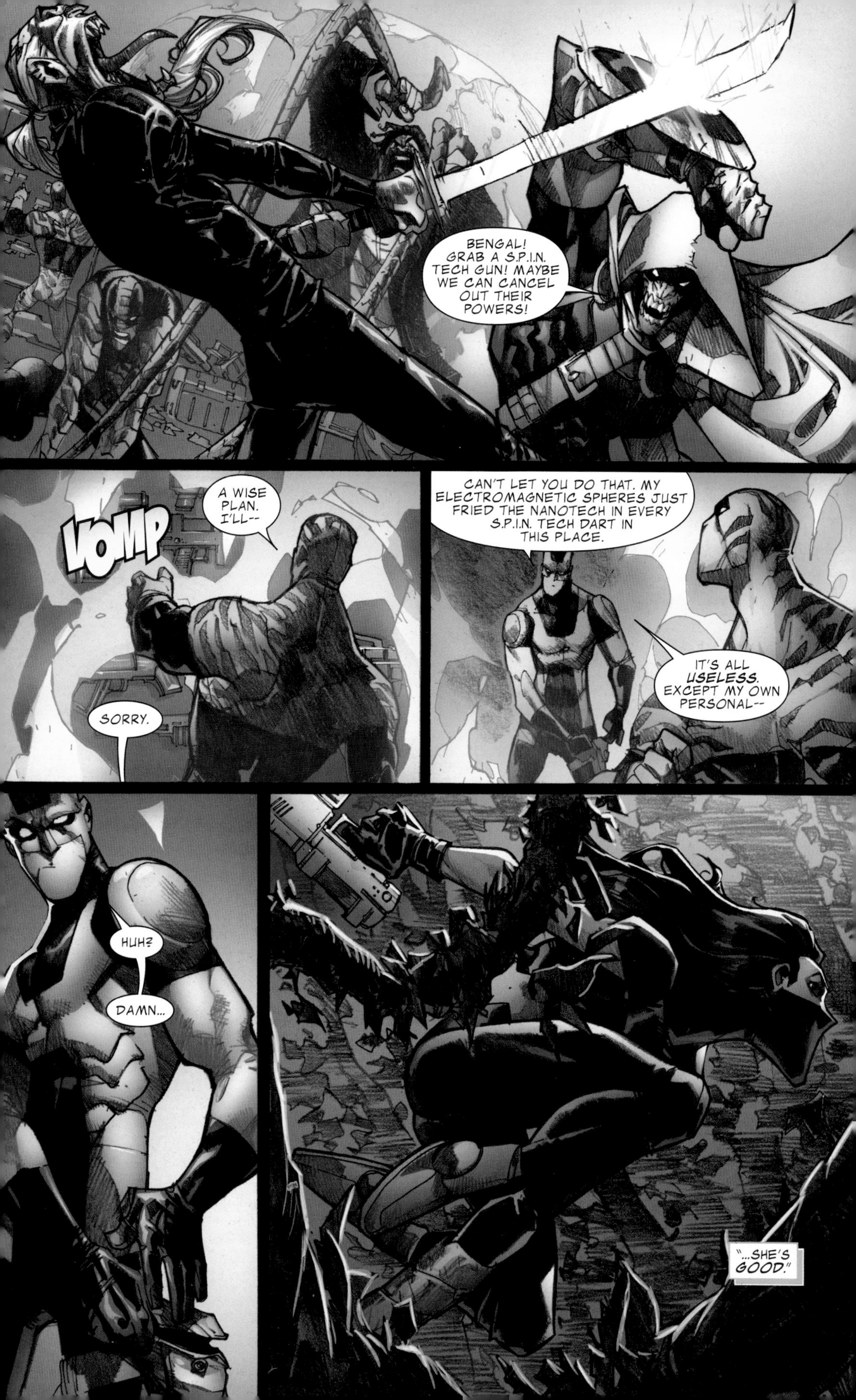
BENGAL! GRAB A S.P.I.N. TECH GUN! MAYBE WE CAN CANCEL OUT THEIR POWERS!
VOMP
A WISE PLAN. I'LL--
SORRY.
CAN'T LET YOU DO THAT. MY ELECTROMAGNETIC SPHERES JUST FRIED THE NANOTECH IN EVERY S.P.I.N. TECH DART IN THIS PLACE.
IT'S ALL USELESS. EXCEPT MY OWN PERSONAL--
HUH?
DAMN...
"...SHE'S GOOD."

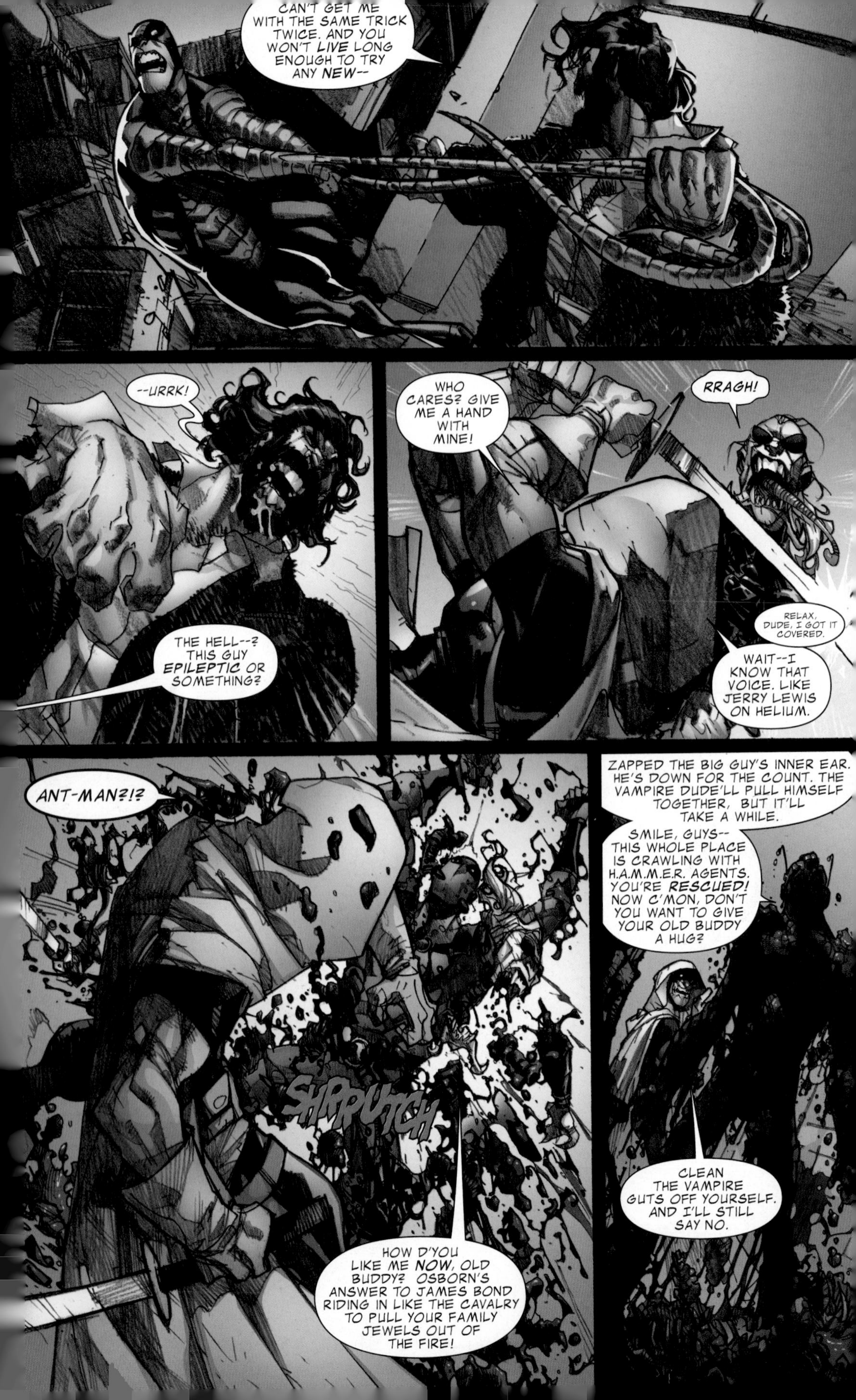
CAN'T GET ME WITH THE SAME TRICK TWICE. AND YOU WON'T LIVE LONG ENOUGH TO TRY ANY NEW--
--URRK!
THE HELL--? THIS GUY EPILEPTIC OR SOMETHING?
WHO CARES? GIVE ME A HAND WITH MINE!
RRAGH!
RELAX, DUDE, I GOT IT COVERED.
WAIT--I KNOW THAT VOICE. LIKE JERRY LEWIS ON HELIUM.
ANT-MAN?!?
SHRRUTCH
HOW D'YOU LIKE ME NOW, OLD BUDDY? OSBORN'S ANSWER TO JAMES BOND RIDING IN LIKE THE CAVALRY TO PULL YOUR FAMILY JEWELS OUT OF THE FIRE!
ZAPPED THE BIG GUY'S INNER EAR. HE'S DOWN FOR THE COUNT. THE VAMPIRE DUDE'LL PULL HIMSELF TOGETHER, BUT IT'LL TAKE A WHILE.
SMILE, GUYS-- THIS WHOLE PLACE IS CRAWLING WITH H.A.M.M.E.R. AGENTS. YOU'RE RESCUED! NOW C'MON, DON'T YOU WANT TO GIVE YOUR OLD BUDDY A HUG?
CLEAN THE VAMPIRE GUTS OFF YOURSELF. AND I'LL STILL SAY NO.

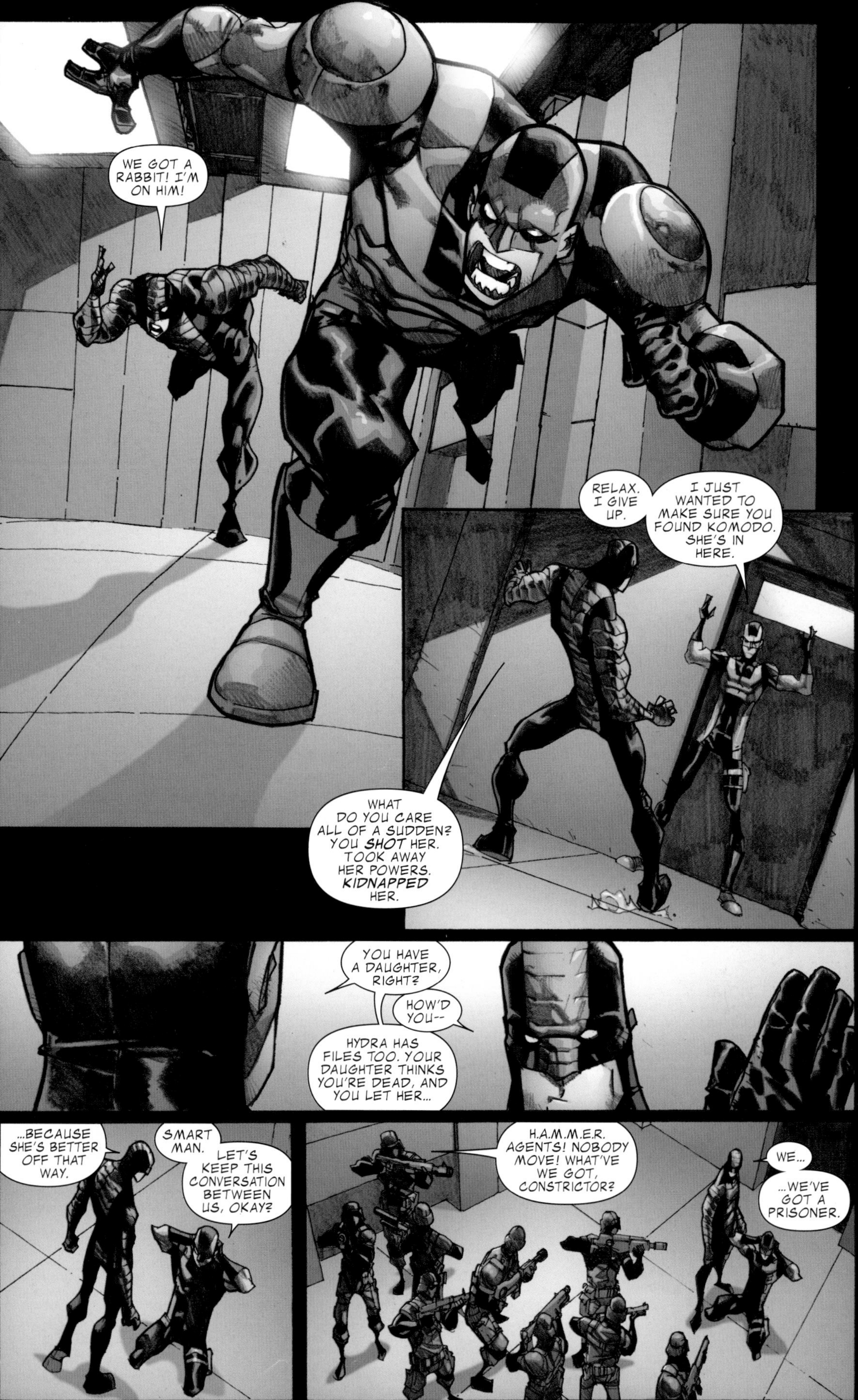
WE GOT A RABBIT! I'M ON HIM!
RELAX. I GIVE UP.
I JUST WANTED TO MAKE SURE YOU FOUND KOMODO. SHE'S IN HERE.
WHAT DO YOU CARE ALL OF A SUDDEN? YOU SHOT HER. TOOK AWAY HER POWERS. KIDNAPPED HER.
YOU HAVE A DAUGHTER, RIGHT?
HOW'D YOU--
HYDRA HAS FILES TOO. YOUR DAUGHTER THINKS YOU'RE DEAD, AND YOU LET HER...
...BECAUSE SHE'S BETTER OFF THAT WAY.
SMART MAN.
LET'S KEEP THIS CONVERSATION BETWEEN US, OKAY?
H.A.M.M.E.R. AGENTS! NOBODY MOVE! WHAT'VE WE GOT, CONSTRICTOR?
WE...
...WE'VE GOT A PRISONER.

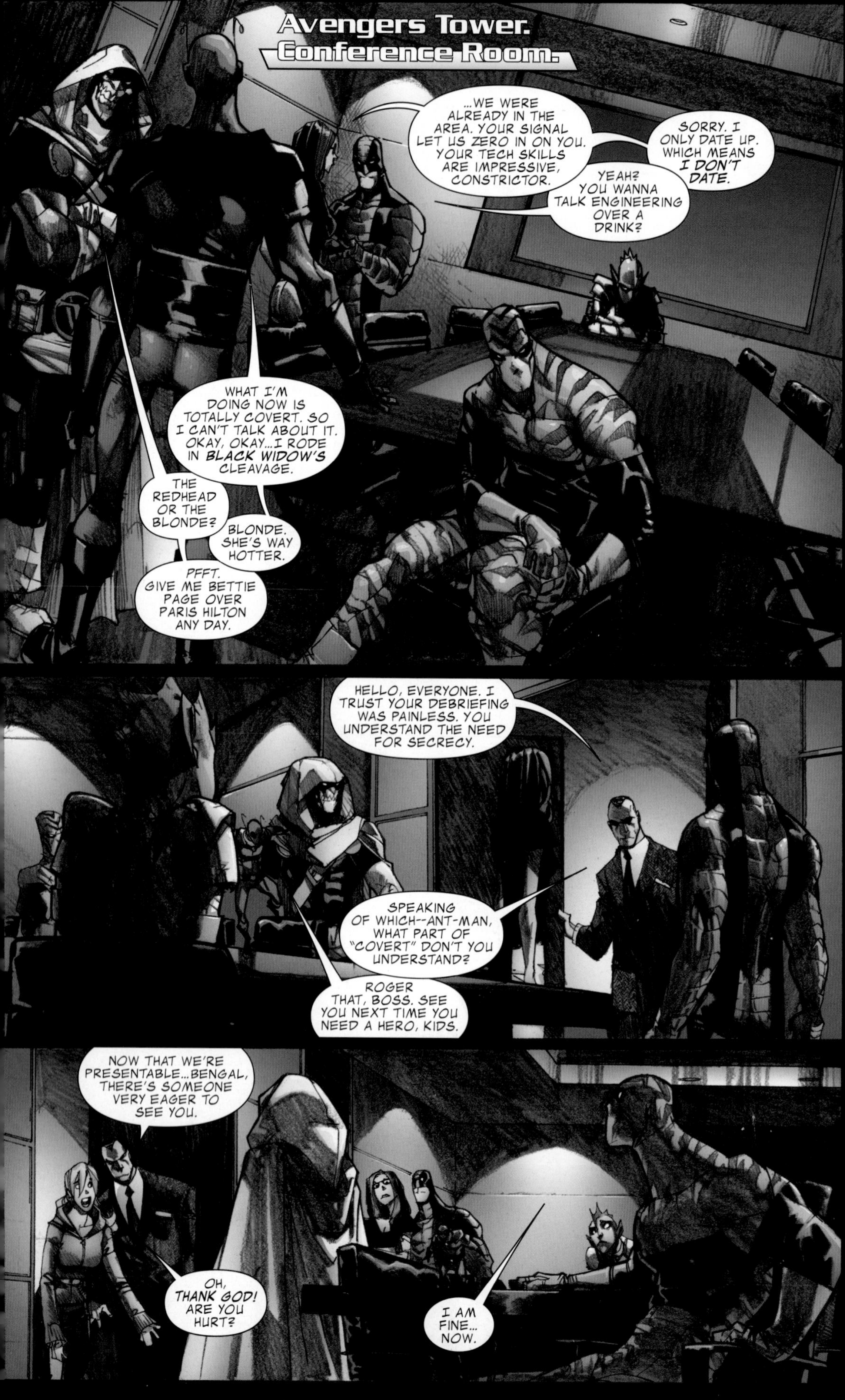
Avengers Tower. Conference Room.
...WE WERE ALREADY IN THE AREA. YOUR SIGNAL LET US ZERO IN ON YOU. YOUR TECH SKILLS ARE IMPRESSIVE, CONSTRICTOR.
YEAH? YOU WANNA TALK ENGINEERING OVER A DRINK?
SORRY. I ONLY DATE UP. WHICH MEANS I DON'T DATE.
WHAT I'M DOING NOW IS TOTALLY COVERT. SO I CAN'T TALK ABOUT IT. OKAY, OKAY...I RODE IN BLACK WIDOW'S CLEAVAGE.
THE REDHEAD OR THE BLONDE?
BLONDE. SHE'S WAY HOTTER.
PFFT. GIVE ME BETTIE PAGE OVER PARIS HILTON ANY DAY.
HELLO, EVERYONE. I TRUST YOUR DEBRIEFING WAS PAINLESS. YOU UNDERSTAND THE NEED FOR SECRECY.
SPEAKING OF WHICH--ANT-MAN, WHAT PART OF "COVERT" DON'T YOU UNDERSTAND?
ROGER THAT, BOSS. SEE YOU NEXT TIME YOU NEED A HERO, KIDS.
NOW THAT WE'RE PRESENTABLE...BENGAL, THERE'S SOMEONE VERY EAGER TO SEE YOU.
OH, THANK GOD! ARE YOU HURT?
I AM FINE... NOW.

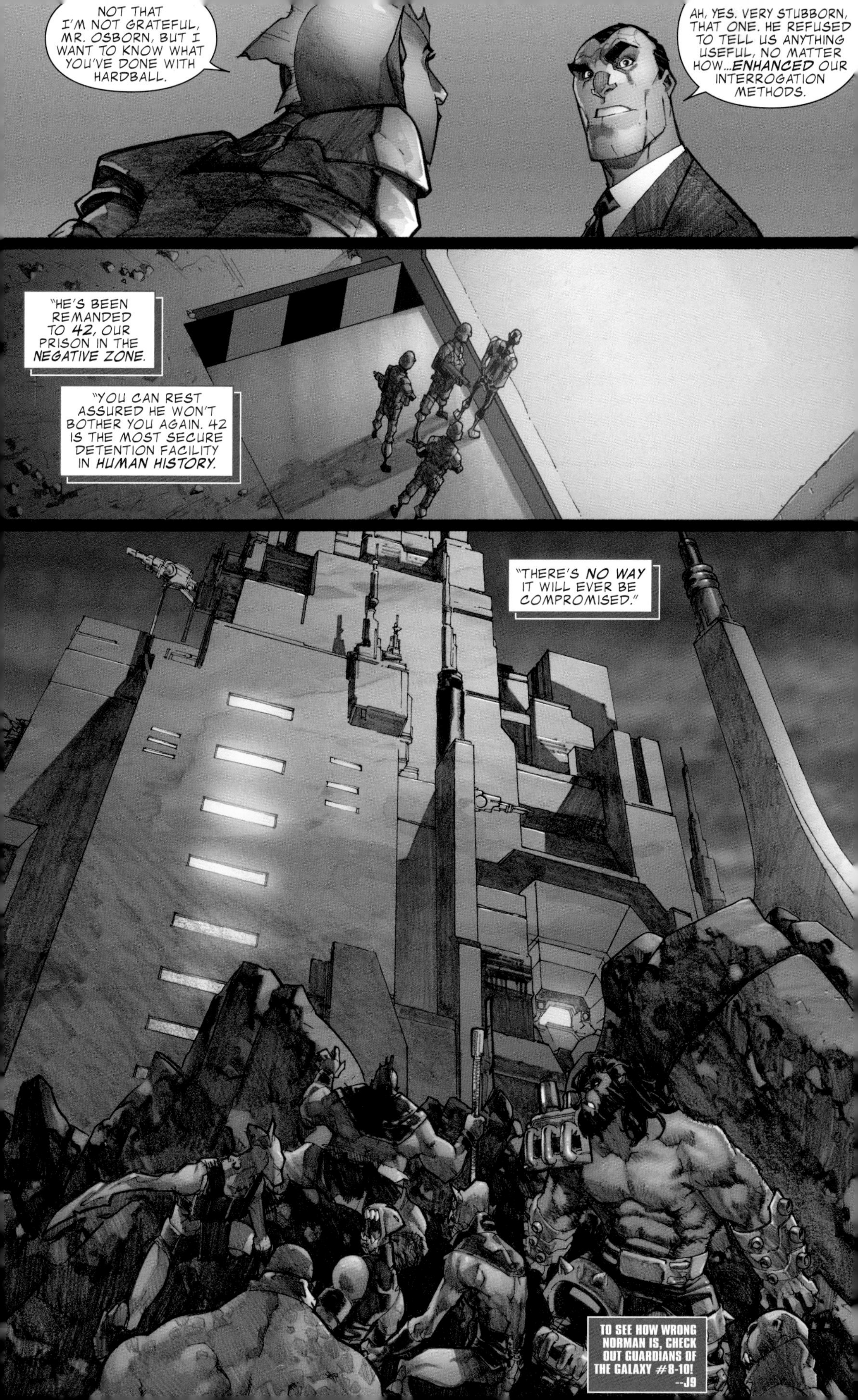
NOT THAT I'M NOT GRATEFUL, MR. OSBORN, BUT I WANT TO KNOW WHAT YOU'VE DONE WITH HARDBALL.
AH, YES. VERY STUBBORN, THAT ONE. HE REFUSED TO TELL US ANYTHING USEFUL, NO MATTER HOW...ENHANCED OUR INTERROGATION METHODS.
"HE'S BEEN REMANDED TO 42, OUR PRISON IN THE NEGATIVE ZONE.
"YOU CAN REST ASSURED HE WON'T BOTHER YOU AGAIN. 42 IS THE MOST SECURE DETENTION FACILITY IN HUMAN HISTORY.
"THERE'S NO WAY IT WILL EVER BE COMPROMISED."
TO SEE HOW WRONG NORMAN IS, CHECK OUT GUARDIANS OF THE GALAXY #8-10! --J9

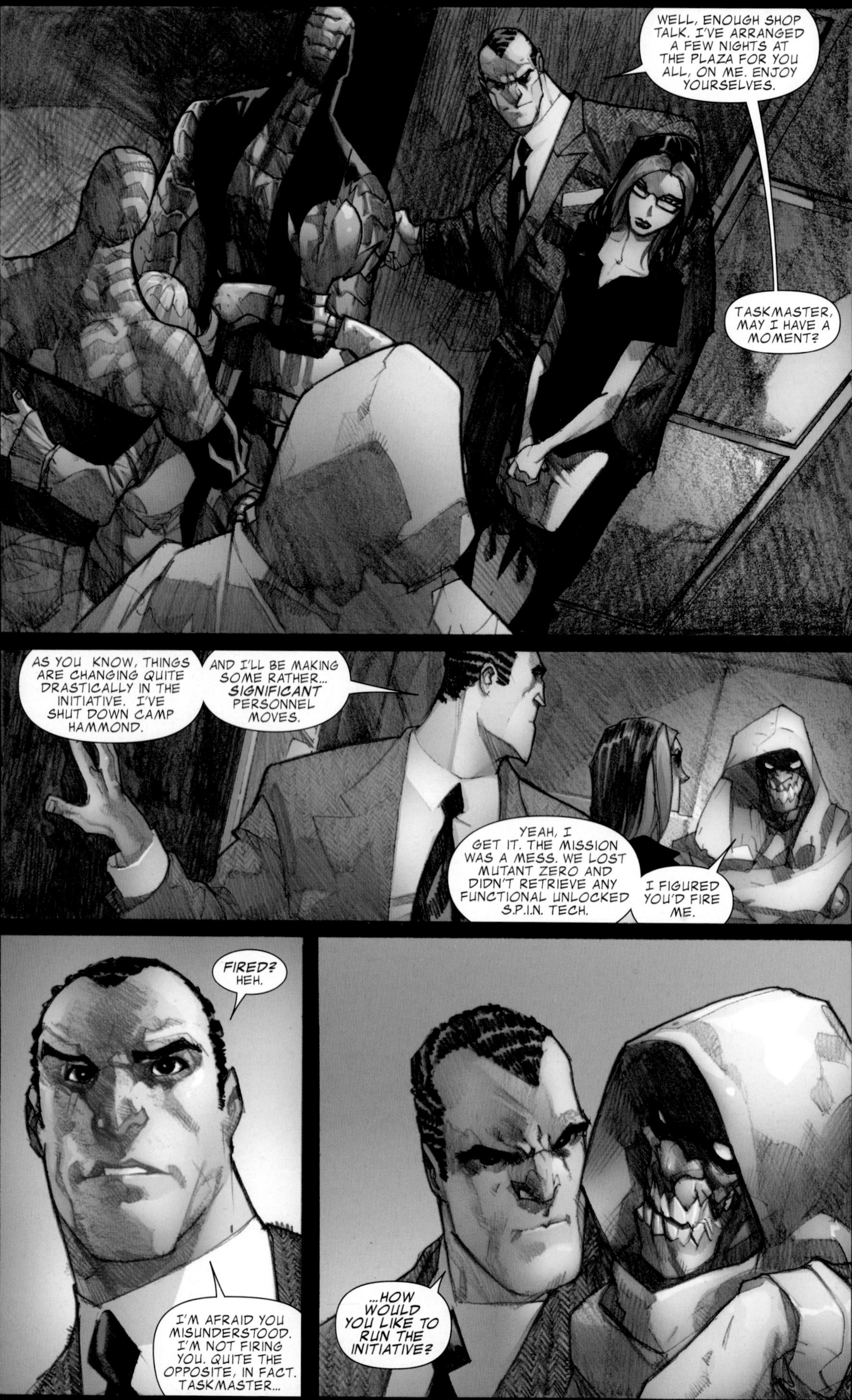
WELL, ENOUGH SHOP TALK. I'VE ARRANGED A FEW NIGHTS AT THE PLAZA FOR YOU ALL, ON ME. ENJOY YOURSELVES.
TASKMASTER, MAY I HAVE A MOMENT?
AS YOU KNOW, THINGS ARE CHANGING QUITE DRASTICALLY IN THE INITIATIVE. I'VE SHUT DOWN CAMP HAMMOND.
AND I'LL BE MAKING SOME RATHER... *SIGNIFICANT* PERSONNEL MOVES.
YEAH, I GET IT. THE MISSION WAS A MESS. WE LOST MUTANT ZERO AND DIDN'T RETRIEVE ANY FUNCTIONAL UNLOCKED S.P.I.N. TECH.
I FIGURED YOU'D FIRE ME.
FIRED? HEH.
I'M AFRAID YOU MISUNDERSTOOD. I'M NOT FIRING YOU. QUITE THE OPPOSITE, IN FACT. TASKMASTER...
...HOW *WOULD* YOU LIKE TO *RUN THE INITIATIVE?*

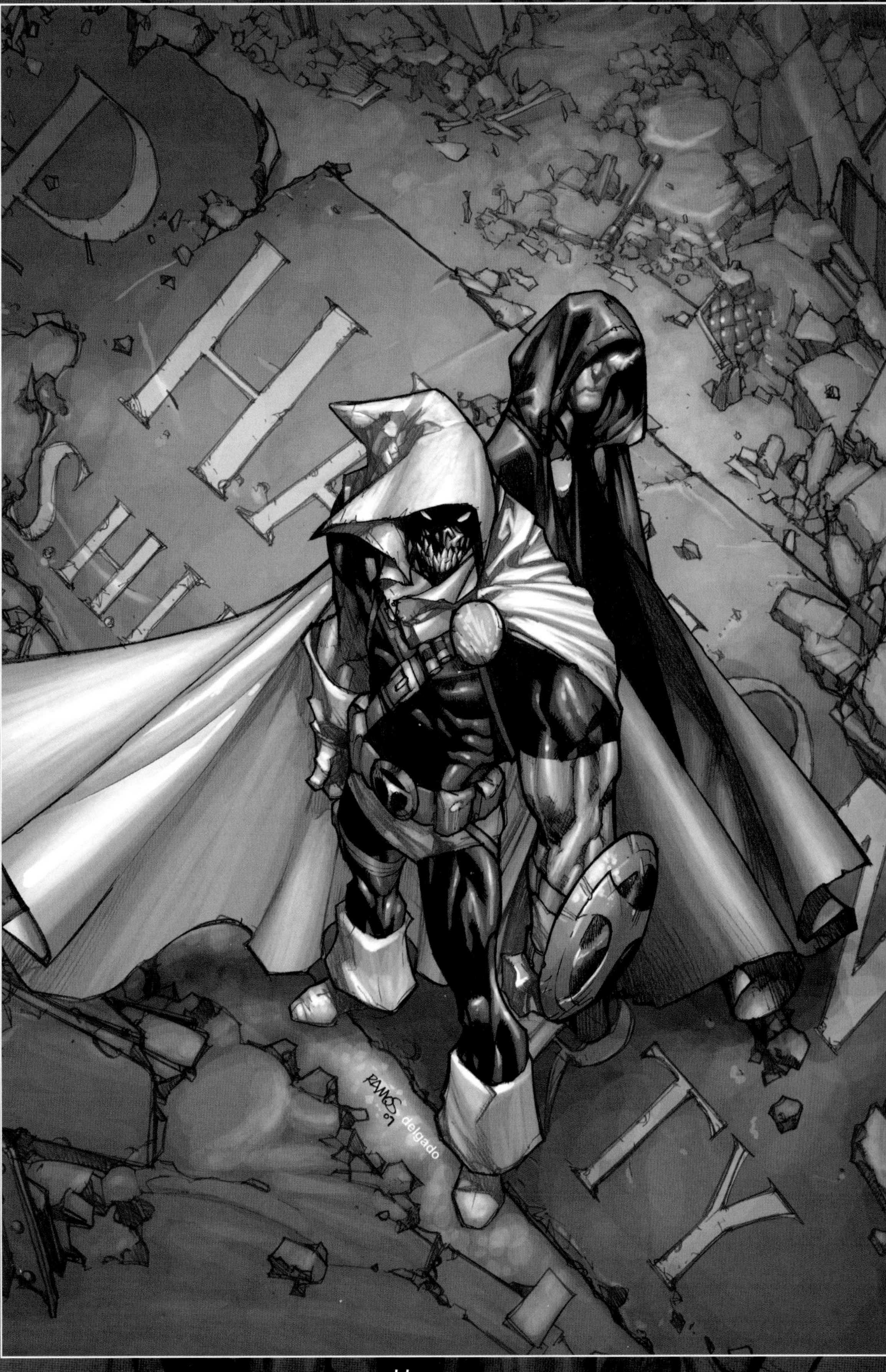

#25

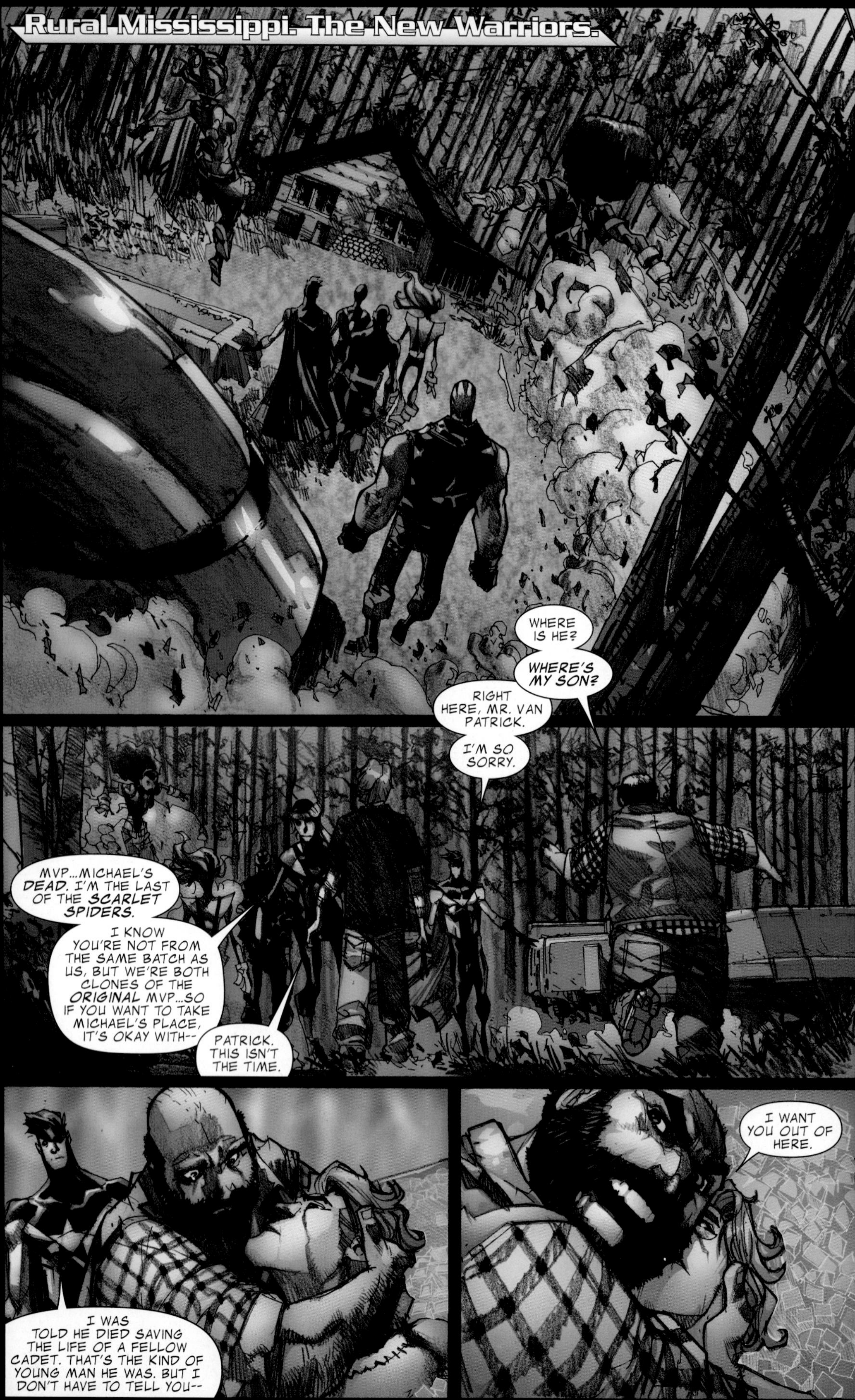
Rural Mississippi. The New Warriors.
WHERE IS HE?
WHERE'S MY SON?
RIGHT HERE, MR. VAN PATRICK.
I'M SO SORRY.
MVP...MICHAEL'S DEAD. I'M THE LAST OF THE SCARLET SPIDERS.
I KNOW YOU'RE NOT FROM THE SAME BATCH AS US, BUT WE'RE BOTH CLONES OF THE ORIGINAL MVP...SO IF YOU WANT TO TAKE MICHAEL'S PLACE, IT'S OKAY WITH--
PATRICK. THIS ISN'T THE TIME.
I WAS TOLD HE DIED SAVING THE LIFE OF A FELLOW CADET. THAT'S THE KIND OF YOUNG MAN HE WAS. BUT I DON'T HAVE TO TELL YOU--
I WANT YOU OUT OF HERE.

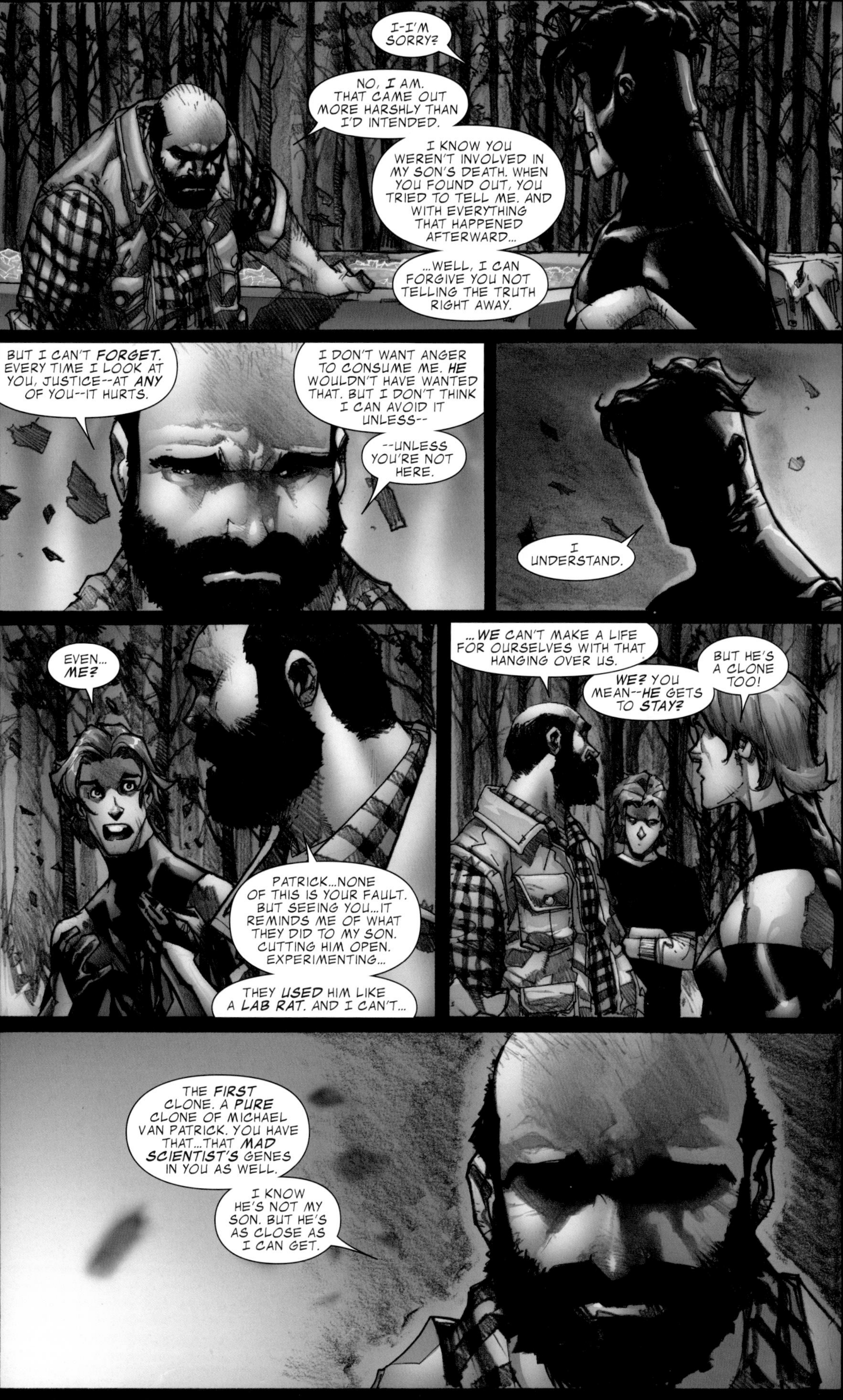
I-I'M SORRY?
NO, I AM. THAT CAME OUT MORE HARSHLY THAN I'D INTENDED.
I KNOW YOU WEREN'T INVOLVED IN MY SON'S DEATH. WHEN YOU FOUND OUT, YOU TRIED TO TELL ME. AND WITH EVERYTHING THAT HAPPENED AFTERWARD...
...WELL, I CAN FORGIVE YOU NOT TELLING THE TRUTH RIGHT AWAY.
BUT I CAN'T FORGET. EVERY TIME I LOOK AT YOU, JUSTICE--AT ANY OF YOU--IT HURTS.
I DON'T WANT ANGER TO CONSUME ME. HE WOULDN'T HAVE WANTED THAT. BUT I DON'T THINK I CAN AVOID IT UNLESS--
--UNLESS YOU'RE NOT HERE.
I UNDERSTAND.
EVEN... ME?
PATRICK...NONE OF THIS IS YOUR FAULT. BUT SEEING YOU...IT REMINDS ME OF WHAT THEY DID TO MY SON. CUTTING HIM OPEN. EXPERIMENTING...
THEY USED HIM LIKE A LAB RAT. AND I CAN'T...
...WE CAN'T MAKE A LIFE FOR OURSELVES WITH THAT HANGING OVER US.
WE? YOU MEAN--HE GETS TO STAY?
BUT HE'S A CLONE TOO!
THE FIRST CLONE. A PURE CLONE OF MICHAEL VAN PATRICK. YOU HAVE THAT...THAT MAD SCIENTIST'S GENES IN YOU AS WELL.
I KNOW HE'S NOT MY SON. BUT HE'S AS CLOSE AS I CAN GET.

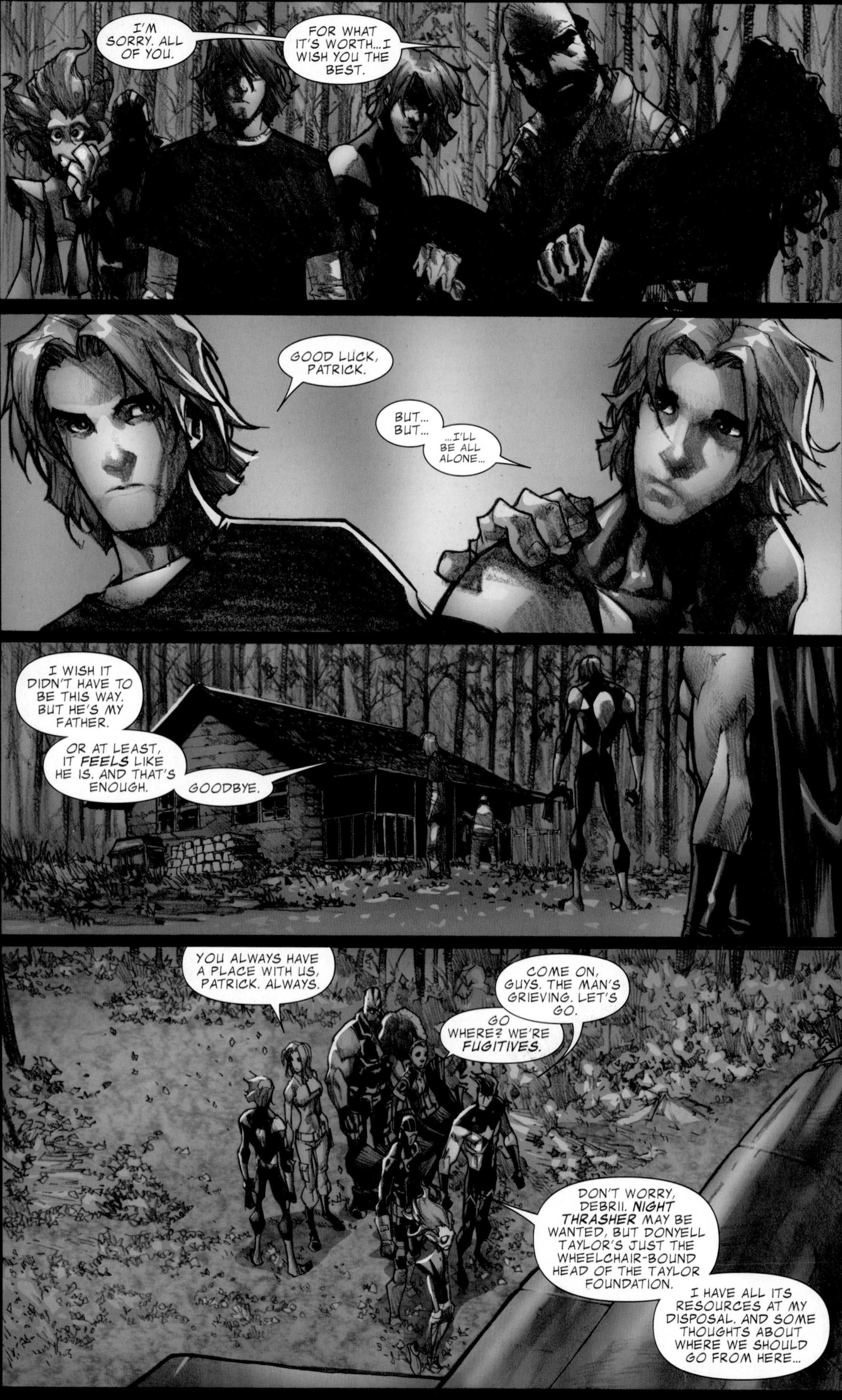

I'M SORRY. ALL OF YOU.
FOR WHAT IT'S WORTH...I WISH YOU THE BEST.
GOOD LUCK, PATRICK.
BUT... BUT...
...I'LL BE ALL ALONE...
I WISH IT DIDN'T HAVE TO BE THIS WAY. BUT HE'S MY FATHER.
OR AT LEAST, IT FEELS LIKE HE IS. AND THAT'S ENOUGH.
GOODBYE.
YOU ALWAYS HAVE A PLACE WITH US, PATRICK. ALWAYS.
COME ON, GUYS. THE MAN'S GRIEVING. LET'S GO.
GO WHERE? WE'RE FUGITIVES.
DON'T WORRY, DEBRII. NIGHT THRASHER MAY BE WANTED, BUT DONYELL TAYLOR'S JUST THE WHEELCHAIR-BOUND HEAD OF THE TAYLOR FOUNDATION.
I HAVE ALL ITS RESOURCES AT MY DISPOSAL. AND SOME THOUGHTS ABOUT WHERE WE SHOULD GO FROM HERE...

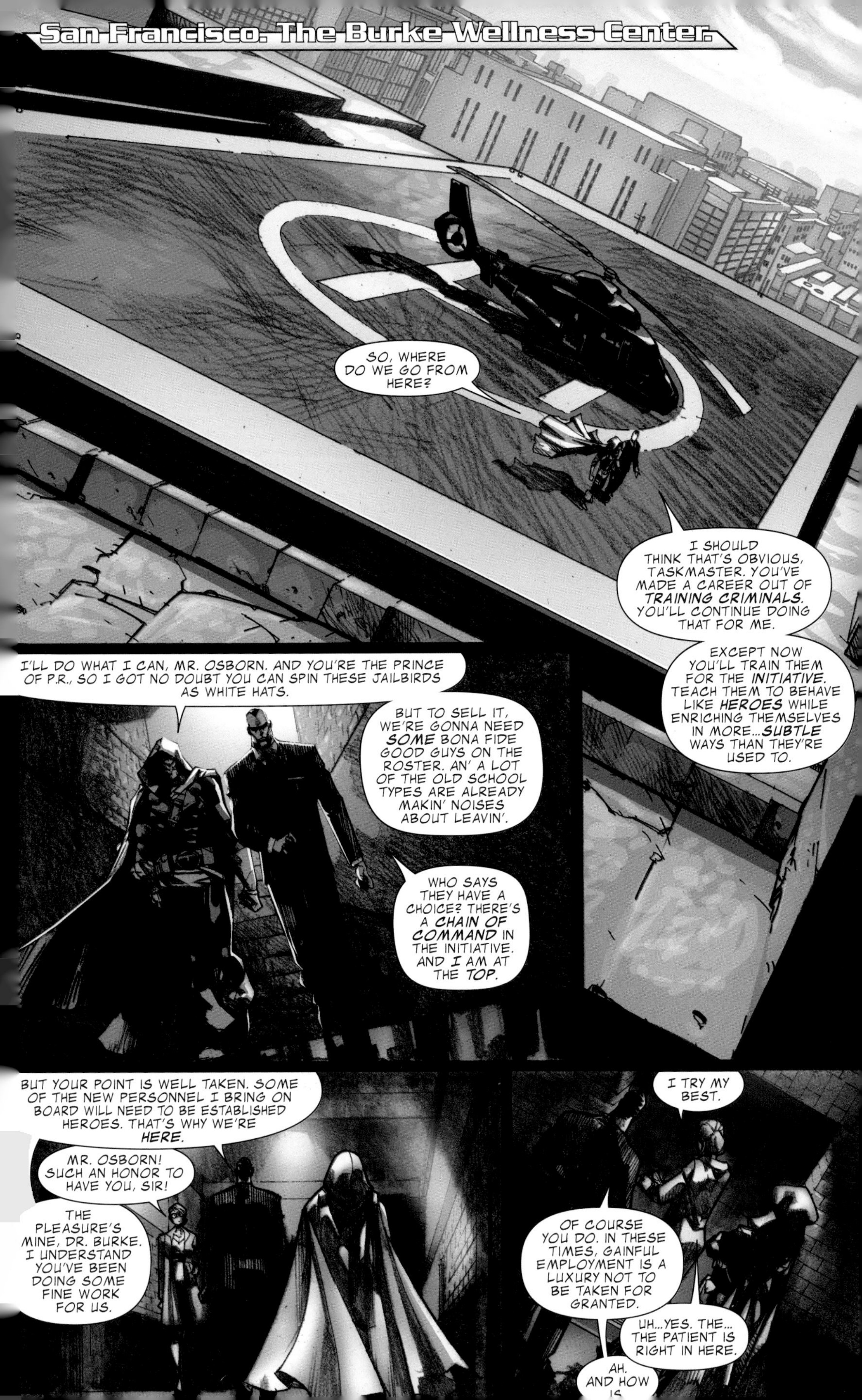
San Francisco. The Burke Wellness Center.
SO, WHERE DO WE GO FROM HERE?
I SHOULD THINK THAT'S OBVIOUS, TASKMASTER. YOU'VE MADE A CAREER OUT OF TRAINING CRIMINALS. YOU'LL CONTINUE DOING THAT FOR ME.
EXCEPT NOW YOU'LL TRAIN THEM FOR THE INITIATIVE. TEACH THEM TO BEHAVE LIKE HEROES WHILE ENRICHING THEMSELVES IN MORE...SUBTLE WAYS THAN THEY'RE USED TO.
I'LL DO WHAT I CAN, MR. OSBORN. AND YOU'RE THE PRINCE OF P.R., SO I GOT NO DOUBT YOU CAN SPIN THESE JAILBIRDS AS WHITE HATS.
BUT TO SELL IT, WE'RE GONNA NEED SOME BONA FIDE GOOD GUYS ON THE ROSTER. AN' A LOT OF THE OLD SCHOOL TYPES ARE ALREADY MAKIN' NOISES ABOUT LEAVIN'.
WHO SAYS THEY HAVE A CHOICE? THERE'S A CHAIN OF COMMAND IN THE INITIATIVE. AND I AM AT THE TOP.
BUT YOUR POINT IS WELL TAKEN. SOME OF THE NEW PERSONNEL I BRING ON BOARD WILL NEED TO BE ESTABLISHED HEROES. THAT'S WHY WE'RE HERE.
MR. OSBORN! SUCH AN HONOR TO HAVE YOU, SIR!
THE PLEASURE'S MINE, DR. BURKE. I UNDERSTAND YOU'VE BEEN DOING SOME FINE WORK FOR US.
I TRY MY BEST.
OF COURSE YOU DO. IN THESE TIMES, GAINFUL EMPLOYMENT IS A LUXURY NOT TO BE TAKEN FOR GRANTED.
UH...YES. THE... THE PATIENT IS RIGHT IN HERE.
AH. AND HOW

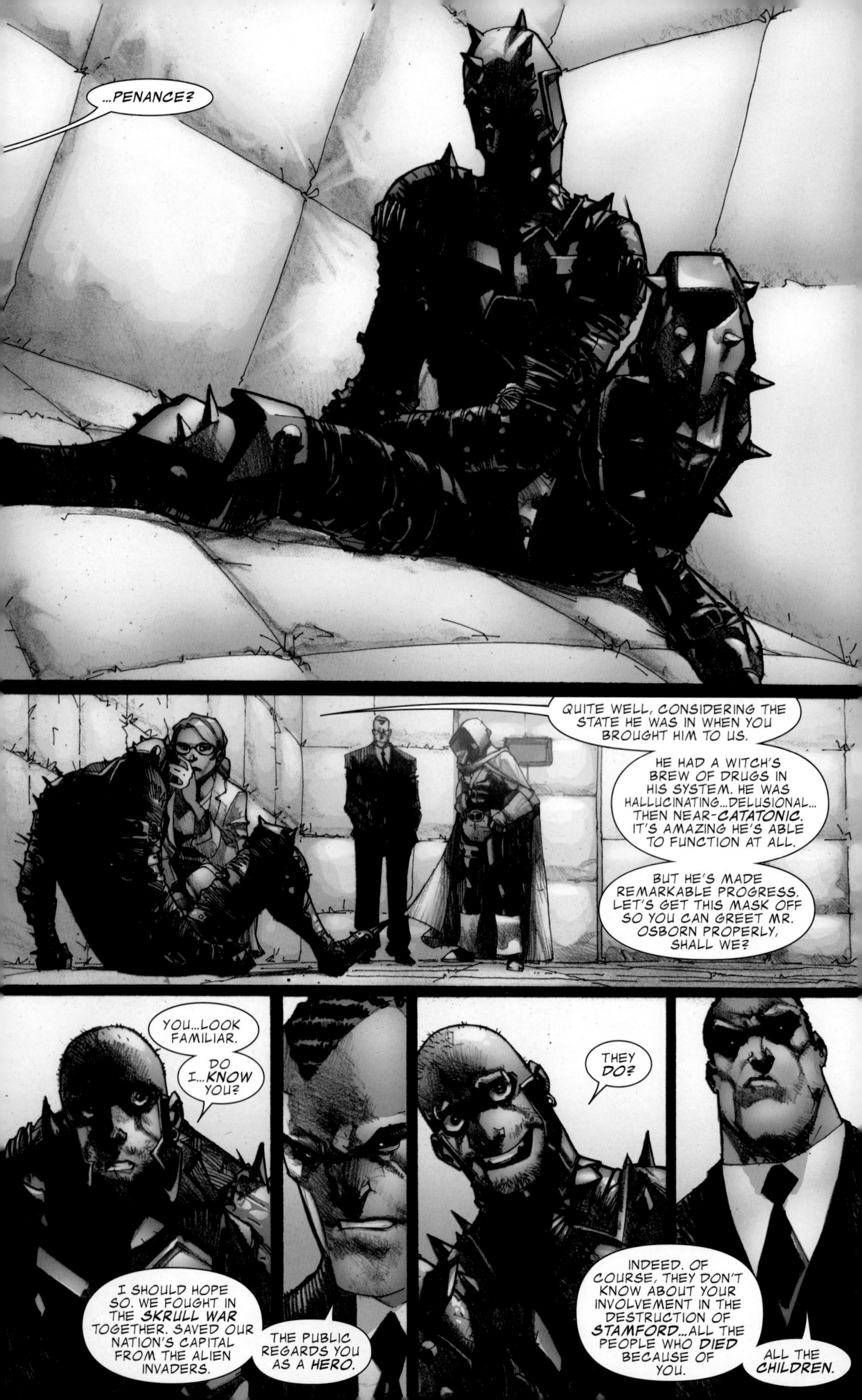
...PENANCE?
QUITE WELL, CONSIDERING THE STATE HE WAS IN WHEN YOU BROUGHT HIM TO US.
HE HAD A WITCH'S BREW OF DRUGS IN HIS SYSTEM. HE WAS HALLUCINATING...DELUSIONAL... THEN NEAR-CATATONIC. IT'S AMAZING HE'S ABLE TO FUNCTION AT ALL.
BUT HE'S MADE REMARKABLE PROGRESS. LET'S GET THIS MASK OFF SO YOU CAN GREET MR. OSBORN PROPERLY, SHALL WE?
YOU...LOOK FAMILIAR.
DO I...KNOW YOU?
I SHOULD HOPE SO. WE FOUGHT IN THE SKRULL WAR TOGETHER. SAVED OUR NATION'S CAPITAL FROM THE ALIEN INVADERS.
THE PUBLIC REGARDS YOU AS A HERO.
THEY DO?
INDEED. OF COURSE, THEY DON'T KNOW ABOUT YOUR INVOLVEMENT IN THE DESTRUCTION OF STAMFORD...ALL THE PEOPLE WHO DIED BECAUSE OF YOU.
ALL THE CHILDREN.

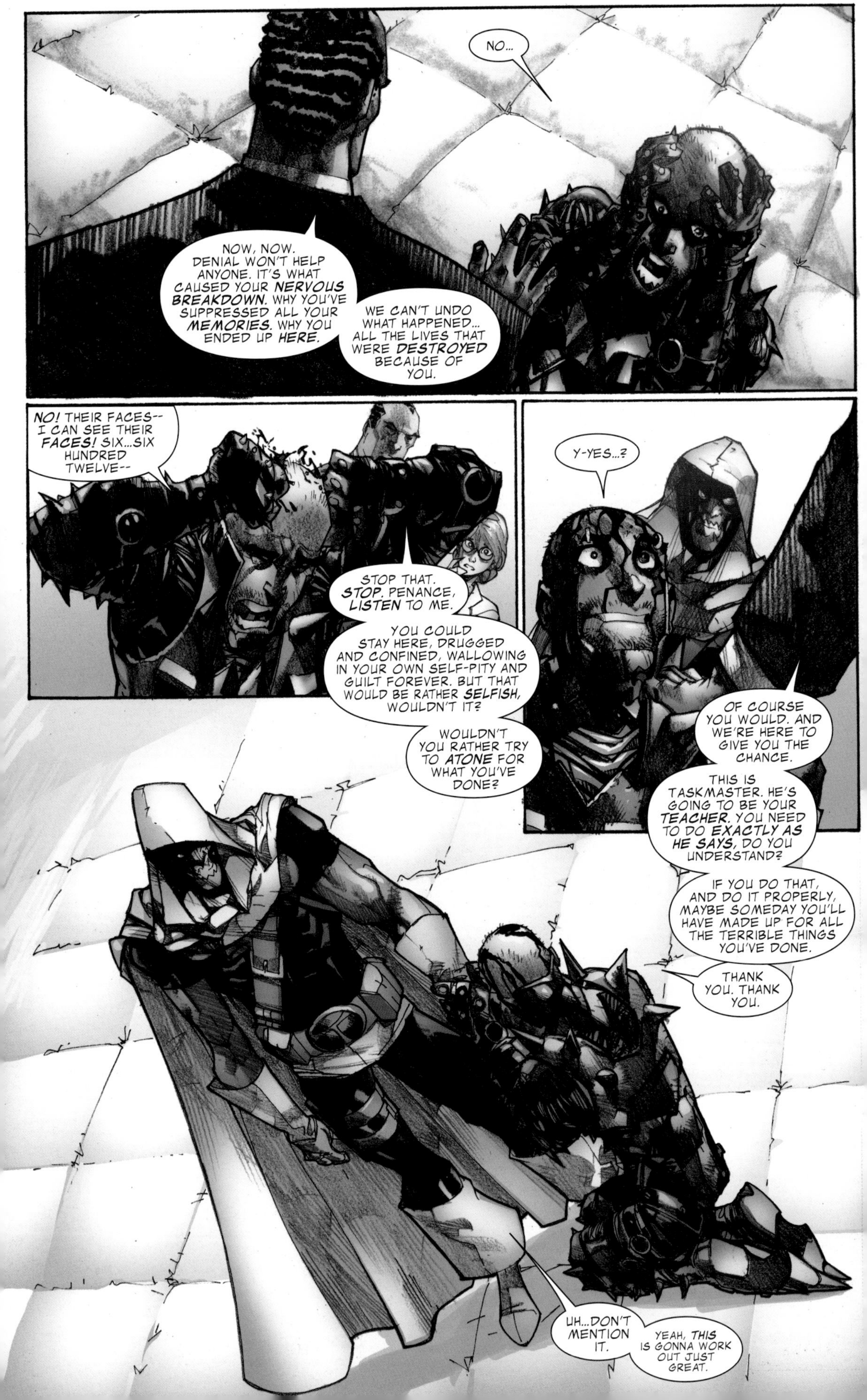
NO...
NOW, NOW. DENIAL WON'T HELP ANYONE. IT'S WHAT CAUSED YOUR NERVOUS BREAKDOWN. WHY YOU'VE SUPPRESSED ALL YOUR MEMORIES. WHY YOU ENDED UP HERE.
WE CAN'T UNDO WHAT HAPPENED... ALL THE LIVES THAT WERE DESTROYED BECAUSE OF YOU.
NO! THEIR FACES-- I CAN SEE THEIR FACES! SIX...SIX HUNDRED TWELVE--
STOP THAT. STOP. PENANCE, LISTEN TO ME.
YOU COULD STAY HERE, DRUGGED AND CONFINED, WALLOWING IN YOUR OWN SELF-PITY AND GUILT FOREVER. BUT THAT WOULD BE RATHER SELFISH, WOULDN'T IT?
WOULDN'T YOU RATHER TRY TO ATONE FOR WHAT YOU'VE DONE?
Y-YES...?
OF COURSE YOU WOULD. AND WE'RE HERE TO GIVE YOU THE CHANCE.
THIS IS TASKMASTER. HE'S GOING TO BE YOUR TEACHER. YOU NEED TO DO EXACTLY AS HE SAYS, DO YOU UNDERSTAND?
IF YOU DO THAT, AND DO IT PROPERLY, MAYBE SOMEDAY YOU'LL HAVE MADE UP FOR ALL THE TERRIBLE THINGS YOU'VE DONE.
THANK YOU. THANK YOU.
UH...DON'T MENTION IT.
YEAH, THIS IS GONNA WORK OUT JUST GREAT.

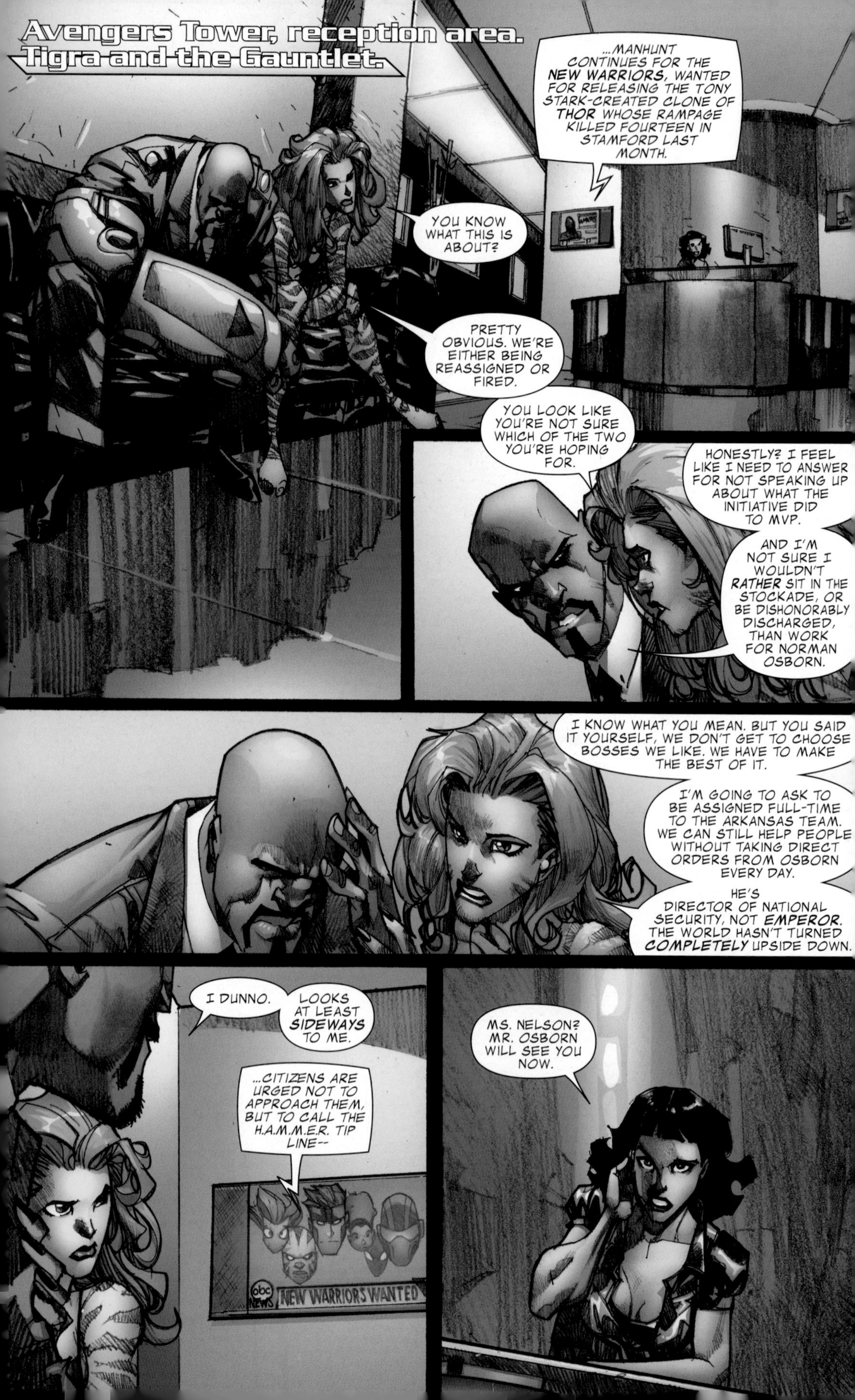
Avengers Tower, reception area.
Tigra and the Gauntlet.
...MANHUNT CONTINUES FOR THE NEW WARRIORS, WANTED FOR RELEASING THE TONY STARK-CREATED CLONE OF THOR WHOSE RAMPAGE KILLED FOURTEEN IN STAMFORD LAST MONTH.
YOU KNOW WHAT THIS IS ABOUT?
PRETTY OBVIOUS. WE'RE EITHER BEING REASSIGNED OR FIRED.
YOU LOOK LIKE YOU'RE NOT SURE WHICH OF THE TWO YOU'RE HOPING FOR.
HONESTLY? I FEEL LIKE I NEED TO ANSWER FOR NOT SPEAKING UP ABOUT WHAT THE INITIATIVE DID TO MVP.
AND I'M NOT SURE I WOULDN'T RATHER SIT IN THE STOCKADE, OR BE DISHONORABLY DISCHARGED, THAN WORK FOR NORMAN OSBORN.
I KNOW WHAT YOU MEAN. BUT YOU SAID IT YOURSELF, WE DON'T GET TO CHOOSE BOSSES WE LIKE. WE HAVE TO MAKE THE BEST OF IT.
I'M GOING TO ASK TO BE ASSIGNED FULL-TIME TO THE ARKANSAS TEAM. WE CAN STILL HELP PEOPLE WITHOUT TAKING DIRECT ORDERS FROM OSBORN EVERY DAY.
HE'S DIRECTOR OF NATIONAL SECURITY, NOT EMPEROR. THE WORLD HASN'T TURNED COMPLETELY UPSIDE DOWN.
I DUNNO.
LOOKS AT LEAST SIDEWAYS TO ME.
...CITIZENS ARE URGED NOT TO APPROACH THEM, BUT TO CALL THE H.A.M.M.E.R. TIP LINE--
NEW WARRIORS WANTED
MS. NELSON? MR. OSBORN WILL SEE YOU NOW.

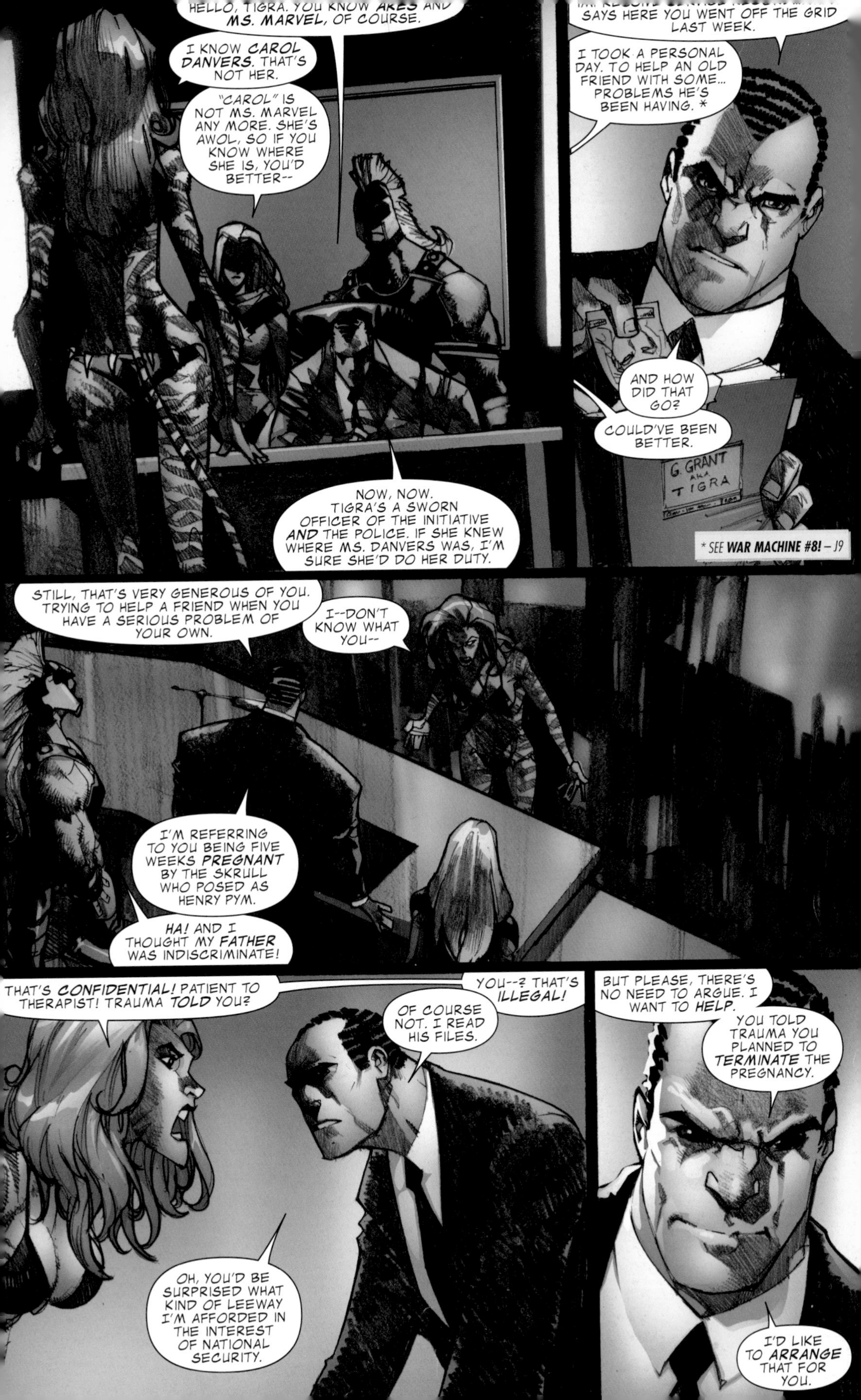
HELLO, TIGRA. YOU KNOW ARES AND MS. MARVEL, OF COURSE.
I KNOW CAROL DANVERS. THAT'S NOT HER.
"CAROL" IS NOT MS. MARVEL ANY MORE. SHE'S AWOL, SO IF YOU KNOW WHERE SHE IS, YOU'D BETTER--
NOW, NOW. TIGRA'S A SWORN OFFICER OF THE INITIATIVE AND THE POLICE. IF SHE KNEW WHERE MS. DANVERS WAS, I'M SURE SHE'D DO HER DUTY.
SAYS HERE YOU WENT OFF THE GRID LAST WEEK.
I TOOK A PERSONAL DAY. TO HELP AN OLD FRIEND WITH SOME... PROBLEMS HE'S BEEN HAVING. *
AND HOW DID THAT GO?
COULD'VE BEEN BETTER.
G. GRANT AKA TIGRA
* SEE WAR MACHINE #8! – J9
STILL, THAT'S VERY GENEROUS OF YOU. TRYING TO HELP A FRIEND WHEN YOU HAVE A SERIOUS PROBLEM OF YOUR OWN.
I--DON'T KNOW WHAT YOU--
I'M REFERRING TO YOU BEING FIVE WEEKS PREGNANT BY THE SKRULL WHO POSED AS HENRY PYM.
HA! AND I THOUGHT MY FATHER WAS INDISCRIMINATE!
THAT'S CONFIDENTIAL! PATIENT TO THERAPIST! TRAUMA TOLD YOU?
YOU--? THAT'S ILLEGAL!
OF COURSE NOT. I READ HIS FILES.
OH, YOU'D BE SURPRISED WHAT KIND OF LEEWAY I'M AFFORDED IN THE INTEREST OF NATIONAL SECURITY.
BUT PLEASE, THERE'S NO NEED TO ARGUE. I WANT TO HELP.
YOU TOLD TRAUMA YOU PLANNED TO TERMINATE THE PREGNANCY.
I'D LIKE TO ARRANGE THAT FOR YOU.

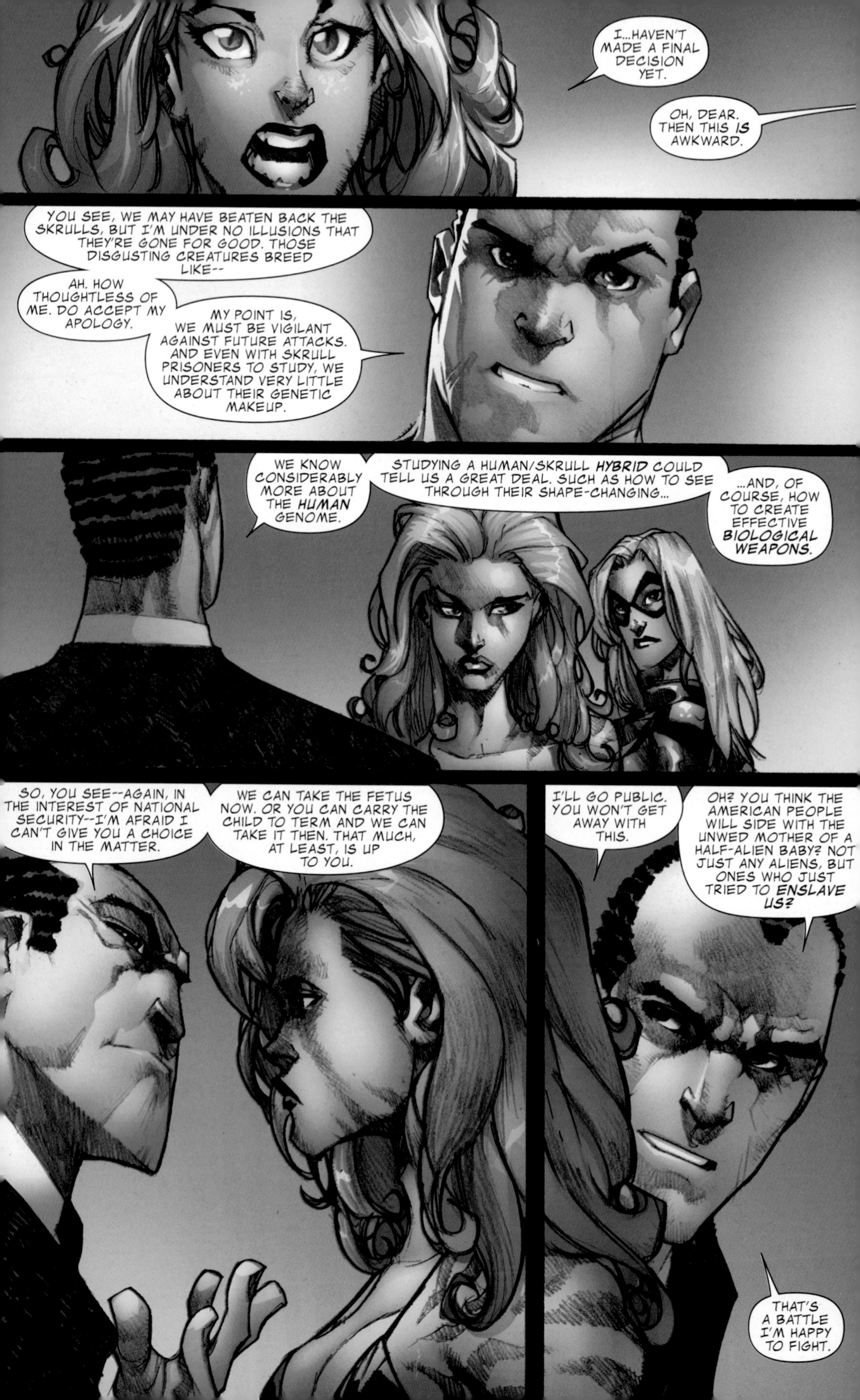
I...HAVEN'T MADE A FINAL DECISION YET.
OH, DEAR. THEN THIS **IS** AWKWARD.
YOU SEE, WE MAY HAVE BEATEN BACK THE SKRULLS, BUT I'M UNDER NO ILLUSIONS THAT THEY'RE GONE FOR GOOD. THOSE DISGUSTING CREATURES BREED LIKE--
AH. HOW THOUGHTLESS OF ME. DO ACCEPT MY APOLOGY.
MY POINT IS, WE MUST BE VIGILANT AGAINST FUTURE ATTACKS. AND EVEN WITH SKRULL PRISONERS TO STUDY, WE UNDERSTAND VERY LITTLE ABOUT THEIR GENETIC MAKEUP.
WE KNOW CONSIDERABLY MORE ABOUT THE **HUMAN** GENOME.
STUDYING A HUMAN/SKRULL **HYBRID** COULD TELL US A GREAT DEAL. SUCH AS HOW TO SEE THROUGH THEIR SHAPE-CHANGING...
...AND, OF COURSE, HOW TO CREATE EFFECTIVE **BIOLOGICAL WEAPONS**.
SO, YOU SEE--AGAIN, IN THE INTEREST OF NATIONAL SECURITY--I'M AFRAID I CAN'T GIVE YOU A CHOICE IN THE MATTER.
WE CAN TAKE THE FETUS NOW. OR YOU CAN CARRY THE CHILD TO TERM AND WE CAN TAKE IT THEN. THAT MUCH, AT LEAST, IS UP TO YOU.
I'LL GO PUBLIC. YOU WON'T GET AWAY WITH THIS.
OH? YOU THINK THE AMERICAN PEOPLE WILL SIDE WITH THE UNWED MOTHER OF A HALF-ALIEN BABY? NOT JUST ANY ALIENS, BUT ONES WHO JUST TRIED TO **ENSLAVE US?**
THAT'S A BATTLE I'M HAPPY TO FIGHT.

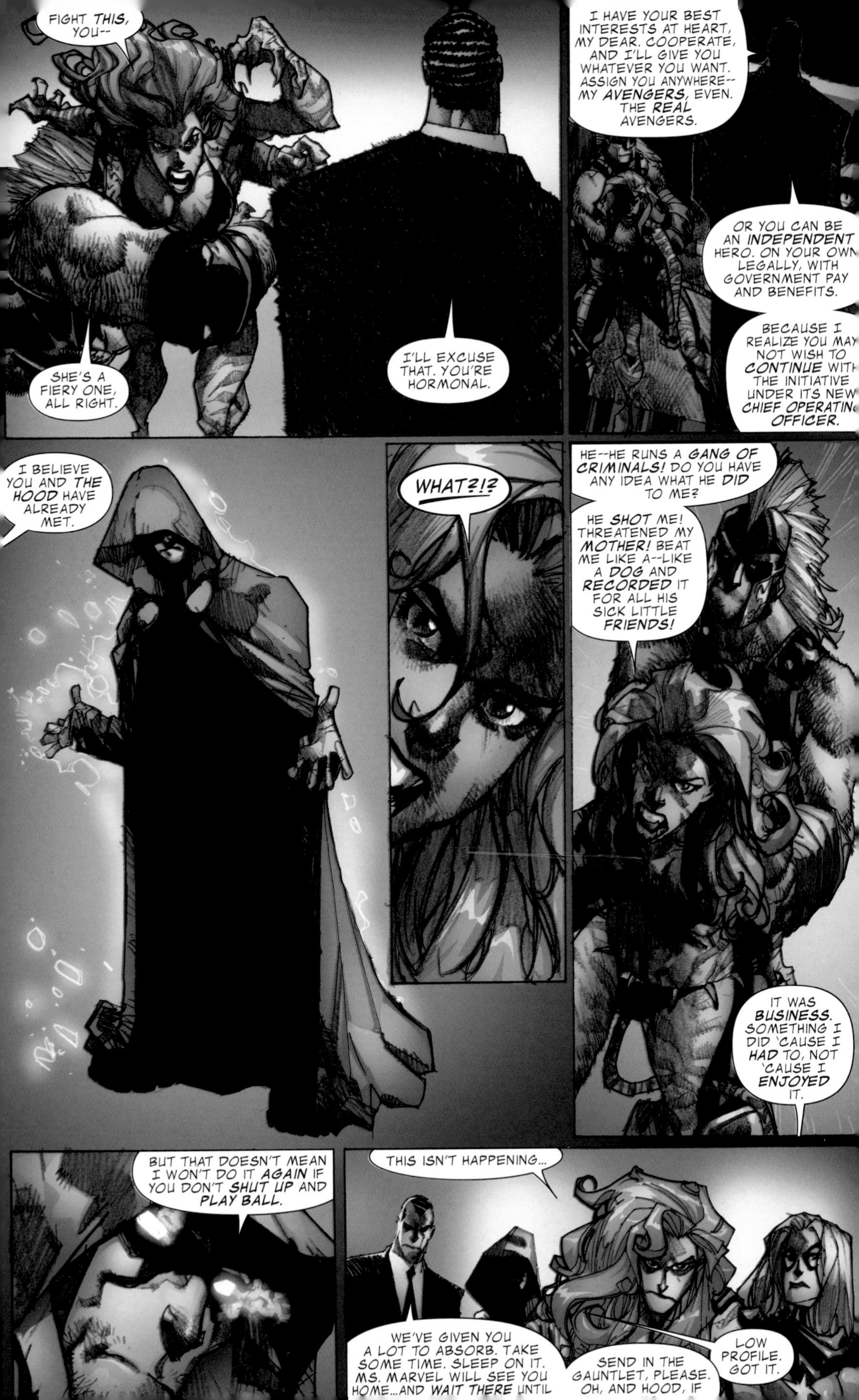
FIGHT THIS, YOU--
I HAVE YOUR BEST INTERESTS AT HEART, MY DEAR. COOPERATE, AND I'LL GIVE YOU WHATEVER YOU WANT. ASSIGN YOU ANYWHERE-- MY AVENGERS, EVEN. THE REAL AVENGERS.
SHE'S A FIERY ONE, ALL RIGHT.
I'LL EXCUSE THAT. YOU'RE HORMONAL.
OR YOU CAN BE AN INDEPENDENT HERO. ON YOUR OWN LEGALLY, WITH GOVERNMENT PAY AND BENEFITS.
BECAUSE I REALIZE YOU MAY NOT WISH TO CONTINUE WITH THE INITIATIVE UNDER ITS NEW CHIEF OPERATING OFFICER.
I BELIEVE YOU AND THE HOOD HAVE ALREADY MET.
WHAT?!?
HE--HE RUNS A GANG OF CRIMINALS! DO YOU HAVE ANY IDEA WHAT HE DID TO ME?
HE SHOT ME! THREATENED MY MOTHER! BEAT ME LIKE A--LIKE A DOG AND RECORDED IT FOR ALL HIS SICK LITTLE FRIENDS!
IT WAS BUSINESS. SOMETHING I DID 'CAUSE I HAD TO, NOT 'CAUSE I ENJOYED IT.
BUT THAT DOESN'T MEAN I WON'T DO IT AGAIN IF YOU DON'T SHUT UP AND PLAY BALL.
THIS ISN'T HAPPENING...
WE'VE GIVEN YOU A LOT TO ABSORB. TAKE SOME TIME. SLEEP ON IT. MS. MARVEL WILL SEE YOU HOME...AND WAIT THERE UNTIL
SEND IN THE GAUNTLET, PLEASE. OH, AND HOOD, IF
LOW PROFILE. GOT IT.

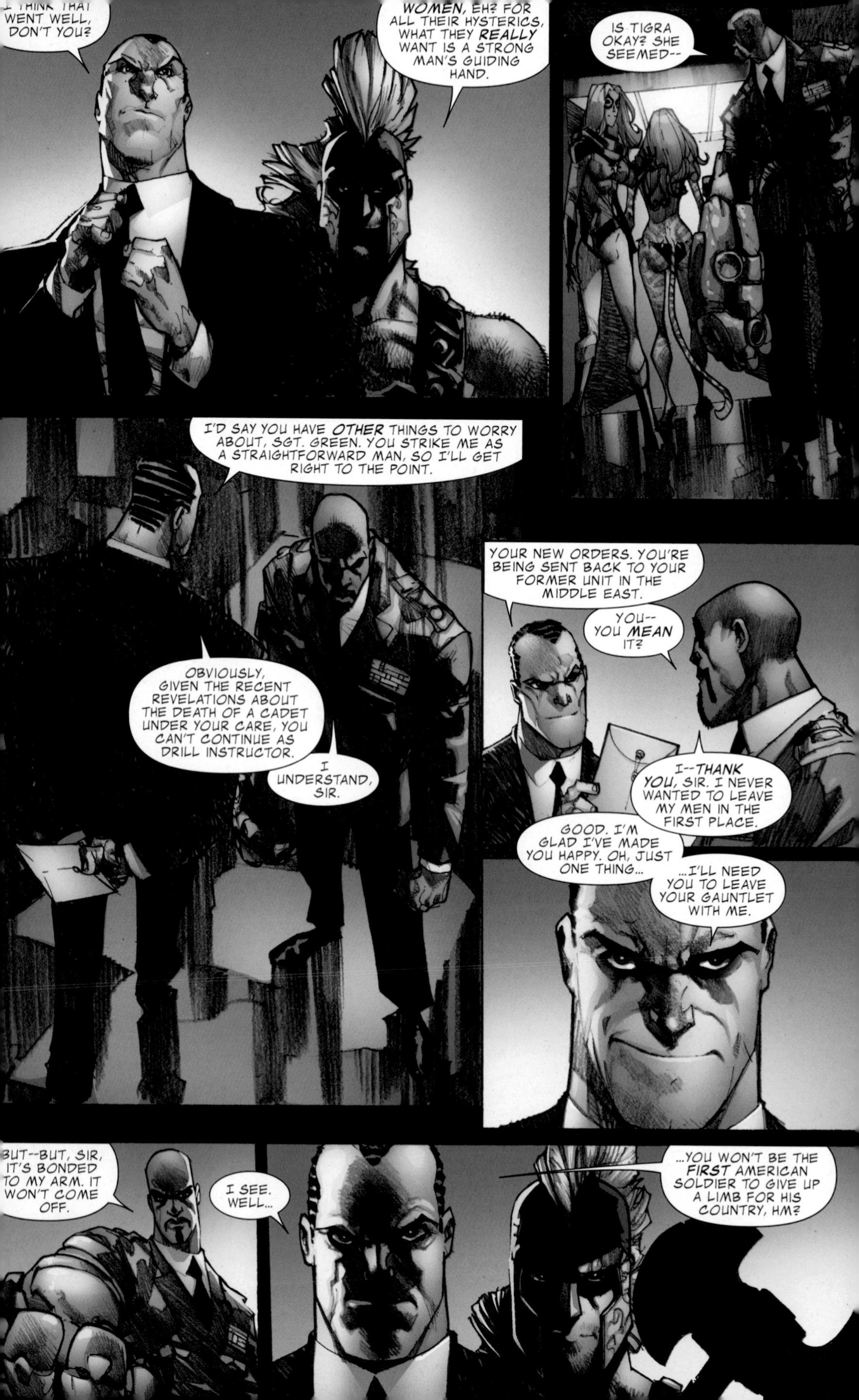
I THINK THAT WENT WELL, DON'T YOU?
WOMEN, EH? FOR ALL THEIR HYSTERICS, WHAT THEY REALLY WANT IS A STRONG MAN'S GUIDING HAND.
IS TIGRA OKAY? SHE SEEMED--
I'D SAY YOU HAVE OTHER THINGS TO WORRY ABOUT, SGT. GREEN. YOU STRIKE ME AS A STRAIGHTFORWARD MAN, SO I'LL GET RIGHT TO THE POINT.
OBVIOUSLY, GIVEN THE RECENT REVELATIONS ABOUT THE DEATH OF A CADET UNDER YOUR CARE, YOU CAN'T CONTINUE AS DRILL INSTRUCTOR.
I UNDERSTAND, SIR.
YOUR NEW ORDERS. YOU'RE BEING SENT BACK TO YOUR FORMER UNIT IN THE MIDDLE EAST.
YOU-- YOU MEAN IT?
I--THANK YOU, SIR. I NEVER WANTED TO LEAVE MY MEN IN THE FIRST PLACE.
GOOD. I'M GLAD I'VE MADE YOU HAPPY. OH, JUST ONE THING...
...I'LL NEED YOU TO LEAVE YOUR GAUNTLET WITH ME.
BUT--BUT, SIR, IT'S BONDED TO MY ARM. IT WON'T COME OFF.
I SEE. WELL...
...YOU WON'T BE THE FIRST AMERICAN SOLDIER TO GIVE UP A LIMB FOR HIS COUNTRY, HM?

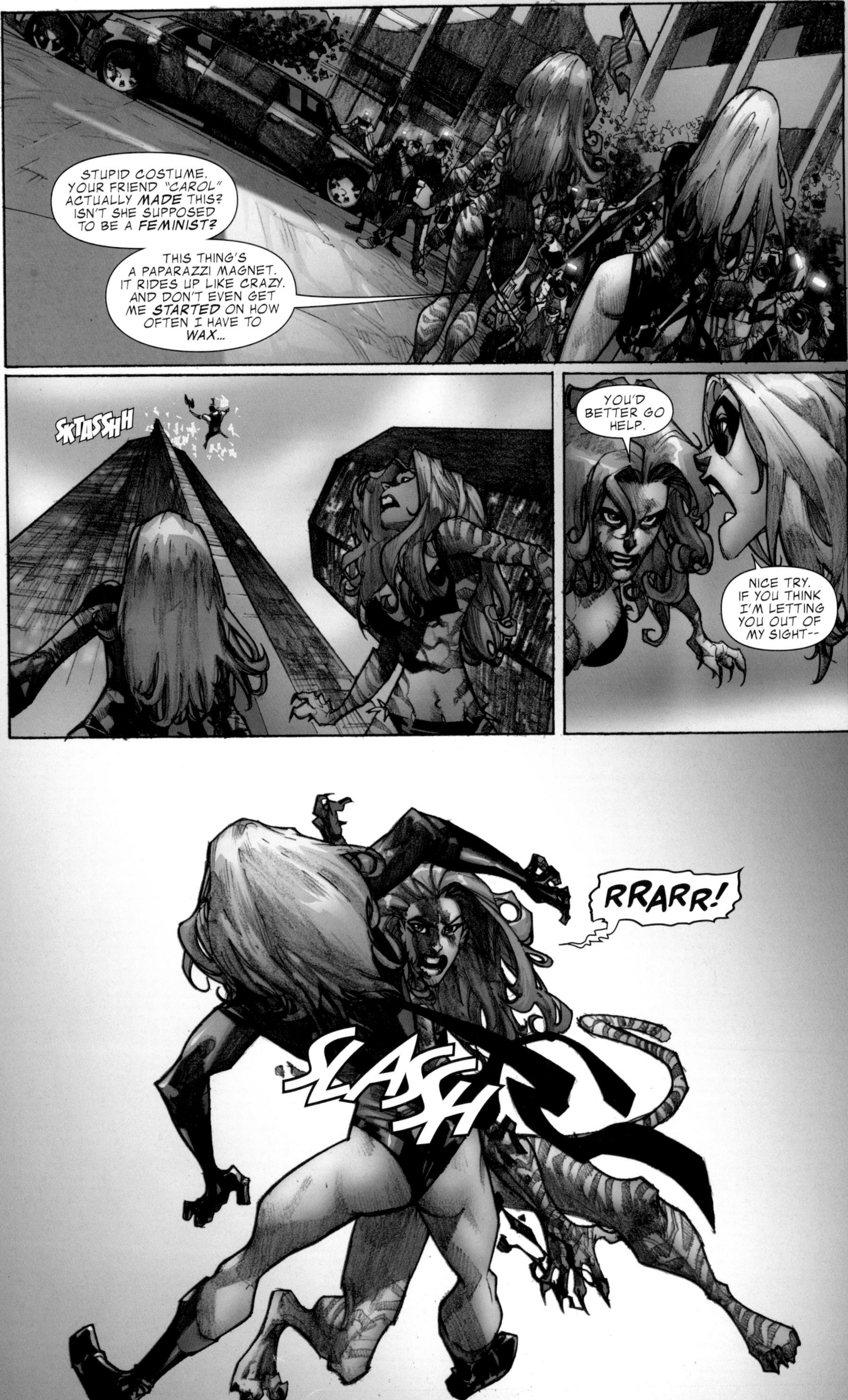
STUPID COSTUME. YOUR FRIEND "CAROL" ACTUALLY MADE THIS? ISN'T SHE SUPPOSED TO BE A FEMINIST?
THIS THING'S A PAPARAZZI MAGNET. IT RIDES UP LIKE CRAZY. AND DON'T EVEN GET ME STARTED ON HOW OFTEN I HAVE TO WAX...
SKTASSHH
YOU'D BETTER GO HELP.
NICE TRY. IF YOU THINK I'M LETTING YOU OUT OF MY SIGHT--
RRARR!
SLASH

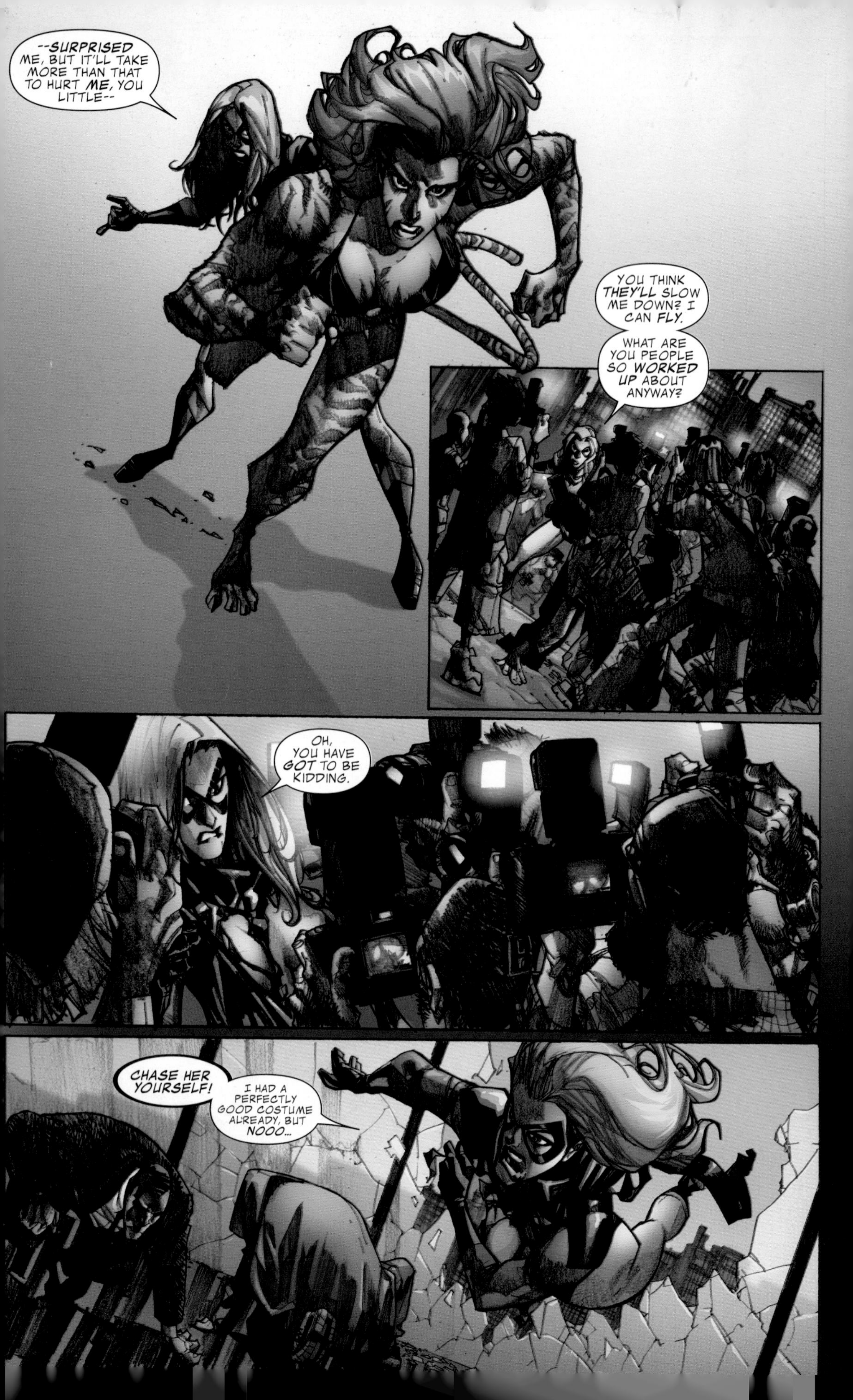
--SURPRISED ME, BUT IT'LL TAKE MORE THAN THAT TO HURT ME, YOU LITTLE--
YOU THINK THEY'LL SLOW ME DOWN? I CAN FLY.
WHAT ARE YOU PEOPLE SO WORKED UP ABOUT ANYWAY?
OH, YOU HAVE GOT TO BE KIDDING.
CHASE HER YOURSELF!
I HAD A PERFECTLY GOOD COSTUME ALREADY, BUT NOOO...

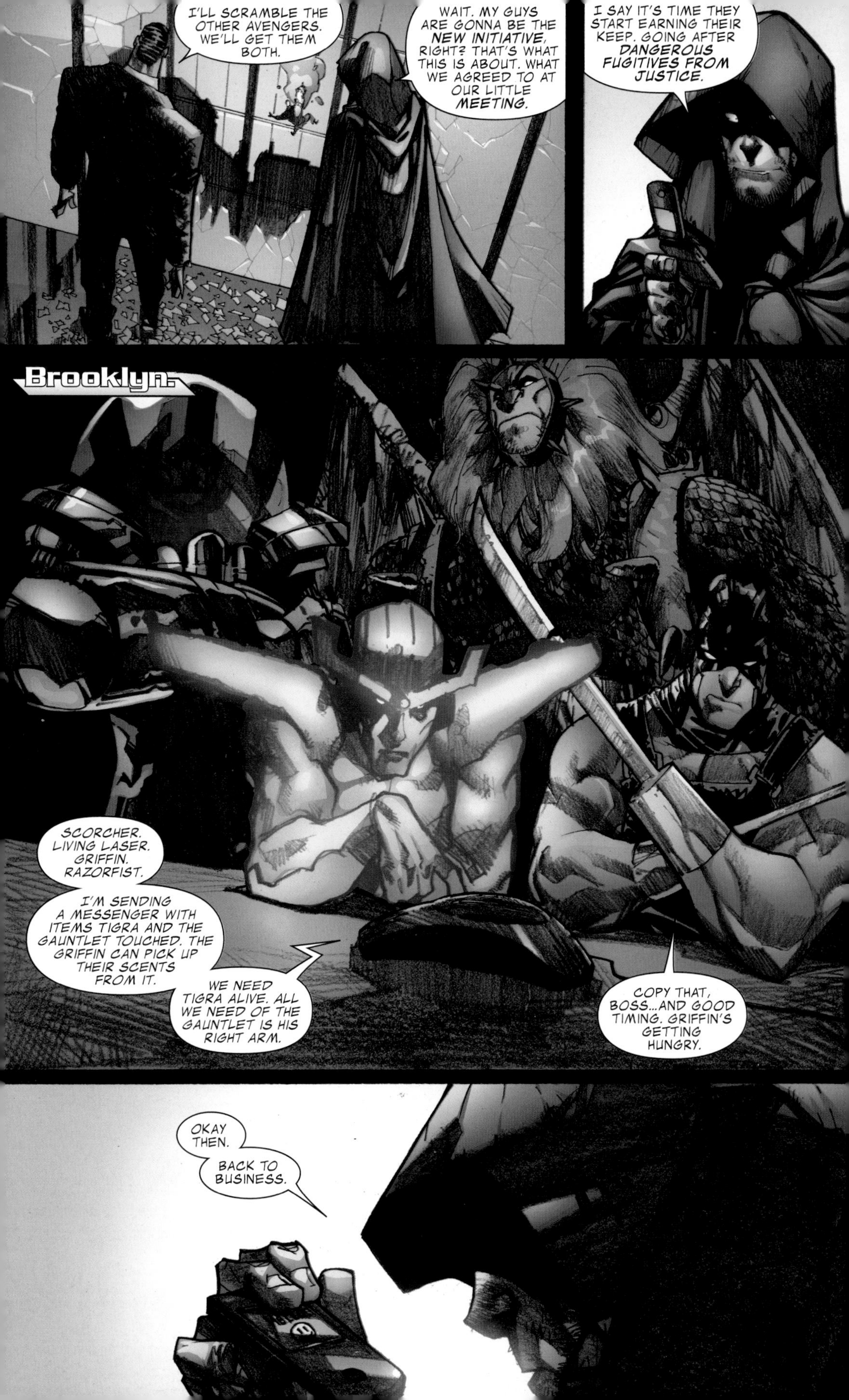
I'LL SCRAMBLE THE OTHER AVENGERS. WE'LL GET THEM BOTH.
WAIT. MY GUYS ARE GONNA BE THE NEW INITIATIVE, RIGHT? THAT'S WHAT THIS IS ABOUT. WHAT WE AGREED TO AT OUR LITTLE MEETING.
I SAY IT'S TIME THEY START EARNING THEIR KEEP. GOING AFTER DANGEROUS FUGITIVES FROM JUSTICE.
Brooklyn.
SCORCHER. LIVING LASER. GRIFFIN. RAZORFIST.
I'M SENDING A MESSENGER WITH ITEMS TIGRA AND THE GAUNTLET TOUCHED. THE GRIFFIN CAN PICK UP THEIR SCENTS FROM IT.
WE NEED TIGRA ALIVE. ALL WE NEED OF THE GAUNTLET IS HIS RIGHT ARM.
COPY THAT, BOSS...AND GOOD TIMING. GRIFFIN'S GETTING HUNGRY.
OKAY THEN.
BACK TO BUSINESS.

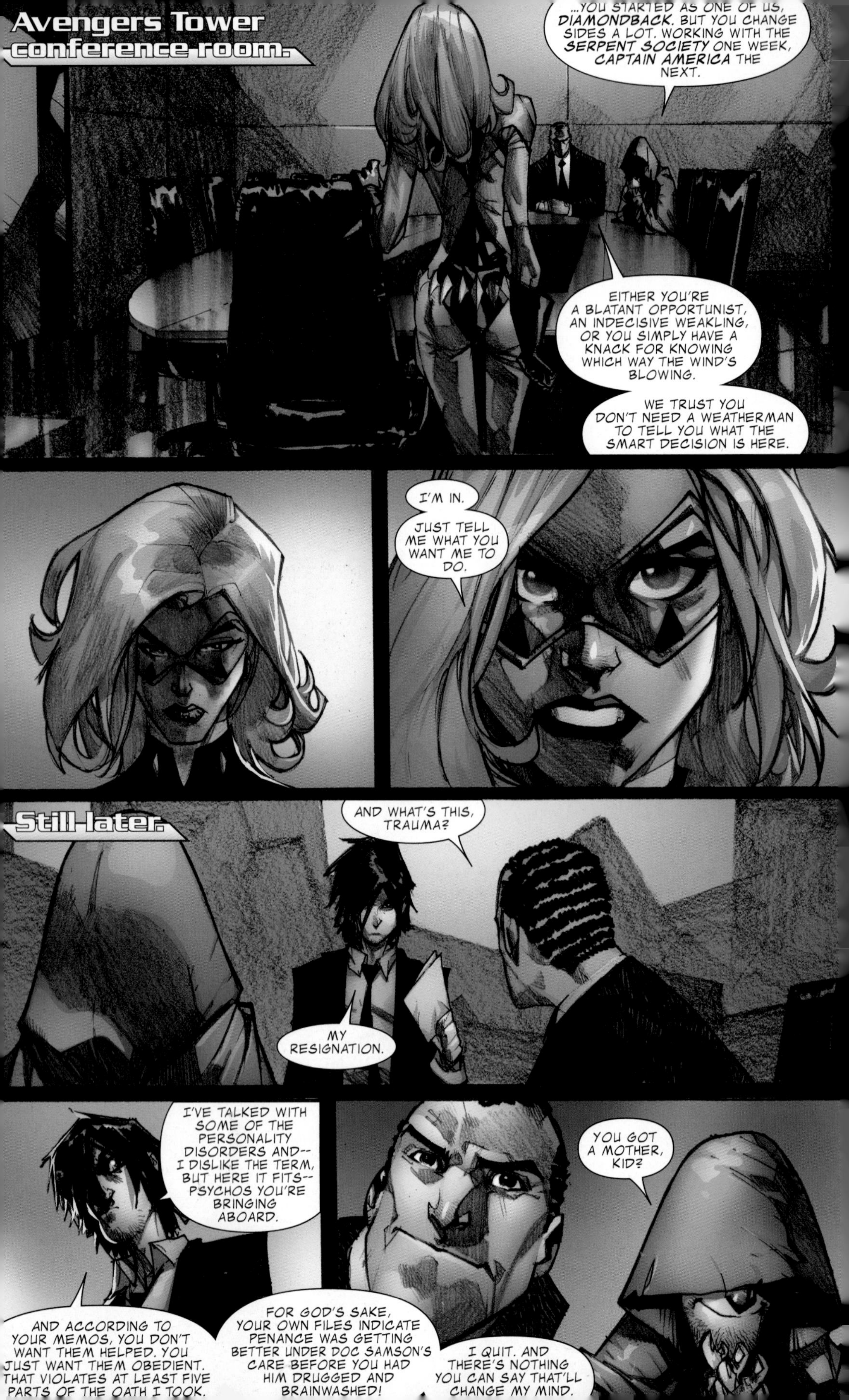
Avengers Tower conference room.
...YOU STARTED AS ONE OF US, DIAMONDBACK. BUT YOU CHANGE SIDES A LOT. WORKING WITH THE SERPENT SOCIETY ONE WEEK, CAPTAIN AMERICA THE NEXT.
EITHER YOU'RE A BLATANT OPPORTUNIST, AN INDECISIVE WEAKLING, OR YOU SIMPLY HAVE A KNACK FOR KNOWING WHICH WAY THE WIND'S BLOWING.
WE TRUST YOU DON'T NEED A WEATHERMAN TO TELL YOU WHAT THE SMART DECISION IS HERE.
I'M IN.
JUST TELL ME WHAT YOU WANT ME TO DO.
Still later.
AND WHAT'S THIS, TRAUMA?
MY RESIGNATION.
I'VE TALKED WITH SOME OF THE PERSONALITY DISORDERS AND-- I DISLIKE THE TERM, BUT HERE IT FITS-- PSYCHOS YOU'RE BRINGING ABOARD.
AND ACCORDING TO YOUR MEMOS, YOU DON'T WANT THEM HELPED. YOU JUST WANT THEM OBEDIENT. THAT VIOLATES AT LEAST FIVE PARTS OF THE OATH I TOOK.
FOR GOD'S SAKE, YOUR OWN FILES INDICATE PENANCE WAS GETTING BETTER UNDER DOC SAMSON'S CARE BEFORE YOU HAD HIM DRUGGED AND BRAINWASHED!
I QUIT. AND THERE'S NOTHING YOU CAN SAY THAT'LL CHANGE MY MIND.
YOU GOT A MOTHER, KID?

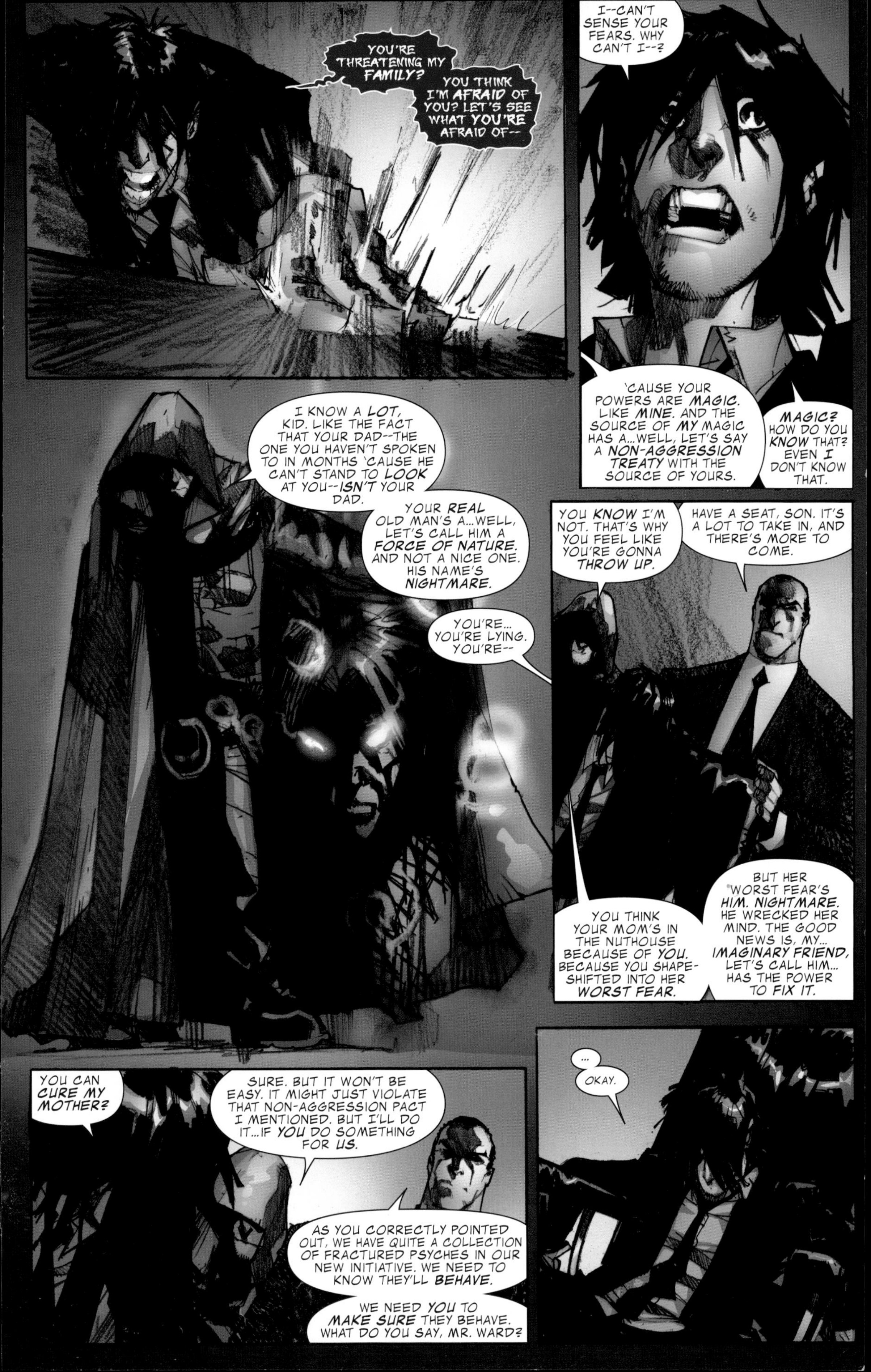

YOU'RE THREATENING MY FAMILY?
YOU THINK I'M AFRAID OF YOU? LET'S SEE WHAT YOU'RE AFRAID OF--
I--CAN'T SENSE YOUR FEARS. WHY CAN'T I--?
'CAUSE YOUR POWERS ARE MAGIC. LIKE MINE. AND THE SOURCE OF MY MAGIC HAS A...WELL, LET'S SAY A NON-AGGRESSION TREATY WITH THE SOURCE OF YOURS.
MAGIC? HOW DO YOU KNOW THAT? EVEN I DON'T KNOW THAT.
I KNOW A LOT, KID. LIKE THE FACT THAT YOUR DAD--THE ONE YOU HAVEN'T SPOKEN TO IN MONTHS 'CAUSE HE CAN'T STAND TO LOOK AT YOU--ISN'T YOUR DAD.
YOUR REAL OLD MAN'S A...WELL, LET'S CALL HIM A FORCE OF NATURE. AND NOT A NICE ONE. HIS NAME'S NIGHTMARE.
YOU'RE... YOU'RE LYING. YOU'RE--
YOU KNOW I'M NOT. THAT'S WHY YOU FEEL LIKE YOU'RE GONNA THROW UP.
HAVE A SEAT, SON. IT'S A LOT TO TAKE IN, AND THERE'S MORE TO COME.
YOU THINK YOUR MOM'S IN THE NUTHOUSE BECAUSE OF YOU. BECAUSE YOU SHAPE-SHIFTED INTO HER WORST FEAR.
BUT HER WORST FEAR'S HIM. NIGHTMARE. HE WRECKED HER MIND. THE GOOD NEWS IS, MY... IMAGINARY FRIEND, LET'S CALL HIM... HAS THE POWER TO FIX IT.
YOU CAN CURE MY MOTHER?
SURE. BUT IT WON'T BE EASY. IT MIGHT JUST VIOLATE THAT NON-AGGRESSION PACT I MENTIONED. BUT I'LL DO IT...IF YOU DO SOMETHING FOR US.
AS YOU CORRECTLY POINTED OUT, WE HAVE QUITE A COLLECTION OF FRACTURED PSYCHES IN OUR NEW INITIATIVE. WE NEED TO KNOW THEY'LL BEHAVE.
WE NEED YOU TO MAKE SURE THEY BEHAVE. WHAT DO YOU SAY, MR. WARD?
...
OKAY.

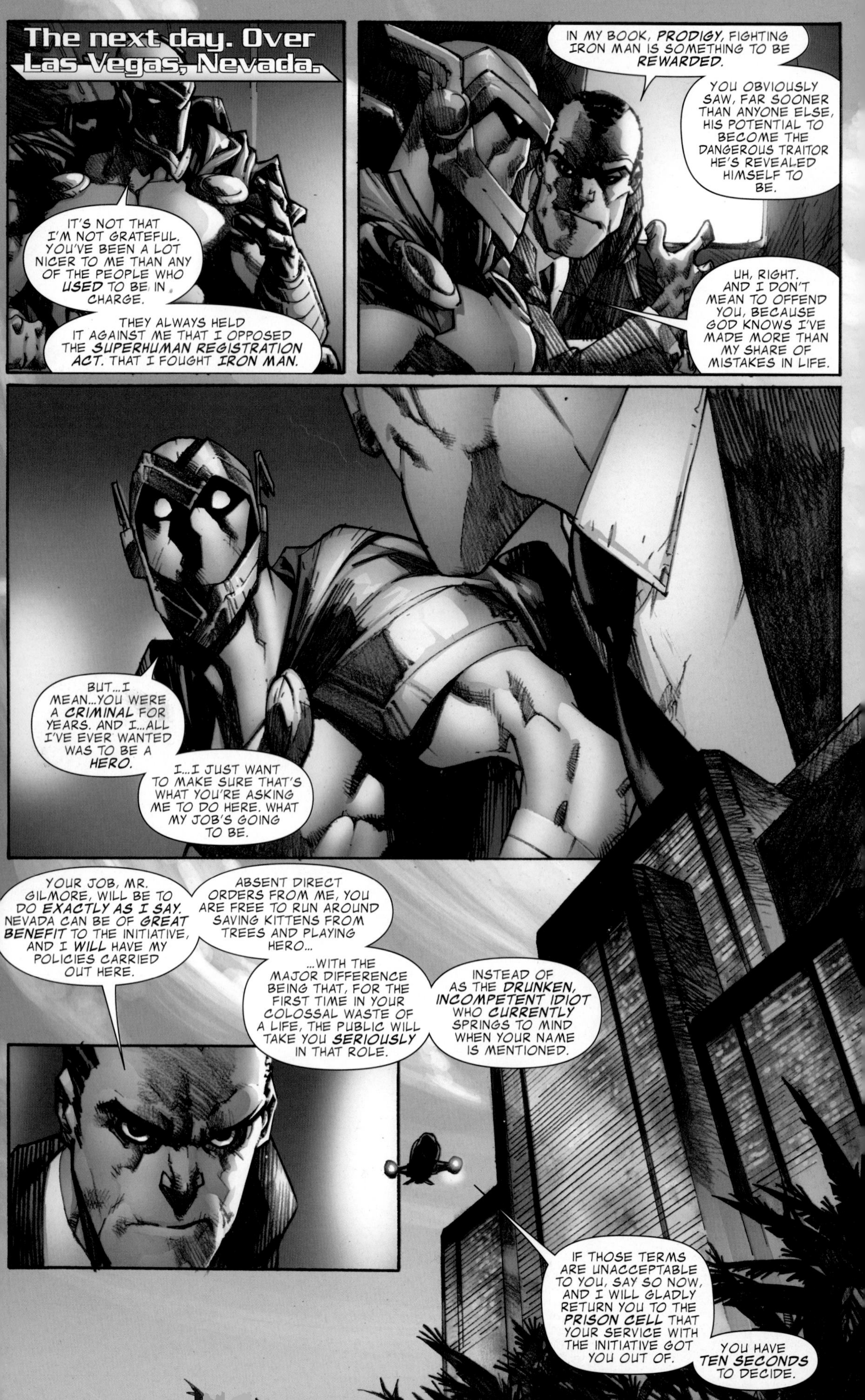
The next day. Over Las Vegas, Nevada.
IT'S NOT THAT I'M NOT GRATEFUL. YOU'VE BEEN A LOT NICER TO ME THAN ANY OF THE PEOPLE WHO USED TO BE IN CHARGE.
THEY ALWAYS HELD IT AGAINST ME THAT I OPPOSED THE SUPERHUMAN REGISTRATION ACT. THAT I FOUGHT IRON MAN.
IN MY BOOK, PRODIGY, FIGHTING IRON MAN IS SOMETHING TO BE REWARDED.
YOU OBVIOUSLY SAW, FAR SOONER THAN ANYONE ELSE, HIS POTENTIAL TO BECOME THE DANGEROUS TRAITOR HE'S REVEALED HIMSELF TO BE.
UH, RIGHT. AND I DON'T MEAN TO OFFEND YOU, BECAUSE GOD KNOWS I'VE MADE MORE THAN MY SHARE OF MISTAKES IN LIFE.
BUT...I MEAN...YOU WERE A CRIMINAL FOR YEARS. AND I...ALL I'VE EVER WANTED WAS TO BE A HERO.
I...I JUST WANT TO MAKE SURE THAT'S WHAT YOU'RE ASKING ME TO DO HERE. WHAT MY JOB'S GOING TO BE.
YOUR JOB, MR. GILMORE, WILL BE TO DO EXACTLY AS I SAY. NEVADA CAN BE OF GREAT BENEFIT TO THE INITIATIVE, AND I WILL HAVE MY POLICIES CARRIED OUT HERE.
ABSENT DIRECT ORDERS FROM ME, YOU ARE FREE TO RUN AROUND SAVING KITTENS FROM TREES AND PLAYING HERO...
...WITH THE MAJOR DIFFERENCE BEING THAT, FOR THE FIRST TIME IN YOUR COLOSSAL WASTE OF A LIFE, THE PUBLIC WILL TAKE YOU SERIOUSLY IN THAT ROLE.
INSTEAD OF AS THE DRUNKEN, INCOMPETENT IDIOT WHO CURRENTLY SPRINGS TO MIND WHEN YOUR NAME IS MENTIONED.
IF THOSE TERMS ARE UNACCEPTABLE TO YOU, SAY SO NOW, AND I WILL GLADLY RETURN YOU TO THE PRISON CELL THAT YOUR SERVICE WITH THE INITIATIVE GOT YOU OUT OF.
YOU HAVE TEN SECONDS TO DECIDE.

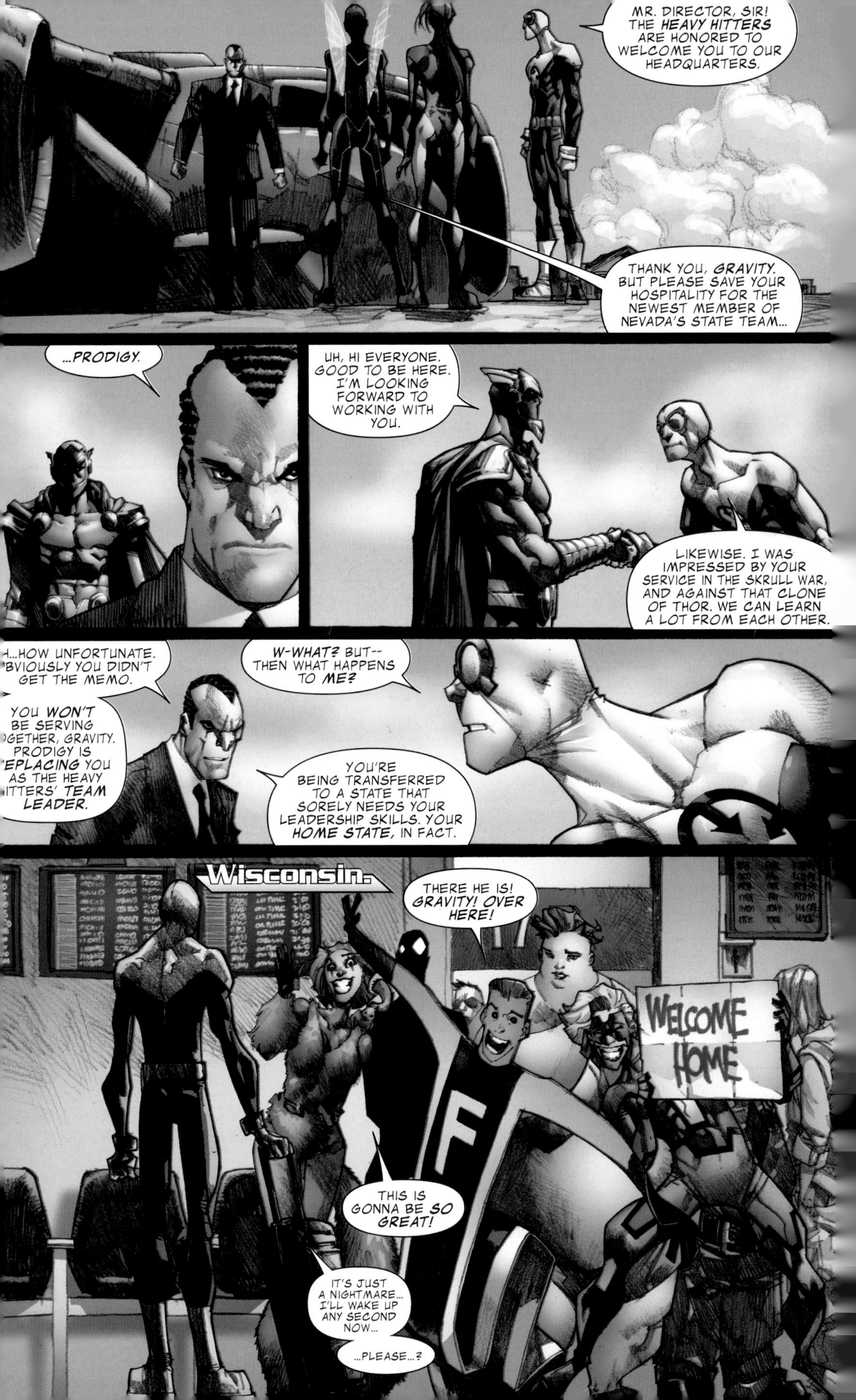
MR. DIRECTOR, SIR! THE HEAVY HITTERS ARE HONORED TO WELCOME YOU TO OUR HEADQUARTERS.
THANK YOU, GRAVITY. BUT PLEASE SAVE YOUR HOSPITALITY FOR THE NEWEST MEMBER OF NEVADA'S STATE TEAM...
...PRODIGY.
UH, HI EVERYONE. GOOD TO BE HERE. I'M LOOKING FORWARD TO WORKING WITH YOU.
LIKEWISE. I WAS IMPRESSED BY YOUR SERVICE IN THE SKRULL WAR, AND AGAINST THAT CLONE OF THOR. WE CAN LEARN A LOT FROM EACH OTHER.
H...HOW UNFORTUNATE. BVIOUSLY YOU DIDN'T GET THE MEMO.
YOU WON'T BE SERVING GETHER, GRAVITY. PRODIGY IS EPLACING YOU AS THE HEAVY ITTERS' TEAM LEADER.
W-WHAT? BUT-- THEN WHAT HAPPENS TO ME?
YOU'RE BEING TRANSFERRED TO A STATE THAT SORELY NEEDS YOUR LEADERSHIP SKILLS. YOUR HOME STATE, IN FACT.
Wisconsin.
THERE HE IS! GRAVITY! OVER HERE!
WELCOME HOME
THIS IS GONNA BE SO GREAT!
IT'S JUST A NIGHTMARE... I'LL WAKE UP ANY SECOND NOW...
...PLEASE...?

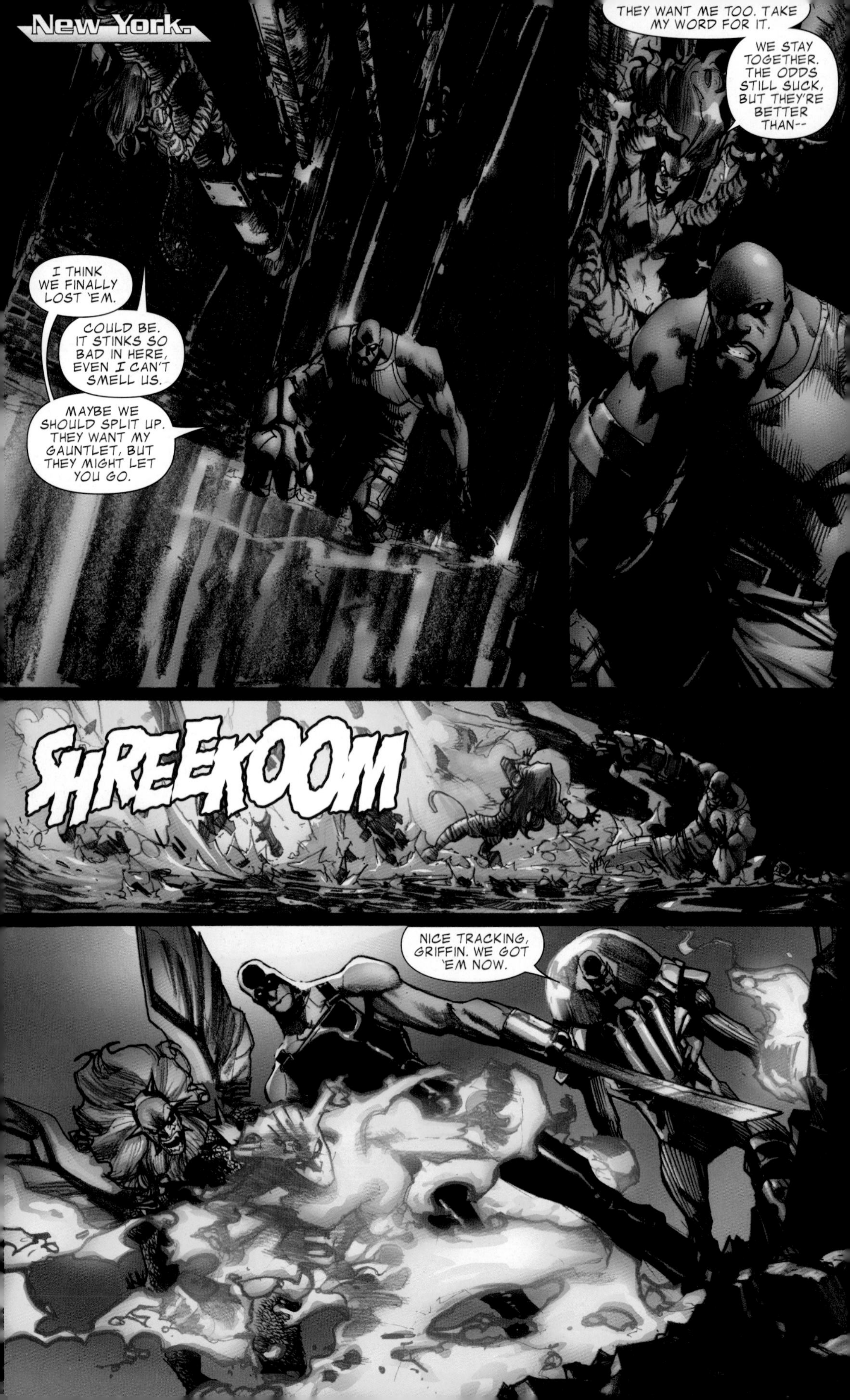
New York.
I THINK WE FINALLY LOST 'EM.
COULD BE. IT STINKS SO BAD IN HERE, EVEN I CAN'T SMELL US.
MAYBE WE SHOULD SPLIT UP. THEY WANT MY GAUNTLET, BUT THEY MIGHT LET YOU GO.
THEY WANT ME TOO. TAKE MY WORD FOR IT.
WE STAY TOGETHER. THE ODDS STILL SUCK, BUT THEY'RE BETTER THAN--
SHREEKOOM
NICE TRACKING, GRIFFIN. WE GOT 'EM NOW.

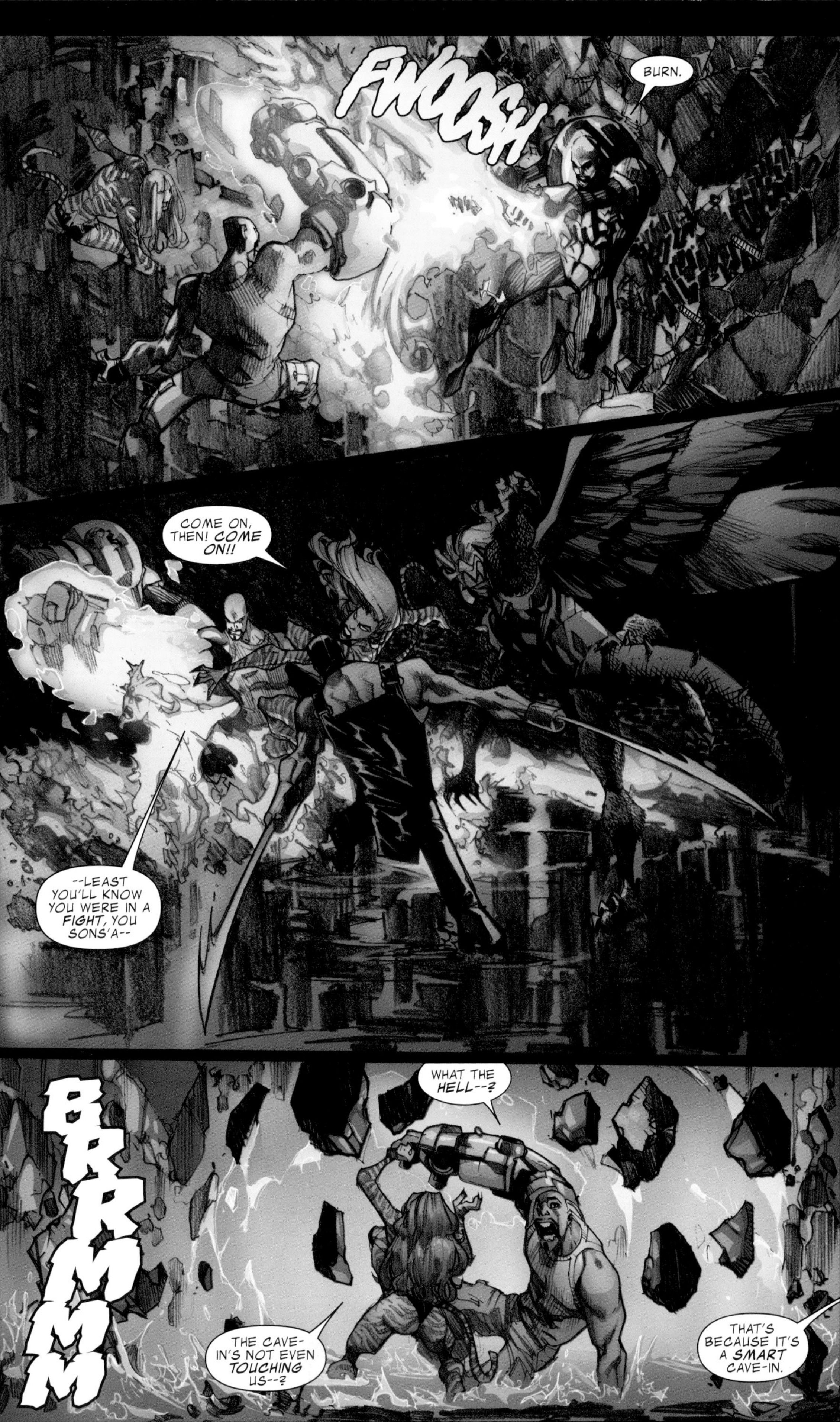
FWOOSH
BURN.
COME ON, THEN! COME ON!!
--LEAST YOU'LL KNOW YOU WERE IN A FIGHT, YOU SONS'A--
BRRMMM
WHAT THE HELL--?
THE CAVE-IN'S NOT EVEN TOUCHING US--?
THAT'S BECAUSE IT'S A SMART CAVE-IN.

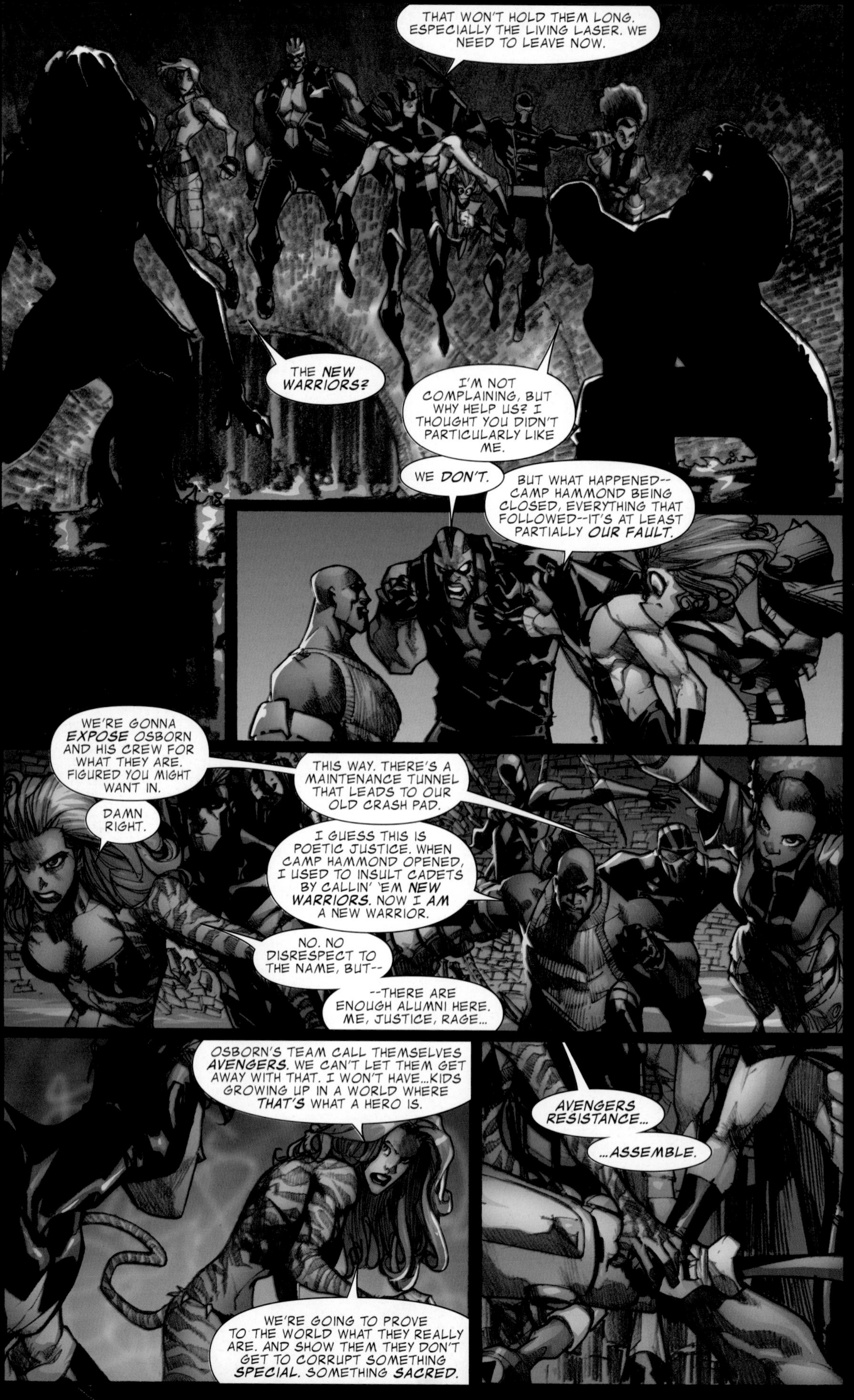
THAT WON'T HOLD THEM LONG. ESPECIALLY THE LIVING LASER. WE NEED TO LEAVE NOW.
THE *NEW WARRIORS?*
I'M NOT COMPLAINING, BUT WHY HELP US? I THOUGHT YOU DIDN'T PARTICULARLY LIKE ME.
WE *DON'T.*
BUT WHAT HAPPENED--CAMP HAMMOND BEING CLOSED, EVERYTHING THAT FOLLOWED--IT'S AT LEAST PARTIALLY *OUR FAULT.*
WE'RE GONNA *EXPOSE* OSBORN AND HIS CREW FOR WHAT THEY ARE. FIGURED YOU MIGHT WANT IN.
DAMN RIGHT.
THIS WAY. THERE'S A MAINTENANCE TUNNEL THAT LEADS TO OUR OLD CRASH PAD.
I GUESS THIS IS POETIC JUSTICE. WHEN CAMP HAMMOND OPENED, I USED TO INSULT CADETS BY CALLIN' 'EM *NEW WARRIORS.* NOW I *AM* A NEW WARRIOR.
NO. NO DISRESPECT TO THE NAME, BUT--
--THERE ARE ENOUGH ALUMNI HERE. ME, JUSTICE, RAGE...
OSBORN'S TEAM CALL THEMSELVES *AVENGERS.* WE CAN'T LET THEM GET AWAY WITH THAT. I WON'T HAVE...KIDS GROWING UP IN A WORLD WHERE *THAT'S* WHAT A HERO IS.
WE'RE GOING TO PROVE TO THE WORLD WHAT THEY REALLY ARE. AND SHOW THEM THEY DON'T GET TO CORRUPT SOMETHING *SPECIAL.* SOMETHING *SACRED.*
AVENGERS RESISTANCE...
...ASSEMBLE.

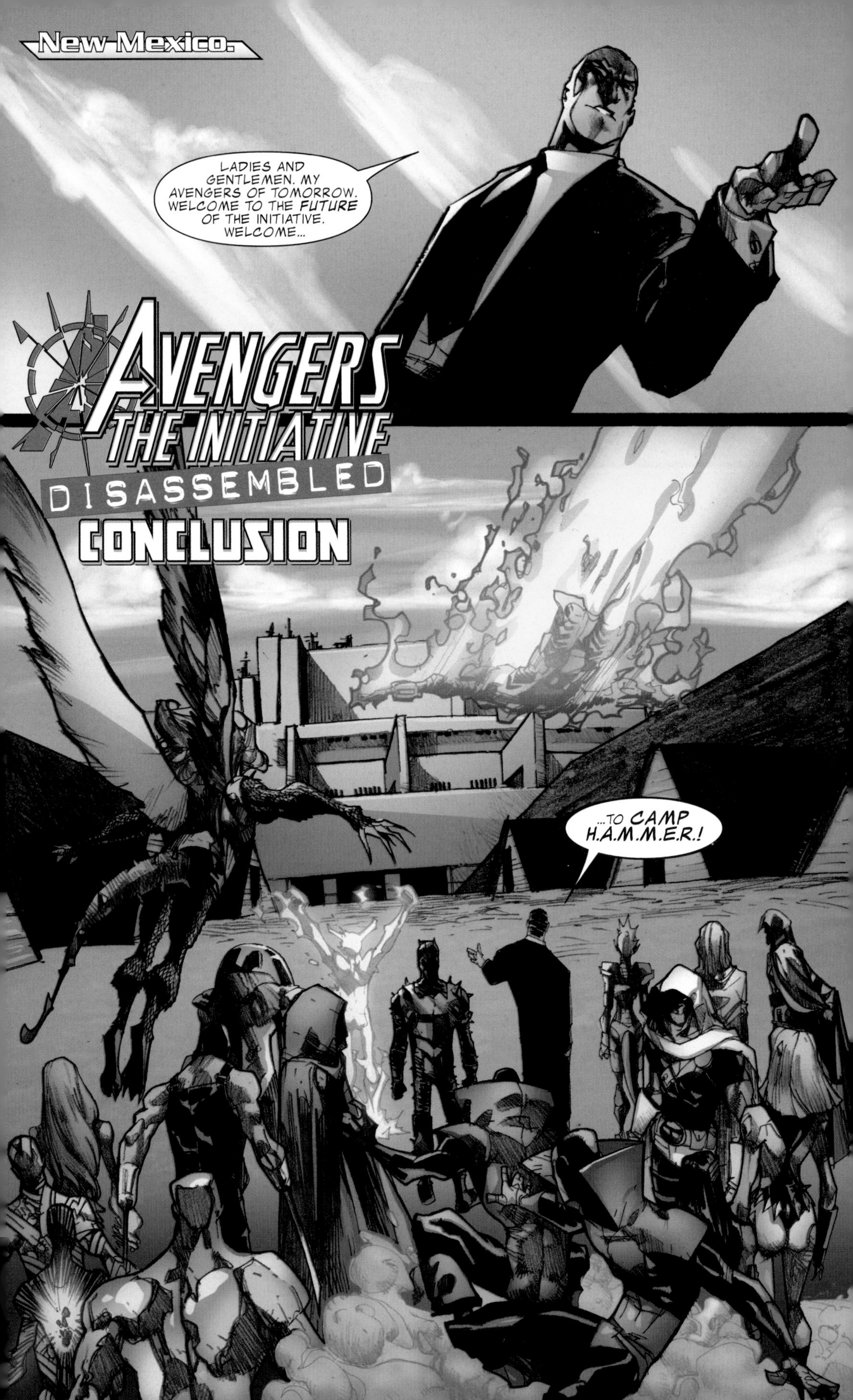
New Mexico.
LADIES AND GENTLEMEN. MY AVENGERS OF TOMORROW. WELCOME TO THE FUTURE OF THE INITIATIVE. WELCOME...
AVENGERS THE INITIATIVE
DISASSEMBLED
CONCLUSION
...TO CAMP H.A.M.M.E.R.!

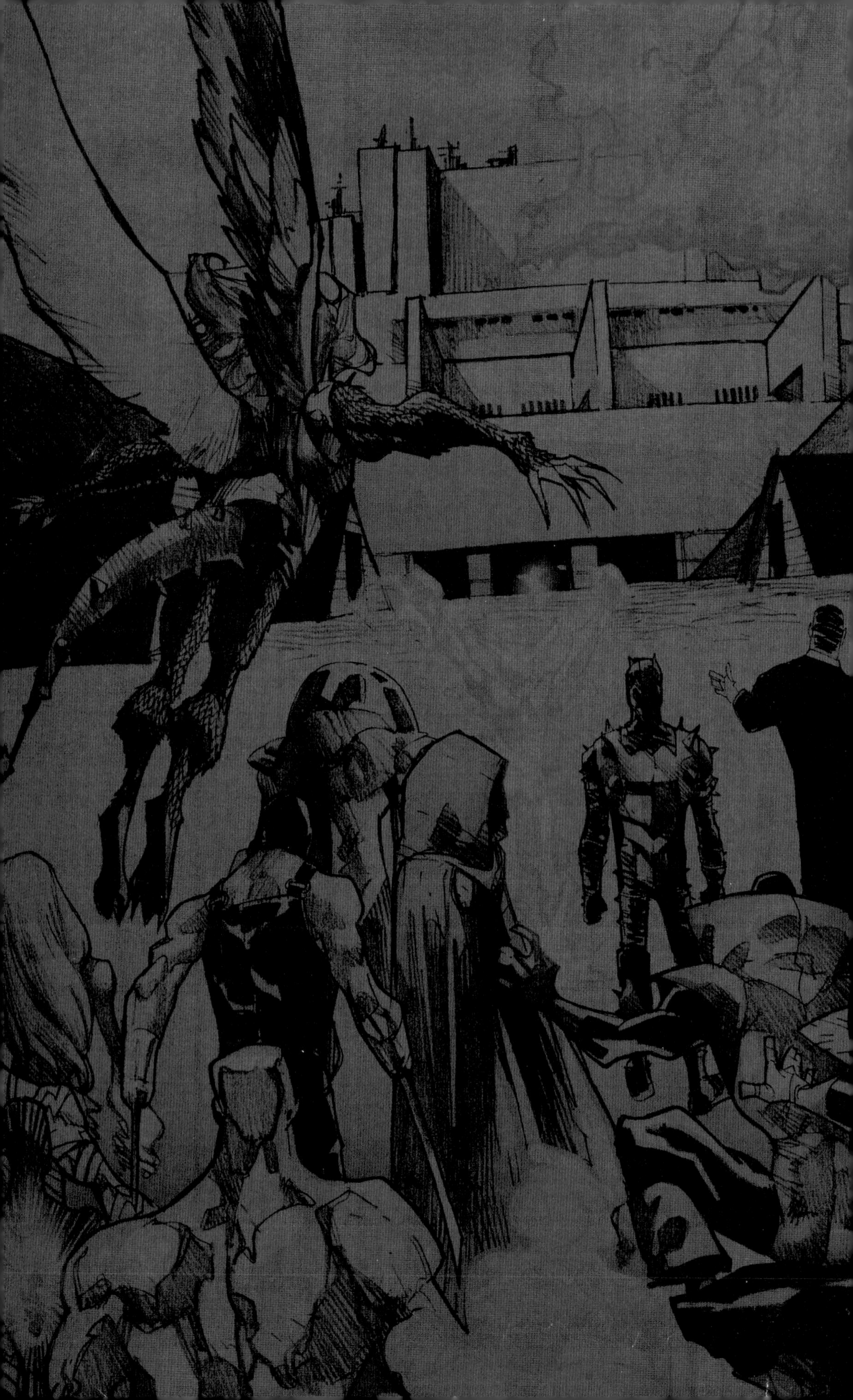

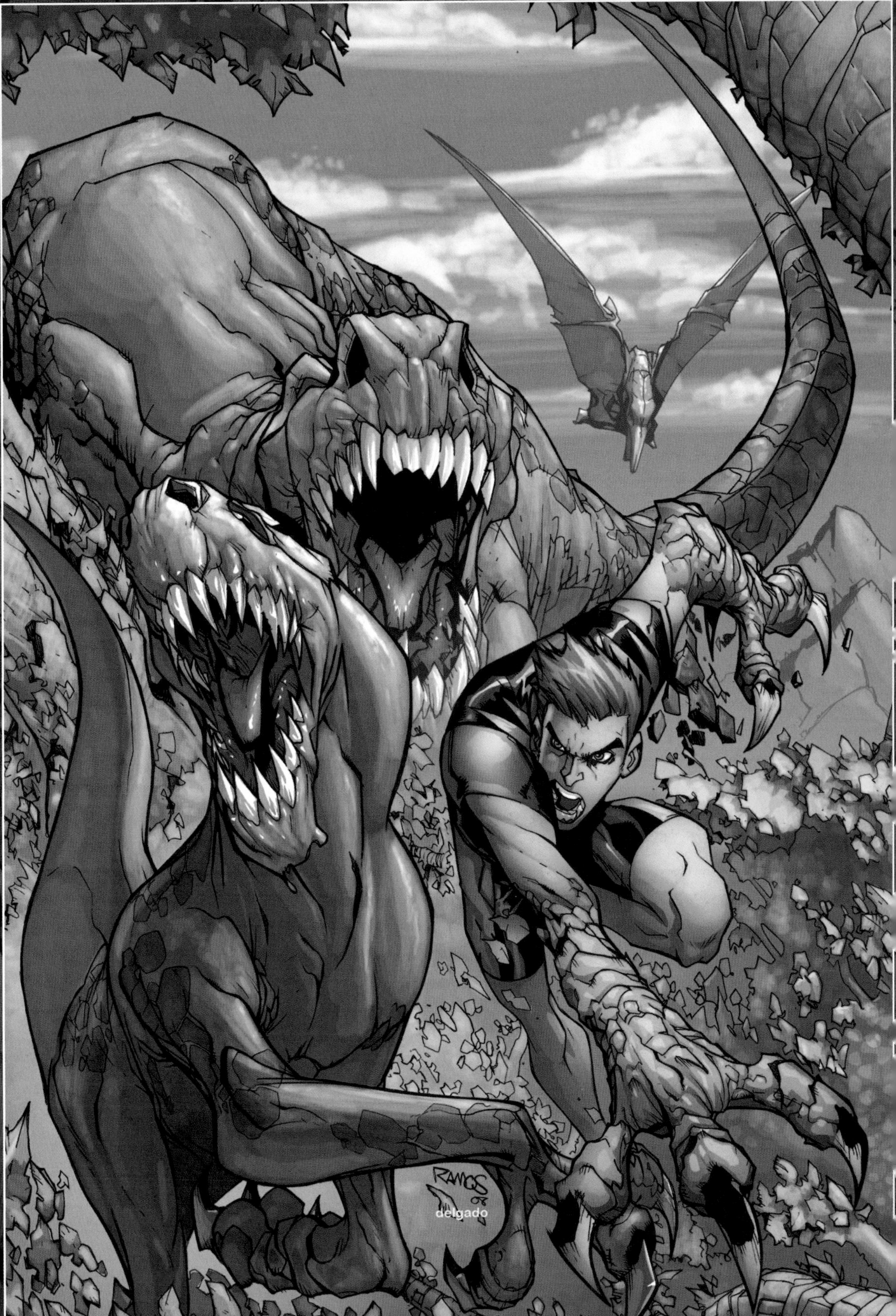
RAMOS 08
delgado

AVENGERS: THE INITIATIVE FEATURING REPTIL

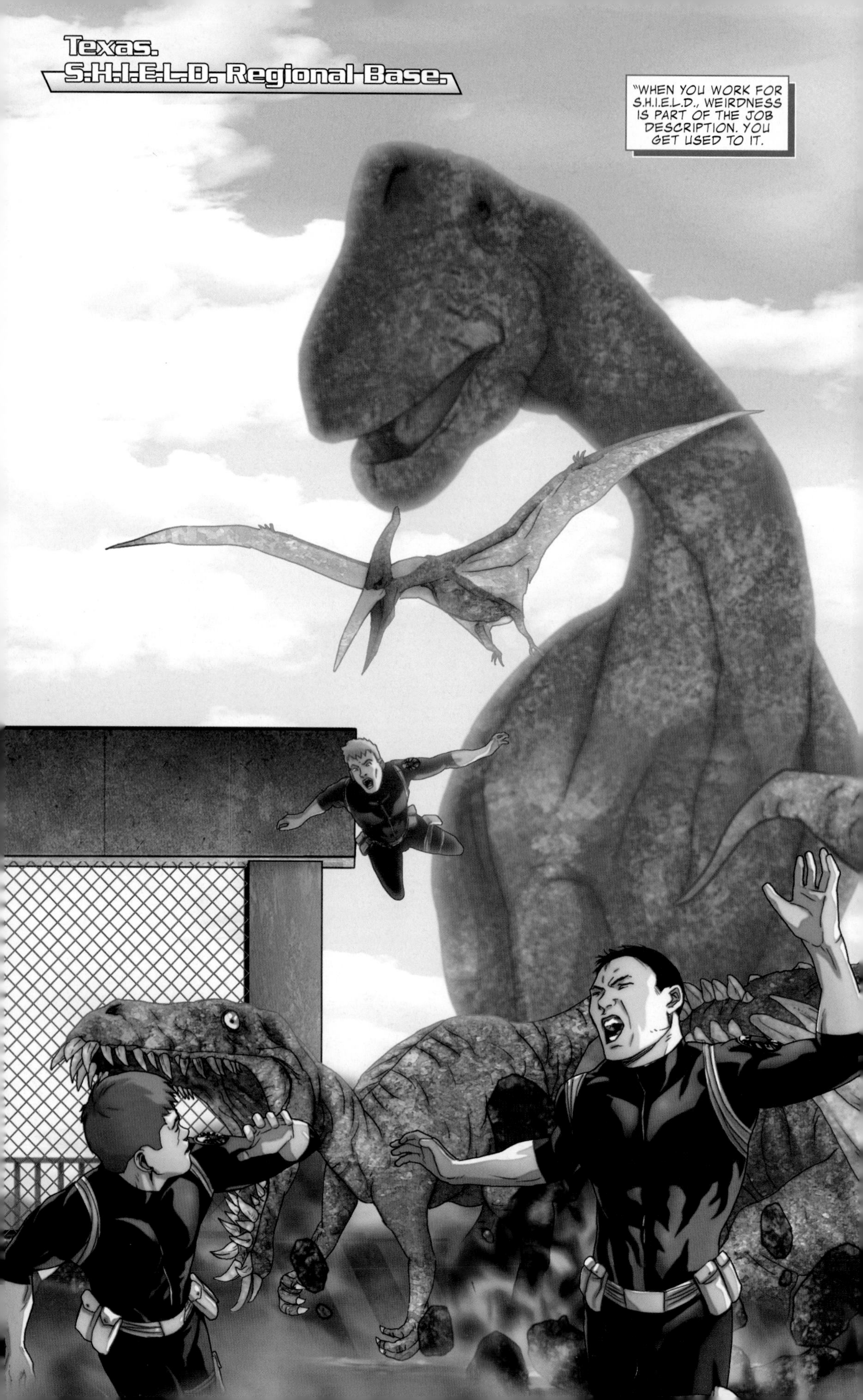
Texas.
S.H.I.E.L.D. Regional Base.
"WHEN YOU WORK FOR S.H.I.E.L.D., WEIRDNESS IS PART OF THE JOB DESCRIPTION. YOU GET USED TO IT.

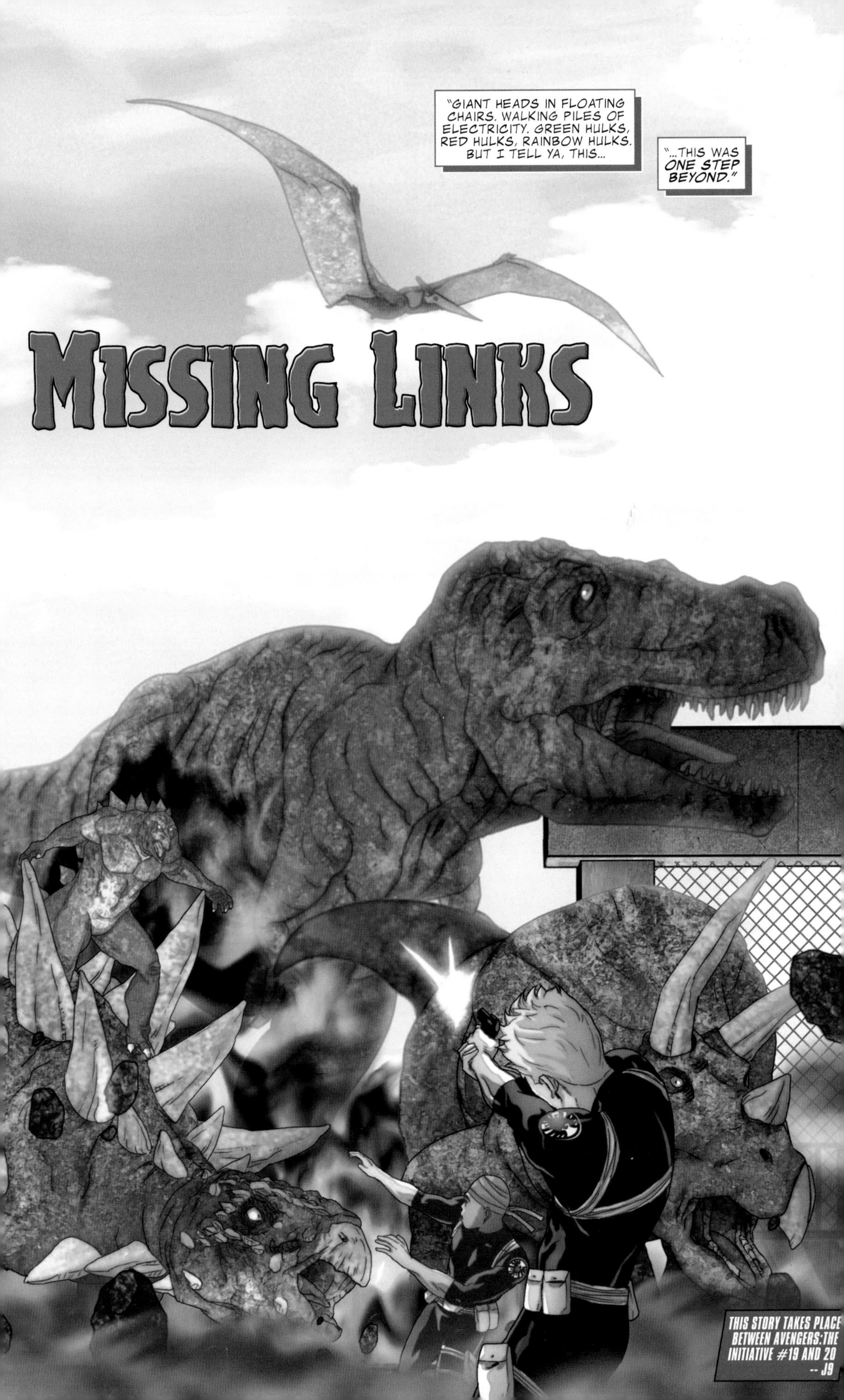

"GIANT HEADS IN FLOATING CHAIRS. WALKING PILES OF ELECTRICITY. GREEN HULKS, RED HULKS, RAINBOW HULKS. BUT I TELL YA, THIS...
"...THIS WAS ONE STEP BEYOND."
MISSING LINKS
THIS STORY TAKES PLACE BETWEEN AVENGERS: THE INITIATIVE #19 AND 20 -- J9

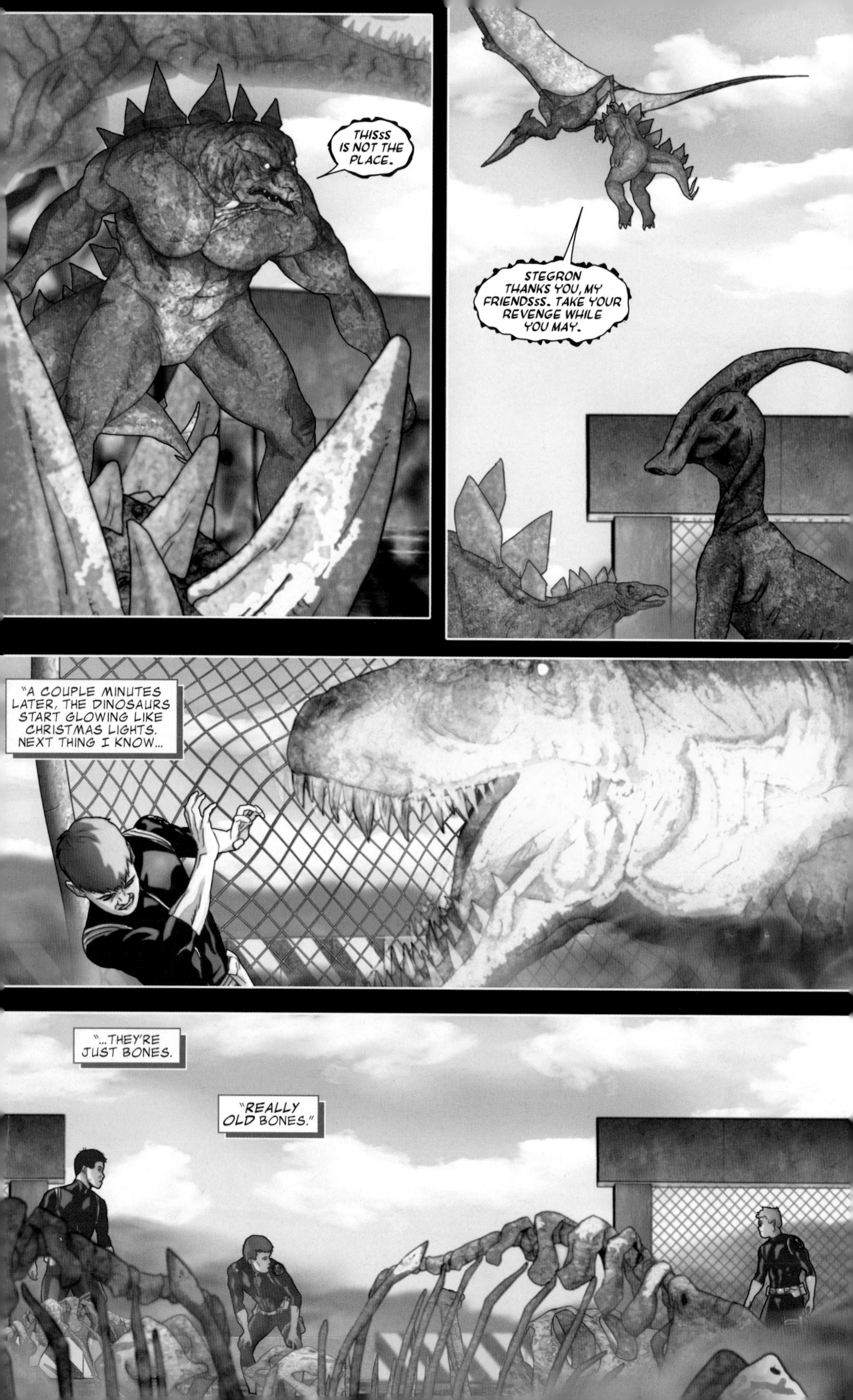
THISSS IS NOT THE PLACE.
STEGRON THANKS YOU, MY FRIENDSSS. TAKE YOUR REVENGE WHILE YOU MAY.
"A COUPLE MINUTES LATER, THE DINOSAURS START GLOWING LIKE CHRISTMAS LIGHTS. NEXT THING I KNOW...
"...THEY'RE JUST BONES.
"REALLY OLD BONES."

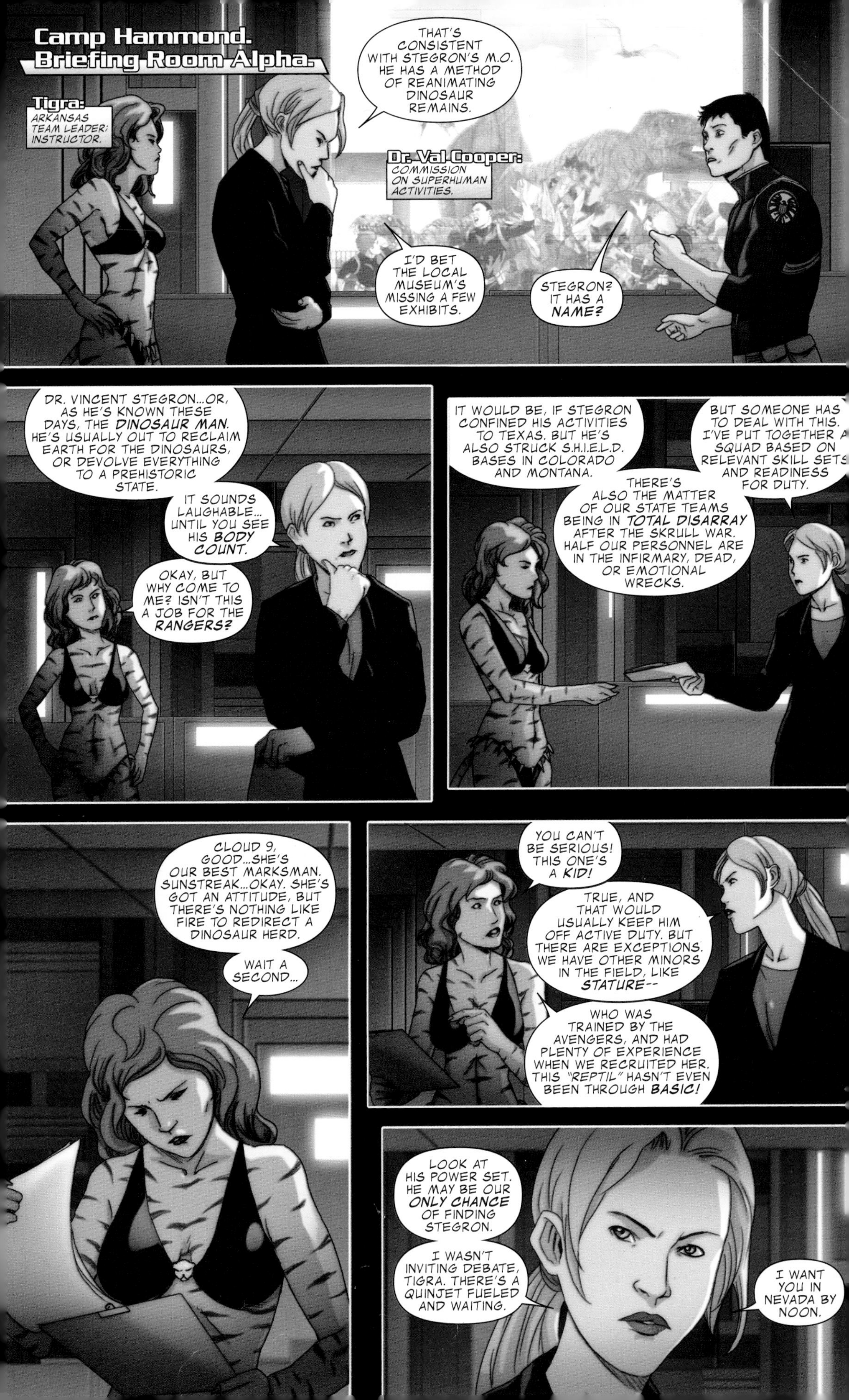
Camp Hammond. Briefing Room Alpha.
Tigra: ARKANSAS TEAM LEADER; INSTRUCTOR.
THAT'S CONSISTENT WITH STEGRON'S M.O. HE HAS A METHOD OF REANIMATING DINOSAUR REMAINS.
Dr. Val Cooper: COMMISSION ON SUPERHUMAN ACTIVITIES.
I'D BET THE LOCAL MUSEUM'S MISSING A FEW EXHIBITS.
STEGRON? IT HAS A NAME?
DR. VINCENT STEGRON...OR, AS HE'S KNOWN THESE DAYS, THE DINOSAUR MAN. HE'S USUALLY OUT TO RECLAIM EARTH FOR THE DINOSAURS, OR DEVOLVE EVERYTHING TO A PREHISTORIC STATE.
IT SOUNDS LAUGHABLE... UNTIL YOU SEE HIS BODY COUNT.
OKAY, BUT WHY COME TO ME? ISN'T THIS A JOB FOR THE RANGERS?
IT WOULD BE, IF STEGRON CONFINED HIS ACTIVITIES TO TEXAS. BUT HE'S ALSO STRUCK S.H.I.E.L.D. BASES IN COLORADO AND MONTANA.
THERE'S ALSO THE MATTER OF OUR STATE TEAMS BEING IN TOTAL DISARRAY AFTER THE SKRULL WAR. HALF OUR PERSONNEL ARE IN THE INFIRMARY, DEAD, OR EMOTIONAL WRECKS.
BUT SOMEONE HAS TO DEAL WITH THIS. I'VE PUT TOGETHER A SQUAD BASED ON RELEVANT SKILL SETS AND READINESS FOR DUTY.
CLOUD 9, GOOD...SHE'S OUR BEST MARKSMAN. SUNSTREAK...OKAY. SHE'S GOT AN ATTITUDE, BUT THERE'S NOTHING LIKE FIRE TO REDIRECT A DINOSAUR HERD.
WAIT A SECOND...
YOU CAN'T BE SERIOUS! THIS ONE'S A KID!
TRUE, AND THAT WOULD USUALLY KEEP HIM OFF ACTIVE DUTY. BUT THERE ARE EXCEPTIONS. WE HAVE OTHER MINORS IN THE FIELD, LIKE STATURE--
WHO WAS TRAINED BY THE AVENGERS, AND HAD PLENTY OF EXPERIENCE WHEN WE RECRUITED HER. THIS "REPTIL" HASN'T EVEN BEEN THROUGH BASIC!
LOOK AT HIS POWER SET. HE MAY BE OUR ONLY CHANCE OF FINDING STEGRON.
I WASN'T INVITING DEBATE, TIGRA. THERE'S A QUINJET FUELED AND WAITING.
I WANT YOU IN NEVADA BY NOON.

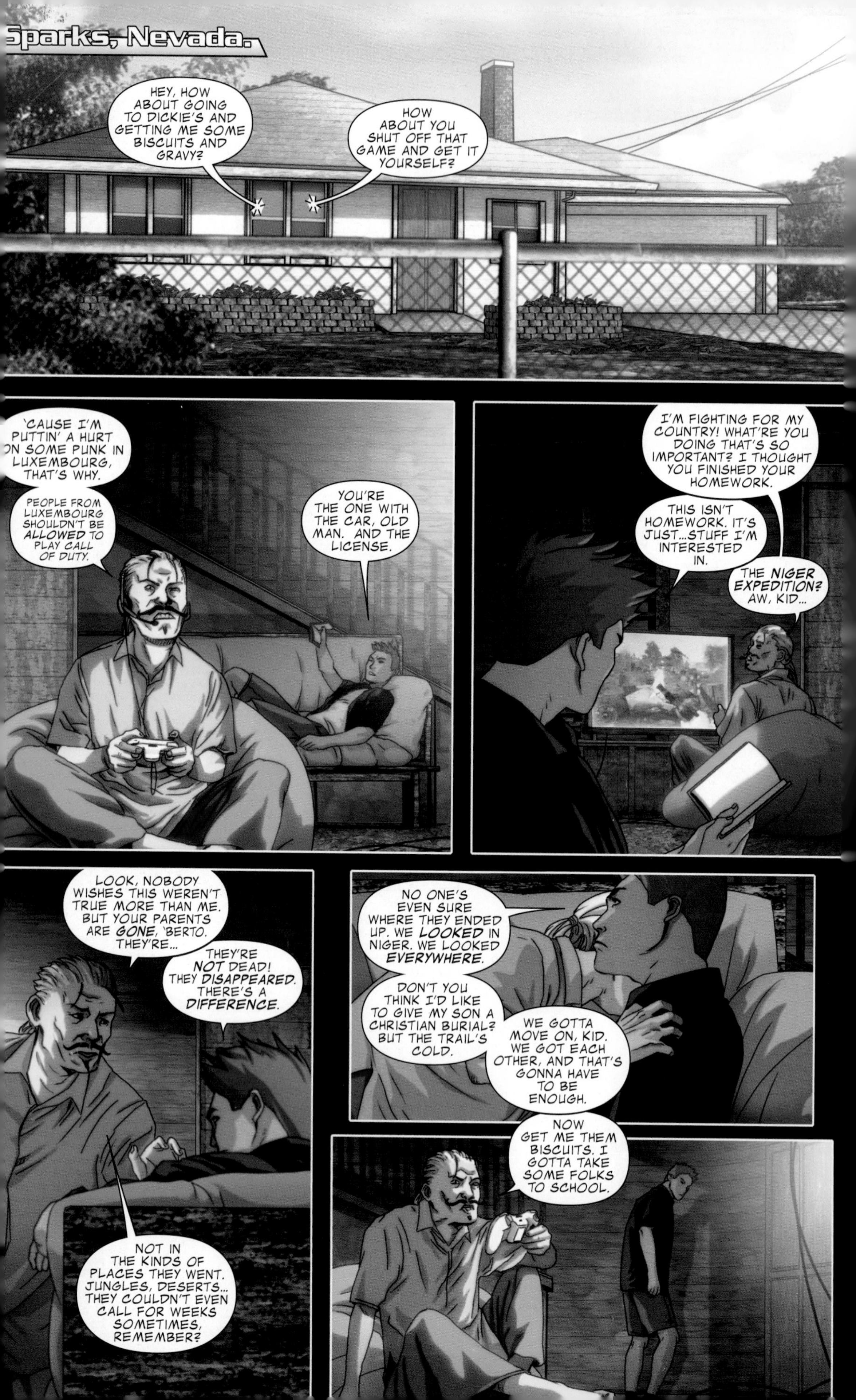
Sparks, Nevada.
HEY, HOW ABOUT GOING TO DICKIE'S AND GETTING ME SOME BISCUITS AND GRAVY?
HOW ABOUT YOU SHUT OFF THAT GAME AND GET IT YOURSELF?
'CAUSE I'M PUTTIN' A HURT ON SOME PUNK IN LUXEMBOURG, THAT'S WHY.
PEOPLE FROM LUXEMBOURG SHOULDN'T BE ALLOWED TO PLAY CALL OF DUTY.
YOU'RE THE ONE WITH THE CAR, OLD MAN. AND THE LICENSE.
I'M FIGHTING FOR MY COUNTRY! WHAT'RE YOU DOING THAT'S SO IMPORTANT? I THOUGHT YOU FINISHED YOUR HOMEWORK.
THIS ISN'T HOMEWORK. IT'S JUST...STUFF I'M INTERESTED IN.
THE NIGER EXPEDITION? AW, KID...
LOOK, NOBODY WISHES THIS WEREN'T TRUE MORE THAN ME. BUT YOUR PARENTS ARE GONE, 'BERTO. THEY'RE...
THEY'RE NOT DEAD! THEY DISAPPEARED. THERE'S A DIFFERENCE.
NOT IN THE KINDS OF PLACES THEY WENT. JUNGLES, DESERTS... THEY COULDN'T EVEN CALL FOR WEEKS SOMETIMES, REMEMBER?
NO ONE'S EVEN SURE WHERE THEY ENDED UP. WE LOOKED IN NIGER. WE LOOKED EVERYWHERE.
DON'T YOU THINK I'D LIKE TO GIVE MY SON A CHRISTIAN BURIAL? BUT THE TRAIL'S COLD.
WE GOTTA MOVE ON, KID. WE GOT EACH OTHER, AND THAT'S GONNA HAVE TO BE ENOUGH.
NOW GET ME THEM BISCUITS. I GOTTA TAKE SOME FOLKS TO SCHOOL.

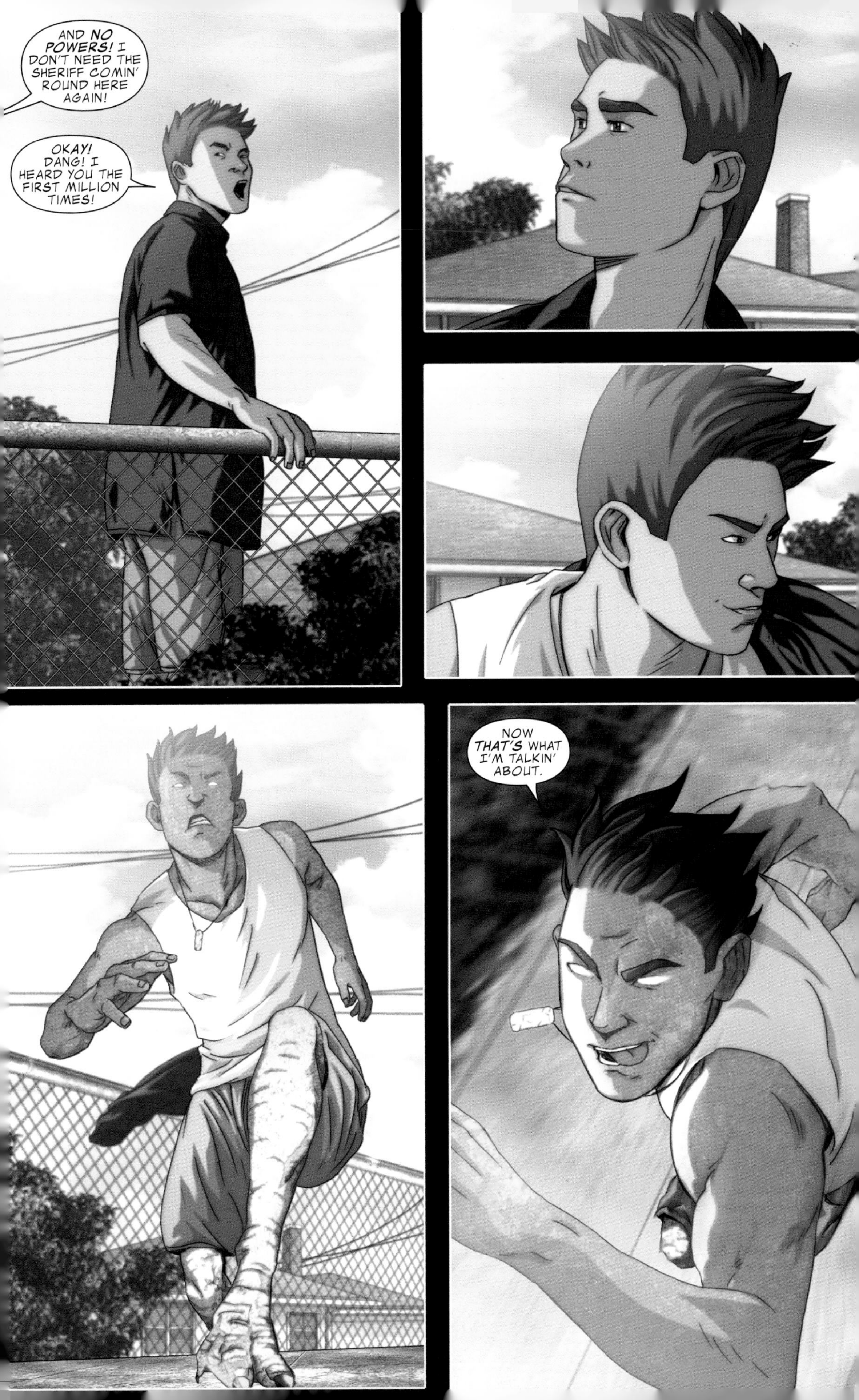
AND NO POWERS! I DON'T NEED THE SHERIFF COMIN' ROUND HERE AGAIN!
OKAY! DANG! I HEARD YOU THE FIRST MILLION TIMES!
NOW THAT'S WHAT I'M TALKIN' ABOUT.

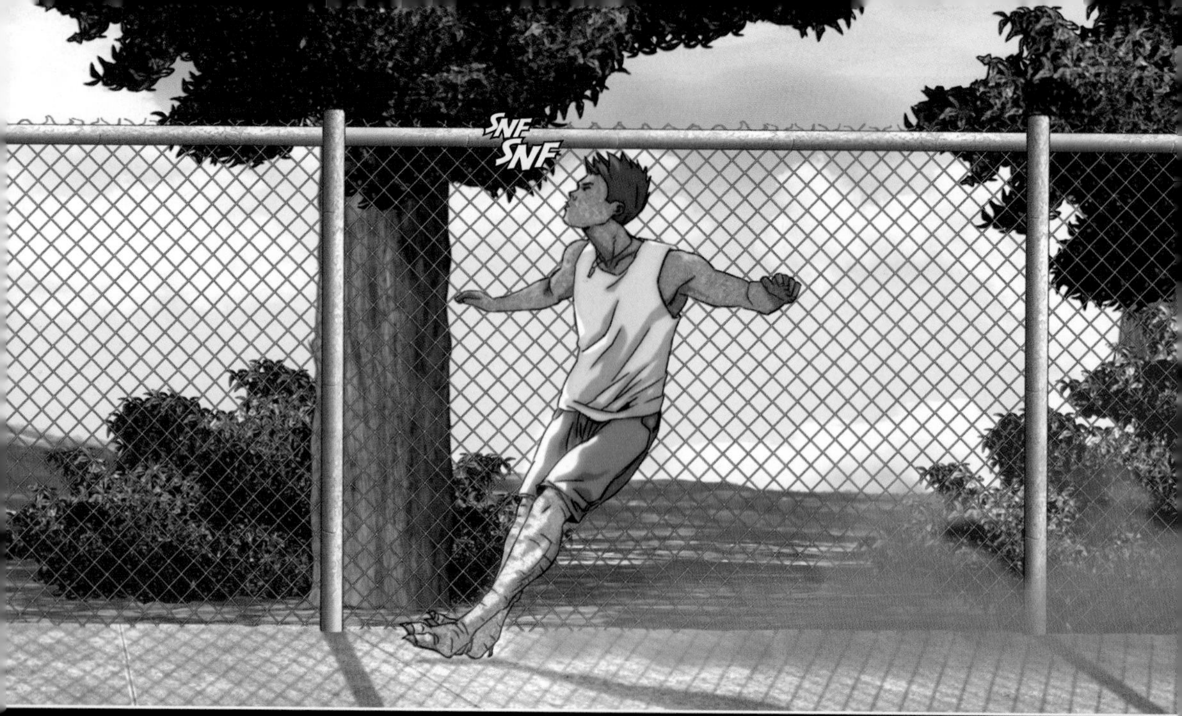
SNF SNF

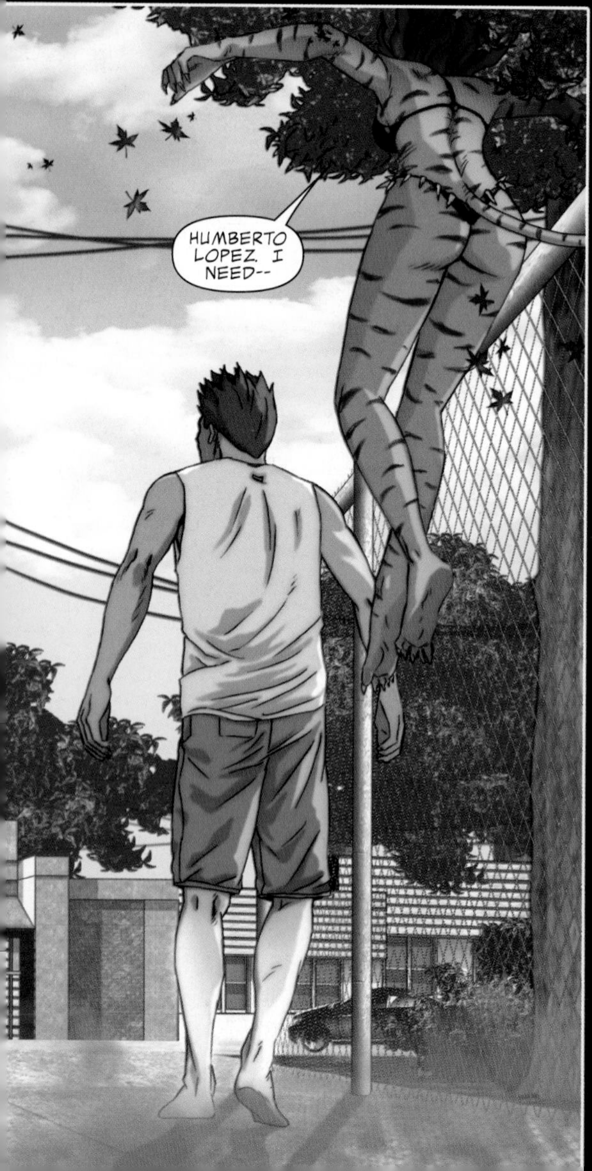
HUMBERTO LOPEZ. I NEED--

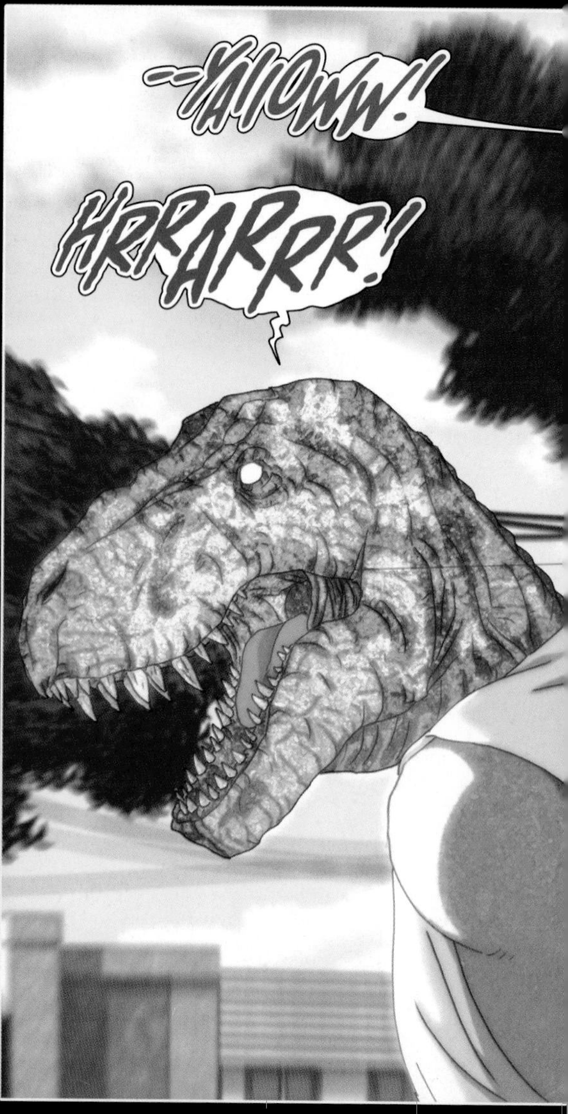
--YAIIOWW!
HRRARRR!

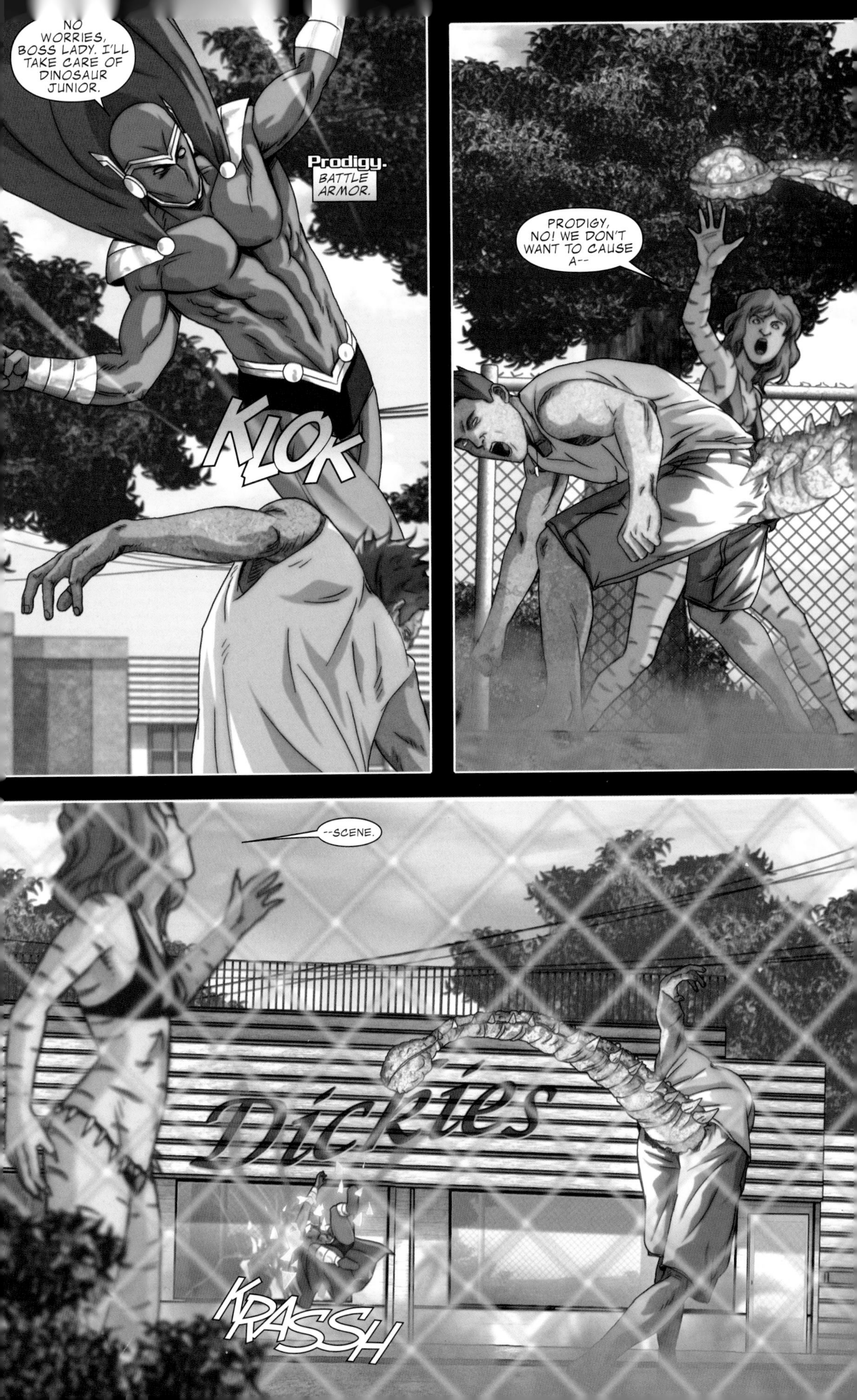
NO WORRIES, BOSS LADY. I'LL TAKE CARE OF DINOSAUR JUNIOR.
Prodigy.
BATTLE ARMOR.
KLOK
PRODIGY, NO! WE DON'T WANT TO CAUSE A--
--SCENE.
Dickies
KRASSH

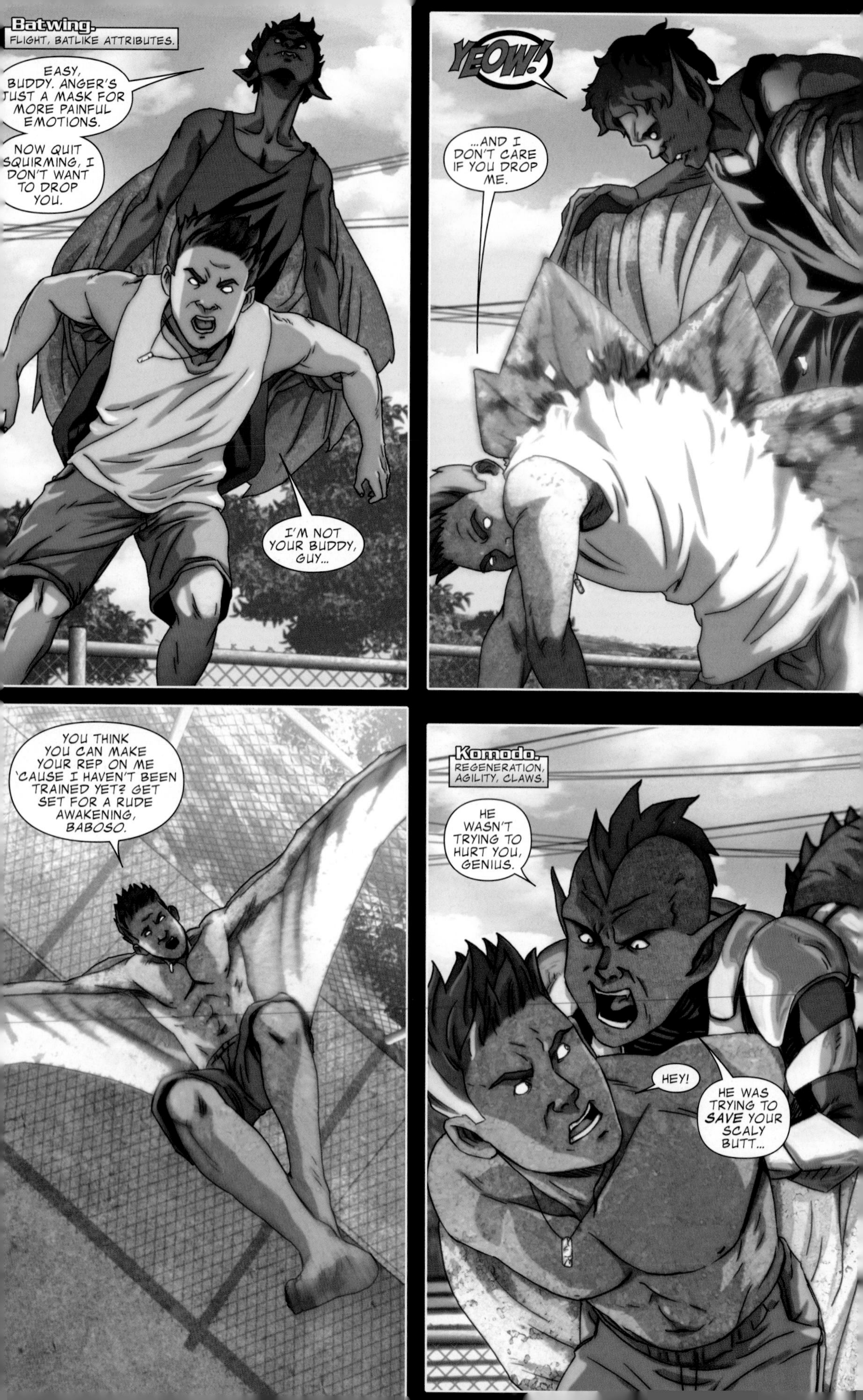
Batwing.
FLIGHT, BATLIKE ATTRIBUTES.
EASY, BUDDY. ANGER'S JUST A MASK FOR MORE PAINFUL EMOTIONS.
NOW QUIT SQUIRMING, I DON'T WANT TO DROP YOU.
I'M NOT YOUR BUDDY, GUY...
YEOW!
...AND I DON'T CARE IF YOU DROP ME.
YOU THINK YOU CAN MAKE YOUR REP ON ME 'CAUSE I HAVEN'T BEEN TRAINED YET? GET SET FOR A RUDE AWAKENING, BABOSO.
Komodo.
REGENERATION, AGILITY, CLAWS.
HE WASN'T TRYING TO HURT YOU, GENIUS.
HEY!
HE WAS TRYING TO SAVE YOUR SCALY BUTT...

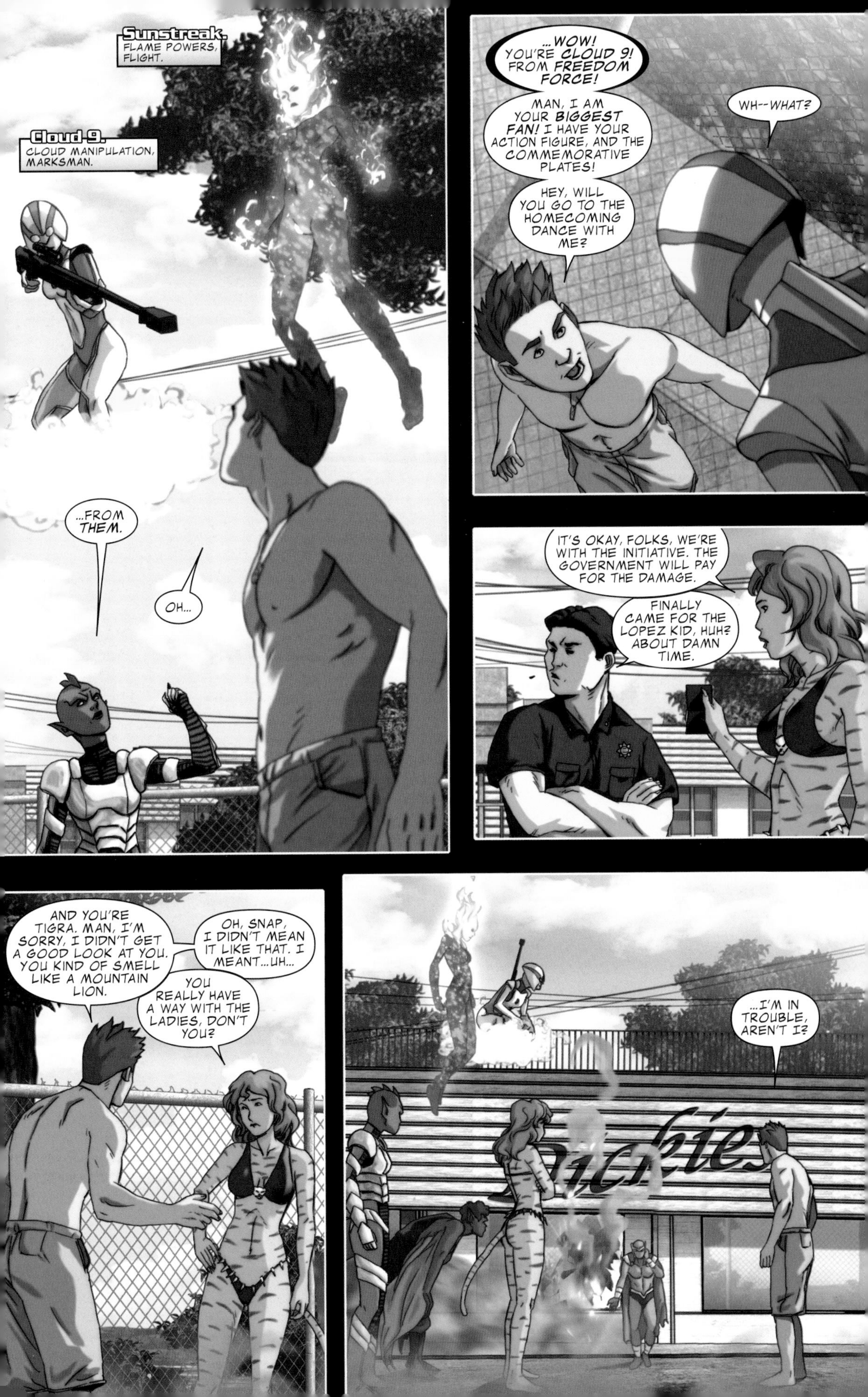

Sunstreak.
FLAME POWERS, FLIGHT.
Cloud 9.
CLOUD MANIPULATION, MARKSMAN.
...FROM THEM.
OH...
...WOW! YOU'RE CLOUD 9! FROM FREEDOM FORCE!
MAN, I AM YOUR BIGGEST FAN! I HAVE YOUR ACTION FIGURE, AND THE COMMEMORATIVE PLATES!
HEY, WILL YOU GO TO THE HOMECOMING DANCE WITH ME?
WH--WHAT?
IT'S OKAY, FOLKS, WE'RE WITH THE INITIATIVE. THE GOVERNMENT WILL PAY FOR THE DAMAGE.
FINALLY CAME FOR THE LOPEZ KID, HUH? ABOUT DAMN TIME.
AND YOU'RE TIGRA. MAN, I'M SORRY, I DIDN'T GET A GOOD LOOK AT YOU. YOU KIND OF SMELL LIKE A MOUNTAIN LION.
OH, SNAP, I DIDN'T MEAN IT LIKE THAT. I MEANT...UH...
YOU REALLY HAVE A WAY WITH THE LADIES, DON'T YOU?
...I'M IN TROUBLE, AREN'T I?

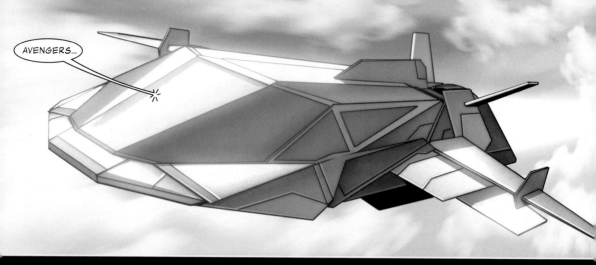

AVENGERS...

...ASSEMBLE!!

WILL SOMEONE **PLEASE** SHUT HIM UP?

YOU'RE A LONG WAY FROM BEING AN AVENGER, HUMBERTO.

CALL ME **REPTIL.** MY GRANDFATHER TRADEMARKED IT AND EVERYTHING.

AND I'M **ON THE WAY,** RIGHT? THIS IS THE FIRST STEP TO BEING A FULL-ON SUPER HERO, LIKE YOU AND CLOUD 9.

I HAVE COMMEMORATIVE PLATES?

LET'S SLOW DOWN A LITTLE, REPTIL. TELL ME HOW YOU GOT YOUR POWERS.

WELL, UH, MY PARENTS WERE--*ARE* PALEONTOLOGISTS. I LIKE TO GO OUT TO THE DESERT AND LOOK FOR FOSSILS. YOU CAN FIND TRILOBITES, BRACHIOPODS...

ANYWAY, ONE DAY I DUG UP **THIS.**

LOOKS LIKE A PIECE OF CRYSTALLIZED BONE.

THERE WAS A ROCKSLIDE...I RAN TO GET OUT OF THE WAY. IT WAS ONLY WHEN I WAS SAFE THAT I REALIZED HOW FAR I'D GONE AND HOW **FAST.**

I CAN TAKE ON THE ABILITIES OF DIFFERENT DINOSAURS JUST BY THINKING ABOUT IT.

BUT ONLY ONE THING AT A TIME, RIGHT? YOU CAN'T SHIFT COMPLETELY INTO DINOSAUR FORM.

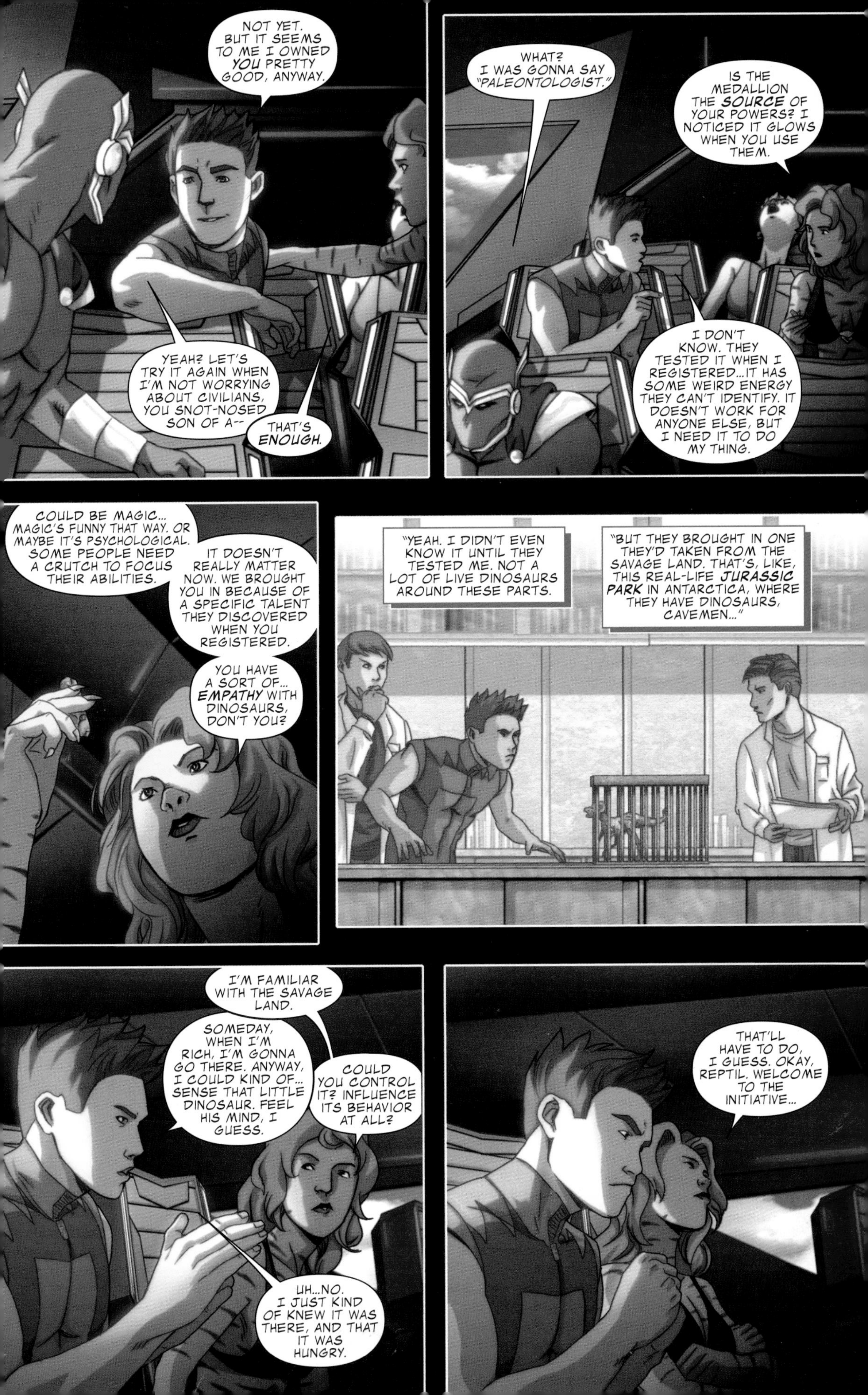
NOT YET. BUT IT SEEMS TO ME I OWNED YOU PRETTY GOOD, ANYWAY.
YEAH? LET'S TRY IT AGAIN WHEN I'M NOT WORRYING ABOUT CIVILIANS, YOU SNOT-NOSED SON OF A--
THAT'S ENOUGH.
WHAT? I WAS GONNA SAY "PALEONTOLOGIST."
IS THE MEDALLION THE SOURCE OF YOUR POWERS? I NOTICED IT GLOWS WHEN YOU USE THEM.
I DON'T KNOW. THEY TESTED IT WHEN I REGISTERED...IT HAS SOME WEIRD ENERGY THEY CAN'T IDENTIFY. IT DOESN'T WORK FOR ANYONE ELSE, BUT I NEED IT TO DO MY THING.
COULD BE MAGIC... MAGIC'S FUNNY THAT WAY. OR MAYBE IT'S PSYCHOLOGICAL. SOME PEOPLE NEED A CRUTCH TO FOCUS THEIR ABILITIES.
IT DOESN'T REALLY MATTER NOW. WE BROUGHT YOU IN BECAUSE OF A SPECIFIC TALENT THEY DISCOVERED WHEN YOU REGISTERED.
YOU HAVE A SORT OF... EMPATHY WITH DINOSAURS, DON'T YOU?
"YEAH. I DIDN'T EVEN KNOW IT UNTIL THEY TESTED ME. NOT A LOT OF LIVE DINOSAURS AROUND THESE PARTS.
"BUT THEY BROUGHT IN ONE THEY'D TAKEN FROM THE SAVAGE LAND. THAT'S, LIKE, THIS REAL-LIFE JURASSIC PARK IN ANTARCTICA, WHERE THEY HAVE DINOSAURS, CAVEMEN..."
I'M FAMILIAR WITH THE SAVAGE LAND.
SOMEDAY, WHEN I'M RICH, I'M GONNA GO THERE. ANYWAY, I COULD KIND OF... SENSE THAT LITTLE DINOSAUR. FEEL HIS MIND, I GUESS.
COULD YOU CONTROL IT? INFLUENCE ITS BEHAVIOR AT ALL?
UH...NO. I JUST KIND OF KNEW IT WAS THERE, AND THAT IT WAS HUNGRY.
THAT'LL HAVE TO DO, I GUESS. OKAY, REPTIL. WELCOME TO THE INITIATIVE...

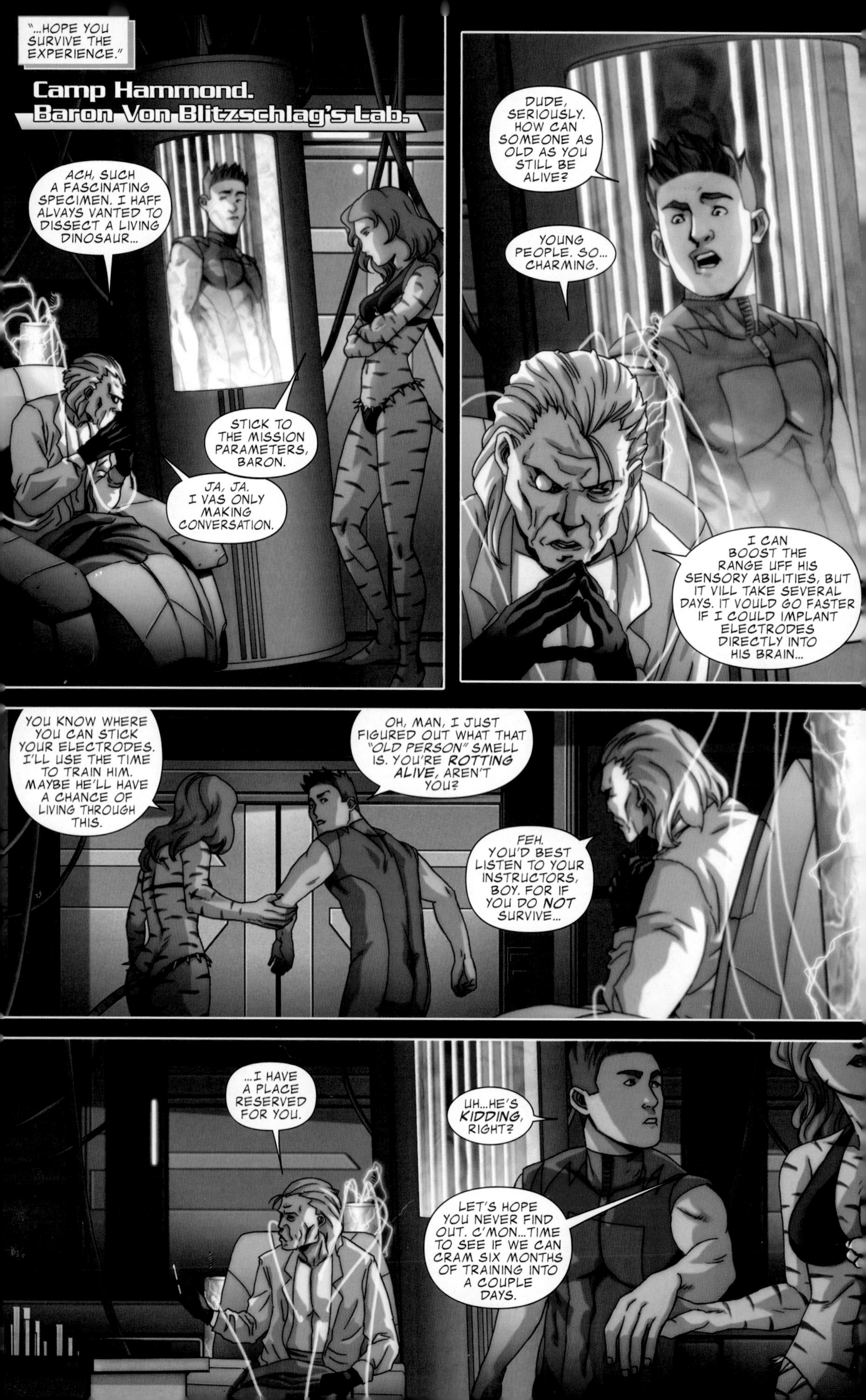
"...HOPE YOU SURVIVE THE EXPERIENCE."
Camp Hammond. Baron Von Blitzschlag's Lab.
ACH, SUCH A FASCINATING SPECIMEN. I HAFF ALVAYS VANTED TO DISSECT A LIVING DINOSAUR...
STICK TO THE MISSION PARAMETERS, BARON.
JA, JA. I VAS ONLY MAKING CONVERSATION.
DUDE, SERIOUSLY. HOW CAN SOMEONE AS OLD AS YOU STILL BE ALIVE?
YOUNG PEOPLE. SO... CHARMING.
I CAN BOOST THE RANGE UFF HIS SENSORY ABILITIES, BUT IT VILL TAKE SEVERAL DAYS. IT VOULD GO FASTER IF I COULD IMPLANT ELECTRODES DIRECTLY INTO HIS BRAIN...
YOU KNOW WHERE YOU CAN STICK YOUR ELECTRODES. I'LL USE THE TIME TO TRAIN HIM. MAYBE HE'LL HAVE A CHANCE OF LIVING THROUGH THIS.
OH, MAN, I JUST FIGURED OUT WHAT THAT "OLD PERSON" SMELL IS. YOU'RE ROTTING ALIVE, AREN'T YOU?
FEH. YOU'D BEST LISTEN TO YOUR INSTRUCTORS, BOY. FOR IF YOU DO NOT SURVIVE...
...I HAVE A PLACE RESERVED FOR YOU.
UH...HE'S KIDDING, RIGHT?
LET'S HOPE YOU NEVER FIND OUT. C'MON...TIME TO SEE IF WE CAN CRAM SIX MONTHS OF TRAINING INTO A COUPLE DAYS.

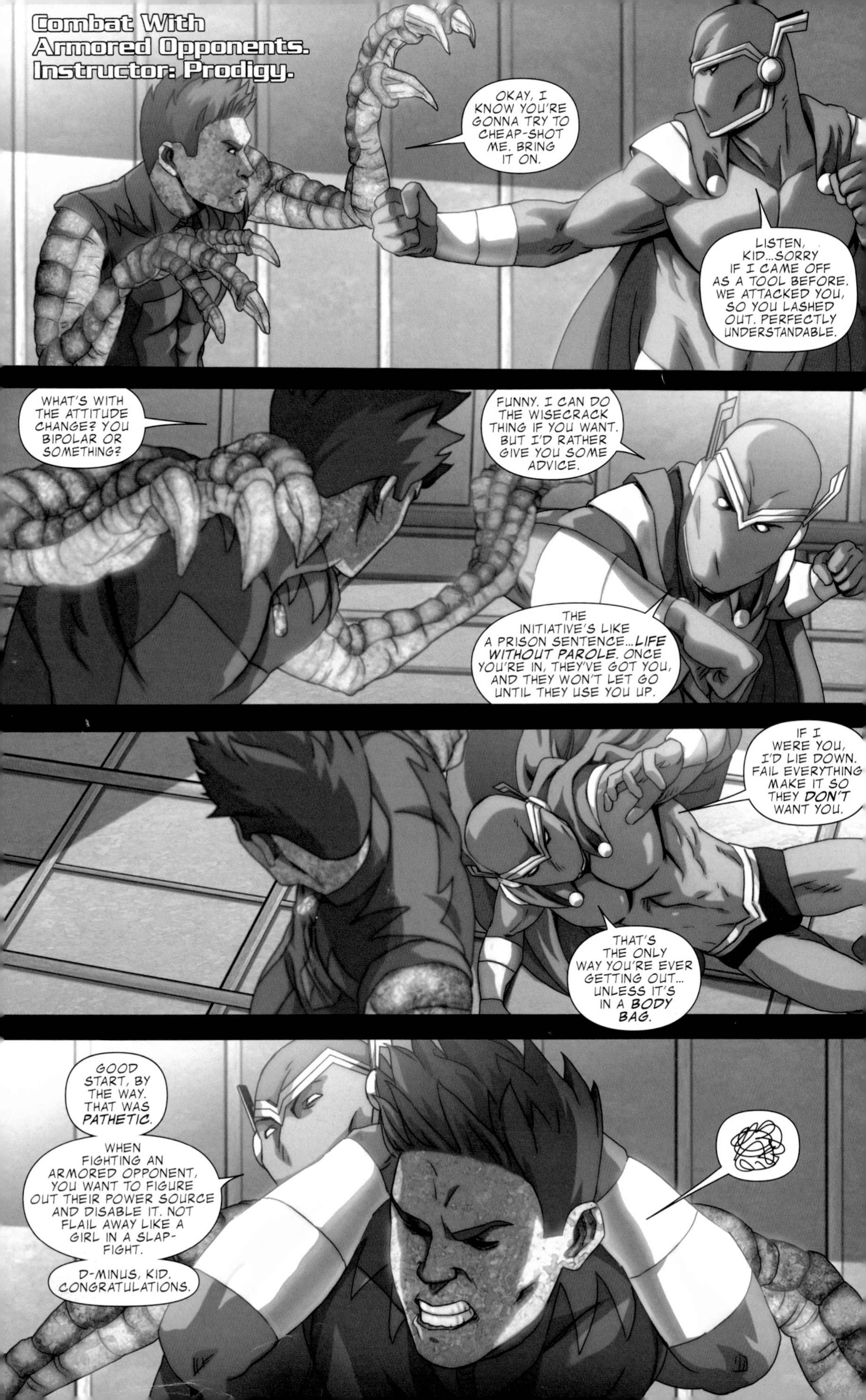
Combat With Armored Opponents. Instructor: Prodigy.
OKAY, I KNOW YOU'RE GONNA TRY TO CHEAP-SHOT ME. BRING IT ON.
LISTEN, KID...SORRY IF I CAME OFF AS A TOOL BEFORE. WE ATTACKED YOU, SO YOU LASHED OUT. PERFECTLY UNDERSTANDABLE.
WHAT'S WITH THE ATTITUDE CHANGE? YOU BIPOLAR OR SOMETHING?
FUNNY. I CAN DO THE WISECRACK THING IF YOU WANT. BUT I'D RATHER GIVE YOU SOME ADVICE.
THE INITIATIVE'S LIKE A PRISON SENTENCE...LIFE WITHOUT PAROLE. ONCE YOU'RE IN, THEY'VE GOT YOU, AND THEY WON'T LET GO UNTIL THEY USE YOU UP.
IF I WERE YOU, I'D LIE DOWN. FAIL EVERYTHING MAKE IT SO THEY DON'T WANT YOU.
THAT'S THE ONLY WAY YOU'RE EVER GETTING OUT... UNLESS IT'S IN A BODY BAG.
GOOD START, BY THE WAY. THAT WAS PATHETIC.
WHEN FIGHTING AN ARMORED OPPONENT, YOU WANT TO FIGURE OUT THEIR POWER SOURCE AND DISABLE IT. NOT FLAIL AWAY LIKE A GIRL IN A SLAP-FIGHT.
D-MINUS, KID. CONGRATULATIONS.

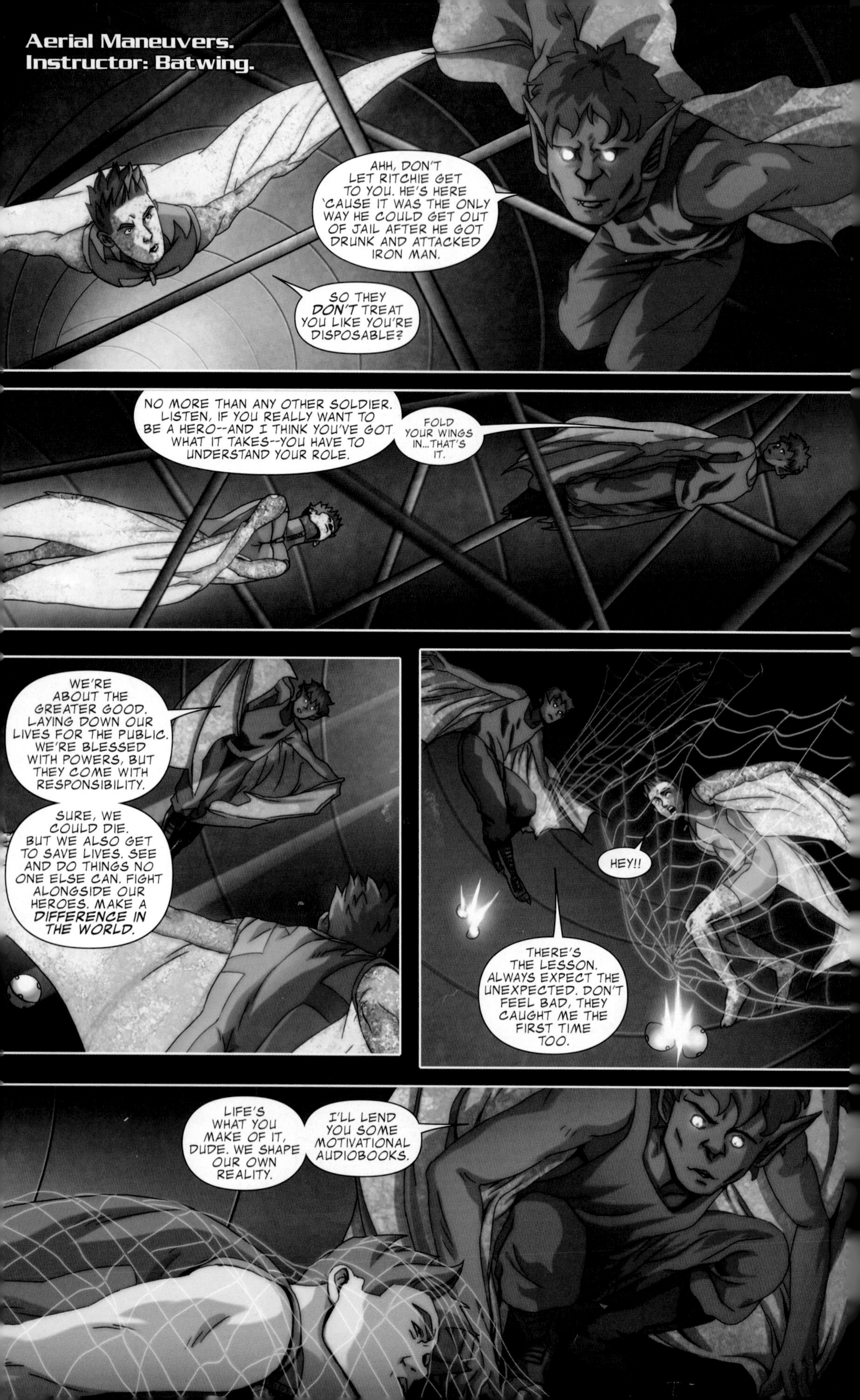
Aerial Maneuvers.
Instructor: Batwing.
AHH, DON'T LET RITCHIE GET TO YOU. HE'S HERE 'CAUSE IT WAS THE ONLY WAY HE COULD GET OUT OF JAIL AFTER HE GOT DRUNK AND ATTACKED IRON MAN.
SO THEY DON'T TREAT YOU LIKE YOU'RE DISPOSABLE?
NO MORE THAN ANY OTHER SOLDIER. LISTEN, IF YOU REALLY WANT TO BE A HERO--AND I THINK YOU'VE GOT WHAT IT TAKES--YOU HAVE TO UNDERSTAND YOUR ROLE.
FOLD YOUR WINGS IN...THAT'S IT.
WE'RE ABOUT THE GREATER GOOD. LAYING DOWN OUR LIVES FOR THE PUBLIC. WE'RE BLESSED WITH POWERS, BUT THEY COME WITH RESPONSIBILITY.
SURE, WE COULD DIE. BUT WE ALSO GET TO SAVE LIVES. SEE AND DO THINGS NO ONE ELSE CAN. FIGHT ALONGSIDE OUR HEROES. MAKE A DIFFERENCE IN THE WORLD.
HEY!!
THERE'S THE LESSON. ALWAYS EXPECT THE UNEXPECTED. DON'T FEEL BAD, THEY CAUGHT ME THE FIRST TIME TOO.
LIFE'S WHAT YOU MAKE OF IT, DUDE. WE SHAPE OUR OWN REALITY.
I'LL LEND YOU SOME MOTIVATIONAL AUDIOBOOKS.

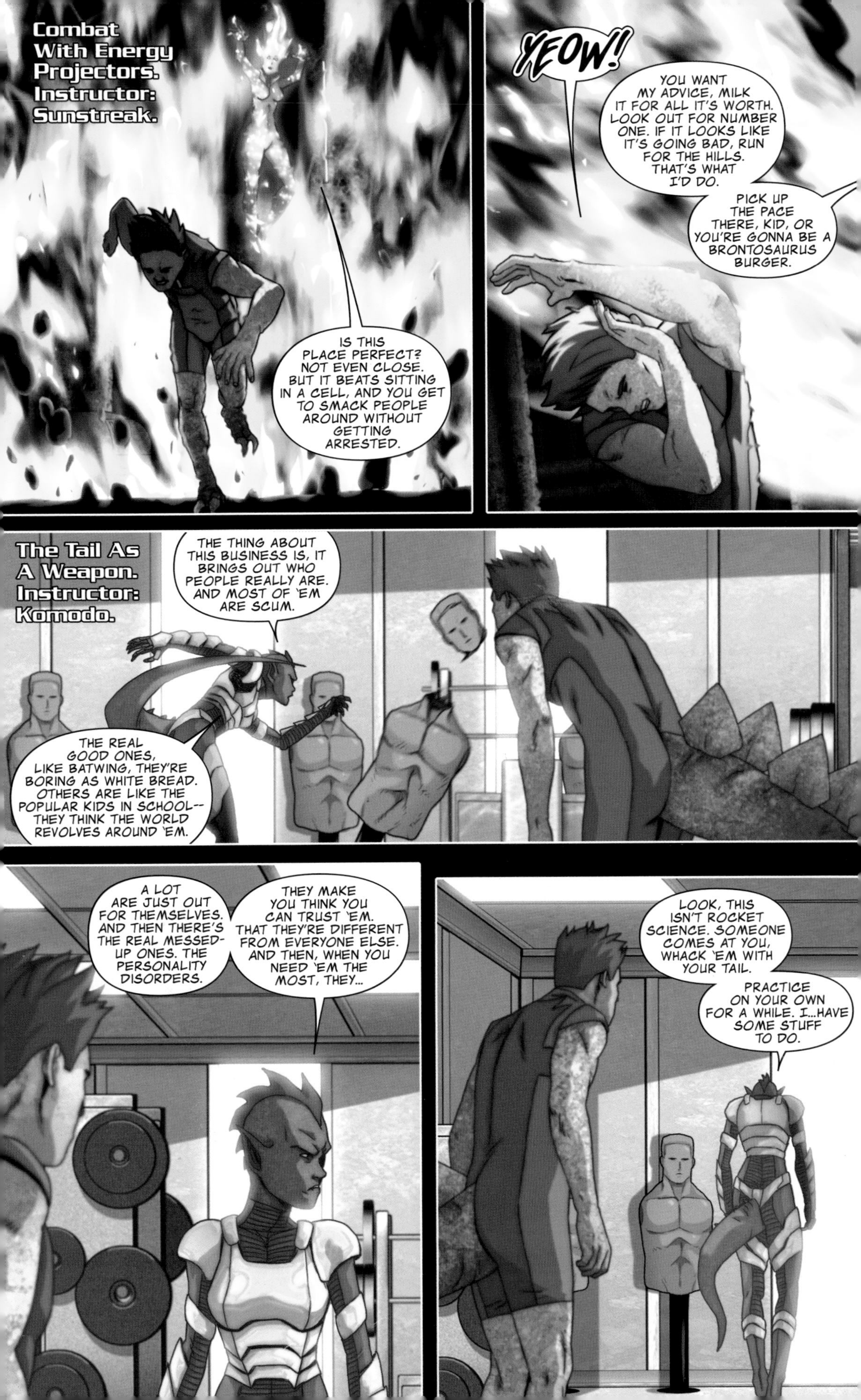
Combat With Energy Projectors. Instructor: Sunstreak.
IS THIS PLACE PERFECT? NOT EVEN CLOSE. BUT IT BEATS SITTING IN A CELL, AND YOU GET TO SMACK PEOPLE AROUND WITHOUT GETTING ARRESTED.
YEOW!
YOU WANT MY ADVICE, MILK IT FOR ALL IT'S WORTH. LOOK OUT FOR NUMBER ONE. IF IT LOOKS LIKE IT'S GOING BAD, RUN FOR THE HILLS. THAT'S WHAT I'D DO.
PICK UP THE PACE THERE, KID, OR YOU'RE GONNA BE A BRONTOSAURUS BURGER.
The Tail As A Weapon. Instructor: Komodo.
THE THING ABOUT THIS BUSINESS IS, IT BRINGS OUT WHO PEOPLE REALLY ARE. AND MOST OF 'EM ARE SCUM.
THE REAL GOOD ONES, LIKE BATWING, THEY'RE BORING AS WHITE BREAD. OTHERS ARE LIKE THE POPULAR KIDS IN SCHOOL-- THEY THINK THE WORLD REVOLVES AROUND 'EM.
A LOT ARE JUST OUT FOR THEMSELVES. AND THEN THERE'S THE REAL MESSED-UP ONES. THE PERSONALITY DISORDERS.
THEY MAKE YOU THINK YOU CAN TRUST 'EM. THAT THEY'RE DIFFERENT FROM EVERYONE ELSE. AND THEN, WHEN YOU NEED 'EM THE MOST, THEY...
LOOK, THIS ISN'T ROCKET SCIENCE. SOMEONE COMES AT YOU, WHACK 'EM WITH YOUR TAIL.
PRACTICE ON YOUR OWN FOR A WHILE. I...HAVE SOME STUFF TO DO.

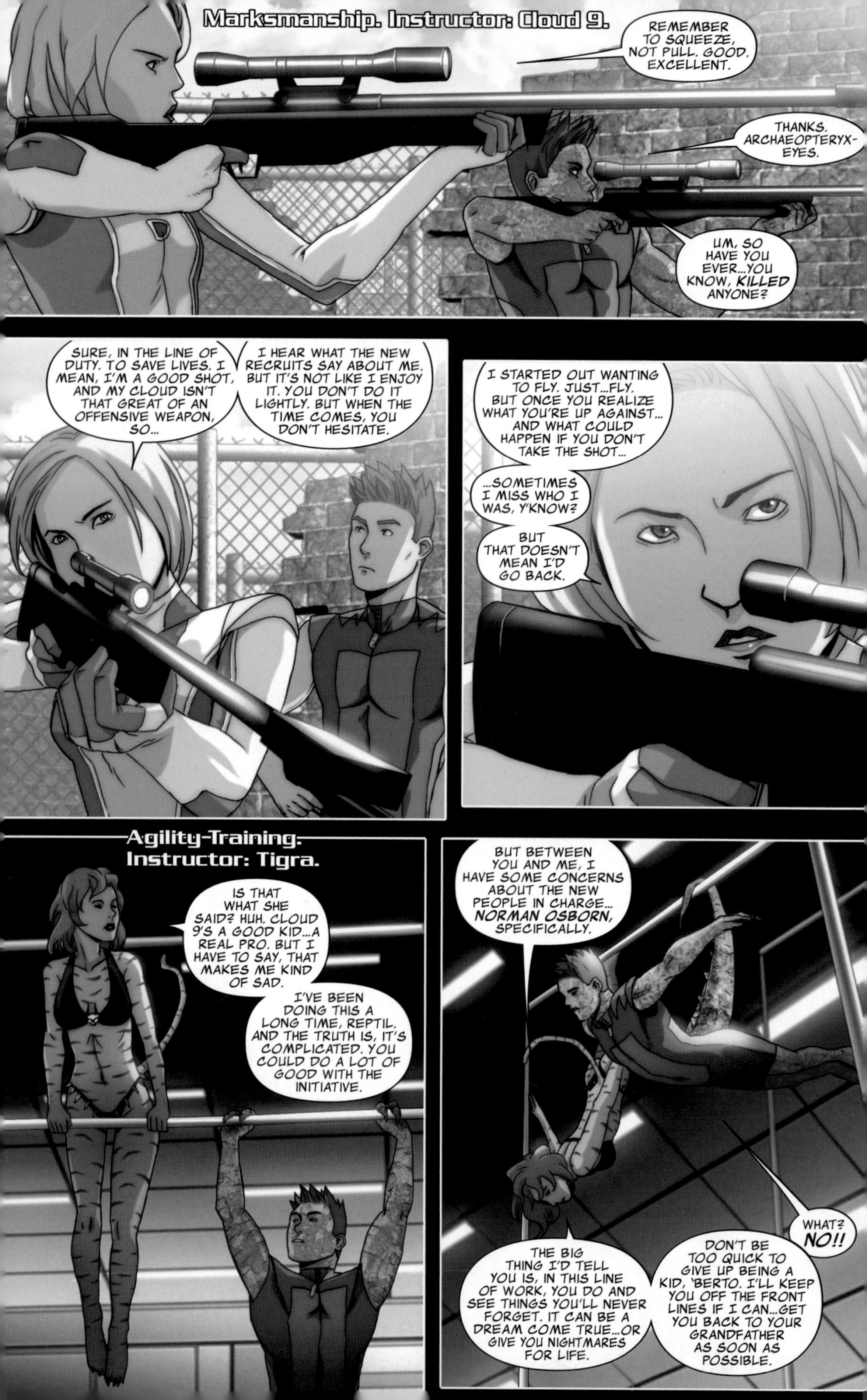
Marksmanship. Instructor: Cloud 9.
REMEMBER TO SQUEEZE, NOT PULL. GOOD. EXCELLENT.
THANKS. ARCHAEOPTERYX-EYES.
UM, SO HAVE YOU EVER...YOU KNOW, KILLED ANYONE?
SURE, IN THE LINE OF DUTY. TO SAVE LIVES. I MEAN, I'M A GOOD SHOT, AND MY CLOUD ISN'T THAT GREAT OF AN OFFENSIVE WEAPON, SO...
I HEAR WHAT THE NEW RECRUITS SAY ABOUT ME. BUT IT'S NOT LIKE I ENJOY IT. YOU DON'T DO IT LIGHTLY. BUT WHEN THE TIME COMES, YOU DON'T HESITATE.
I STARTED OUT WANTING TO FLY. JUST...FLY. BUT ONCE YOU REALIZE WHAT YOU'RE UP AGAINST... AND WHAT COULD HAPPEN IF YOU DON'T TAKE THE SHOT...
...SOMETIMES I MISS WHO I WAS, Y'KNOW?
BUT THAT DOESN'T MEAN I'D GO BACK.
Agility-Training. Instructor: Tigra.
IS THAT WHAT SHE SAID? HUH. CLOUD 9'S A GOOD KID...A REAL PRO. BUT I HAVE TO SAY, THAT MAKES ME KIND OF SAD.
I'VE BEEN DOING THIS A LONG TIME, REPTIL. AND THE TRUTH IS, IT'S COMPLICATED. YOU COULD DO A LOT OF GOOD WITH THE INITIATIVE.
BUT BETWEEN YOU AND ME, I HAVE SOME CONCERNS ABOUT THE NEW PEOPLE IN CHARGE... NORMAN OSBORN, SPECIFICALLY.
WHAT? NO!!
THE BIG THING I'D TELL YOU IS, IN THIS LINE OF WORK, YOU DO AND SEE THINGS YOU'LL NEVER FORGET. IT CAN BE A DREAM COME TRUE...OR GIVE YOU NIGHTMARES FOR LIFE.
DON'T BE TOO QUICK TO GIVE UP BEING A KID, 'BERTO. I'LL KEEP YOU OFF THE FRONT LINES IF I CAN...GET YOU BACK TO YOUR GRANDFATHER AS SOON AS POSSIBLE.

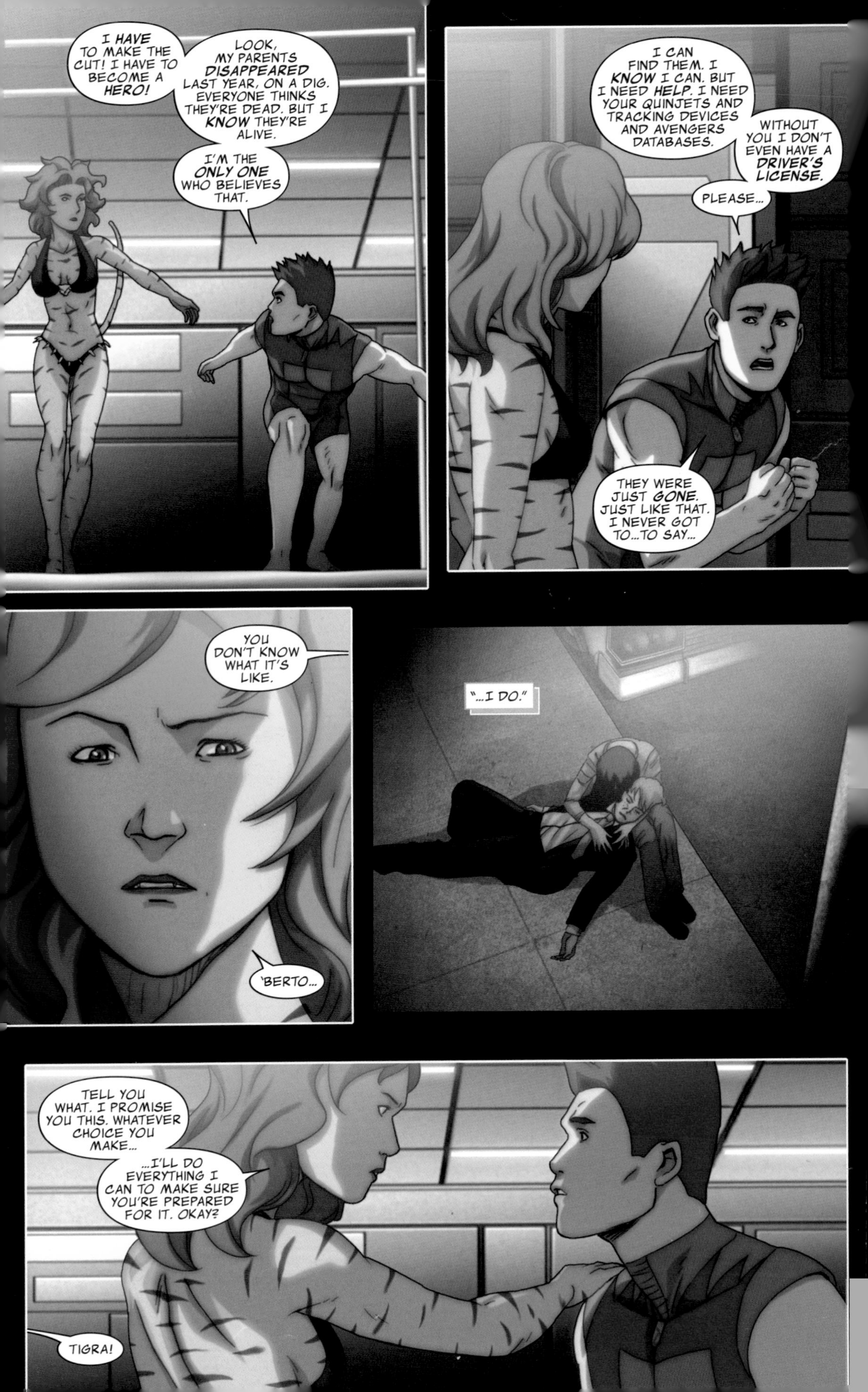
I HAVE TO MAKE THE CUT! I HAVE TO BECOME A HERO!
LOOK, MY PARENTS DISAPPEARED LAST YEAR, ON A DIG. EVERYONE THINKS THEY'RE DEAD. BUT I KNOW THEY'RE ALIVE.
I'M THE ONLY ONE WHO BELIEVES THAT.
I CAN FIND THEM. I KNOW I CAN. BUT I NEED HELP. I NEED YOUR QUINJETS AND TRACKING DEVICES AND AVENGERS DATABASES.
WITHOUT YOU I DON'T EVEN HAVE A DRIVER'S LICENSE.
PLEASE...
THEY WERE JUST GONE. JUST LIKE THAT. I NEVER GOT TO...TO SAY...
YOU DON'T KNOW WHAT IT'S LIKE.
'BERTO...
"...I DO."
TELL YOU WHAT. I PROMISE YOU THIS. WHATEVER CHOICE YOU MAKE...
...I'LL DO EVERYTHING I CAN TO MAKE SURE YOU'RE PREPARED FOR IT. OKAY?
TIGRA!

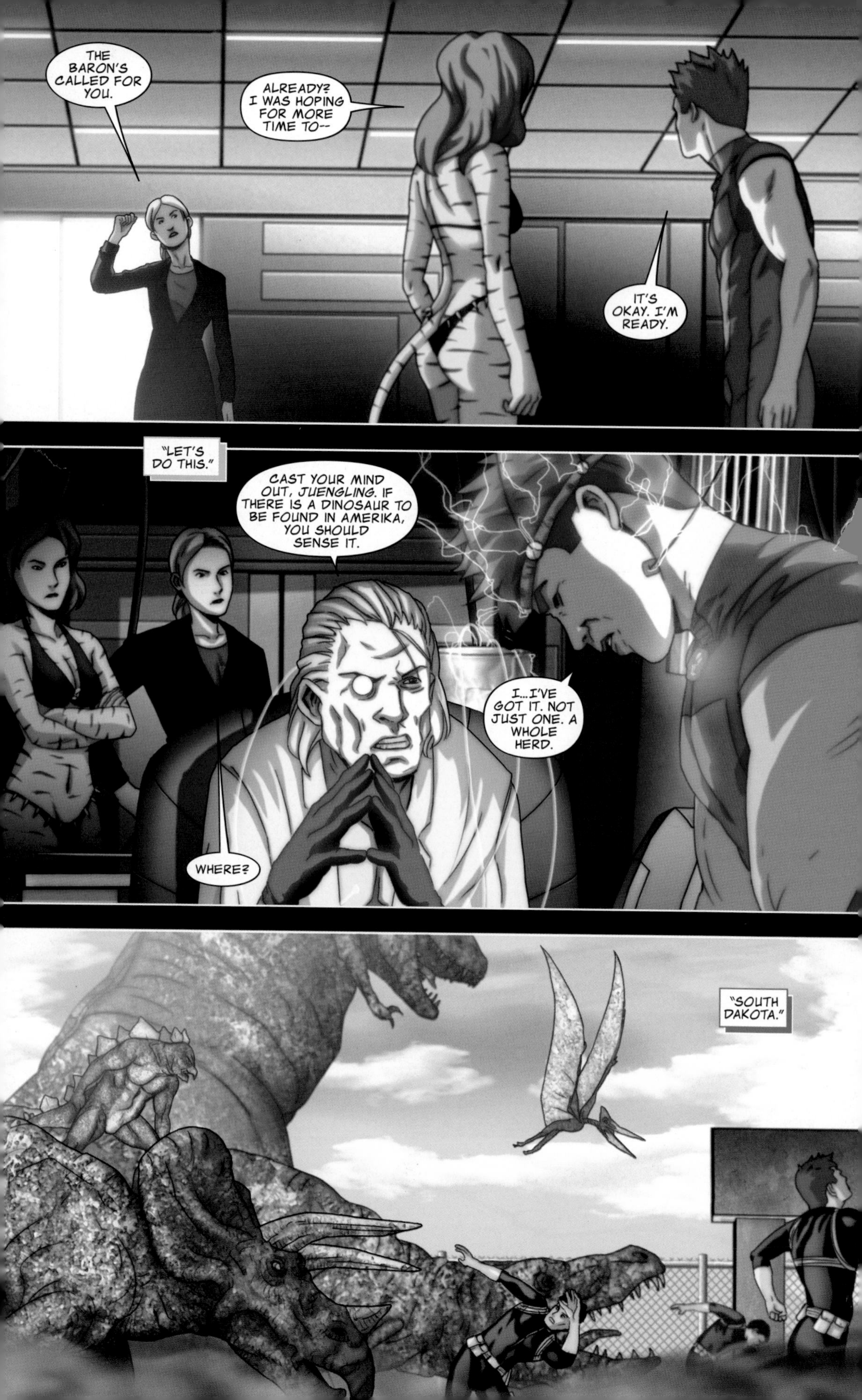
THE BARON'S CALLED FOR YOU.
ALREADY? I WAS HOPING FOR MORE TIME TO--
IT'S OKAY. I'M READY.
"LET'S DO THIS."
CAST YOUR MIND OUT, JUENGLING. IF THERE IS A DINOSAUR TO BE FOUND IN AMERIKA, YOU SHOULD SENSE IT.
I...I'VE GOT IT. NOT JUST ONE. A WHOLE HERD.
WHERE?
"SOUTH DAKOTA."

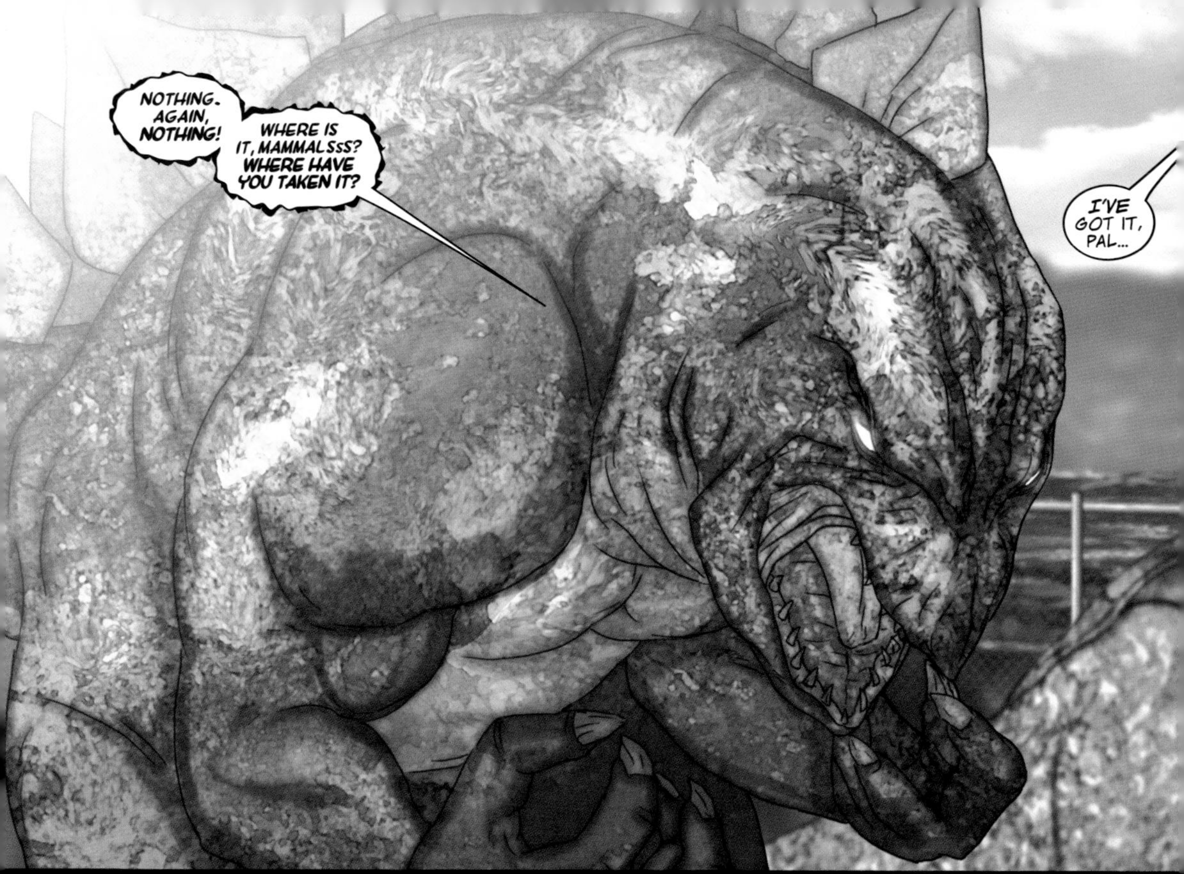
NOTHING. AGAIN, NOTHING!
WHERE IS IT, MAMMALSsS? WHERE HAVE YOU TAKEN IT?
I'VE GOT IT, PAL...

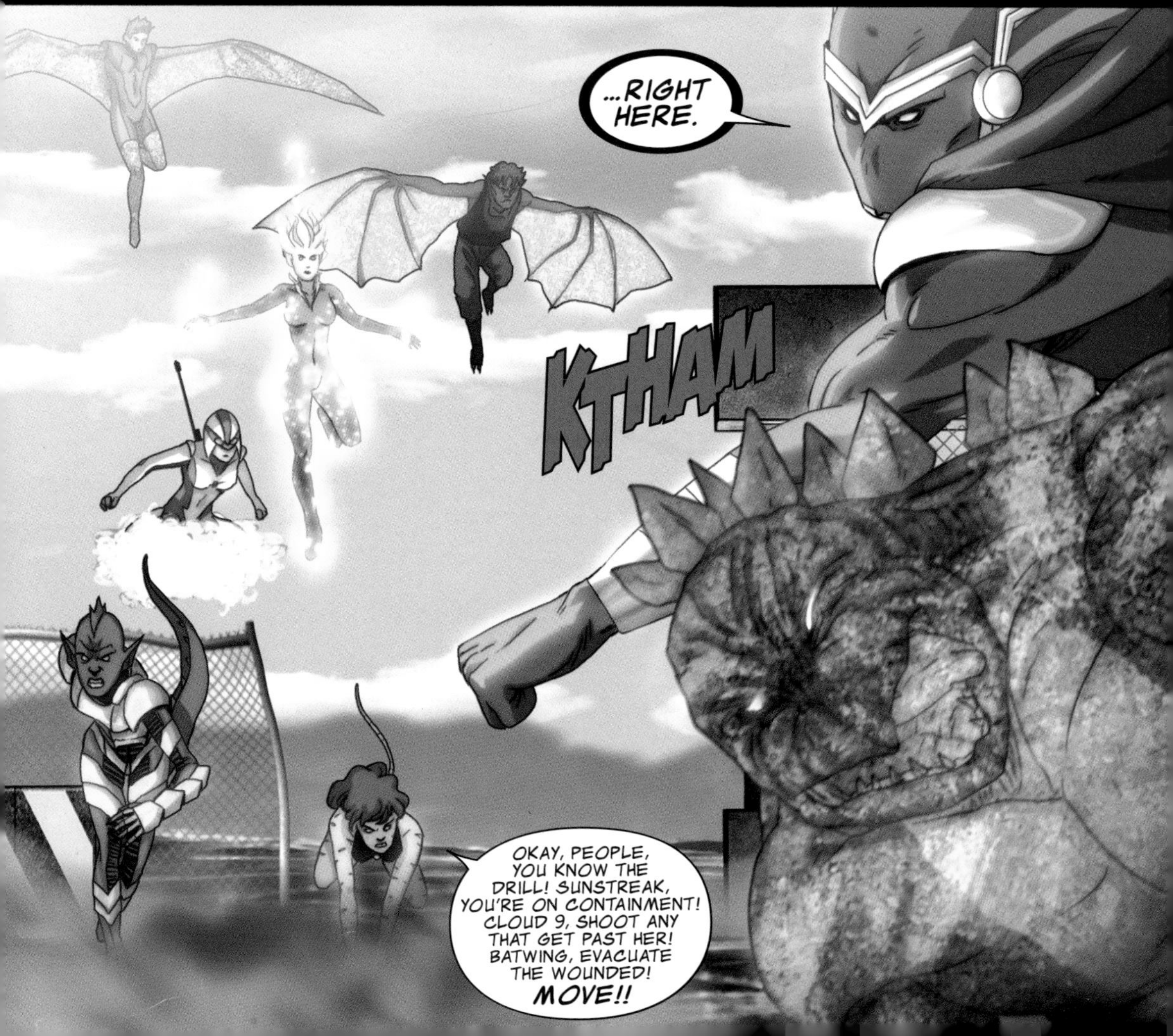
...RIGHT HERE.
KTHAM
OKAY, PEOPLE, YOU KNOW THE DRILL! SUNSTREAK, YOU'RE ON CONTAINMENT! CLOUD 9, SHOOT ANY THAT GET PAST HER! BATWING, EVACUATE THE WOUNDED! MOVE!!

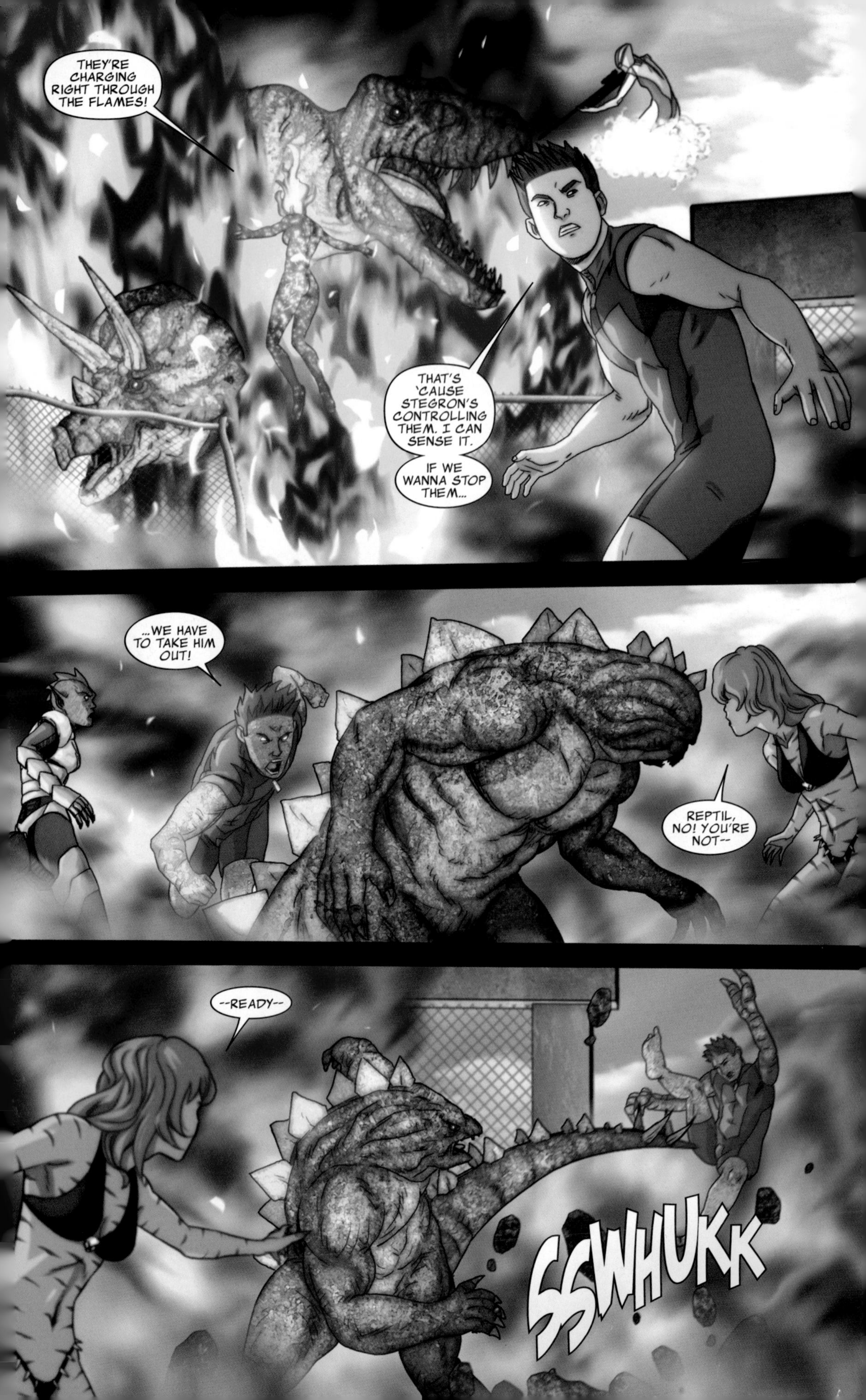
THEY'RE CHARGING RIGHT THROUGH THE FLAMES!
THAT'S 'CAUSE STEGRON'S CONTROLLING THEM. I CAN SENSE IT.
IF WE WANNA STOP THEM...
...WE HAVE TO TAKE HIM OUT!
REPTIL, NO! YOU'RE NOT--
--READY--
SSWHUKK

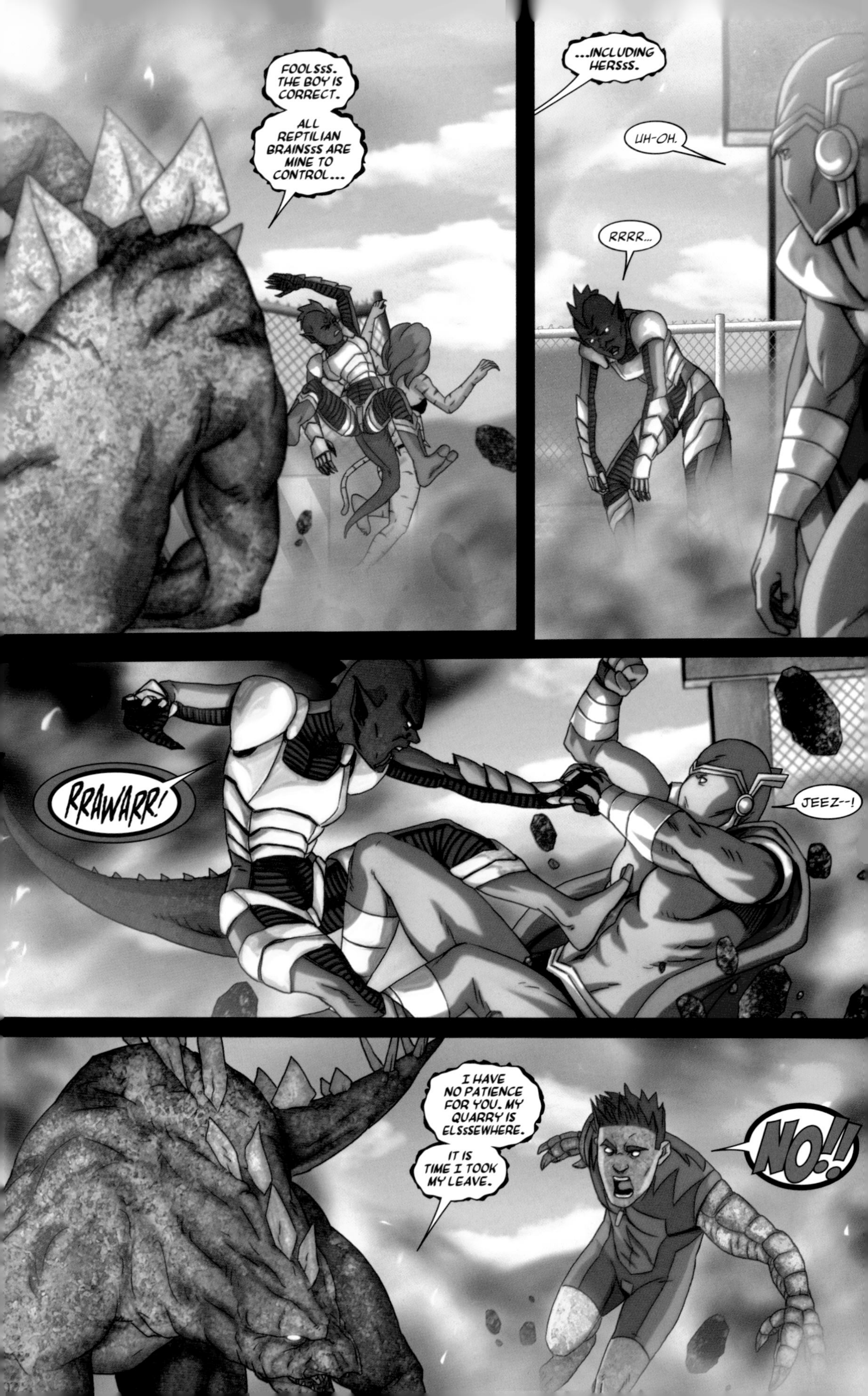
FOOLSSS. THE BOY IS CORRECT.
ALL REPTILIAN BRAINSSS ARE MINE TO CONTROL...
...INCLUDING HERSSS.
UH-OH.
RRRR...
RRAWARR!
JEEZ--!
I HAVE NO PATIENCE FOR YOU. MY QUARRY IS ELSSSEWHERE.
IT IS TIME I TOOK MY LEAVE.
NO!!

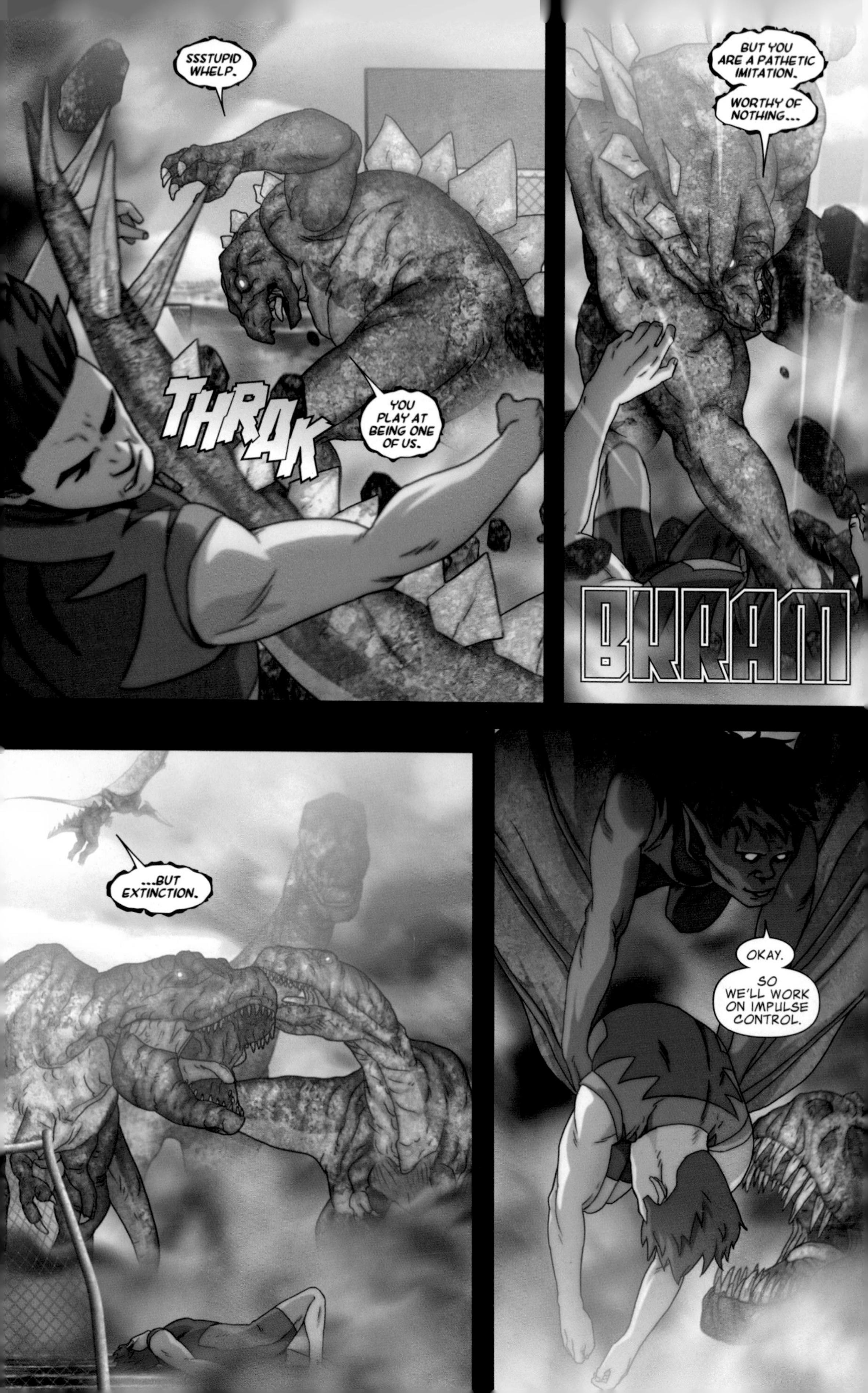
SSSTUPID WHELP.
THRAK
YOU PLAY AT BEING ONE OF US.
BUT YOU ARE A PATHETIC IMITATION.
WORTHY OF NOTHING...
BKRAM
...BUT EXTINCTION.
OKAY.
SO WE'LL WORK ON IMPULSE CONTROL.

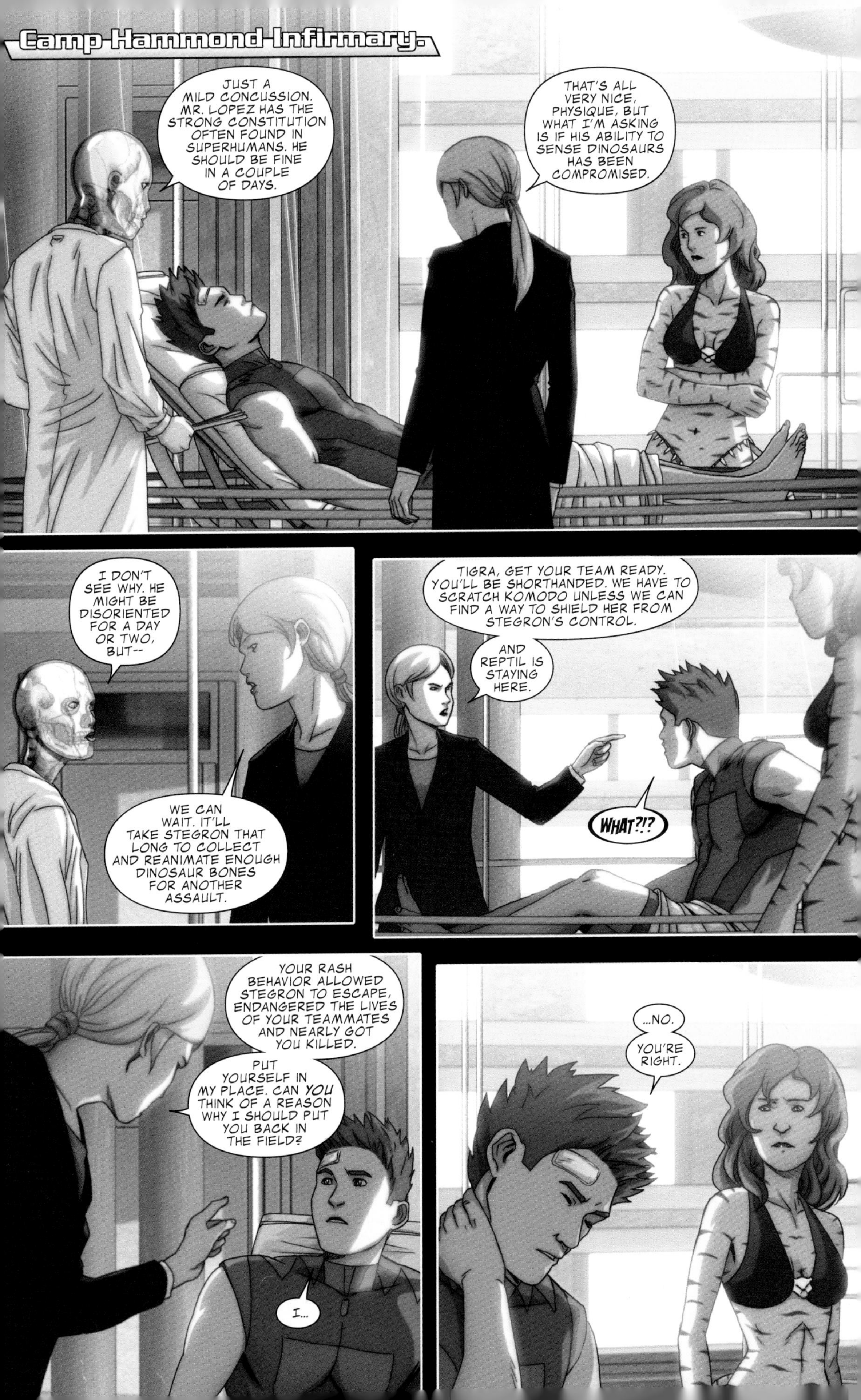
Camp Hammond Infirmary.
JUST A MILD CONCUSSION. MR. LOPEZ HAS THE STRONG CONSTITUTION OFTEN FOUND IN SUPERHUMANS. HE SHOULD BE FINE IN A COUPLE OF DAYS.
THAT'S ALL VERY NICE, PHYSIQUE, BUT WHAT I'M ASKING IS IF HIS ABILITY TO SENSE DINOSAURS HAS BEEN COMPROMISED.
I DON'T SEE WHY. HE MIGHT BE DISORIENTED FOR A DAY OR TWO, BUT--
WE CAN WAIT. IT'LL TAKE STEGRON THAT LONG TO COLLECT AND REANIMATE ENOUGH DINOSAUR BONES FOR ANOTHER ASSAULT.
TIGRA, GET YOUR TEAM READY. YOU'LL BE SHORTHANDED. WE HAVE TO SCRATCH KOMODO UNLESS WE CAN FIND A WAY TO SHIELD HER FROM STEGRON'S CONTROL.
AND REPTIL IS STAYING HERE.
WHAT?!?
YOUR RASH BEHAVIOR ALLOWED STEGRON TO ESCAPE, ENDANGERED THE LIVES OF YOUR TEAMMATES AND NEARLY GOT YOU KILLED.
PUT YOURSELF IN MY PLACE. CAN YOU THINK OF A REASON WHY I SHOULD PUT YOU BACK IN THE FIELD?
I...
...NO.
YOU'RE RIGHT.

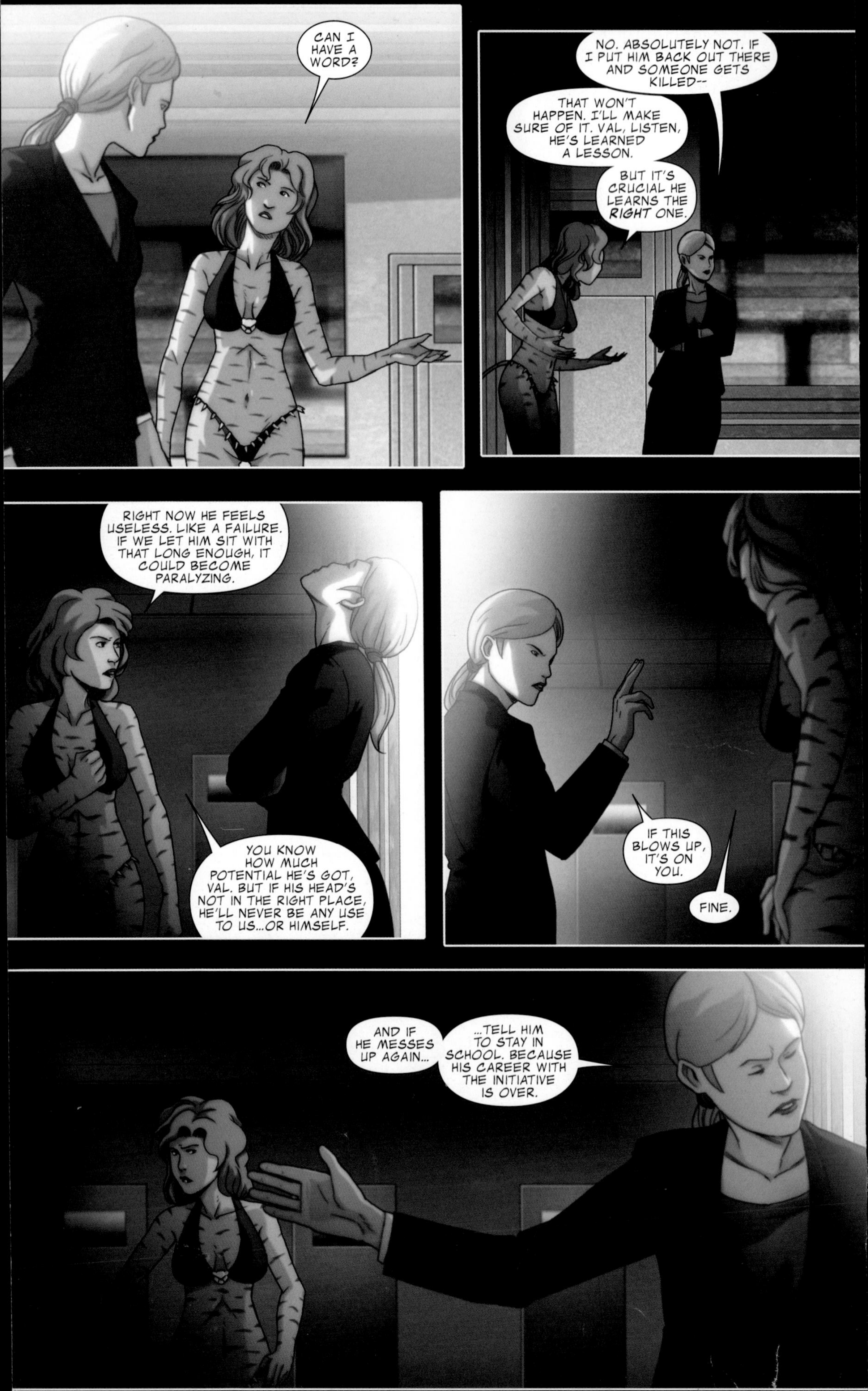
CAN I HAVE A WORD?
NO. ABSOLUTELY NOT. IF I PUT HIM BACK OUT THERE AND SOMEONE GETS KILLED--
THAT WON'T HAPPEN. I'LL MAKE SURE OF IT. VAL, LISTEN, HE'S LEARNED A LESSON.
BUT IT'S CRUCIAL HE LEARNS THE *RIGHT* ONE.
RIGHT NOW HE FEELS USELESS. LIKE A FAILURE. IF WE LET HIM SIT WITH THAT LONG ENOUGH, IT COULD BECOME PARALYZING.
YOU KNOW HOW MUCH POTENTIAL HE'S GOT, VAL. BUT IF HIS HEAD'S NOT IN THE RIGHT PLACE, HE'LL NEVER BE ANY USE TO US...OR HIMSELF.
IF THIS BLOWS UP, IT'S ON YOU.
FINE.
AND IF HE MESSES UP AGAIN...
...TELL HIM TO STAY IN SCHOOL. BECAUSE HIS CAREER WITH THE INITIATIVE IS OVER.

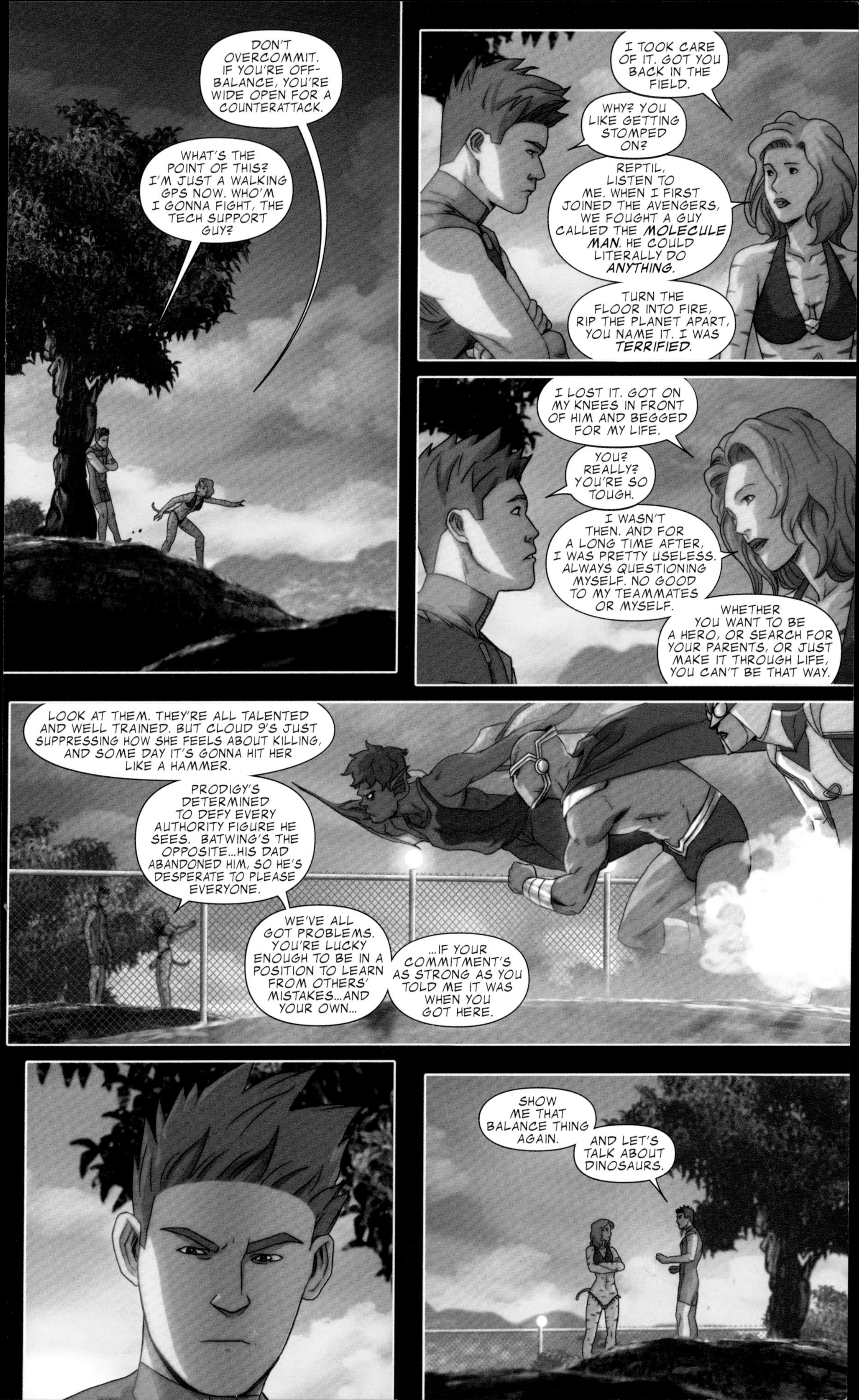
DON'T OVERCOMMIT. IF YOU'RE OFF-BALANCE, YOU'RE WIDE OPEN FOR A COUNTERATTACK.
WHAT'S THE POINT OF THIS? I'M JUST A WALKING GPS NOW. WHO'M I GONNA FIGHT, THE TECH SUPPORT GUY?
I TOOK CARE OF IT. GOT YOU BACK IN THE FIELD.
WHY? YOU LIKE GETTING STOMPED ON?
REPTIL, LISTEN TO ME. WHEN I FIRST JOINED THE AVENGERS, WE FOUGHT A GUY CALLED THE MOLECULE MAN. HE COULD LITERALLY DO ANYTHING.
TURN THE FLOOR INTO FIRE, RIP THE PLANET APART, YOU NAME IT. I WAS TERRIFIED.
I LOST IT. GOT ON MY KNEES IN FRONT OF HIM AND BEGGED FOR MY LIFE.
YOU? REALLY? YOU'RE SO TOUGH.
I WASN'T THEN. AND FOR A LONG TIME AFTER, I WAS PRETTY USELESS. ALWAYS QUESTIONING MYSELF. NO GOOD TO MY TEAMMATES OR MYSELF.
WHETHER YOU WANT TO BE A HERO, OR SEARCH FOR YOUR PARENTS, OR JUST MAKE IT THROUGH LIFE, YOU CAN'T BE THAT WAY.
LOOK AT THEM. THEY'RE ALL TALENTED AND WELL TRAINED. BUT CLOUD 9'S JUST SUPPRESSING HOW SHE FEELS ABOUT KILLING, AND SOME DAY IT'S GONNA HIT HER LIKE A HAMMER.
PRODIGY'S DETERMINED TO DEFY EVERY AUTHORITY FIGURE HE SEES. BATWING'S THE OPPOSITE...HIS DAD ABANDONED HIM, SO HE'S DESPERATE TO PLEASE EVERYONE.
WE'VE ALL GOT PROBLEMS. YOU'RE LUCKY ENOUGH TO BE IN A POSITION TO LEARN FROM OTHERS' MISTAKES...AND YOUR OWN...
...IF YOUR COMMITMENT'S AS STRONG AS YOU TOLD ME IT WAS WHEN YOU GOT HERE.
SHOW ME THAT BALANCE THING AGAIN.
AND LET'S TALK ABOUT DINOSAURS.

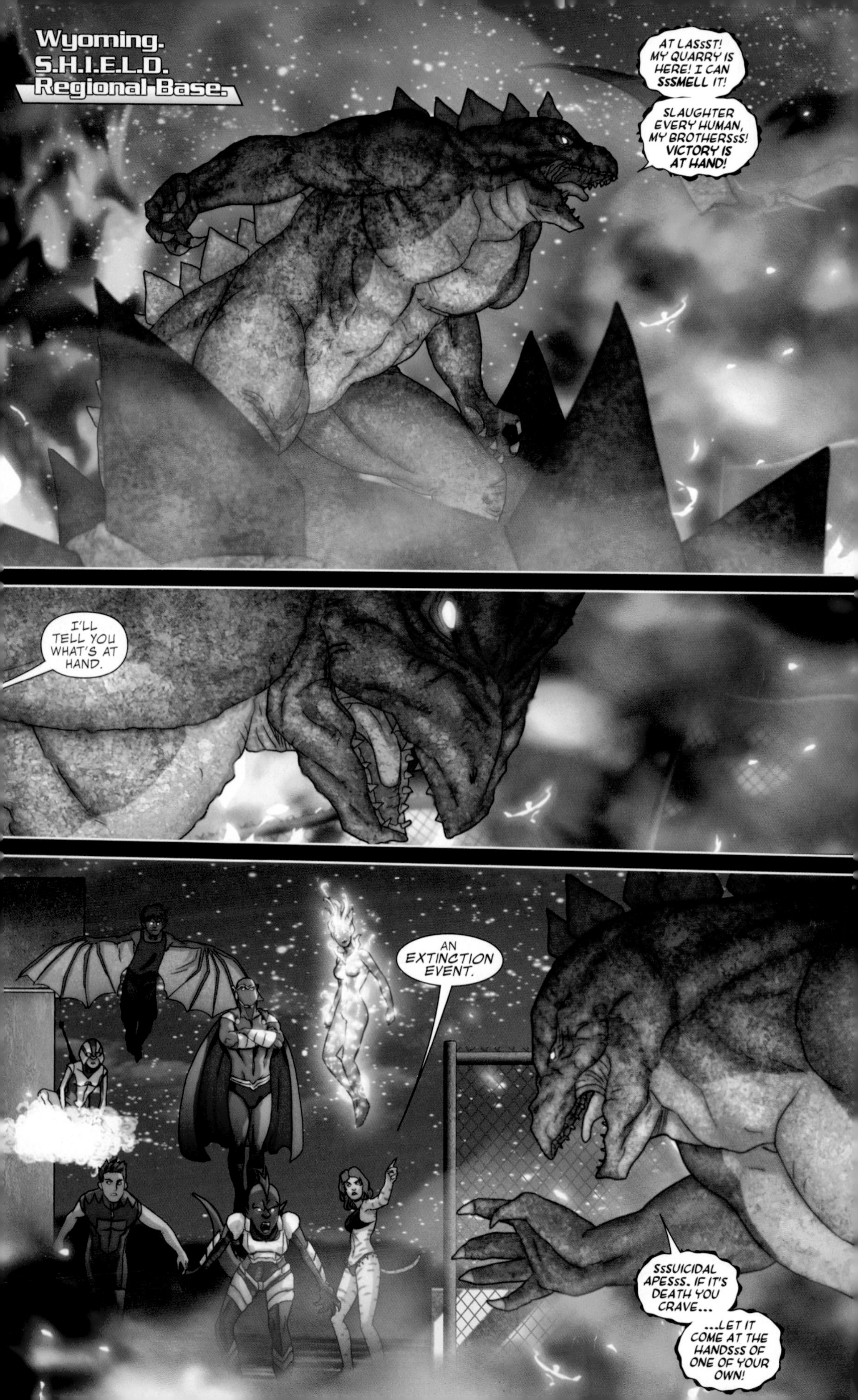

Wyoming. S.H.I.E.L.D. Regional Base.
AT LASSST! MY QUARRY IS HERE! I CAN SsSMELL IT!
SLAUGHTER EVERY HUMAN, MY BROTHERSsS! VICTORY IS AT HAND!
I'LL TELL YOU WHAT'S AT HAND.
AN EXTINCTION EVENT.
SsSUICIDAL APESsS. IF IT'S DEATH YOU CRAVE...
...LET IT COME AT THE HANDSsS OF ONE OF YOUR OWN!

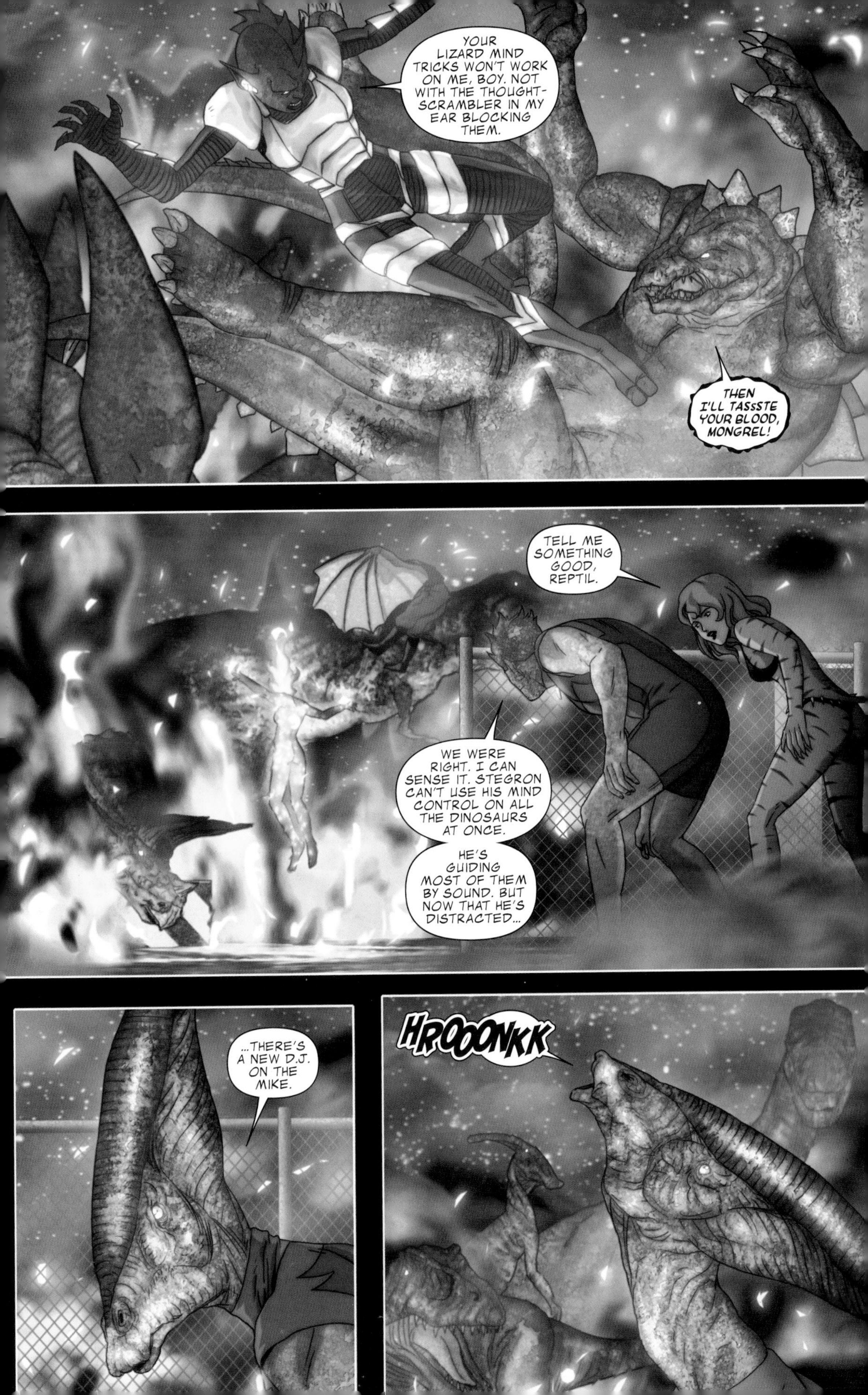
YOUR LIZARD MIND TRICKS WON'T WORK ON ME, BOY. NOT WITH THE THOUGHT-SCRAMBLER IN MY EAR BLOCKING THEM.
THEN I'LL TASSSTE YOUR BLOOD, MONGREL!
TELL ME SOMETHING GOOD, REPTIL.
WE WERE RIGHT. I CAN SENSE IT. STEGRON CAN'T USE HIS MIND CONTROL ON ALL THE DINOSAURS AT ONCE.
HE'S GUIDING MOST OF THEM BY SOUND. BUT NOW THAT HE'S DISTRACTED...
...THERE'S A NEW D.J. ON THE MIKE.
HROOONKK

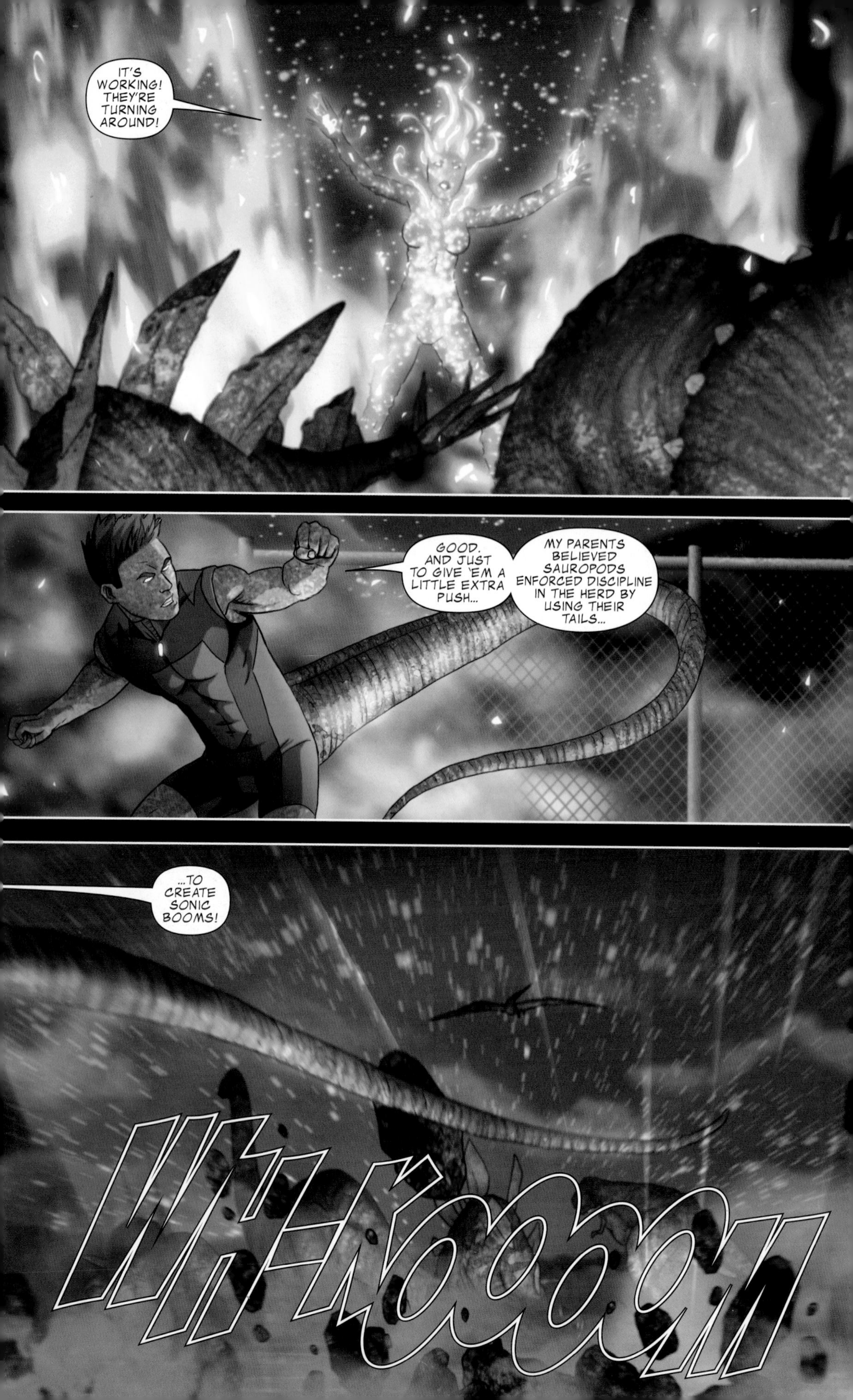
IT'S WORKING! THEY'RE TURNING AROUND!
GOOD. AND JUST TO GIVE 'EM A LITTLE EXTRA PUSH...
MY PARENTS BELIEVED SAUROPODS ENFORCED DISCIPLINE IN THE HERD BY USING THEIR TAILS...
...TO CREATE SONIC BOOMS!
WHOOOOM

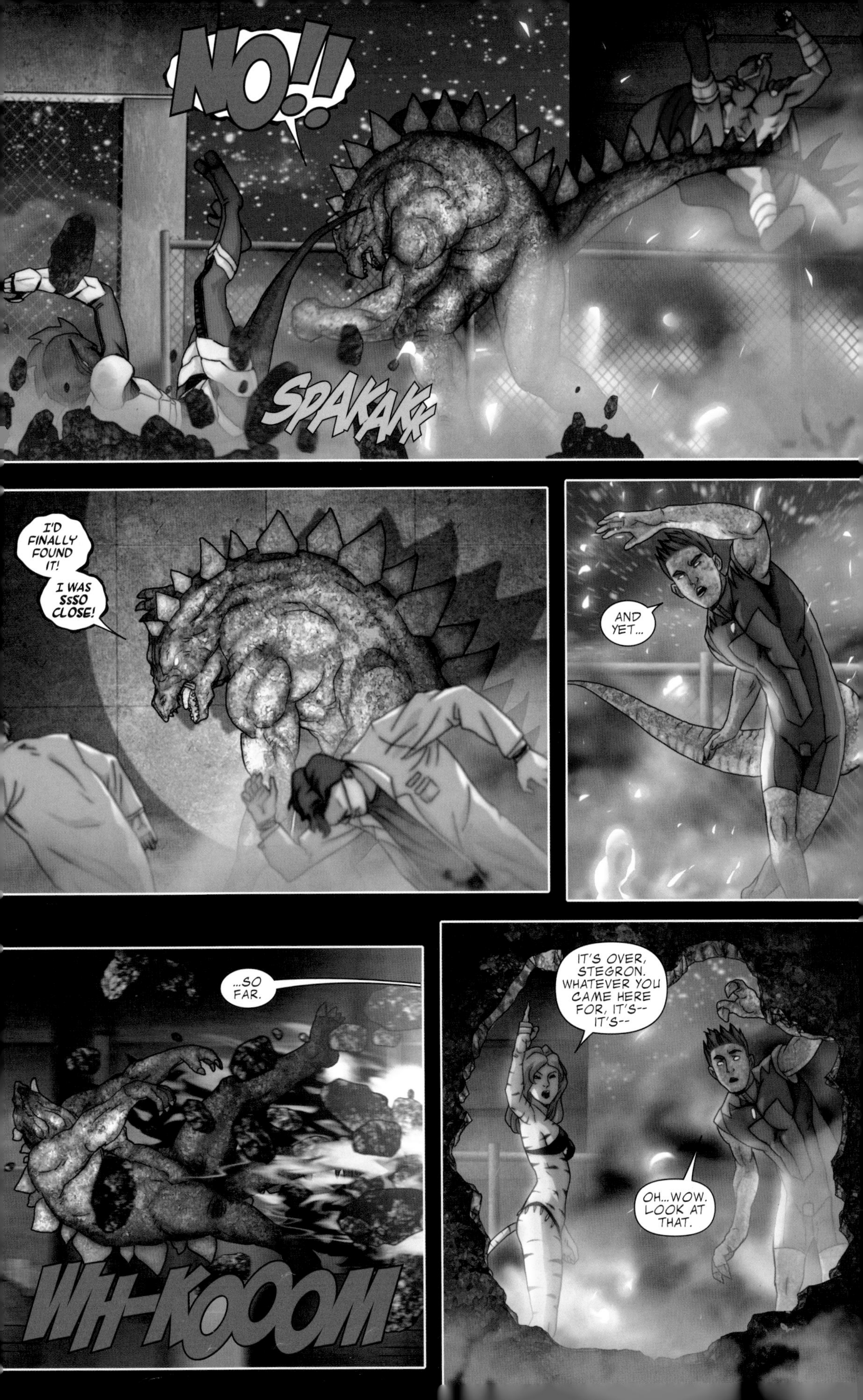

NO!!
SPAKAKK
I'D FINALLY FOUND IT!
I WAS SSSO CLOSE!
AND YET...
...SO FAR.
WH-KOOOM
IT'S OVER, STEGRON. WHATEVER YOU CAME HERE FOR, IT'S-- IT'S--
OH...WOW. LOOK AT THAT.

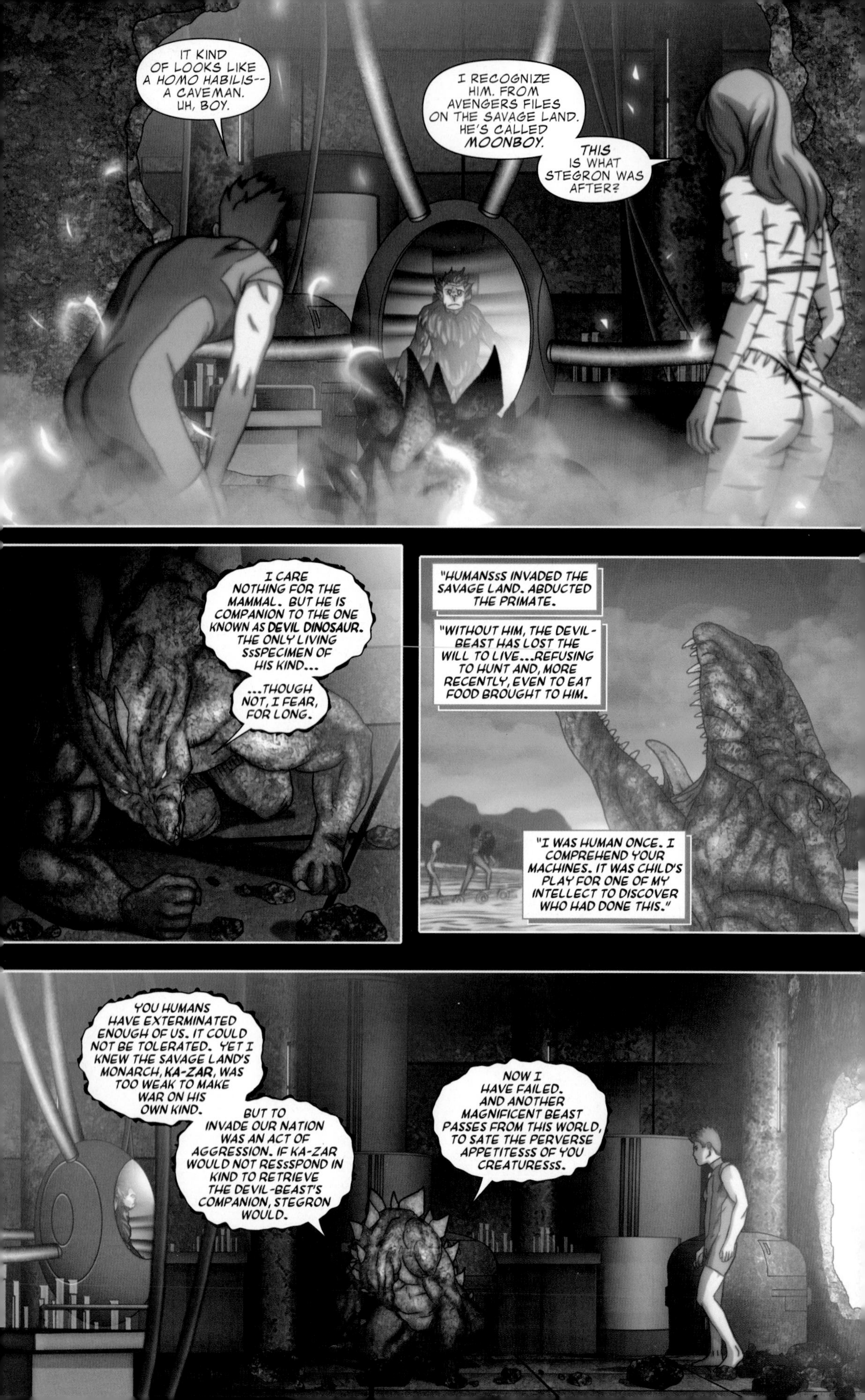
IT KIND OF LOOKS LIKE A HOMO HABILIS-- A CAVEMAN. UH, BOY.
I RECOGNIZE HIM. FROM AVENGERS FILES ON THE SAVAGE LAND. HE'S CALLED MOONBOY.
THIS IS WHAT STEGRON WAS AFTER?
I CARE NOTHING FOR THE MAMMAL. BUT HE IS COMPANION TO THE ONE KNOWN AS DEVIL DINOSAUR. THE ONLY LIVING SsSPECIMEN OF HIS KIND...
...THOUGH NOT, I FEAR, FOR LONG.
"HUMANSsS INVADED THE SAVAGE LAND. ABDUCTED THE PRIMATE.
"WITHOUT HIM, THE DEVIL-BEAST HAS LOST THE WILL TO LIVE...REFUSING TO HUNT AND, MORE RECENTLY, EVEN TO EAT FOOD BROUGHT TO HIM.
"I WAS HUMAN ONCE. I COMPREHEND YOUR MACHINES. IT WAS CHILD'S PLAY FOR ONE OF MY INTELLECT TO DISCOVER WHO HAD DONE THIS."
YOU HUMANS HAVE EXTERMINATED ENOUGH OF US. IT COULD NOT BE TOLERATED. YET I KNEW THE SAVAGE LAND'S MONARCH, KA-ZAR, WAS TOO WEAK TO MAKE WAR ON HIS OWN KIND.
BUT TO INVADE OUR NATION WAS AN ACT OF AGGRESSION. IF KA-ZAR WOULD NOT RESsSPOND IN KIND TO RETRIEVE THE DEVIL-BEAST'S COMPANION, STEGRON WOULD.
NOW I HAVE FAILED. AND ANOTHER MAGNIFICENT BEAST PASSES FROM THIS WORLD, TO SATE THE PERVERSE APPETITESsS OF YOU CREATURESsS.

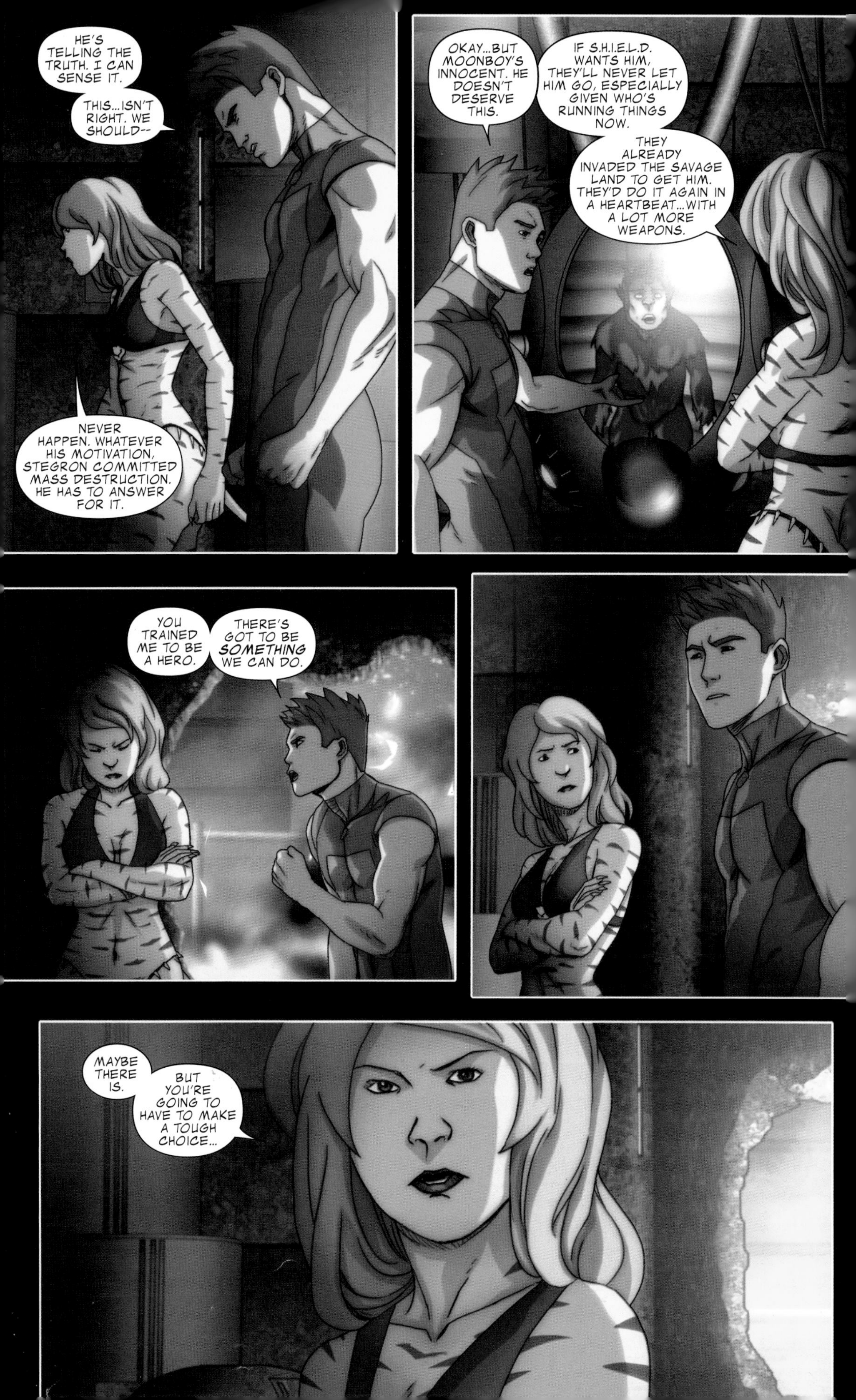
HE'S TELLING THE TRUTH. I CAN SENSE IT.
THIS...ISN'T RIGHT. WE SHOULD--
NEVER HAPPEN. WHATEVER HIS MOTIVATION, STEGRON COMMITTED MASS DESTRUCTION. HE HAS TO ANSWER FOR IT.
OKAY...BUT MOONBOY'S INNOCENT. HE DOESN'T DESERVE THIS.
IF S.H.I.E.L.D. WANTS HIM, THEY'LL NEVER LET HIM GO, ESPECIALLY GIVEN WHO'S RUNNING THINGS NOW.
THEY ALREADY INVADED THE SAVAGE LAND TO GET HIM. THEY'D DO IT AGAIN IN A HEARTBEAT...WITH A LOT MORE WEAPONS.
YOU TRAINED ME TO BE A HERO.
THERE'S GOT TO BE SOMETHING WE CAN DO.
MAYBE THERE IS.
BUT YOU'RE GOING TO HAVE TO MAKE A TOUGH CHOICE...

WELL DONE, TIGRA. IS HE STILL DANGEROUS?

I DON'T THINK SO. HE KNOWS WHEN HE'S BEATEN.

STEGRON SHALL SSSUBMIT TO IMPRISONMENT, MAMMAL. THOUGH HE MAKESSS NO PROMISE TO REMAIN.

THINK YOU CAN BUST OUT OF PRISON 42, HUH, LIZARD LIPS? I'LL ENJOY WATCHING YOU TRY.

WHERE IS HE? WHAT HAVE YOU DONE WITH HIM?

WHERE'S THE HOMO HABILIS?

WHAT, THE MONKEY? ONE OF THE DINOSAURS ATE HIM.

YOU'RE LYING! YOU'VE STOLEN HIM!

ARE YOU SERIOUS? LOOK AT MY OUTFIT, DOC. WHERE EXACTLY DO YOU THINK I'M HIDING HIM?

SEE THAT BLOODSTAIN? TEST IT. I GUARANTEE IT'S A MATCH FOR HIS DNA.

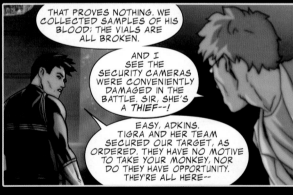

THAT PROVES NOTHING. WE COLLECTED SAMPLES OF HIS BLOOD; THE VIALS ARE ALL BROKEN.

AND I SEE THE SECURITY CAMERAS WERE CONVENIENTLY DAMAGED IN THE BATTLE. SIR, SHE'S A THIEF--!

EASY, ADKINS. TIGRA AND HER TEAM SECURED OUR TARGET, AS ORDERED. THEY HAVE NO MOTIVE TO TAKE YOUR MONKEY, NOR DO THEY HAVE OPPORTUNITY. THEY'RE ALL HERE--

WAIT. THERE'S ONE MISSING. CODE-NAME REPTIL.

THE KID? I SENT HIM HOME.

DR. COOPER WAS RIGHT. ALL HE DID WAS GET IN THE WAY.

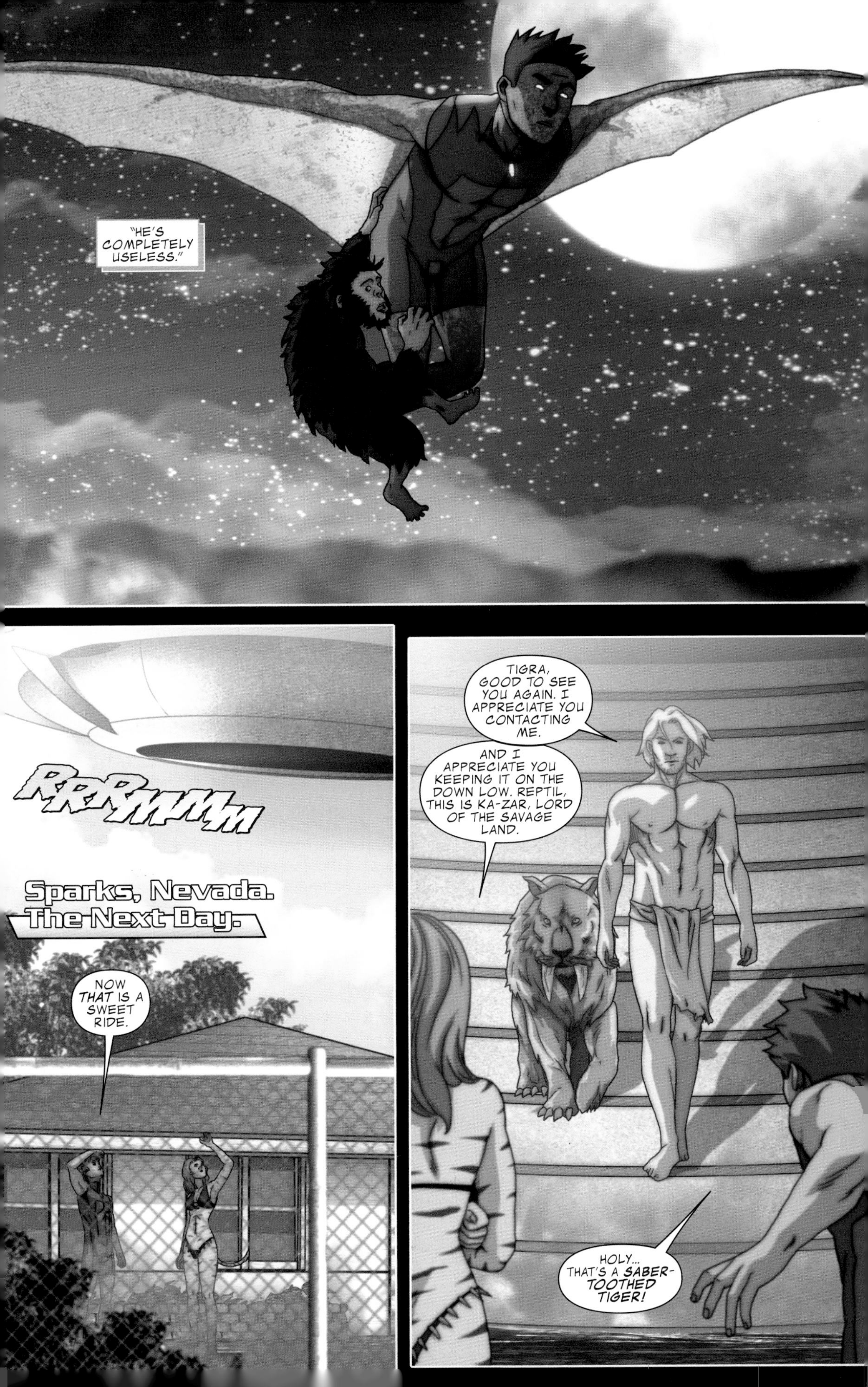
"HE'S COMPLETELY USELESS."
RRRMMMM
Sparks, Nevada. The Next Day.
NOW THAT IS A SWEET RIDE.
TIGRA, GOOD TO SEE YOU AGAIN. I APPRECIATE YOU CONTACTING ME.
AND I APPRECIATE YOU KEEPING IT ON THE DOWN LOW. REPTIL, THIS IS KA-ZAR, LORD OF THE SAVAGE LAND.
HOLY... THAT'S A SABER-TOOTHED TIGER!

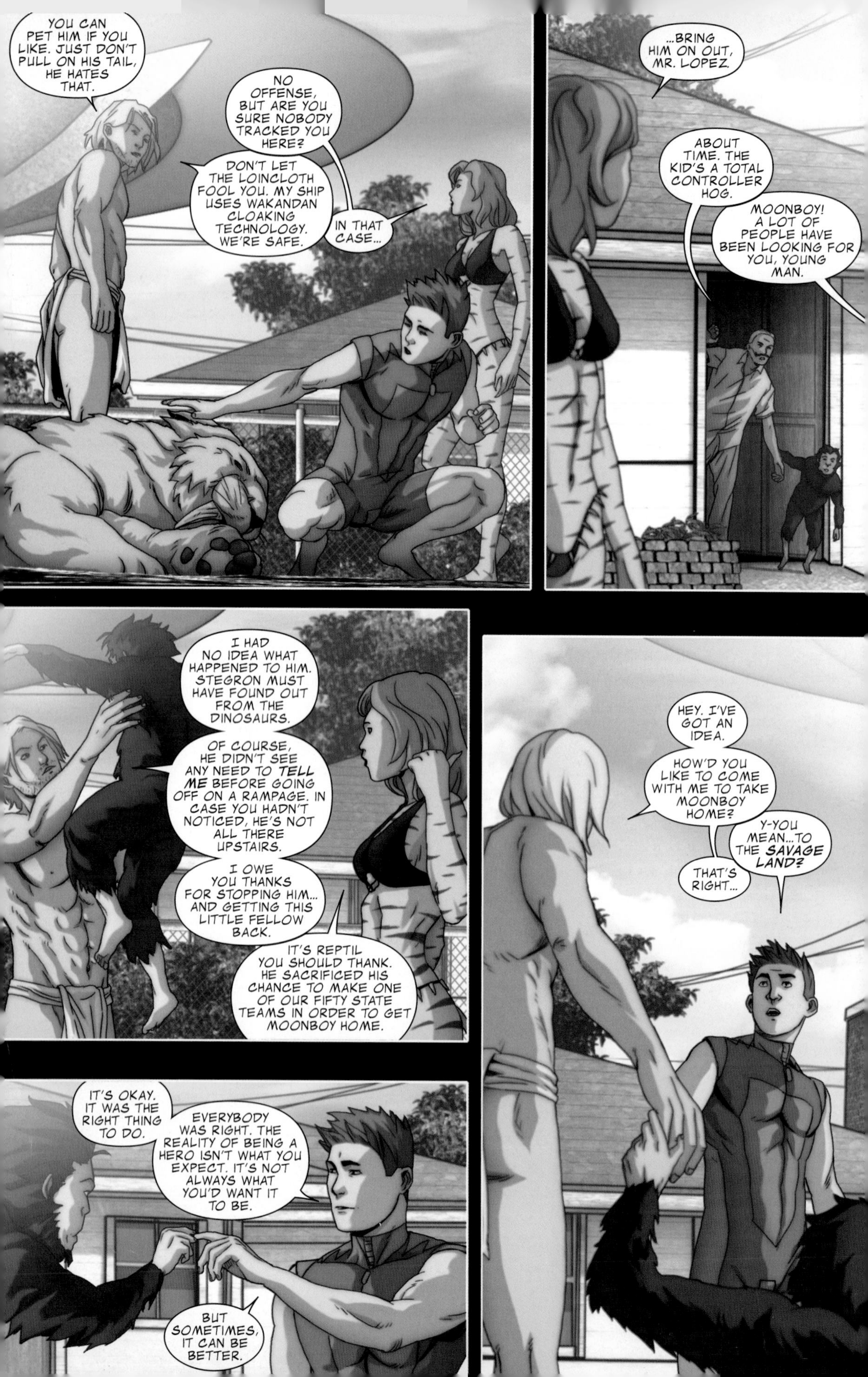
YOU CAN PET HIM IF YOU LIKE. JUST DON'T PULL ON HIS TAIL, HE HATES THAT.
NO OFFENSE, BUT ARE YOU SURE NOBODY TRACKED YOU HERE?
DON'T LET THE LOINCLOTH FOOL YOU. MY SHIP USES WAKANDAN CLOAKING TECHNOLOGY. WE'RE SAFE.
IN THAT CASE...
...BRING HIM ON OUT, MR. LOPEZ.
ABOUT TIME. THE KID'S A TOTAL CONTROLLER HOG.
MOONBOY! A LOT OF PEOPLE HAVE BEEN LOOKING FOR YOU, YOUNG MAN.
I HAD NO IDEA WHAT HAPPENED TO HIM. STEGRON MUST HAVE FOUND OUT FROM THE DINOSAURS.
OF COURSE, HE DIDN'T SEE ANY NEED TO TELL ME BEFORE GOING OFF ON A RAMPAGE. IN CASE YOU HADN'T NOTICED, HE'S NOT ALL THERE UPSTAIRS.
I OWE YOU THANKS FOR STOPPING HIM... AND GETTING THIS LITTLE FELLOW BACK.
IT'S REPTIL YOU SHOULD THANK. HE SACRIFICED HIS CHANCE TO MAKE ONE OF OUR FIFTY STATE TEAMS IN ORDER TO GET MOONBOY HOME.
IT'S OKAY. IT WAS THE RIGHT THING TO DO.
EVERYBODY WAS RIGHT. THE REALITY OF BEING A HERO ISN'T WHAT YOU EXPECT. IT'S NOT ALWAYS WHAT YOU'D WANT IT TO BE.
BUT SOMETIMES, IT CAN BE BETTER.
HEY. I'VE GOT AN IDEA.
HOW'D YOU LIKE TO COME WITH ME TO TAKE MOONBOY HOME?
Y-YOU MEAN...TO THE SAVAGE LAND?
THAT'S RIGHT...

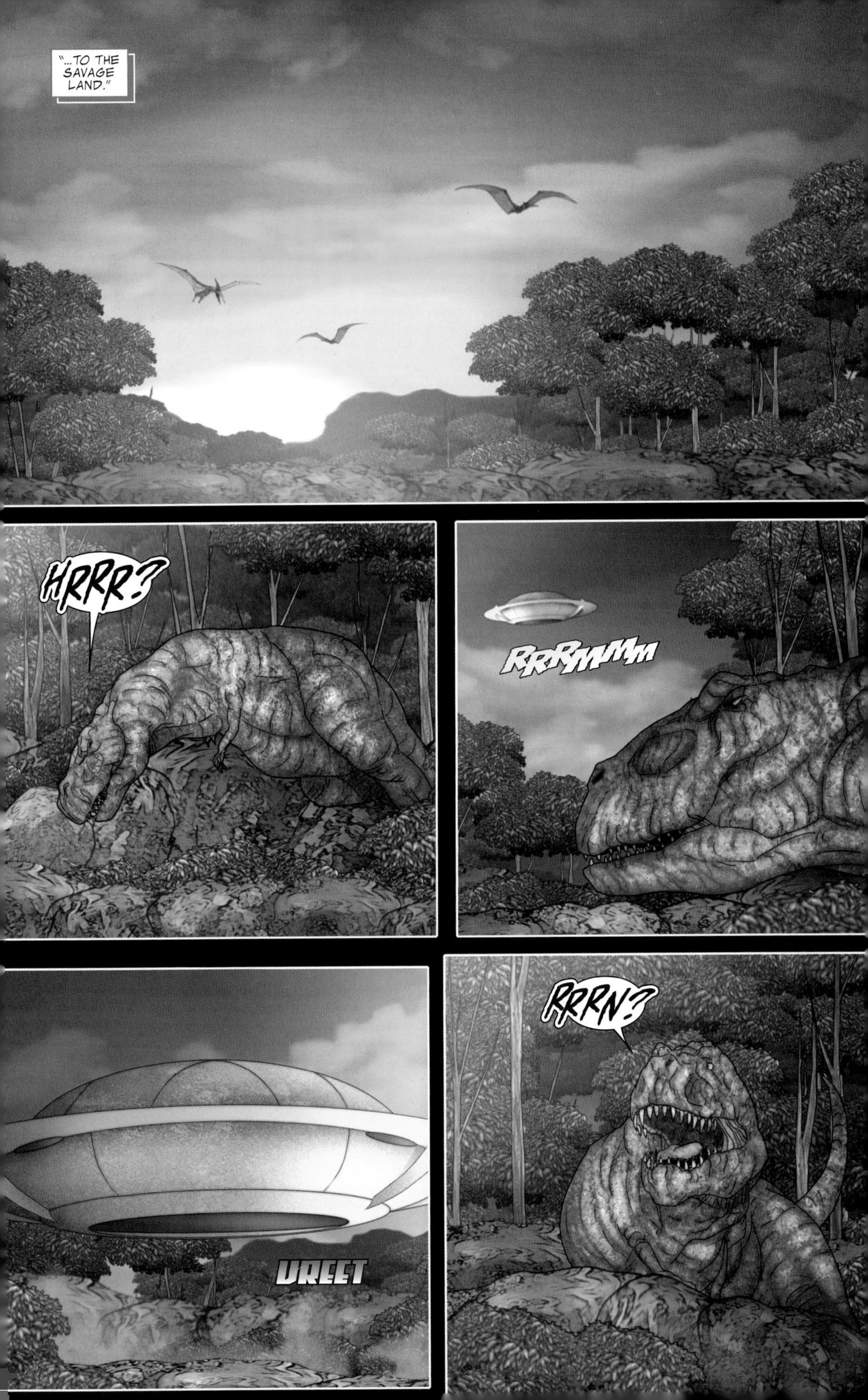
"...TO THE SAVAGE LAND."
HRRR?
RRRMMM
VREET
RRRN?

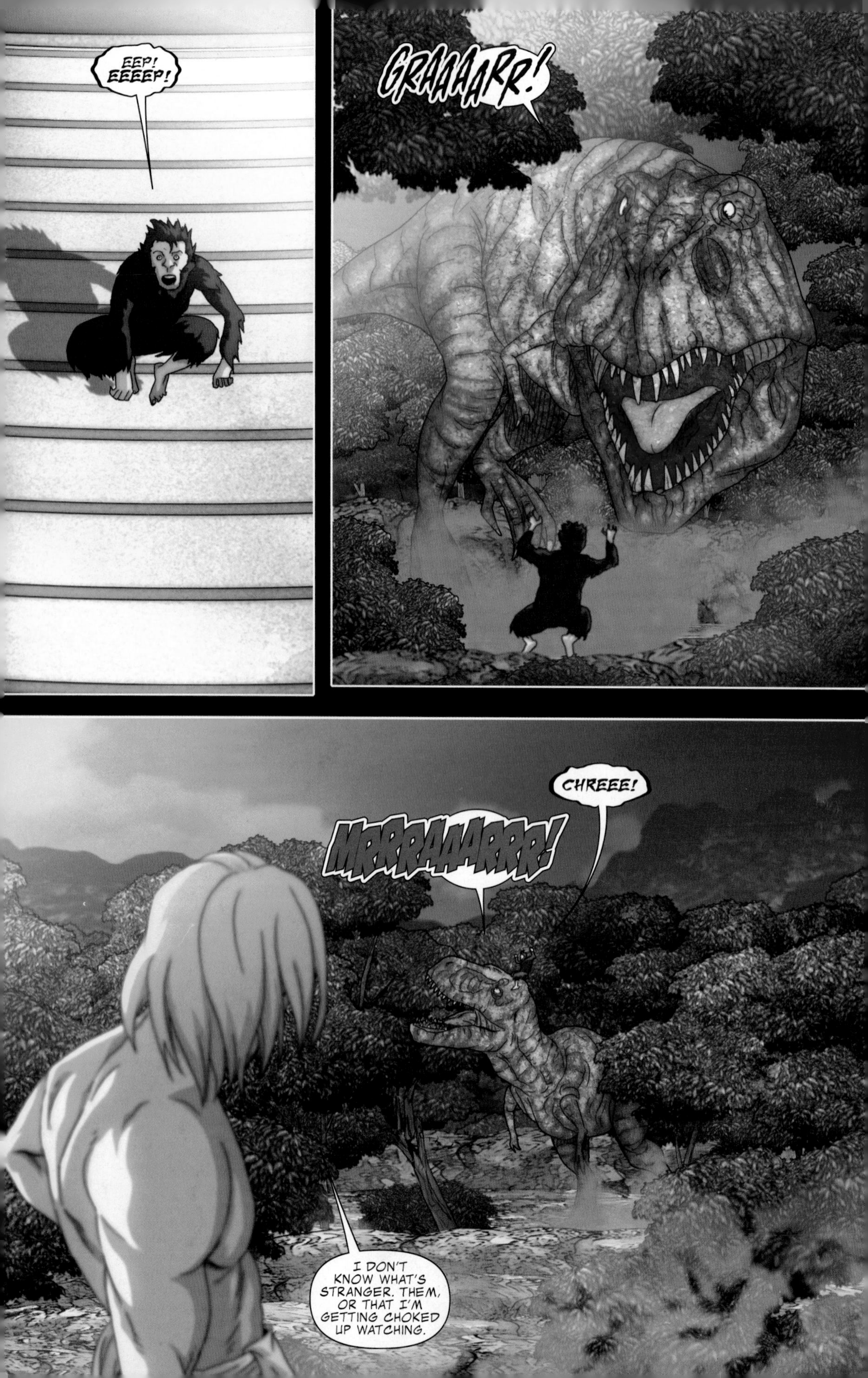
EEP! EEEEP!
GRAAAAARR!
CHREEE!
MRRRAAARRR!
I DON'T KNOW WHAT'S STRANGER. THEM, OR THAT I'M GETTING CHOKED UP WATCHING.

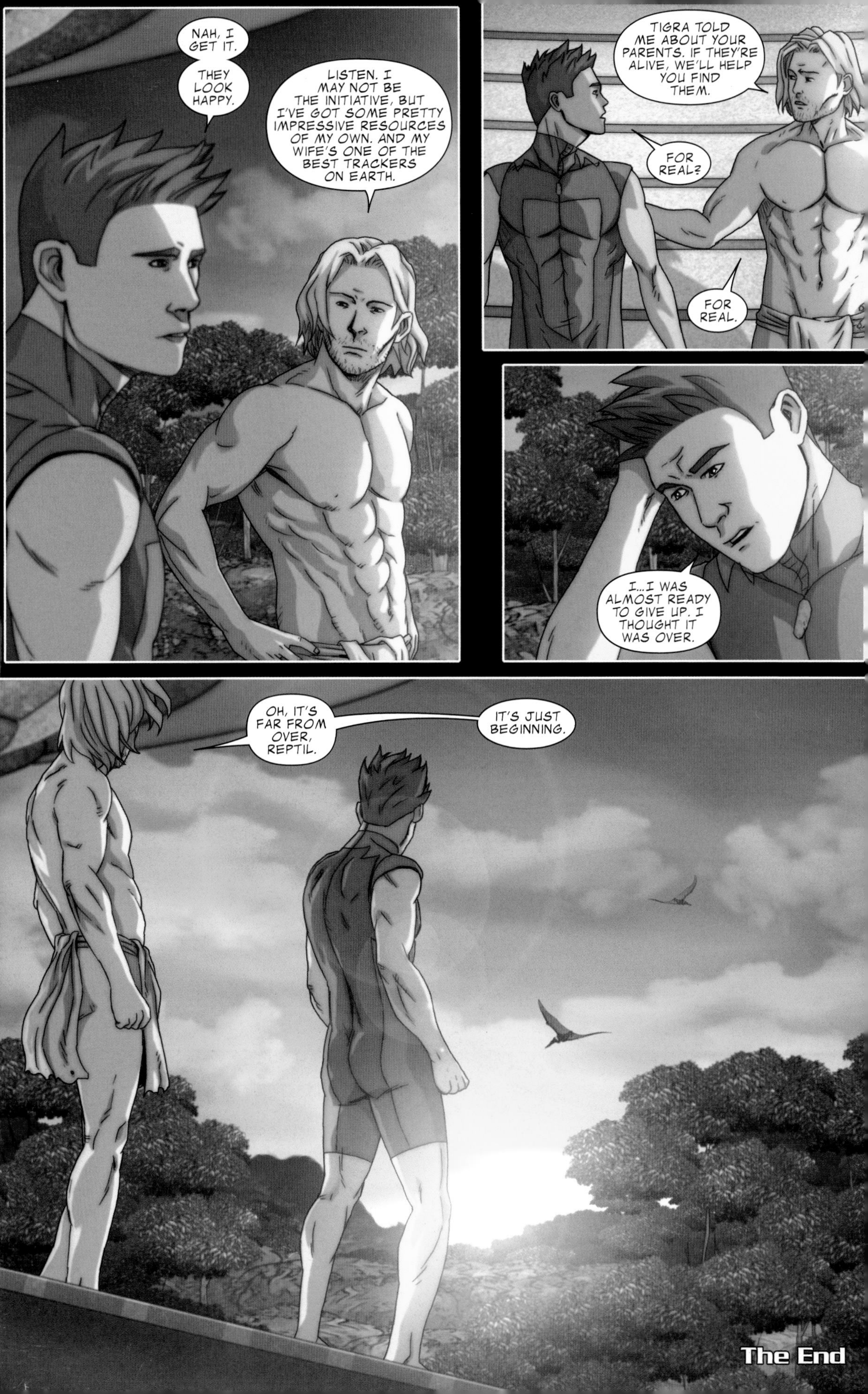
NAH, I GET IT.
THEY LOOK HAPPY.
LISTEN. I MAY NOT BE THE INITIATIVE, BUT I'VE GOT SOME PRETTY IMPRESSIVE RESOURCES OF MY OWN. AND MY WIFE'S ONE OF THE BEST TRACKERS ON EARTH.
TIGRA TOLD ME ABOUT YOUR PARENTS. IF THEY'RE ALIVE, WE'LL HELP YOU FIND THEM.
FOR REAL?
FOR REAL.
I...I WAS ALMOST READY TO GIVE UP. I THOUGHT IT WAS OVER.
OH, IT'S FAR FROM OVER, REPTIL.
IT'S JUST BEGINNING.
The End

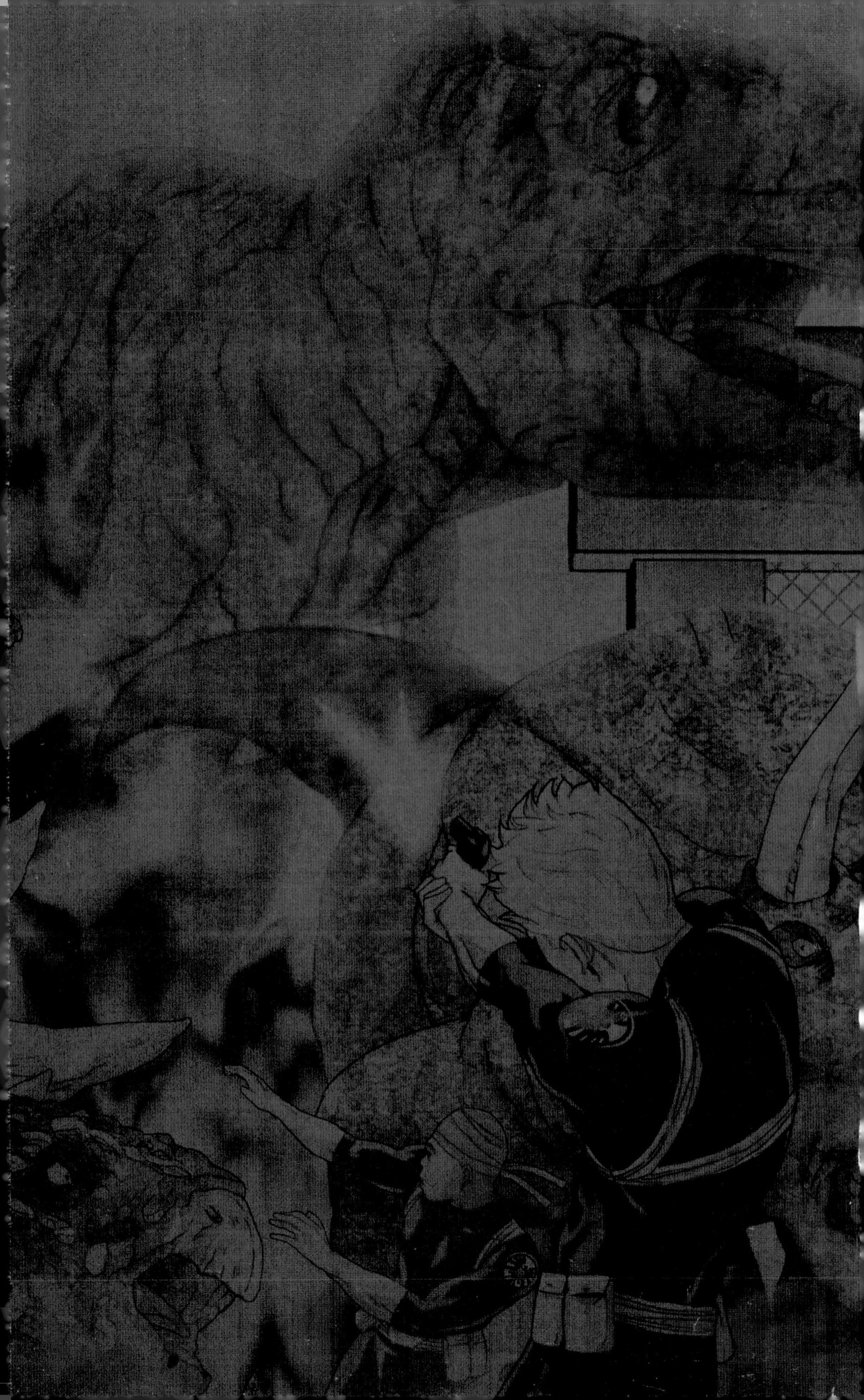